PAINTINGS FROM RAJASTHAN

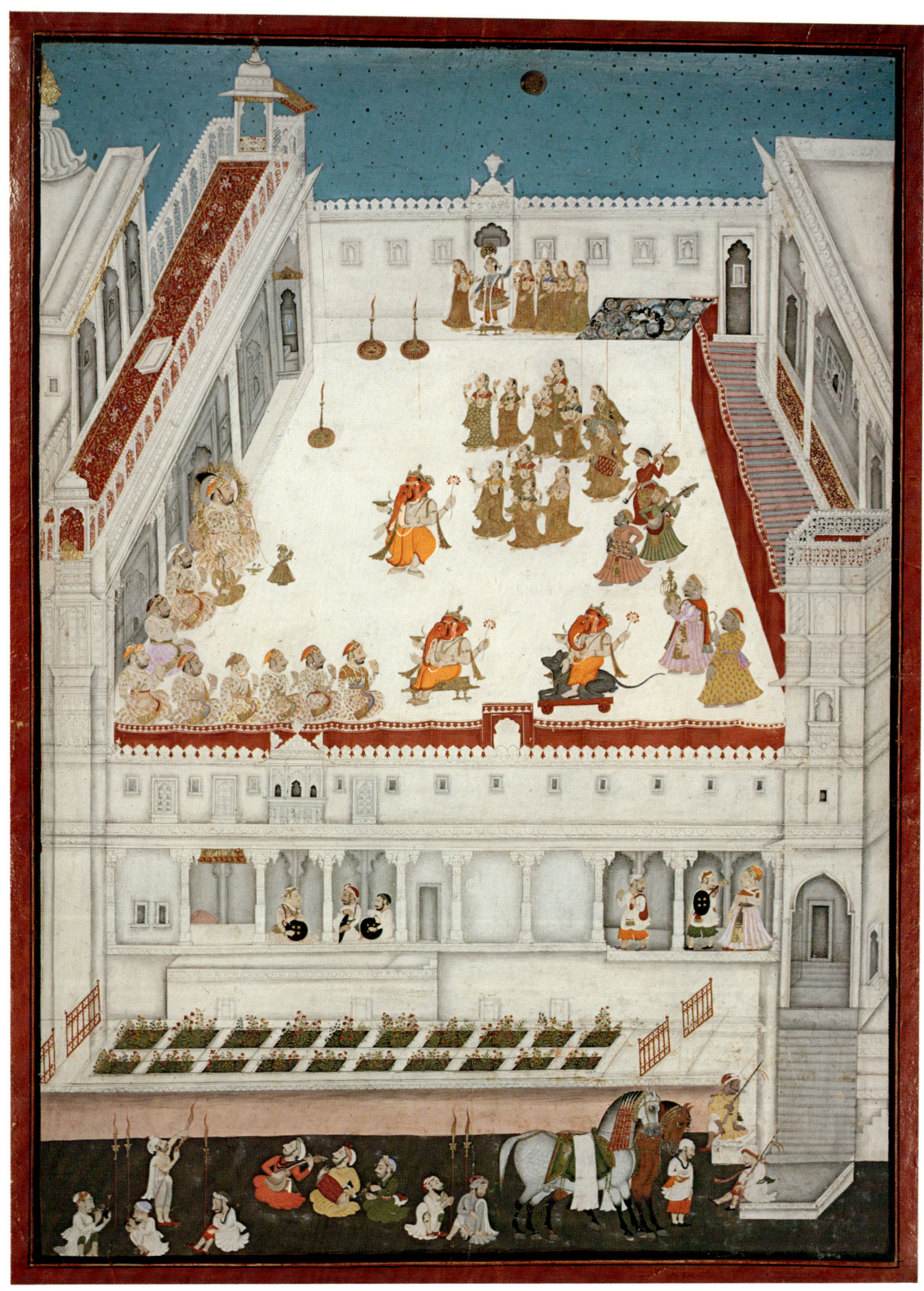

Colour plate No. 1   **Maharana Jagat Singh Attending the** *Rasalila* (cat. no. 114)

PAINTINGS FROM RAJASTHAN

in the National Gallery of Victoria

A Collection acquired through the
Felton Bequests' Committee

by Andrew Topsfield

NGV

Published by the National Gallery of Victoria
180 St. Kilda Road, Melbourne, 1980

This book has been published with the assistance of the Trustees Executors and Agency Company
of Australia Limited, which administers the Felton Bequests' Committee.

National Library of Australia Cataloguing in Publication Data:
Topsfield, Andrew
    Paintings from Rajasthan in the National Gallery of Victoria.

    Index
    Bibliography
    ISBN 0 7241 0072 5

    1. National Gallery of Victoria – Exhibitions.
    2. Rajput painting – Exhibitions. I. National Gallery of Victoria. II. Title.

759.954'4

Front Cover:
'Maharana Amar Singh Playing Holi with his Sardars'
Udaipur, c. 1708-10
Gouache on paper
47 x 40.5 cm
Felton Bequest 1980

Editor: Dorothy McCulloch
Designer: Kathy Richards
Curatorial Co-ordinator: John Guy
Transliteration Consultant: Chintaman Datar
Black and White Photography: Victoria and Albert Museum, London
Colour Photography: Victoria and Albert Museum, London, and Stephen West
Typesetting and Printing: Gardner Printing Co. (Vic.) Pty. Ltd.

Contents

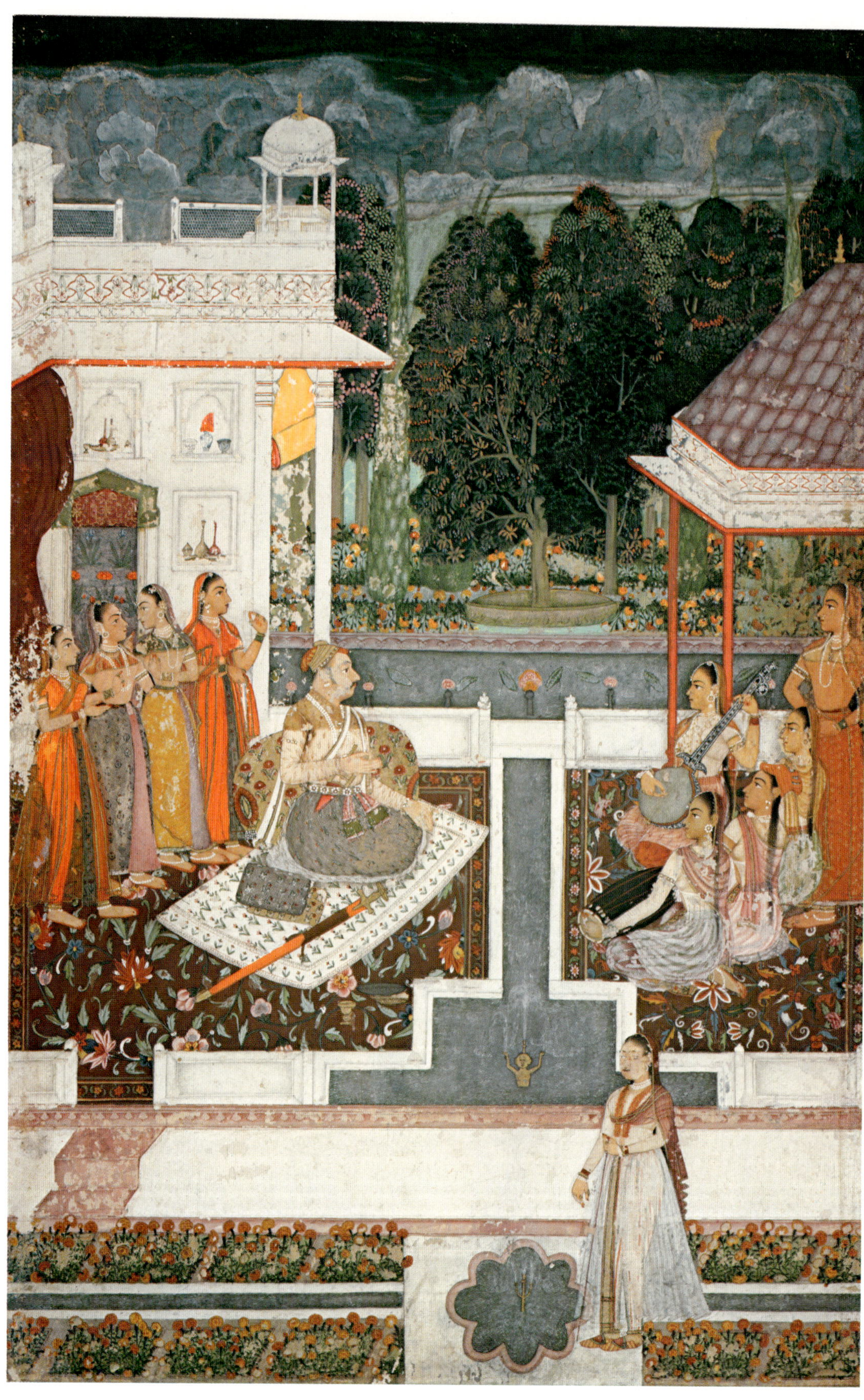

Colour plate No. 2 **Maharaja Jaswant Singh of Jodhpur Listening to Music** (cat. no. 12)

Preface

This collection of mainly Rajasthani paintings, which bears the marks of having at one time formed part of a princely collection, is one of the most important of its kind outside India. Apart from their visual attractions, which are discussed in the Introduction, the paintings are unusually well provided with contemporary clerks' inscriptions, some of them quite lengthy. In preparing this catalogue, which was written within a limited period of time, I have tried to transliterate these inscriptions as precisely as I could, while incorporating the more salient matter in them in the adjoining descriptive notes on the paintings. I have omitted some information of secondary importance, such as the names of some attendant figures, and the names of horses which are often given along with those of their royal riders. A few inscriptions have not been transliterated, either because their length outweighed their interest or because of their impenetrable obscurity. Similarly, I have not attempted translations of the inscriptions, partly because they are frequently repetitious and contain relatively unimportant information, but also partly out of discretion. As students of Rajasthani painting will know, these inscriptions are often far from easy going. Variable legibility, unfamiliar dialect forms and corrupt and inconsistent spelling are among the problems that they present. Although I hope to have extracted any information of direct art historical interest from them, a number have remained in greater or lesser part unintelligible, as the queries, lacunae and sometimes speculative word divisions in my transliterations will reveal. Nevertheless, I hope that these will be of use to students in spite of the errors, omissions and inconsistencies that remain.

Diacritical marks are generally omitted except in passages directly transliterated from inscriptions; a modified form of the Royal Asiatic Society's system is used, with *kh* usually read in place of *s* in accordance with Rajasthani usage. Inscriptions are in the *nagari* script unless otherwise stated. Picture measurements exclude the borders except where large discrepancies exist, as in the case of album pages, when border measurements are also given. All the paintings are executed in gouache on paper. Dates have been computed by the approximately accurate method of deducting 57 from the V.S. year or 56 when the date falls in Magha, Phalguna or the second half of Pausa (a note on the calendar employed in Mewar is given in Shyamaldas, *Vir Vinod*, vol. I, p. 119f.).

I am indebted to the Felton Bequests' Committee for inviting me to write this catalogue, and to Dr Ursula Hoff, London Adviser to the Felton Bequests' Committee and Mrs Dorothy McCulloch, Editor, National Gallery of Victoria, for their co-operation during the preparation of the manuscript and production of the catalogue. I am grateful to a number of colleagues for information and advice, in particular Mr Robert Skelton, Dr John D. Smith, Dr Mildred Archer and Mr Rupert Snell. I would also like to thank Miss Betty Tyers for her patient assistance, Miss Christine Smith for her photographic work, Mr Graham Parlett for providing the map, and Helen and Sophie Topsfield for their encouragement.

Andrew Topsfield
London, June 1980

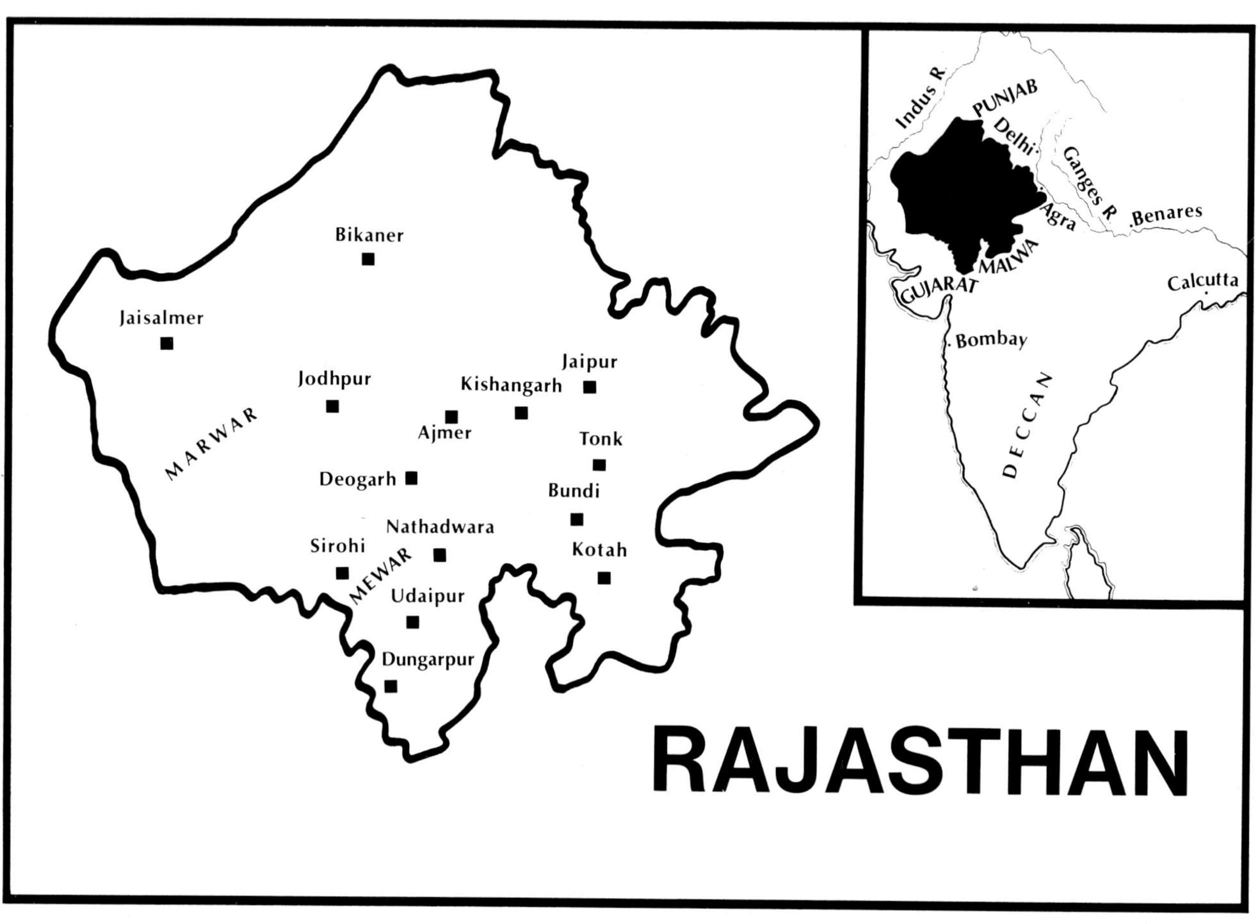

Bikaner
Jaisalmer
Jodhpur
Kishangarh
Jaipur
MARWAR
Ajmer
Tonk
Deogarh
Bundi
Nathadwara
Sirohi
Kotah
MEWAR
Udaipur
Dungarpur
Indus R.
PUNJAB
Delhi
Ganges R.
Agra
Benares
GUJARAT
MALWA
Calcutta
Bombay
DECCAN
RAJASTHAN

Introduction

These paintings from the courts of Rajasthan evoke a way of life, recalling that of medieval Europe in its pageantry and its simple and violent tenor, which has only vanished altogether within living memory. We see the Maharajas as they themselves liked to be shown, portrayed individually in fiercely impassive profile, ranged in solemn durbar groups, giving impetuous chase on the hunting-field, participating in riotous festivals, or, more privately, at their devotions or dallying in the *zenana*. The ruler himself is normally the central figure, to whom all the others defer in hierarchical order; in the case of the Maharana of Mewar he is usually distinguished by a glowing nimbus suggesting his legendary descent from the Sun-god. Bright daylight colours, enclosed by rhythmically adumbrated and boldly accentuated outline drawing, pervade the paintings, even in night scenes, which are only indicated by the muted presence of moon and stars and one or two lamps held by servants. Both in mood and style they embody the cultural values of their Rajput patrons, interpreted by artists who were themselves artisans of low caste.[1] The persistent vitality of this court art in the two centuries of Rajput decline (c. 1650-1850) can in fact be attributed to these artists' closeness to folk traditions which continuously reinvigorated their work, while other more insulated and refined court styles lapsed into inanition.

The Rajputs, 'sons of kings', had originally entered India from the north-west during the first millennium A.D. They established kingdoms in western India in a region that came to be called Rajasthan, 'the abode of kings'. Like previous immigrants from Central Asia, they were assimilated into the all-embracing Hindu social system as Kshatriyas or members of the warrior caste. When northern India fell under the domination of Muslim Turks from the 13th century onwards, the Rajputs were foremost both in resisting the alien invaders and in preserving the surviving traditions of classical Hindu culture at their courts. They have been proverbial in India since those days for their courage, tending to recklessness, and for their code of honour and chivalry. Many heroic legends from Rajput folklore are recounted by James Tod, the first British Political Agent in Mewar (1818-22) and author of a classic history, among them that of the sack of Chitor, the hilltop fortress of the Mewar rulers, by Sultan Alauddin Khalji in 1303. When the besieged Rajputs faced certain defeat by the Muslim forces, the womenfolk are said to have immolated themselves in thousands in a subterranean pyre, while their husbands 'threw open the portals and descended to the plains, and with a reckless despair carried death, or met it... in the crowded ranks of Ala.'[2] Francois Bernier, a French doctor who was at the Mughal court in the 17th century, observed that 'it is an interesting sight to see the Rajputs on the eve of a battle, with the fumes of opium in their heads, embrace and bid adieu to one another, as if certain of death.'[3] Bernier also relates a current story about Maharaja Jaswant Singh of Jodhpur, whose portrait in the present collection (cat. no. 12) shows him taking his ease, respectfully attended by his ladies. On one occasion Jaswant Singh returned exhausted to his castle after fighting valiantly but unsuccessfully on the battlefield, only to find the gates closed in his face by his wife, a princess of the house of Mewar, who averred that he should have chosen a glorious death rather than the humiliation of defeat.[4]

Besides preserving earlier scholarly and artistic traditions, the Rajput rulers themselves initiated new work. Maharana Kumbha of Mewar (r. 1433-68) was one such patron, and it was probably at courts such as his that illustrations of poetical and rhetorical themes, such as *ragamala,* the depiction of visualised musical modes, or *nayakanayikabheda,* the classification of ideal types of lovers, were first developed. A more important influence was the resurgence of popular devotional cults centred on the incarnations of Vishnu, most notably Krishna, the playful, dark-skinned cowherd god, celebrated for his destruction of malignant demons and his wooing of the milkmaids of the Braj country around Mathura. This powerful movement gave rise both to new vernacular literatures and a bold and expressive style of manuscript illustration which was practised in Rajasthan and elsewhere in northern India. Its conventions were to form a foundation for the later Rajasthani styles, whose individual histories only begin to be clear from the 17th century onwards.

The cultural traditions of the Rajput courts were to be profoundly altered by the arrival in India of another, more enduring Muslim dynasty from Central Asia. The Mughal empire, which was to last in name at least until 1857, was established by Babur, a prince descended from both Genghis Khan and Tamerlane, who defeated the Rajput opposition led by Maharana Sanga of Mewar in 1527. It was extended and consolidated by his grandson, the indefatigably energetic Akbar (r. 1556-1605), who subdued all but one of the Rajput kingdoms, and ensured their loyalty by taking the rulers into his service and by marrying into their families. In this way the rulers of Amber (later Jaipur), Jodhpur, Bikaner, Bundi and other Rajput courts attained a new prominence. At the same time the Maharanas of Mewar, who had long been the premier Rajput ruling family, fought a solitary guerilla war against the Mughals until, some forty years later, a qualified submission was finally made to the Emperor Jahangir in 1615. The Maharanas escaped the repugnant duties of attending the imperial court in person or of sending their daughters there as wives. Instead they tended thereafter to remain aloof from external events, living on their memories of past glories and meanwhile sinking into a decline which was hastened in the 18th century by the invasions of the Marathas from the south, who met little resistance from the increasingly enervated Rajputs. The political and economic chaos caused by the Maratha depredations was only alleviated by the intervention of the British, whose suzerainty the Rajputs accepted in 1818. While retaining a nominal independence, the Rajput states were in effect preserved as living fossils by British rule until their dissolution at Independence in 1947. The Maharajas of the present day have been divested of their titles and incomes, but as a rule they retain the respect of their people. Some have turned their palaces into successful tourist hotels.

An important feature of the present collection is that the majority of the pictures belong to the relatively late tradition of portraiture and court genre painting rather than the older Rajasthani tradition of mythological and poetical illustration, which to a great extent diminished in importance from the early 18th century onwards. This secular preoccupation with the recording of historical incident instead of the timeless world of the religious epics is entirely attributable to the influence of the Mughal court. Portraiture for its own sake is foreign to the Indian classical tradition, with its predilection for idealised forms based in religious iconography or in the stock conceits of poetic imagery. It is also unknown in the Persian court culture in which the Mughals were grounded, but the individual emperors themselves evolved their own, more modern-minded standards. In his memoirs Babur shows a candid and observant eye for the peculiarities of man and nature, which was shared by Akbar, who brought together a large atelier of Indian artists under the guidance of two Persian masters. Under his supervision a brilliant eclectic style of poetical and historical manuscript illustration was quickly developed, combining Persian technical refinement and Indian vigour and feeling for nature with a gradually increasing influence from European art, which had begun to reach the Mughal court through Jesuit missionaries. Akbar's initiative was further developed by his son Jahangir (r. 1605-27), who, like Babur, reveals an unusually observant and inquiring mind in his memoirs. As a patron, Jahangir's preference was less for illustrated manuscripts than for individual paintings of outstanding quality, often portraits or animal and flower studies, which were mounted in splendidly decorated borders and bound in albums. The art of the portrait was brought to such perfection in his reign that Jahangir was able to boast to Sir Thomas Roe that his painters were the equal of the English miniaturists whose work the ambassador had shown him. The Mughal school had gathered such momentum at this period that it was able to continue, with very high technical standards although with some loss of inspiration, in the reigns of Shah Jahan (1627-58), whose primary concern was for his grandiose architectural projects, and the puritanical Aurangzeb (1658-1707), who was however eventually to banish the arts from his court (cat. nos. 3-6).

The Rajput rulers who spent long periods in residence at the Mughal court inevitably came to adopt many of its customs and fashions, among them a taste for the naturalism and high finish of Mughal painting. When in the course of the 17th century Mughal-trained artists were introduced at their own courts, a number of distinct local styles resulted. The portrait of Maharaja Jaswant Singh listening to music in his *zenana* is one of the best examples of a small group of 17th century Jodhpur portraits showing strong Mughal influence. Similarly, by the late 17th century a number of Muslim artists are known to have been working at the desert-locked court of Bikaner to the north-west, in a style showing close affinities both with the Mughal school and with those of the Muslim kingdoms of the Deccan recently conquered by Aurangzeb. In its cool palette, delicate drawing and restrained expression Bikaner is the least Rajput in character of the Rajasthani schools (cat. nos. 16, 18-20). The court of Amber, later moved by Sawai Jai Singh to the new town of Jaipur in 1727, also had close ties with the Mughal court and patronised secular portraiture as a complement to its existing tradition of mythological illustration; several examples in the hard late 18th century style, influenced by late Mughal painting, are included here (cat. nos. 27-30). At Kishangarh the same sensuous and increasingly world-weary late Mughal style was adapted by a process of expressive distortion in poetic scenes of the love of Krishna and Radha in palace and pastoral settings (cat. no. 24). At the neighbouring courts of Bundi and Kotah, in south-east Rajasthan, strong initial Mughal influences were even more thoroughly assimilated and adapted to native Rajput modes of expression during the 17th and 18th centuries. The tumultuous painting, by Kisan Das, of Ram Singh II of Kotah celebrating the spring festival of Holi with his townspeople (cat. no. 35) shows a typical late reassertion of the dramatic colour sense and swaggering, ebullient use of line of the Rajput artist.

Although the historical development of few (perhaps none) of the many schools and sub-schools of Rajasthani painting is yet fully understood — and many pictures remain difficult to assign to any particular school — this constant interplay between Mughal sobriety and refinement and Rajput verve and expression is implicit in all of them. On the cultural level it reflects the Rajput patrons' intermediary position between the insular and ultimately alien world of the imperial court, to which they were politically affiliated, and their more deep-rooted participation in the life and culture of their own people. It is again evident in the development of painting at Udaipur, which had become the capital of the Maharanas of Mewar after the fall of Chitor to Akbar in 1568. As has been mentioned, the Maharanas were both implacable opponents of the Mughals and the chief upholders of Rajput traditionalism. Nevertheless by the end of the 17th century a flourishing stream of portraiture and court genre painting had become established at Udaipur as elsewhere, which soon overshadowed the long-established local tradition of manuscript illustration. Its continuous development down to the time of its extinction in the present century has hitherto received little attention, and it will, in conclusion, be appropriate to give some account of this. The very ample body of evidence in the present collection particularly serves to bear out the main principle of Rajput life enunciated by Tod, namely that the fortunes of a Rajput kingdom are chiefly dependent on the character of its ruler. In the long history of court painting at Udaipur the interest and discrimination of individual Maharanas did most to determine the quality of artistic work produced for them.

After their submission to the Mughals in 1615, the Maharanas were able to enjoy the pursuits of peace for the first time in forty years, 'exchanging the din of arms for voluptuous inactivity', in Tod's phrase.[5] The earlier tradition of religious and poetical manuscript illustration was resumed under Maharana Jagat Singh (r. 1628-52), whose principal artist, Sahibdin, gave the style new vitality by his discreet assimilation of elements from the dilute, so-called Popular Mughal school. Unlike those Rajput rulers who were in the imperial service Jagat Singh seems not to have commissioned portraits of himself.[6] The first evidence of such a commission occurs in the time of his successor, Raj Singh (r. 1652-80), of whom an equestrian portrait dated 1670 is known.[7] It is at first sight surprising that this Mughal fashion should have been introduced by Raj Singh, who was himself the last of the old type of warrior Maharanas, stalemating the Mughal forces by his guerilla tactics in the hilly regions of Mewar during Aurangzeb's inconclusive Rajput War (1679-81). But the small group of portraits made for him are still few in number compared with his patronage of manuscript illustrations, while in style they derive from contemporary work in the more heavily Mughal-influenced Bundi style rather than directly from Mughal example. It is indeed clear that an important cross-fertilisation between Mewar and Bundi painting took place in the later 17th century which is not yet properly understood (cat. nos. 49-52). An early, if enigmatic, example of the adoption of a more ambitious viewpoint and spatial conventions at this time is an unprecedentedly large painting by an Udaipur artist which appears to show a Kotah prince in his palace *zenana* during the festival of Diwali (cat. no. 52). With its profusion of lively detail and its delightfully *ad hoc* perspective, this picture stands at the beginning of a tradition of large panoramic compositions showing courtly ceremonies, festivals and other *tamashas* which lasted, with interruptions, until as late as the early 20th century at Udaipur.

Bundi influence is also evident in a number of unpublished portraits of Maharana Jai Singh (1680-98) and of his son Amar Singh (b. 1672, r. 1698-1710) as a young prince. The latter were painted at a time when Amar Singh, who in spite of the tranquilly hedonistic aspect of his portraits is said to have been both quick-tempered and ruthless, fell out with his father over his neglect of Amar Singh's mother, a Bundi princess.

Amar Singh himself withdrew to Bundi and returned with an army to oppose his father. Civil war was only narrowly averted, and an agreement was made by which Amar Singh held separate court at Rajnagar in the north of Mewar during the last years of his father's life; Jai Singh meanwhile lapsed into 'a state of indolence, having all the effects of imbecility'.[8] Certainly the evidence indicates that Amar Singh was more active than his father as a patron of painting during the 1690s, and that in this time he laid the ground for what, in his short reign of twelve years, was to be the formative period for later painting at Udaipur (cat. nos. 54-58). These paintings show an assured clarity of outline, a cool palette and restrained atmosphere unusual in the Mewar school. Many of them are in the so-called *nim qalam* or grisaille style, deriving from earlier Deccani and Mughal examples but remarkable for its transformation at Udaipur by an expressive use of heavy stippling, which may itself be an adaptation of effects seen in European engravings circulating in India at this time. One of the most sensitive pictures ever painted at Udaipur is a large composition in which Amar Singh is seen, not long before his death at the age of thirty-eight, taking part in a Holi colour-fight with his sardars, while they sit in formal durbar in a darkly luxuriant, cypress-fringed garden (cat. no. 58). Even the attendants and the three musicians playing in the undergrowth are portrayed with a careful veracity attested by an unusually full inscription giving all their names. This picture represents a short-lived moment of perfection in Udaipur court painting, showing its creative assimilation of refining external influences. The freshness of its vision was however soon lost in pedestrian imitations by lesser artists.

Portraits and court scenes had now for the first time begun to supplant mythological manuscript illustration as the mainstream of Udaipur painting. The illustrative style established by Sahibdin under Maharana Jagat Singh had been maintained with relatively little modification under Raj Singh and Jai Singh. Amar Singh also commissioned some finely executed work in the style, including more than one series of the mystical poems of Sur Das, which celebrate the childhood and youthful loves of Krishna (cat. no. 62). His was however the last reign in which a consistently high quality was attained in mythological illustration at Udaipur.

Amar Singh's successor, Sangram Singh (b. 1690, r. 1710-34), was a shrewd, competent and conservative ruler, who was, in general, content to follow the initiatives of his father, without himself possessing the flair that had informed them. Well aware of the growing Maratha threat from the south, he was in frequent conference with Sawai Jai Singh of Jaipur as to how to meet it (cat. no. 84). As events turned out, Sangram Singh was the last of the Maharanas to enjoy both internal stability in his kingdom and freedom from outside interference. As a patron he was if anything excessively prolific. In contrast to his more discriminating father, he commissioned series of poetical and devotional illustrations which often ran into hundreds of pages. Not surprisingly the level of quality declined irrevocably within a few years, as can be seen in several *Rasikapriya* illustrations (cat. nos. 100-106), which are cruder versions of original compositions by Sahibdin of a century earlier. Little new inspiration was forthcoming in this now secondary stream of Udaipur painting, which persisted in much the same form into the 19th century.

Court painting however flourished more than ever under Sangram Singh. The new fashion for large, panoramic, densely peopled scenes of court life, initiated in earlier paintings such as the Diwali (cat. no. 52) and Holi (cat. no. 58) scenes, was pursued with relentless enthusiasm. The subject matter of these ever grander compositions became as it were a celebration and comprehensive documentary record of the public life of the Maharana (who was however noticeably more reticent about his leisure hours in the *zenana* than Amar Singh had been). The smaller stock portraits and procession scenes (cat. nos. 68-71) become less frequent than spectacular set-pieces in which the Maharana and his companions are seen from a distant viewpoint, engaged in their daily activities, sometimes shown in several stages by the archaic device of continuous narration. The most successful of these is the great crane hunt (cat. no. 78), also notable for its sensitive treatment of landscape. In other paintings we see Sangram Singh watching elephant fights at the Chaugan arena (cat. no. 74), attending the daily feeding of crocodiles at Jagmandir island (cat. no. 72) or playing cards with his sardars in camp at night (cat. no. 73). On one occasion the elephant he was riding seized and threw his *huqqa*-bearer, and this too was thought worthy of record in a painting (cat. no. 83). Sangram Singh's initiative in this respect, which was continued by his immediate successors, has in effect preserved for us a unique and lively record of a courtly way of life that was already distantly threatened. The quantity and size of these pictures inevitably led to a falling off in technical quality; but pleasing archaistic improvisations also began to occur, such as the movable viewpoint from which the royal hunting party is seen as it goes to visit the Gosain Nilakanthaji (cat. no. 76). As in Amar Singh's time, no artists' names are recorded in the increasingly prolix clerks' inscriptions on the paintings. Several individual hands are however discernible, one of which, notable for finely delineated drawing and a frequent use of three-quarter faces, can be identified as that of Jai Ram (cat. nos. 83, 84) by comparison with his later, signed work.

After the death of Sangram Singh in 1734, Mewar, like the other Rajput kingdoms, entered a period of steady decline that was only halted by British intervention in the early 19th century. Maharana Jagat Singh II (b. 1709, r. 1734-51) lacked the experience and stature to lead a concerted Rajput resistance to the Maratha incursions. In 1736 he was forced to entertain the Maratha leader Baji Rao at Udaipur and to begin the large annual payments of tribute that were eventually to destroy the country's economy. Jagat Singh himself only exacerbated this state of affairs by waging a costly war over the disputed Jaipur succession, in which the Marathas also became involved, while at home his sardars began to turn against him. He seems to have showed a blithe insouciance in the midst of these troubles. A few months after his humiliation by Baji Rao, we see him watching dance dramas in a palace courtyard, smiling, as ever slightly sardonically, as he smokes a *huqqa* in the form of a woman (cat. no. 114). Larger compositions of this type begin to lose the more solemnly documentary atmosphere of Sangram Singh's reign, and·take on an air of escapist gaiety which is borne out by Tod's exasperated appraisal of Jagat Singh's character: 'Addicted to pleasure, his habits of levity and profusion totally unfitted him for the task of governing his country at such a juncture; he considered his elephant fights of more importance than keeping down the Mahrattas. Like all his family, he patronized the arts, greatly enlarged the palace, and expended £250,000 in embellishing the islets of the Pichola. The villas scattered over the valley were all erected by him, and many of those festivals devoted to idleness and dissipation, and now firmly rooted at Udaipur, were instituted by Jagat Singh II.'⁹ It is true that seasonal festivals, of which there are normally many in the Hindu calendar, came to assume an unusual prominence in the daily life of Udaipur. Tod remarks elsewhere that 'this determination to be happy amidst calamity... has made the court proverbial in [Rajasthan] in the adage *"sat bara, aur nau teohara"*, *i.e.* nine holidays out of seven days.'[10]

The art historian must feel some gratitude to Jagat Singh, or to his clerks, for the painting inscriptions of his reign begin to include artists' names in some numbers. Those represented here include the gifted Jai Ram (cat. nos. 113, 114), the very competent Naga (cat. no. 111) and the more pedestrian Raghunath, whose masterpiece is perhaps the scene of Jagat Singh's revels in a rose-garden[11] (cat. no. 128). An intriguing, posthumously dated picture of Jagat Singh slaying a boar is an early work by Bakhta (cat. no. 130).

Jagat Singh's immediate successors ruled briefly and ineffectually. The remorseless exactions of the Marathas and the disaffection among the Mewar sardars continued unchecked. Little innovation occurred in the practice of court painting, which continued, if erratically, on the momentum it had gained under Sangram Singh and Jagat Singh. Few paintings seem to have been made for Pratap Singh (r. 1751-54), but a number of good established artists, such as Nuruddin (cat. no. 150), worked for his son Raj Singh (r. 1754-61), who was only ten at the time of his accession. However none of the known dated pictures of Raj Singh's reign are later than 1756; either he lost interest as a patron or, more likely, he could no longer afford to pay the artists. The Maharana's resources were so depleted by this time that he had to borrow money from the Brahmin tribute-collector to pay for his own marriage.

Raj Singh, who had a cruel and unattractive nature, died in 1761, possibly by poison. He was succeeded by his uncle Ari (also known as Arsi) Singh, whose oppressiveness and vile temper had, within a few years, entirely alienated the sardars, contributing further to the disintegration of Mewar. Ari Singh was however responsible for an explosion of painting activity in the early years of his reign. Large numbers of generally stereotyped portraits of himself, riding in procession or giving chase on the hunting-field (cat. nos. 154-57), were produced, as well as a series of somewhat wooden portraits of earlier Maharanas (cat. nos. 181, 182) and an enormous catalogue in pictures of the hundreds of horses and elephants in the royal stables (cat. nos. 185-95). The latter tend not unnaturally to be very monotonous, and a new and unattractive hastiness of execution appears in much of the work of this time. Some paintings of good quality were produced nonetheless, such as a portrait by Shiva (cat. no. 169), and scenes of the Maharana with his sardars by Bhima (cat. no, 166) and Bakhta (cat. no. 167). Other painters represented here include Jugarsi, Jiva, Kesu Ram and Bhopa. An absence of dated paintings in Ari Singh's reign after 1767 is perhaps again attributable to the economic and political disruption of the period. The court artists were presumably compelled to seek other means of subsistence or to find work with the sardars or other patrons. One who took the latter course was Bakhta, who went to the court of the recalcitrant and now virtually independent Rawat of Deogarh, where a vigorous local variant of the Udaipur style became established at this time.

In 1773 Ari Singh was assassinated on the hunting-field by a Bundi prince, probably with the collusion of the Mewar sardars. The brief reign of the juvenile Maharana Hamir Singh (1773-78) was almost entirely unproductive of painting, while the unpretentious quality of two portraits painted early in the reign of Maharana Bhim Singh (b. 1768, r. 1778-1828) was clearly the best that he was able to command (cat.

nos. 202, 203). He too had to borrow to pay for his marriage ceremony. No more flamboyant panoramic paintings were forthcoming, although Bhim Singh might well have desired them, for he shared the incorrigibly escapist mentality of his grandfather, Jagat Singh II. Tod, who knew him well, wrote: '...though able, wise and amiable, his talents were nullified by numerous weak points. Vain shows, frivolous amusements, and an ill-regulated liberality alone occupied him... He had little steadiness of purpose, and was particularly obnoxious to female influence.'[13] One of Bhim Singh's greater achievements was to father more than a hundred children, although only one of his sons survived him. The paintings of his reign are comparatively small in size and restricted in scope. Some of the most pleasing are by Chokha, the son of Bakhta, such as the scene of a buffalo sacrifice, teeming with squat figures, which can be attributed to him (cat. no. 210).

In 1818 the almost complete decline of Mewar was arrested when Bhim Singh and the other Rajput rulers accepted British suzerainty. However even the return of peace and stability, much as it was welcomed, brought about a 'chilling void' and an 'enervating calm'[14] in which the Rajputs could find little play for their natural aggressions apart from hunting, opium-eating and bickering over land disputes. Bhim Singh himself only took advantage of the restoration of his income through Tod's wise administrative measures by indulging in further extravagance which reduced his court to penury yet again. The British had higher hopes of the reliability of the heir apparent, Jawan Singh (r. 1828-38), whom Sir Charles Metcalfe described as 'a prince in appearance, and a gentleman in manners. He bears a high character, and manages his own affairs well.'[15] But these were dispelled when Jawan Singh turned to debauchery soon after his accession. Nor did he distinguish himself as a patron of painting. Both his reign and that of his adopted successor, Sirdar Singh (r. 1838-42), are notable mainly for a lifeless stream of hackneyed equestrian and hunting portraits or else small vapid scenes of court ladies or Krishna and Radha. The prevailing style is an exhausted version of that practised under Bhim Singh, in which dark green tones predominate. The border colouring departs more than before from the standard red, often with the addition of artless embellishment in silver.

At least one of the artists who worked for Jawan Singh was to escape this mediocrity, probably with the encouragement of the more able Maharana Sarup Singh (r. 1842-61). This was Tara, whose period of known activity extends from 1836 to c. 1866. Many pictures ascribed to him survive, and we also have a perhaps unique portrait of the artist himself, described as 'Tara Chund, court painter, Udipur', one of a number of water-colours painted at Udaipur in 1851 by an itinerant English artist, William Carpenter[16] (fig. 1). This warmly sympathetic portrait tempts one to think that the two artists from alien traditions got on well together. Tara's work shows an evolution from stock equestrian portraits to a confident handling of larger compositions such as the boar hunt at Khas Odi (cat. no. 265) and an occasional indulgence in happy conceits such as the double image of the Maharana on horseback hurling powder at Holi (cat. no. 268). In the 1850s European influences begin to appear in Tara's work, for example in the limited use of stippled modelling and recession in his picture of the durbar held for Sir Henry Lawrence (cat. no. 273) and in his increasing use of virulent imported colours, as in the later portrait of Maharana Shambhu Singh (cat. no. 274).

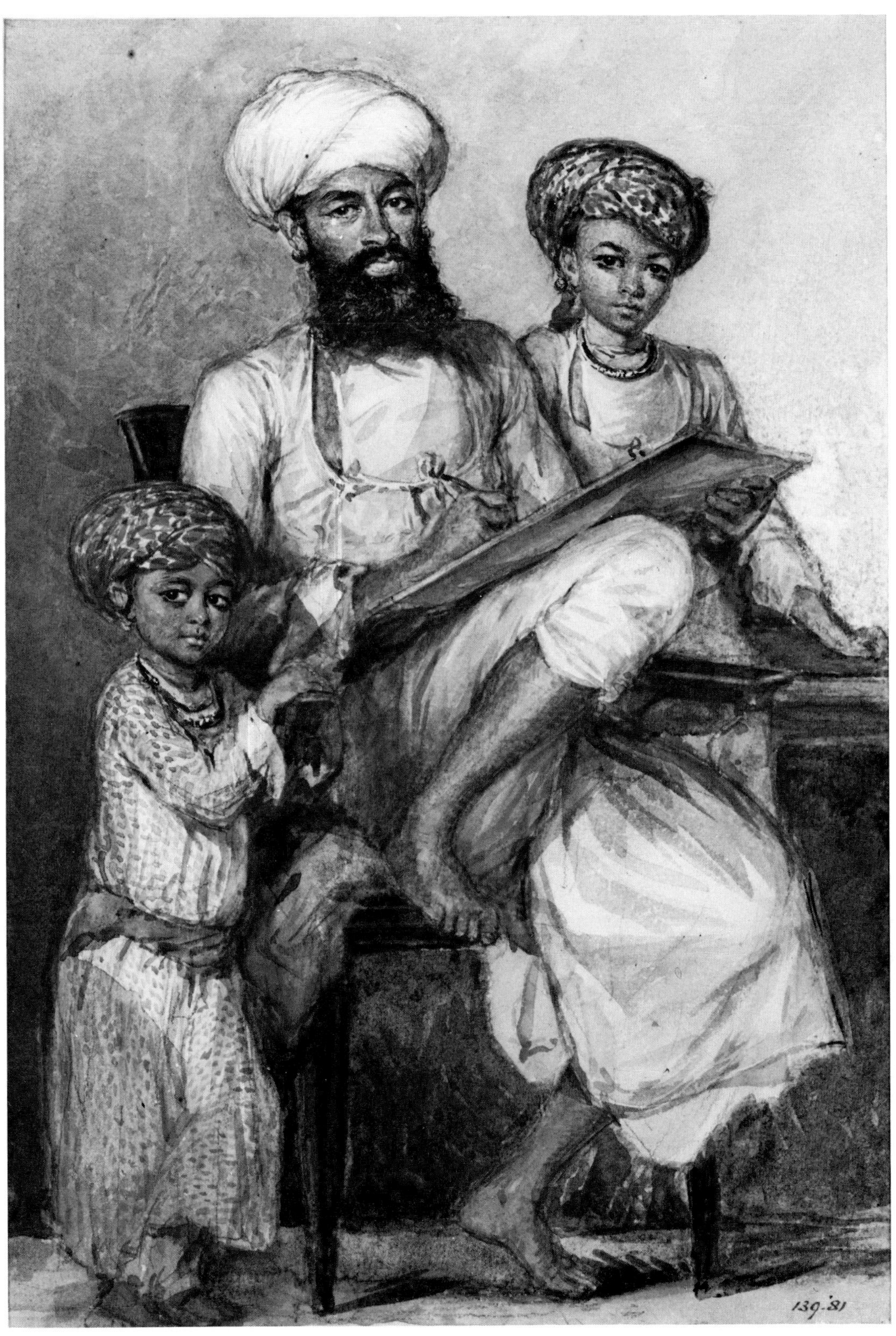

Fig. 1.
Tara Chand, Court Painter at Udaipur
by William Carpenter
Victoria and Albert Museum

Although Sarup Singh maintained generally good relations with the British, earning their gratitude by offering sanctuary to British families fleeing from the Mutiny in 1857, he nevertheless contrived to keep his distance from them. However, in the reign of the youthful and less adroit Shambhu Singh (b. 1847, r. 1861-74) the British Political Agents were able to gain a far greater control over the administration. Social reforms were introduced, including the abolition of suttee, and the Maharana himself learned English;[17] thus the modern age began to enter Udaipur. By the 1880s a European engineer was employed to lay out a public garden, with cricket and football pitches, a zoo and a hall commemorating Queen Victoria's jubilee. The court artists meanwhile became less able to withstand the challenge of European pictorial conventions and the novel attractions of photography. Stylistically hybrid paintings, sometimes showing charm and originality, continued to be produced as late as the 1920s and 1930s. There are still competent artists at Udaipur today painting fakes, mainly in the 18th century style, for the tourist market.

[1] The artists generally belonged to the carpenters' occupational group, as the affix *sutar* to two of their names implies (cat. nos. 127, 158). Next to nothing is known about them as individuals, although some information may one day be forthcoming when the *haqiqat bahis* or daily records in the palace archives are studied by scholars.

[2] J. Tod, *Annals and Antiquities of Rajasthan*, vol. I, p. 311.

[3] F. Bernier, *Travels in the Mughal Empire*, rev. ed., London, 1934, p. 40.

[4] *ibid.*, pp. 40-41.

[5] Tod, *Annals*, vol. I, p. 434.

[6] It is however possible that a mid-17th century equestrian portrait in the National Museum, New Delhi, may be of Jagat Singh; see J. Brijbhushan, *The World of Indian Miniatures*, Tokyo, 1979, pl. 22.

[7] Private collection.

[8] Tod, *Annals*, vol. I, pp. 459-60.

[9] *ibid.*, p. 495.

[10] *ibid.*, vol. II, p. 656. Very full accounts of the annual festivals at Udaipur are given by Shyamaldas, *Vir Vinod*, vol. I, pp. 120-36, and Tod, *loc. cit.*, pp. 656-700.

[11] This picture is loosely based on an earlier composition of the period of Sangram Singh (private collection). Another large painting by Raghunath, dated 1756, and showing Maharana Raj Singh II in the Chini Mahal in the palace, is in the collection of Kumar Sangram Singh of Nawalgarh.

[12] Both Jiva and Jugarsi had previously worked for Maharana Jagat Singh. Pictures dated 1750 by each of them are respectively in the Baroda Museum, (Gangoly, *Critical Catalogue of the Miniature Paintings in the Baroda Museum*, p. 96) and a private collection (an unpublished bear hunt scene by Jugarsi).

[13] Tod, *Annals*, vol. I, p. 558.

[14] *ibid.*, p. 553n.

[15] Brooke(s), *History of Meywar*, p. 33.

[16] William Carpenter (c. 1818-99) travelled widely in northern India between 1850-56; many of his sketches are preserved in the Indian Department of the Victoria and Albert Museum. See also W. G. Archer, *Paintings of the Sikhs*, London, 1966, p. 148.

[17] An illustration in Rousselet's *India and its Native Princes*, p. 167, shows the Political Agent leaning avuncularly on the back of Shambhu Singh's chair at a hunt.

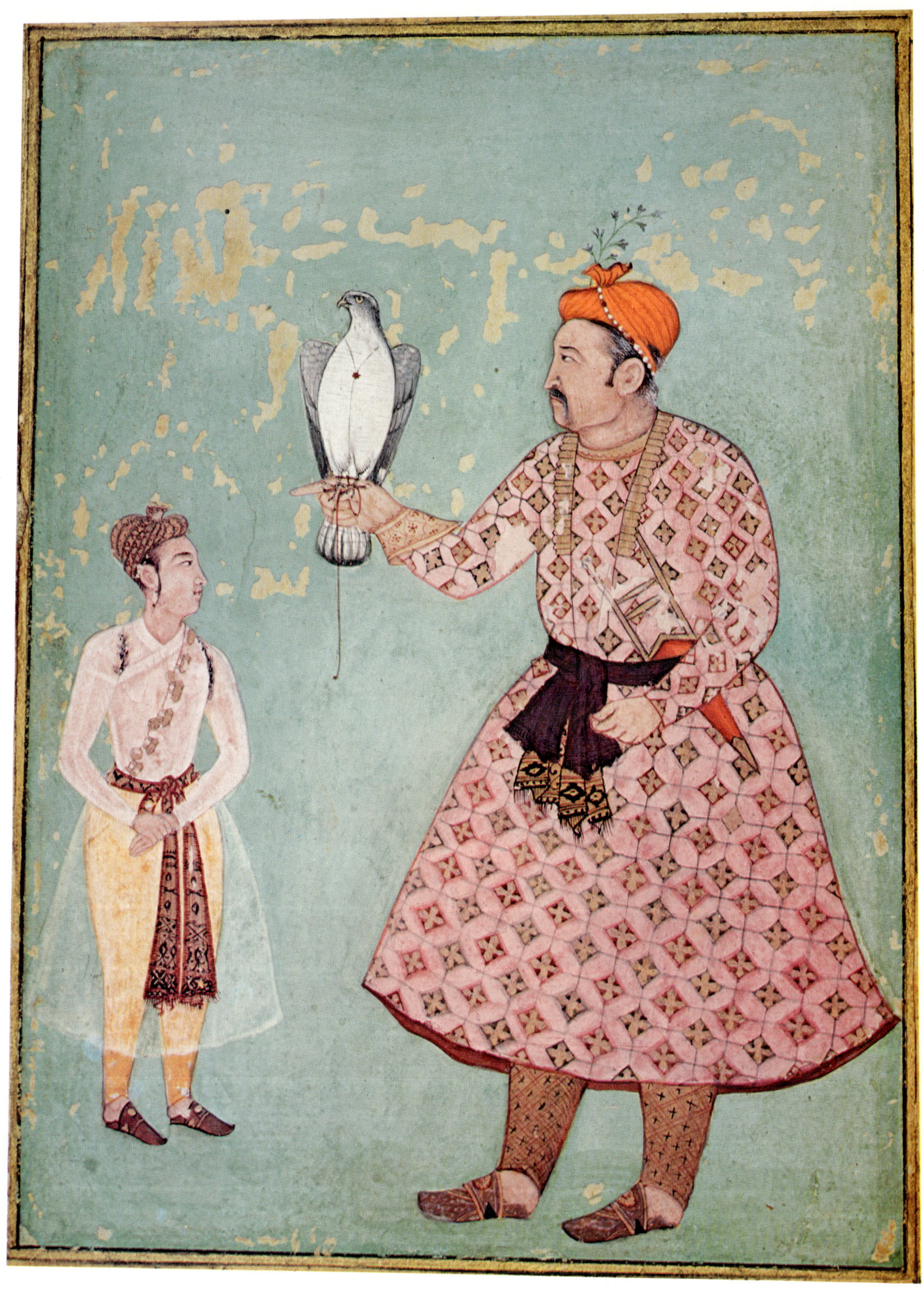

Colour plate No. 3   **The Emperor Akbar with a Hawk** (cat. no. 1)

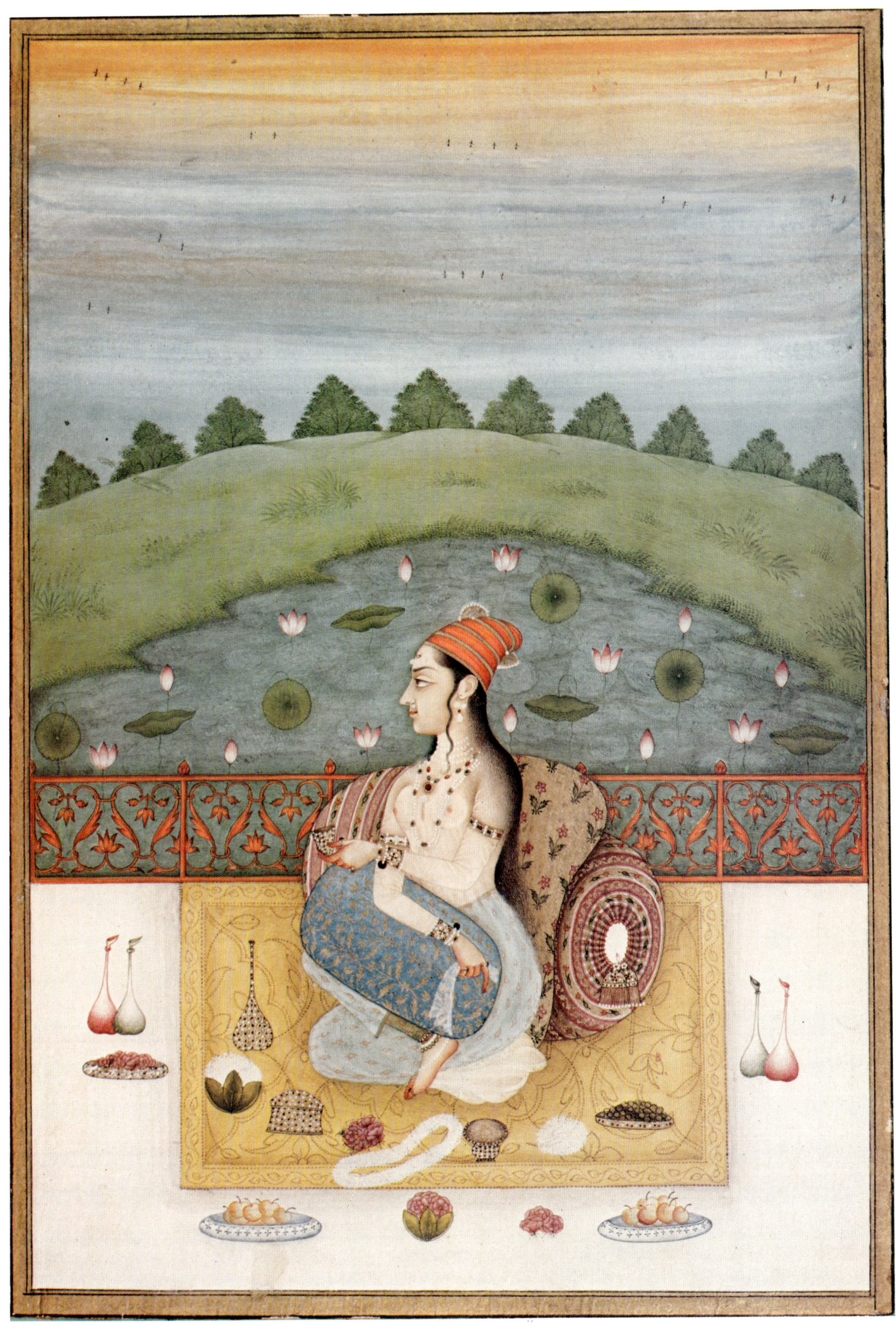

Colour plate No. 4   **A Lady on a Terrace** (cat. no. 18)

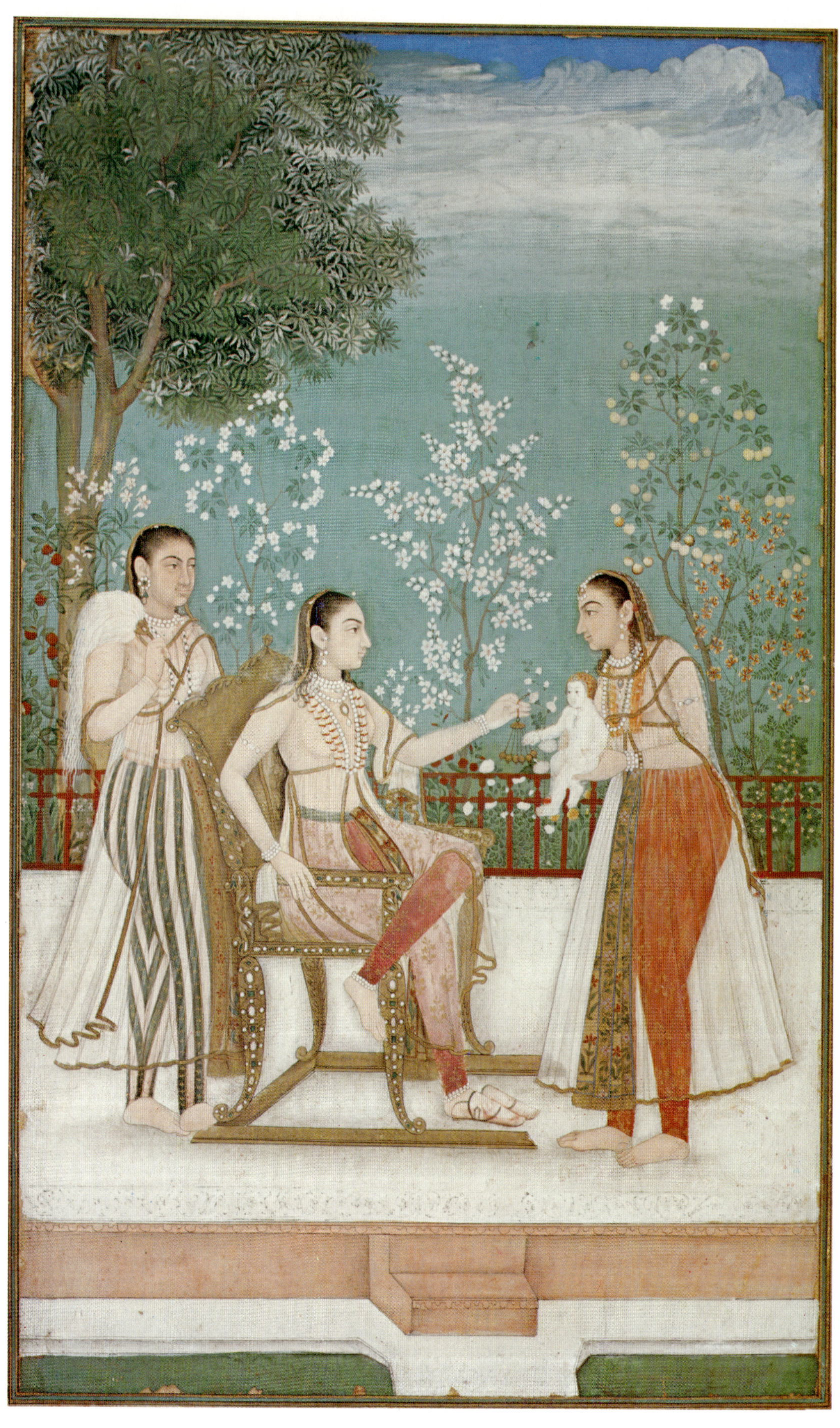

Colour plate No. 5   **A Lady Playing with a Child** (cat. no. 16)

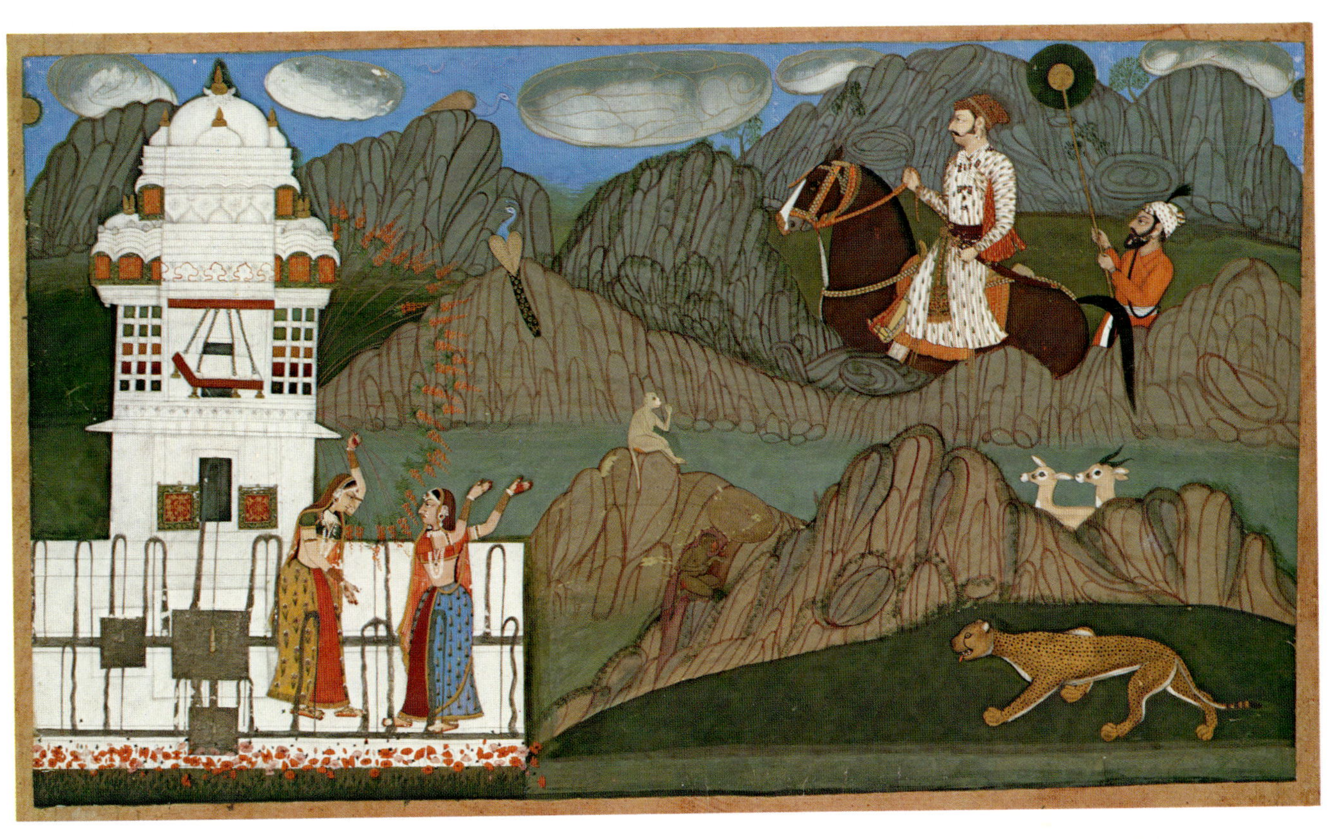

Colour plate No. 6   **A Raja and a Pining Lady** (cat. no. 14)

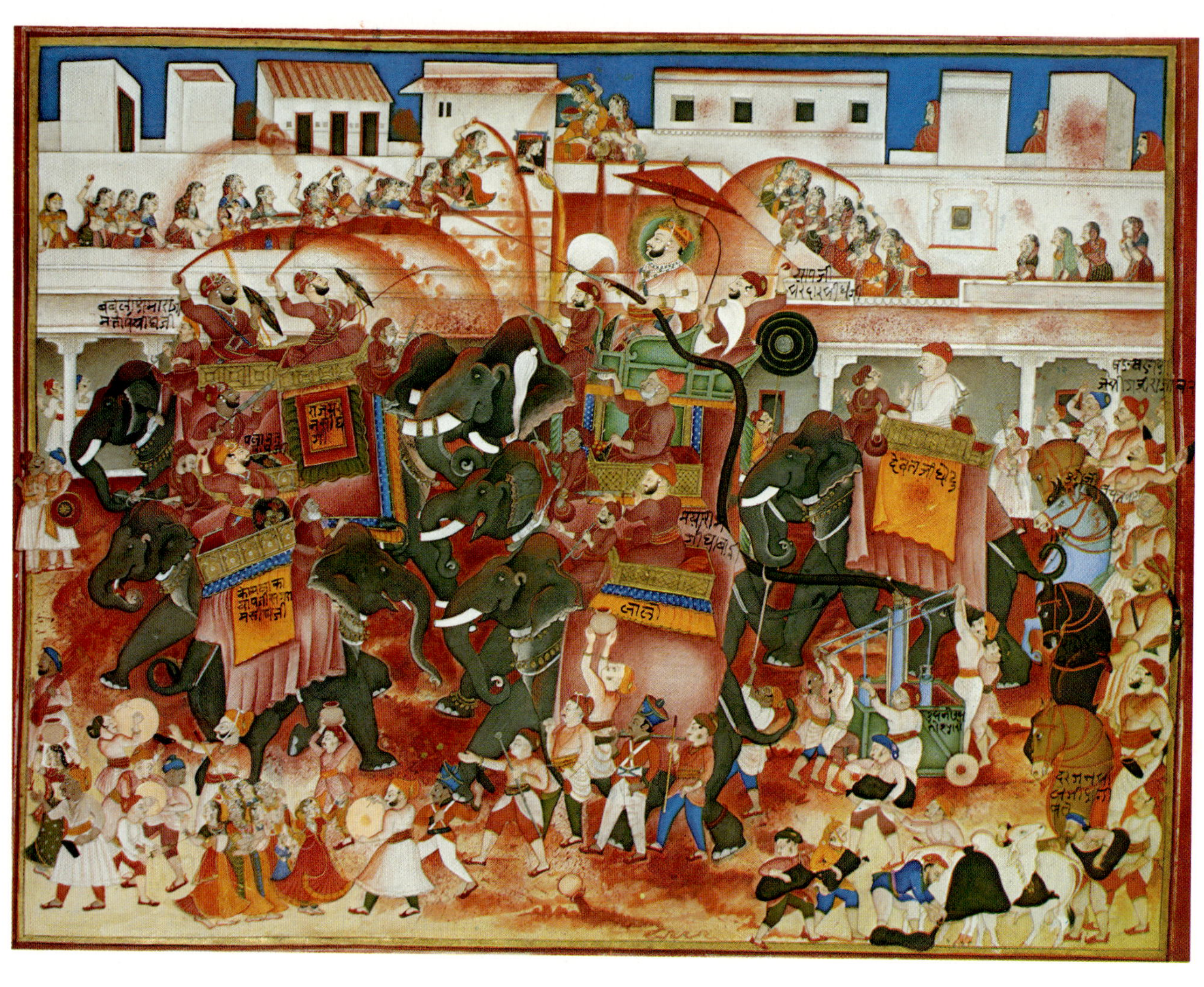

Colour plate No. 7 **Maharao Ram Singh II of Kotah and Companions Playing Holi on Elephants in a Street** (cat. no. 35)

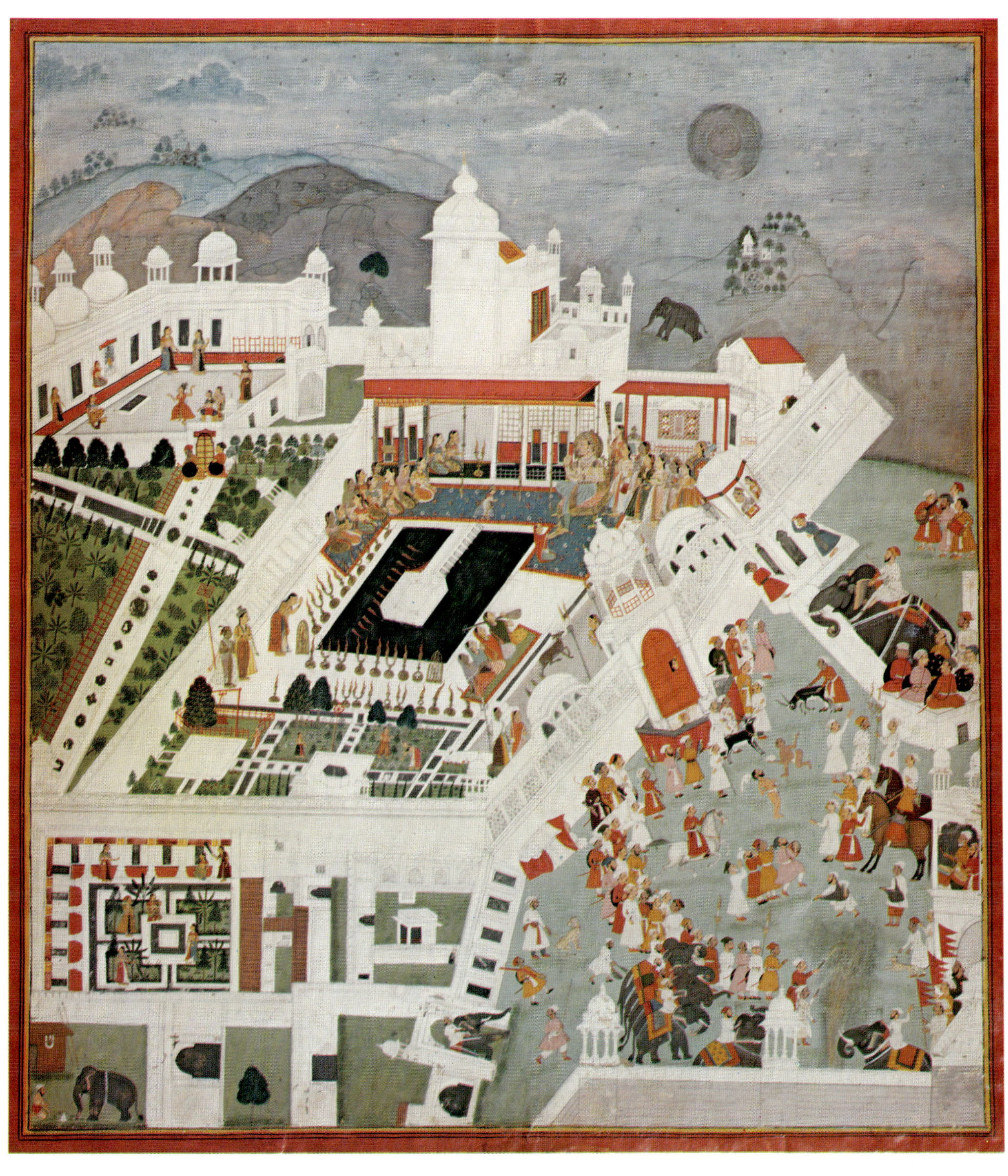

Colour plate No. 8   **Diwali Celebrations at Kotah** (cat. no. 52)

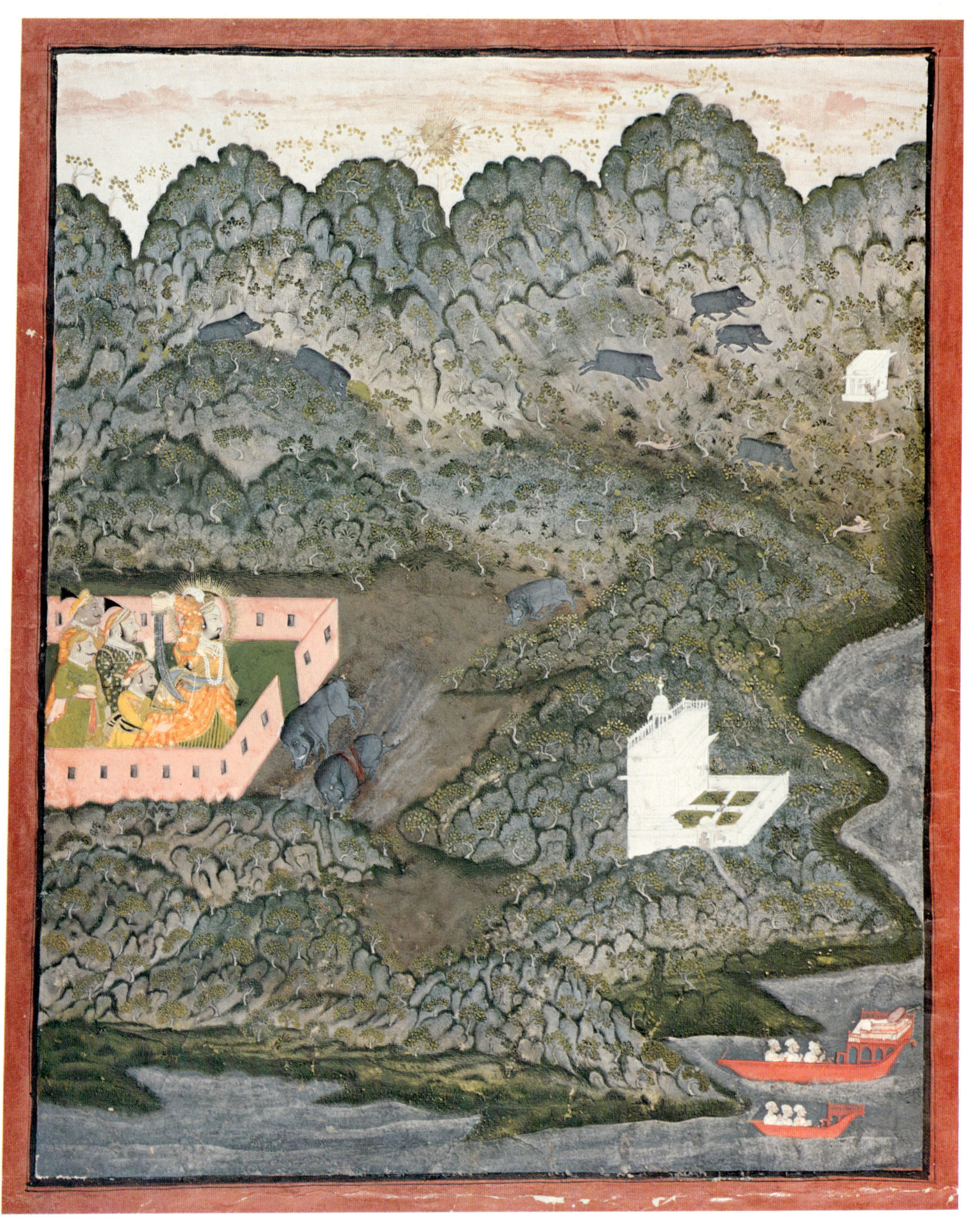

Colour plate No. 9   **Maharana Jagat Singh Slaying a Boar at Khas Odi** (cat. no. 130)

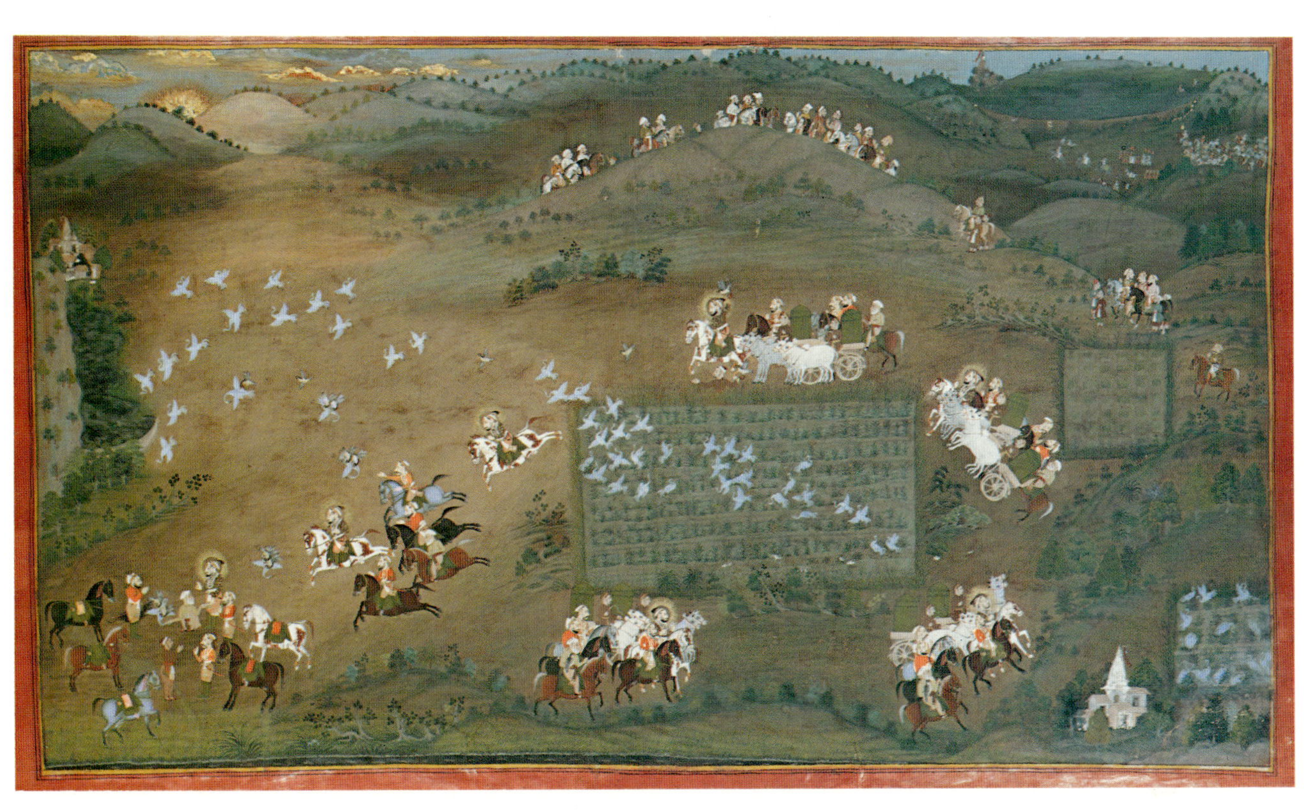

Colour plate No. 10   **Maharana Sangram Singh Hunting Crane at Nahar Magra** (cat. no. 78)

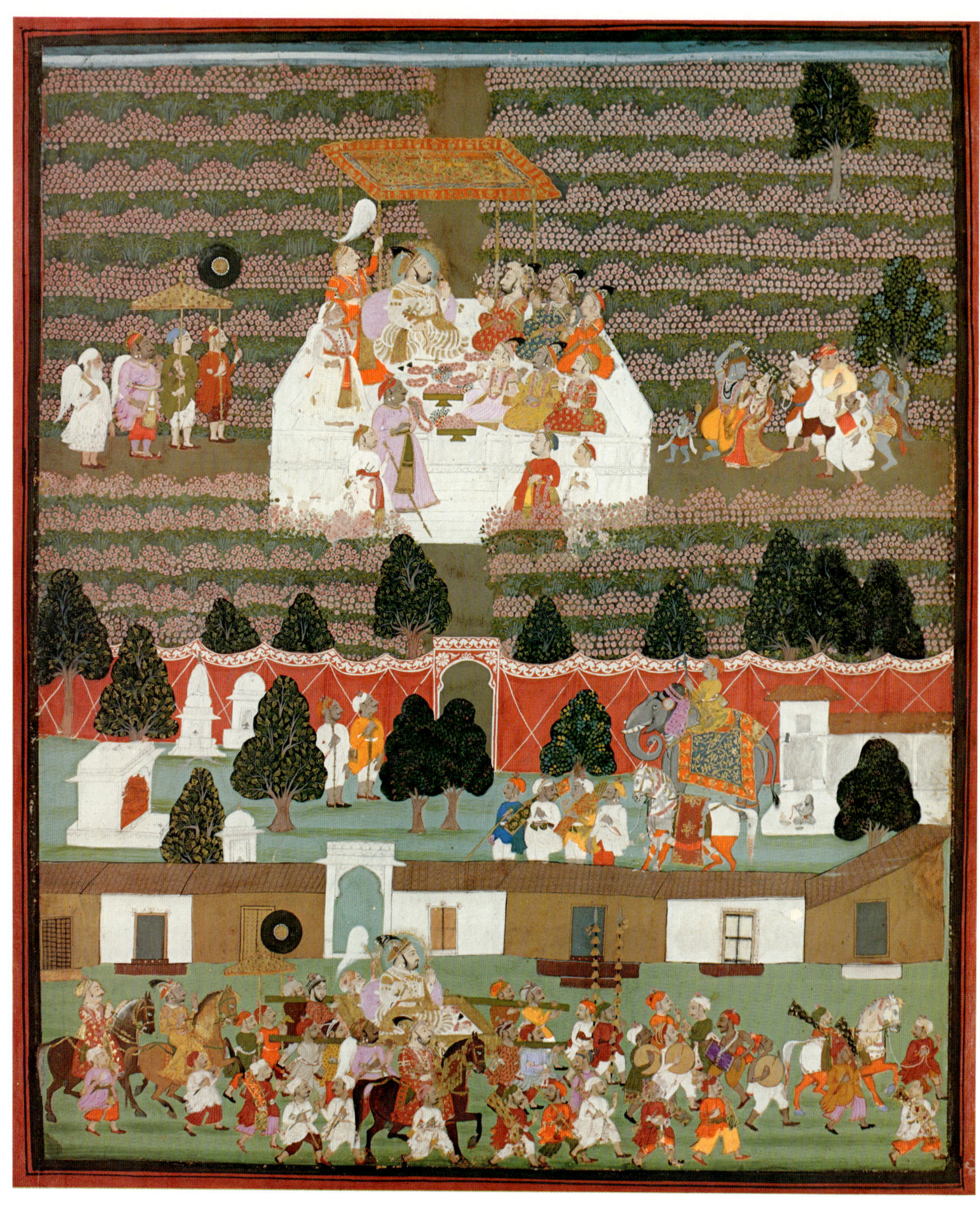

Colour plate No. 11 **Maharana Jagat Singh Celebrating the Festival of Flowers in the Gulab Bari Gardens** (cat. no. 128)

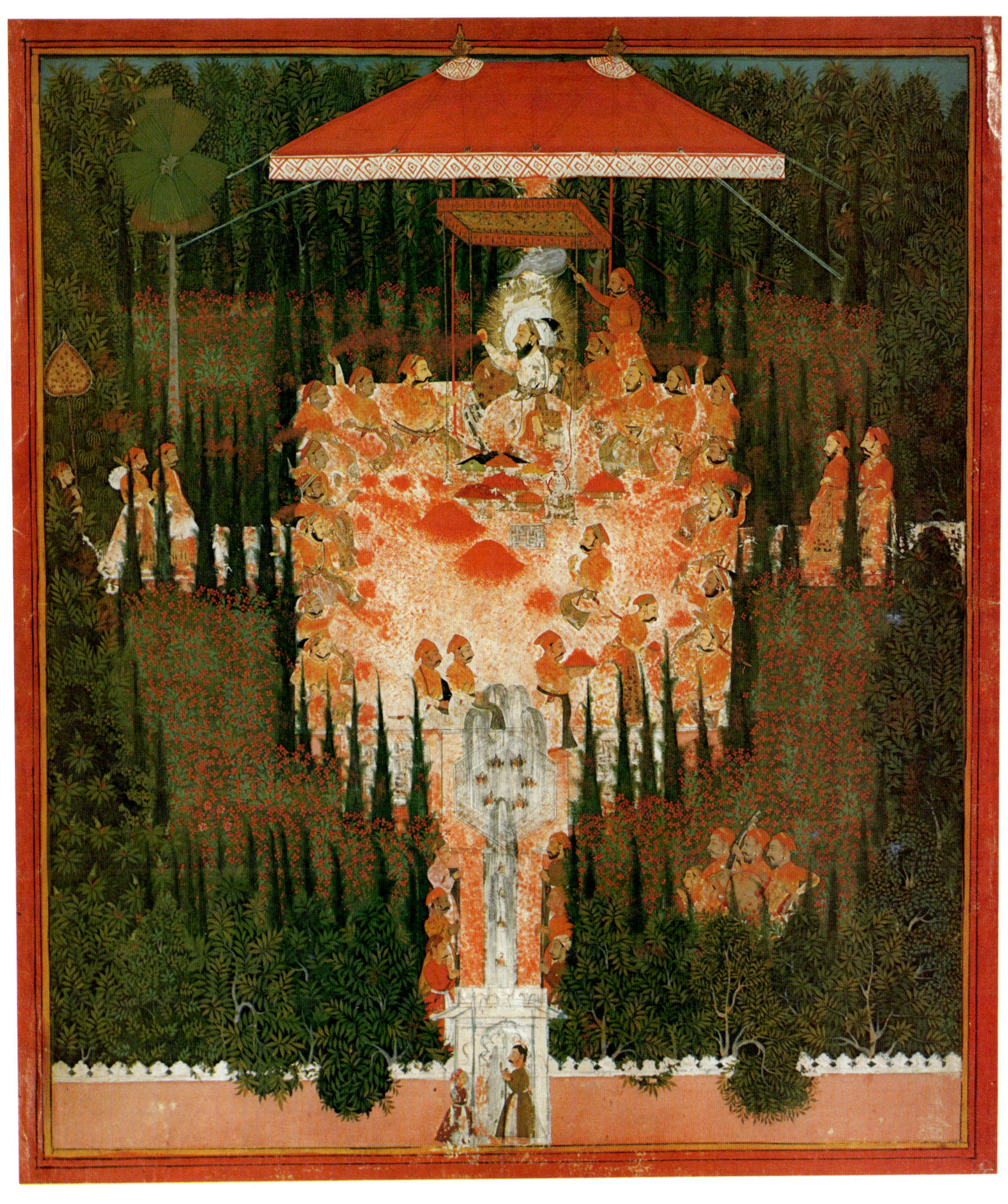

Colour plate No. 12 **Maharana Amar Singh Playing Holi with his Sardars** (cat. no. 58)

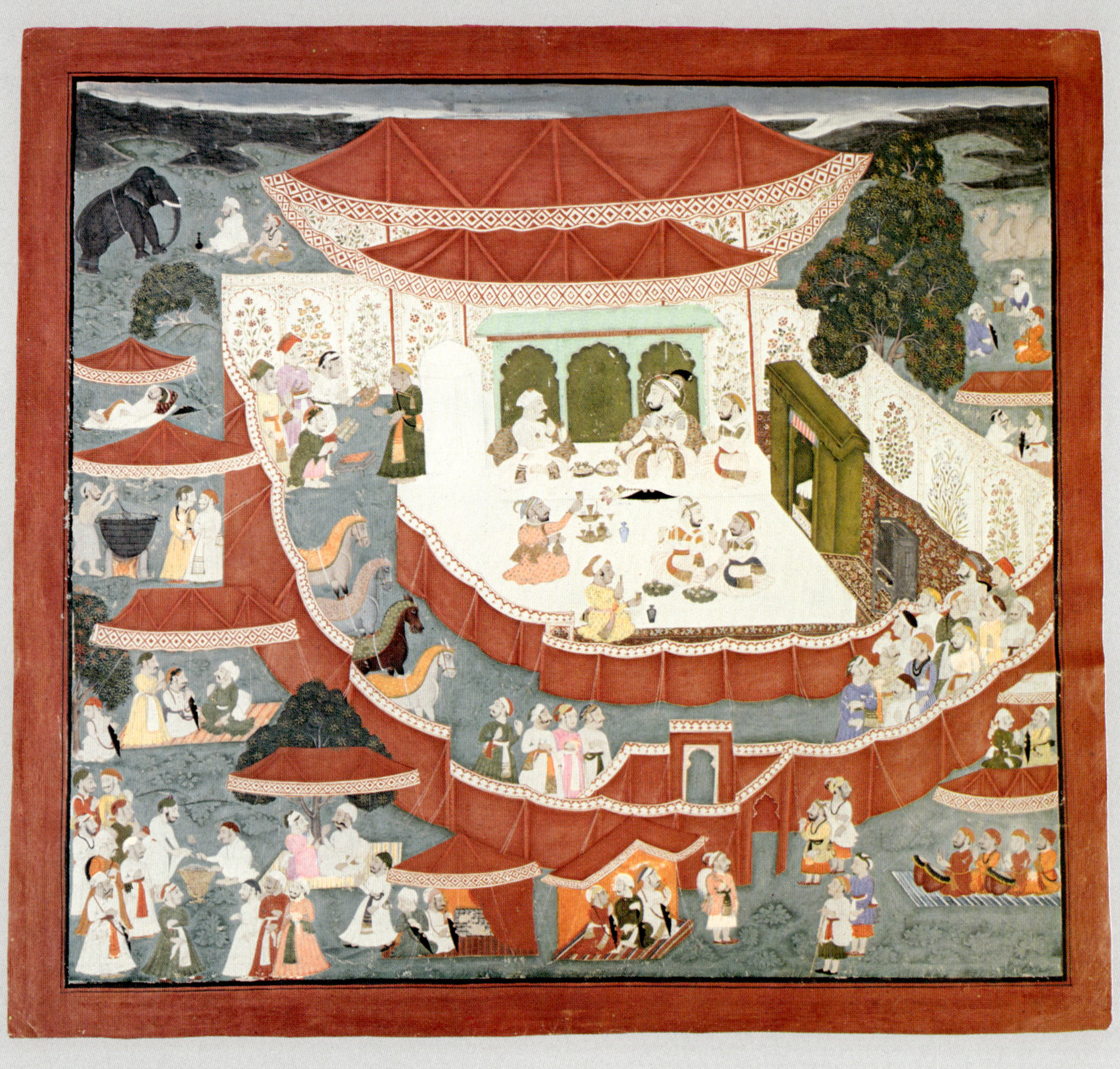

Colour plate No. 13 **Maharana Sangram Singh Receiving Maharaja Sawai Jai Singh in Camp** (cat. no. 84)

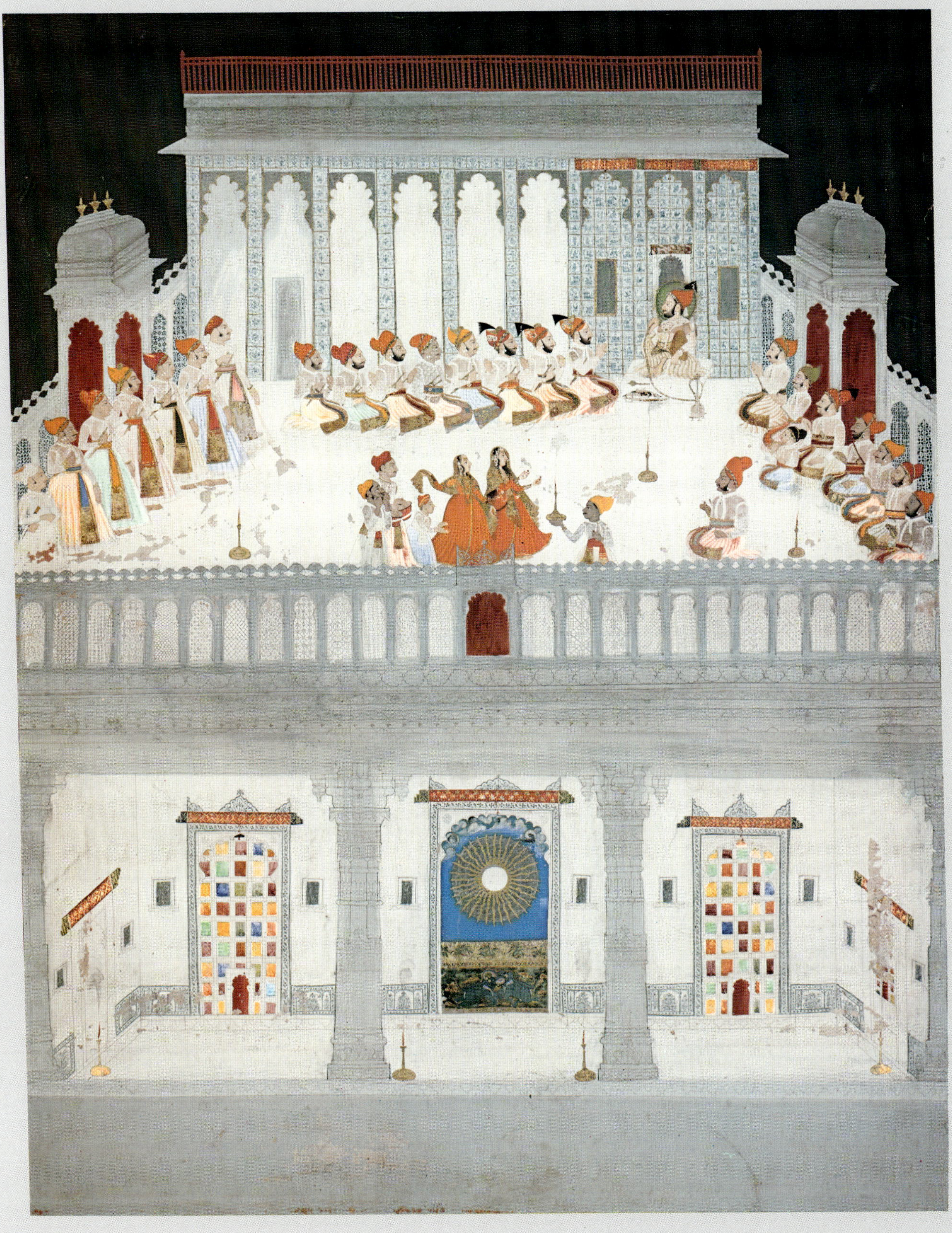

Colour plate No. 14 **Maharana Ari Singh in Durbar** (cat. no. 167)

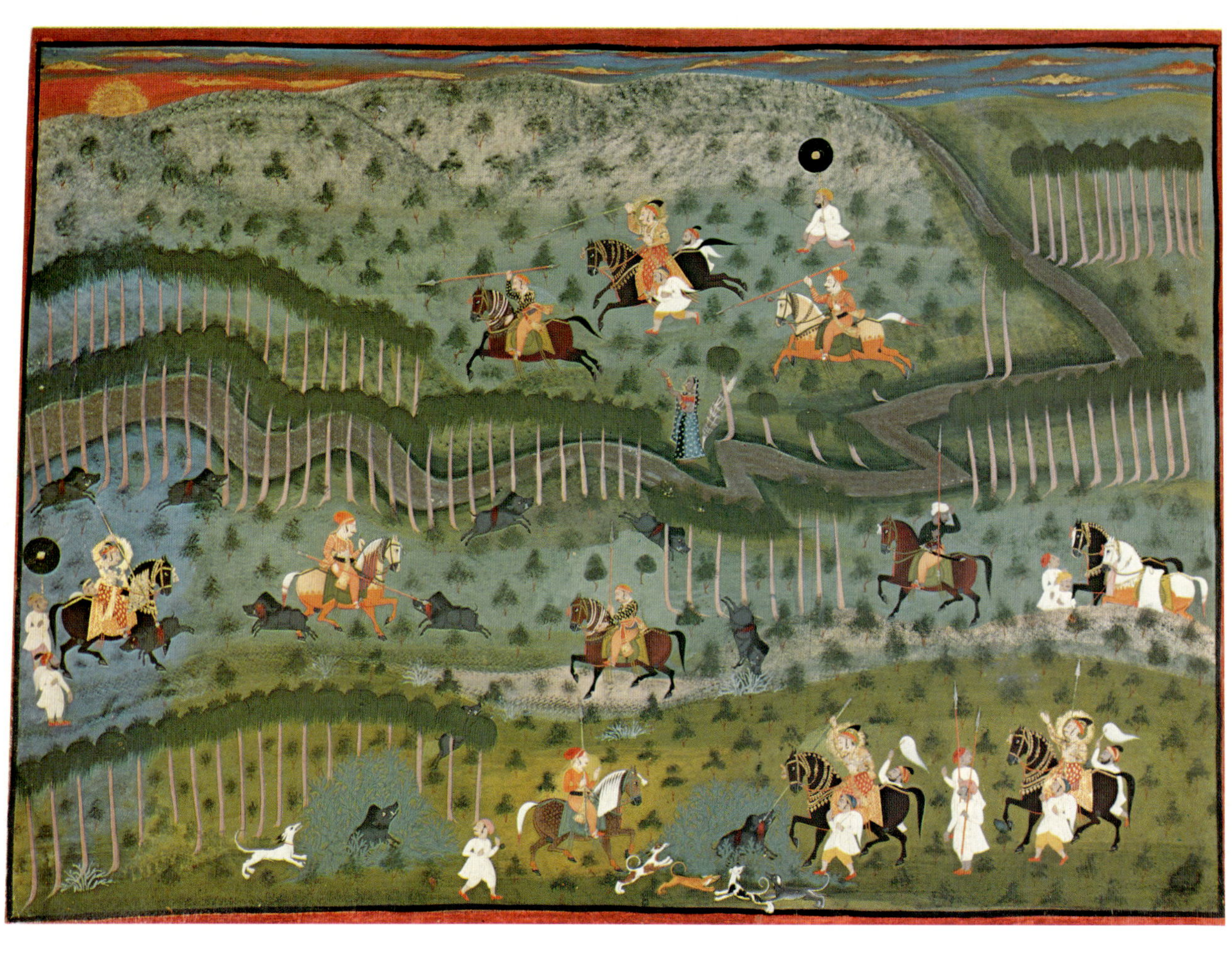

Colour plate No. 15 **Maharana Ari Singh Hunting Boar** (cat. no. 168)

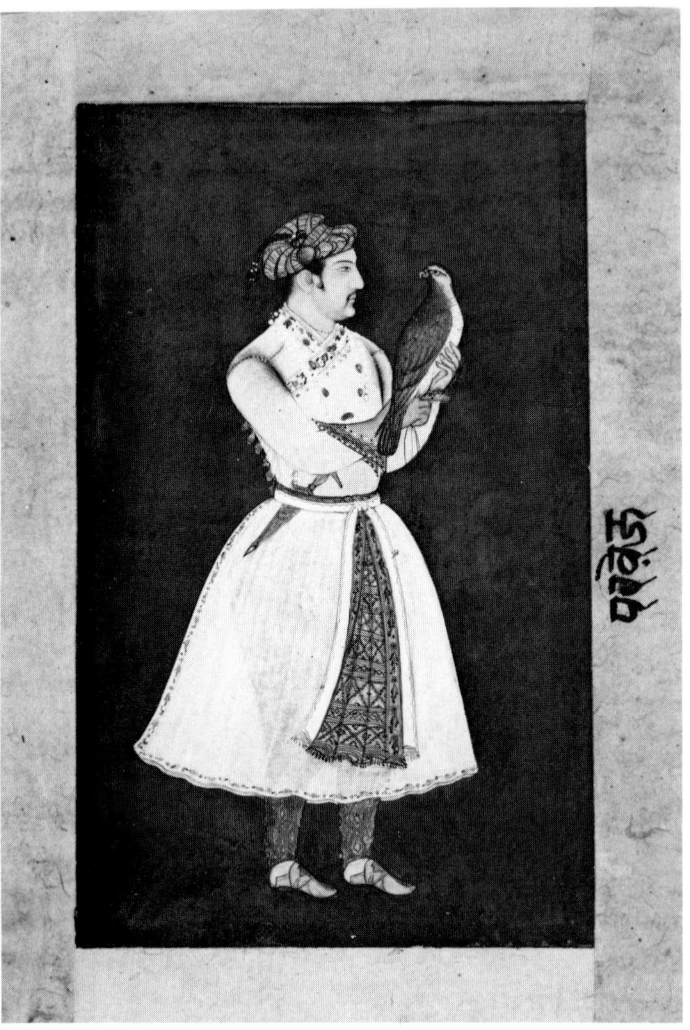

1

The Emperor Akbar with a Hawk
Mughal, c. 1600
12.5 x 9 cm
(Colour Plate No. 3)

Akbar stands holding a hawk, wearing an orange *pagri*, in which a plant sprig is fixed, and a mauve *jama* with gold quatrefoil pattern. A young prince stands beside him. Pale green background. Narrow gold margin; buff border with silver flecks, inscribed in gold: *akabar bādasāh;* a similar Persian inscription on the back.

Cf. Y. A. Godard, 'Un album de portraits des princes timurides de l'Inde', *Athar-e Iran,* vol. II, 1937, fig. 82.

2

Prince Parviz
Mughal, c. 1620-25
10.2 x 6.2 cm

Prince Parviz, son of the Emperor Jahangir, in a pink *pagri* and transparent white *jama*, stands holding a hawk. Dark green background. Buff paper surround, inscribed: *paravej.* The back of the painting is marbled and inscribed in Persian: *sultān parvīz.*

Parviz is here shown in later life; he died of dissipation at the age of thirty-seven in 1626. A Mughal historian observed that 'he had faithfully followed his father in the ways of eating and drinking but was not gifted with the same natural constitution and powers of endurance.' (B. Prasad, *History of Jahangir,* 5th ed., Allahabad, 1962, p. 393).

3

A Negro Musician
Mughal, late 17th century
20.2 x 12 cm

A negro musician with plant sprigs in his turban plays a stringed instrument and dances as he sings. A lightly coloured drawing, evidently a version after an unknown original. Buff border.

The instrument shown is, according to Dr J. R. Widdess, a five-stringed bowl-lyre of a type unknown in India but common in the ancient Mediterranean and at the present day in parts of north-east Africa. 'Abyssinian' *(habshi)* slaves were common in India, particularly in the Deccan, by the 17th century; evidently they brought their own instruments with them.

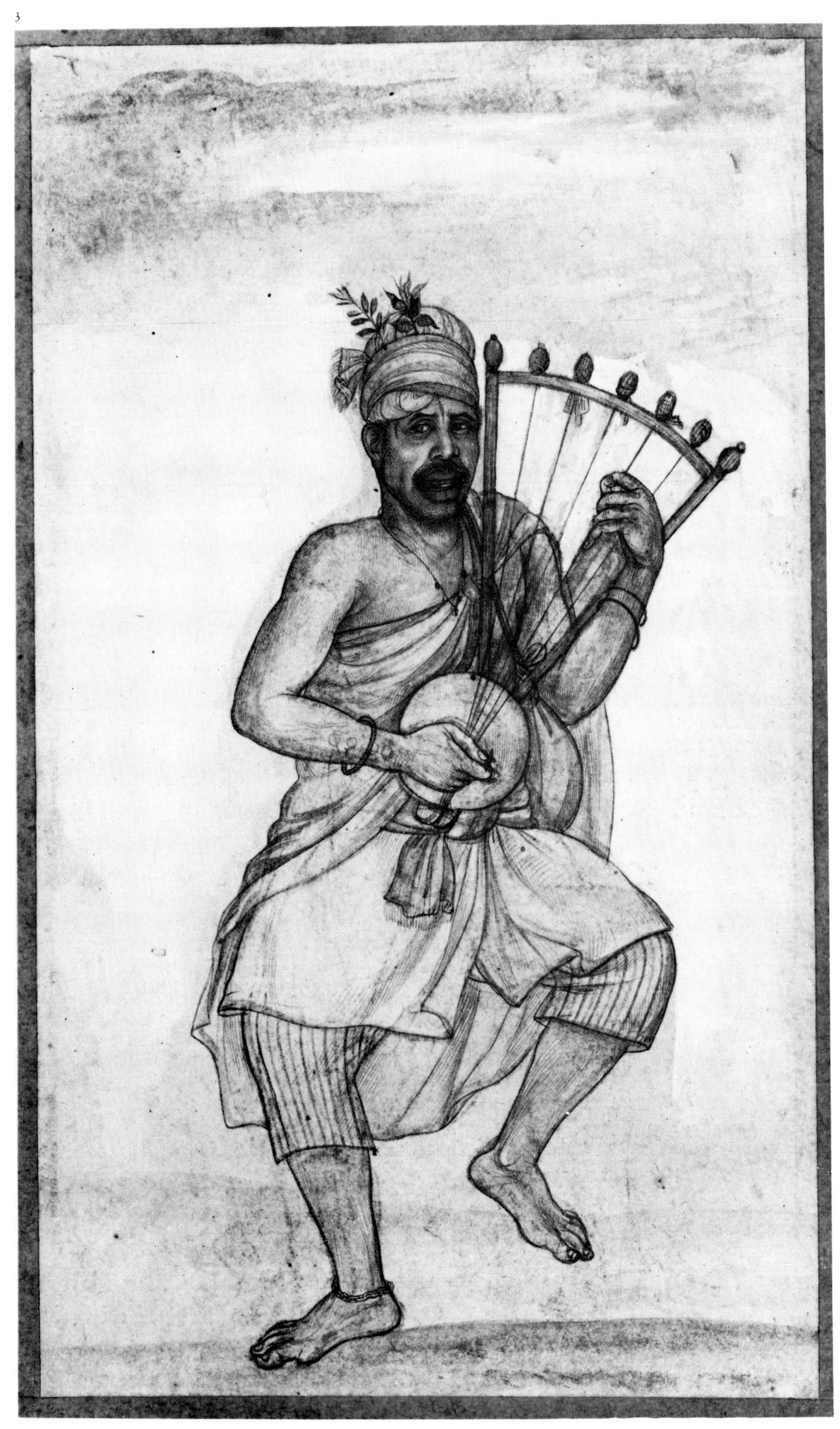

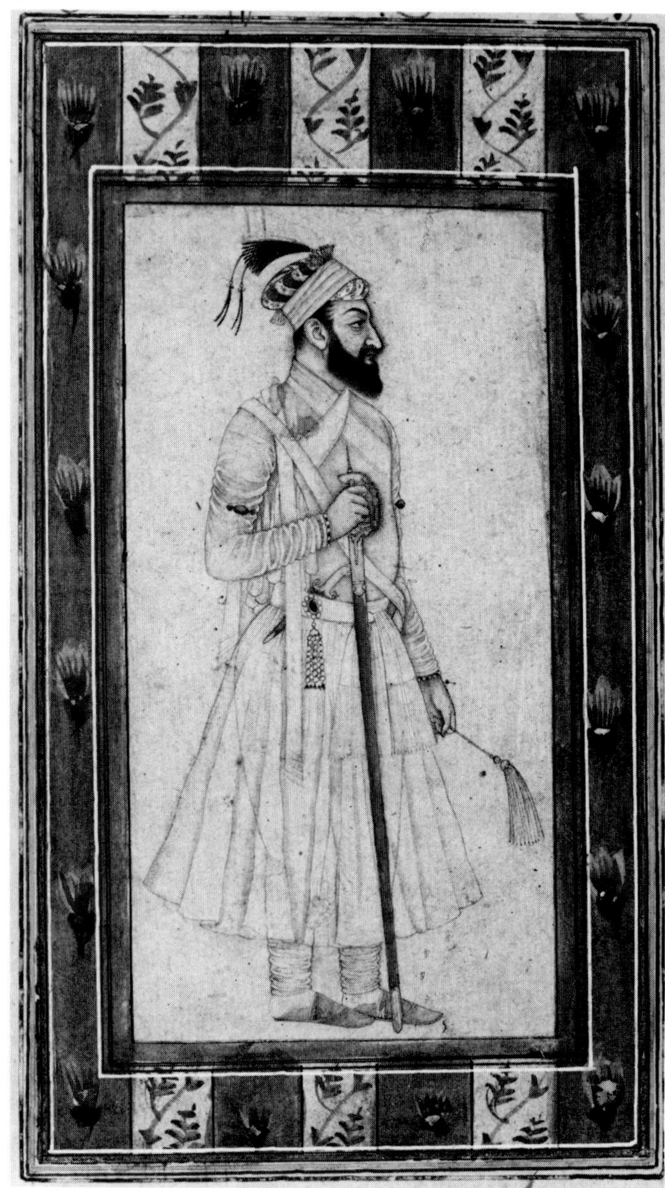

4
An Album Page
Side 1:
A Mughal nobleman, identified as Ja'far Khan (a prominent Mughal officer under Shah Jahan and Aurangzeb, d. 1670) but possibly the Emperor Aurangzeb himself, stands holding his sword-hilt and a fly-whisk.
Mughal, c. 1660
14.6 x 7.7 cm, 42.9 x 31.4 cm with border

Margin with pink flowers on gold stripes and gold, red, white, pale green and blue rules; buff border with gold ruling, numbered 31 and inscribed in Persian: *ja'far khān,* followed by a Persian *bait;* below, in *nagari* script: *sabīh jāphar khan.*
Published: Delhi Museum of Archaeology, *Loan Exhibition of Antiquities, Coronation Durbar, 1911,* Delhi, n.d., p. 124, pl. LIV(d).

Side 2:
Two Persian *baits,* written in *nasta'liq* on buff paper embellished with gold scrollwork, signed by the calligrapher 'Abd al-ghaffar.
Mughal, mid-17th century
17.1 x 9.1 cm

Dark buff inner border with silver floral decoration, gold inner margin and gold, pale green, red and blue rules; buff outer border with gold ruling and a seal of the period of Aurangzeb.

5
The Emperor Aurangzeb
Mughal, c. 1660-70
22.6 x 14.7 cm

The Emperor, with nimbus, stands facing left on a grassy knoll, with both hands on the hilt of his sword. He wears a fur-collared gold coat with floral pattern over a pink *jama* with trefoil pattern. Pale green background with cloud above. Gold marginal ruling; buff border, inscribed in gold: *orangajeb bādasāh.*

Inscribed on the back: *jme ?..utī cetra vadī 6 sam 1738/ oregajeb/ śrī bādasāhajī.* (This is a Rajasthani clerk's inscription dated 1681 A.D.)

6
An Album Page
Side 1:
The Emperor Aurangzeb, with nimbus, seated on a throne reading the Qur'an. Pallidly coloured. Pale green margin with gold, red and black rules; buff border with black and gold rules. Provincial Mughal, c. 1700.
16.8 x 9.8 cm, 38.4 x 27.1 cm with border

Side 2:
Four Persian *baits* written in *nasta'liq,* with meandering floral decoration on a gold background, signed by the calligrapher Sharif, at Akbarabad (Agra). Cream margin with black, red and gold rules; blue border with black and gold rules.

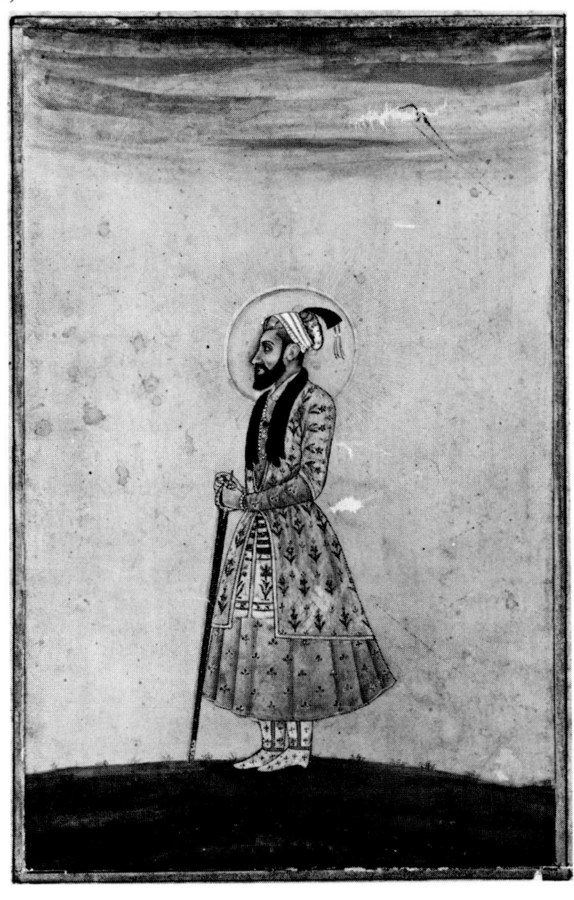

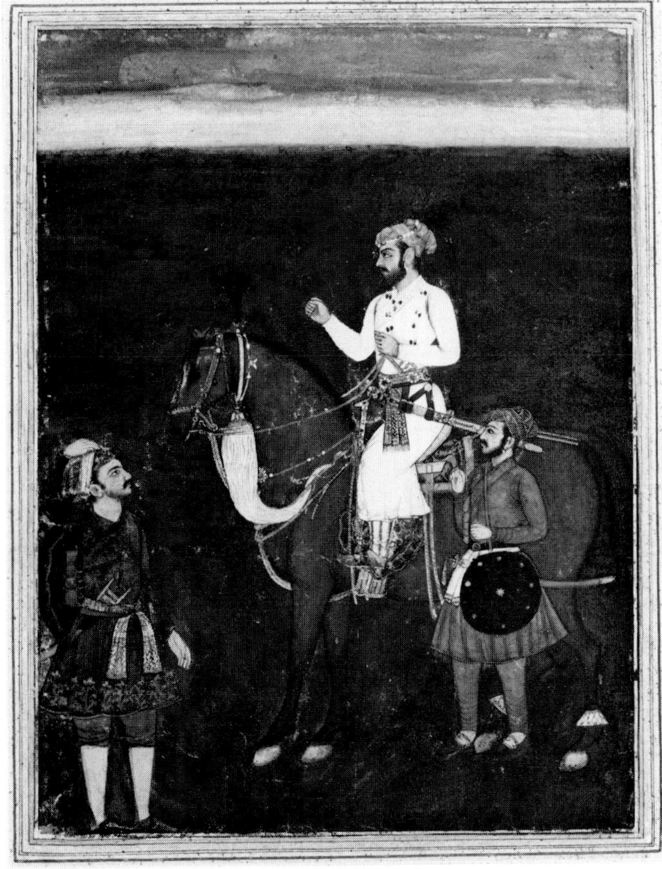

7

An Album Page
Side 1:
A Mughal nobleman, possibly the Emperor Shah Jahan,
on horseback, accompanied by an attendant and a
shikari standing in an attitude of respect. Dark green
background with a blue band above.
Provincial Mughal, late 17th century
21 x 16.3 cm, 33.8 x 27.2 cm with border

Side 2:
Hunters trapping wild elephants, one of which has killed
a horse and rider in the foreground; based on a
composition of the Akbar period.
Provincial Mughal, late 17th century
21.2 x 15 cm

On both sides, gold, pale green and gold marginal rules;
buff border flecked with grey, with black, indigo and
white rules. A mutilated *nagari* clerk's inscription on the
second side.

8

The Emperor Aurangzeb on Horseback
Rajasthan, possibly Mewar, after a Mughal original,
early 18th century
28.7 x 20 cm

The Emperor, in transparent white *jama* and striped
paijama, sits on a grey stallion facing left, holding the
reins in one hand and his sword-hilt in the other. Pale
green background with cloud above. Buff border.

Inscribed on the back: *tarabat 5 patasha norangade sabi.*

9

A Kingfisher
Mughal, mid-17th century
17.4 x 9.3 cm

The kingfisher, with red bill, white throat, blue-green and orange plumage, stands against a plain background with a blue band of sky above and flowering plants in the foreground. Narrow gold margin; buff border.

Inscribed on the back: *kīlakīlai rangīn* ; there is also a *nagari* clerk's inscription, giving the date A.H.1111 = 1699-1700 A.D., of a type discussed by R. Skelton, 'Two Mughal Lion Hunts', *Victoria and Albert Museum Yearbook*, I, 1969, p. 47, n. 32.
Cf. Khandalavala and Chandra, *Miniatures and Sculptures from the Collection of the late Sir Cowasji Jehangir, Bart.*, col. pl. F., and T. Falk *et al.*, *Indian Painting*, Colnaghi & Co., London, 1978, no. 14.

10

A Hawk Taking a Crane in Flight
Rajasthan under Mughal influence, late 17th century
21.4 x 12.6 cm, 40.5 x 30 cm with border

A hawk has seized the head of a sarus crane above a pool with lotuses and flowering plants. Another crane and other water-fowl scatter in flight above. Greyish-ochre background.

11

A Warrior Carrying a Horse
Rajasthan, after a Mughal original, early 18th century
23 x 12.2 cm

Lightly coloured study of a Mongol warrior carrying a white horse across his shoulders. Grey wash background. Pale buff inner border; darker buff outer border.

12

Maharaja Jaswant Singh of Jodhpur Listening to Music
Jodhpur, c. 1660
26.5 x 17.3 cm
(Colour Plate No. 2)

Maharaja Jaswant Singh (b. 1627, r. 1638-78) sits on a carpeted garden terrace with water-courses and fountains, attended by ladies and female musicians. The sun appears among dark rain-clouds above the trees in the background. Flimsy buff border. Some flaking.

Inscribed on the back in Persian script: *bahādur jaswant sang* ; in *nagari* script: *jasut sihajī rajā bīkāner ka rī chabī majal kī.*

A very fine portrait of Jaswant Singh, who spent much of his long reign away from Jodhpur in the service of the Mughal Emperors. Other portraits of him are in the Victoria and Albert Museum (see Welch, *Indian Drawings and Painted Sketches,* no. 64), the British Museum, and the collections of J. P. Goenka, G. K. Kanoria and the late Dr Moti Chandra; see also Christie's sale catalogue, 19 April 1979, lot. 83.

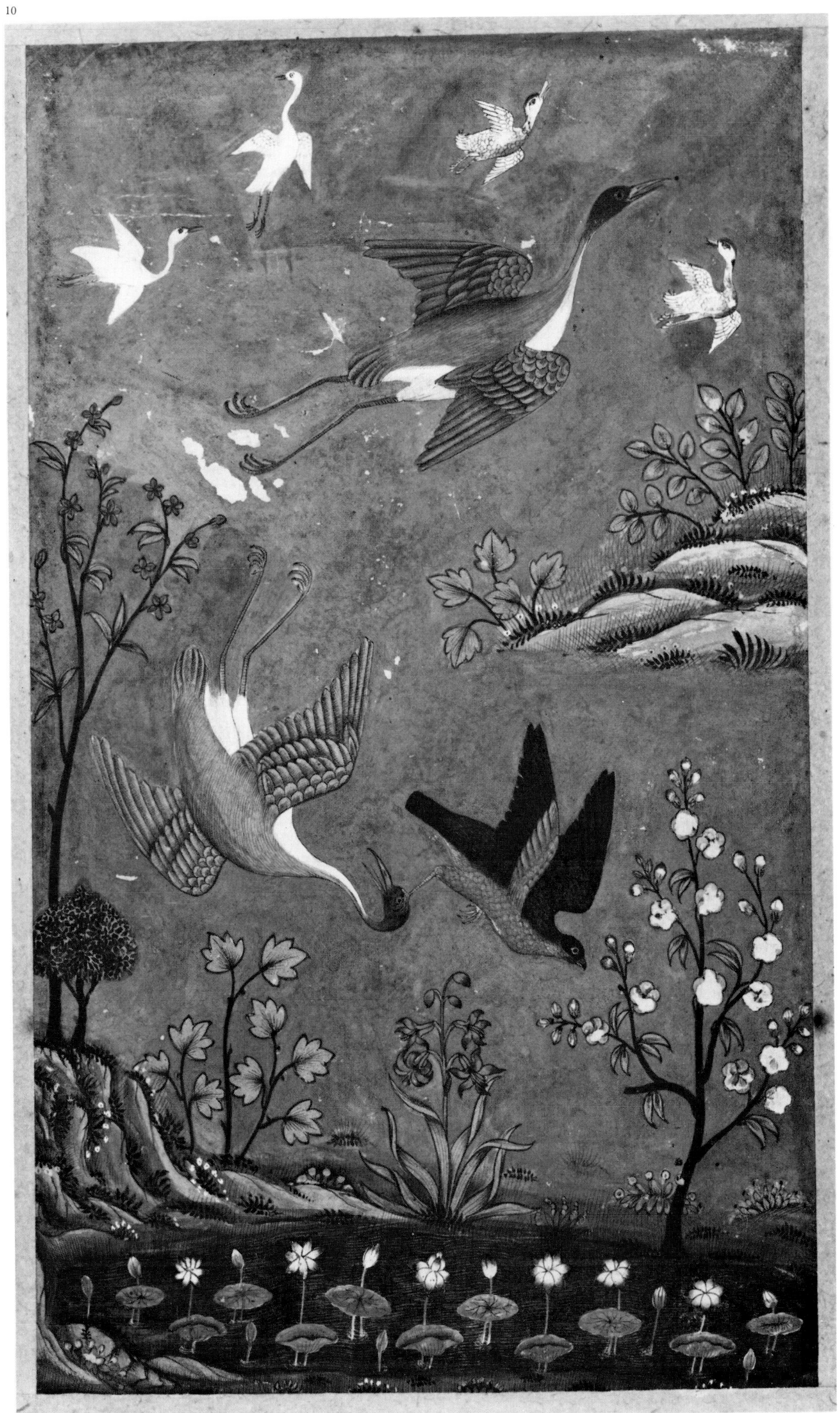

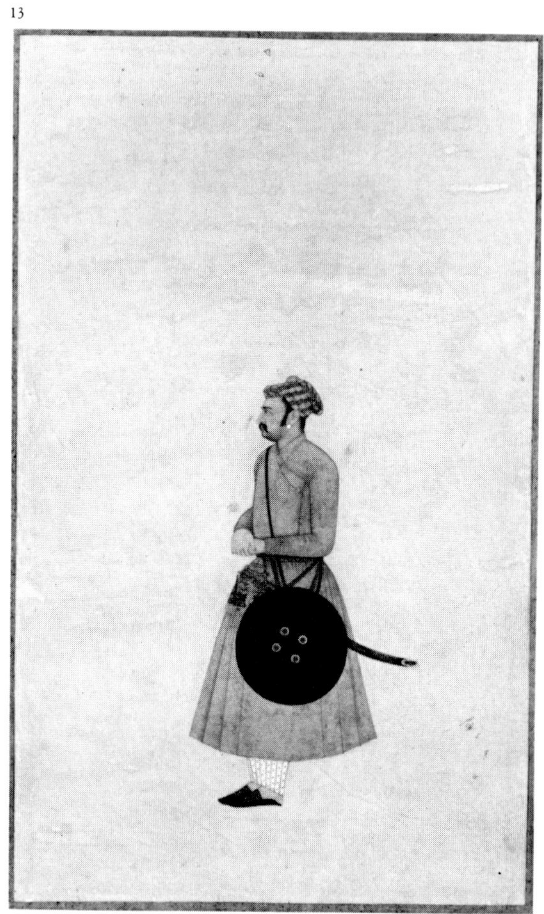

13

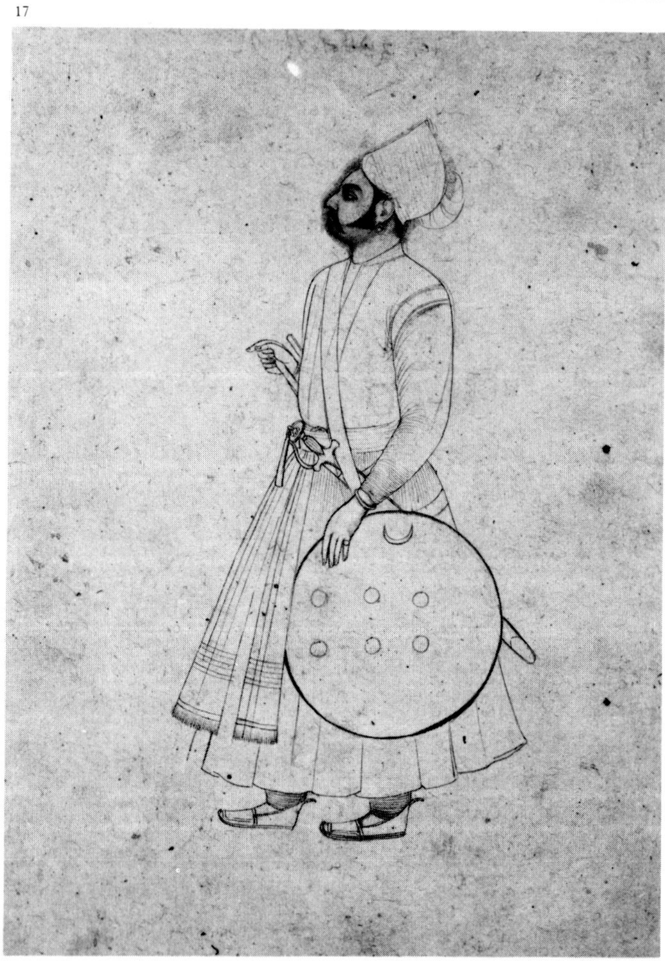

17

13

Maharaja Anup Singh of Bikaner
Mughal style at Bikaner, late 17th century
19.7 x 12.1 cm

Maharaja Anup Singh (r. 1669-98), wearing a pink *jama*,
stands facing left with his hands clasped, a sword and
shield hanging from his belt. Pale green background.
Muted salmon-pink border with fine dark flecks.

Inscribed on the back: [in Persian script:] *rājah atma
rara? gur* [in *nagari* script:] *rāje anop sig/ kalam
sajanāvad/ araja to jaraji lahe jara kimat ru 25 ri.*

Cf. Goetz, *The Art and Architecture of Bikaner State,*
fig. 77.

14

A Raja and a Pining Lady
Rajasthan, c. 1700
25 x 45 cm
(Colour Plate No. 6)

A raja on horseback proceeds through a rocky landscape
with peacocks, monkeys, deer and a prowling leopard.
To the left a languishing lady stands on a palace terrace
with fountains and water-courses, while a maid talks to
her of the absent raja's return. Buff and salmon-pink
border with sparse silver flecks. Probably an illustration
of an unidentified romance.

15

Laila Visiting Majnun
Rajasthan, after a Mughal model, early 18th century
19.9 x 12.6 cm

Laila visits Majnun in a hilly landscape; he is surrounded
by animals both real and fabulous, including lions,
rhinoceroses, elephants, deer, a *makara,* a camel and
others. Buff border; an unidentified verse in *nagari*
script above.

16

A Lady Playing with a Child
Bikaner, late 17th century
23.3 x 14.3 cm
(Colour Plate No. 5)

A lady seated on a gold throne on a terrace dangles a
plaything in front of a small child held before her by a
maid. Another maid holds a chowry. Behind are
flowering trees against a pale green background with
clouds and blue sky above. Buff and blue borders with
fine gold decoration, trimmed on all sides; similar
borders on the back.

17

Rathor Pratap Singh
Nagaur?, c. 1700
32.5 x 22.5 cm

Drawing of Rathor Pratap Singh standing with one hand
on his shield and the other resting on his *katar.* Light
colouring on the face.

Inscribed on the back: *rāthod pratāp sigh amarāvat
gamani badi.*

18

A Lady on a Terrace
Bikaner, late 17th century
18.4 x 12.6 cm
(Colour Plate No. 4)

A lady wearing transparent muslin sits against a bolster
on a terrace, with wine and delicacies spread before her.
Behind her is a lake with lotuses, a tree-fringed hill and
an orange-streaked sky. Gold margin; bright green
border with black rules and gold outer margin. A
modern clerk's inscription on the back.

19

A Lady and a *Yogini*
Bikaner, late 17th century
15 x 9.5 cm

A lady sits beneath a tree while a *yogini* plays a *vina* in
front of her. Another lady stands clasping the trunk of
the tree. A palace is seen in the distance. Orange margin
and bright green border with red rules. A modern
clerk's inscription on the back.

20

Prince Zorawar Singh of Bikaner Riding
Bikaner, c. 1715
24 x 17 cm

Prince Zorawar Singh (b. 1703, r. 1736-45), with
nimbus, rides a chestnut stallion, accompanied by a
chowry-bearer. Green background with streaky cloud
above. Damaged buff border with traces of floral
decoration in gold and indigo.

Inscribed on the back: *kuar joravar sighji sujan sighot
bikaner ro.*

Cf. Goetz, *The Art and Architecture of Bikaner State*,
fig. 88, and Archer, *Indian Miniatures*, pl. 54.

21

A Lady on a Terrace
Bikaner?, c. 1700
14.1 x 7.9 cm

A lady sits against a bolster on a yellow carpet, with
floral pattern, on a green terrace, with red railings and
trees behind. Green background with cloud above.
Flimsy speckled buff border, numbered 18, inscribed
below: *pugal ro padamani ?adi takiya upare betha che.*
On the back is a clerk's inscription, apparently dated
V.S.1777 = 1720 A.D.

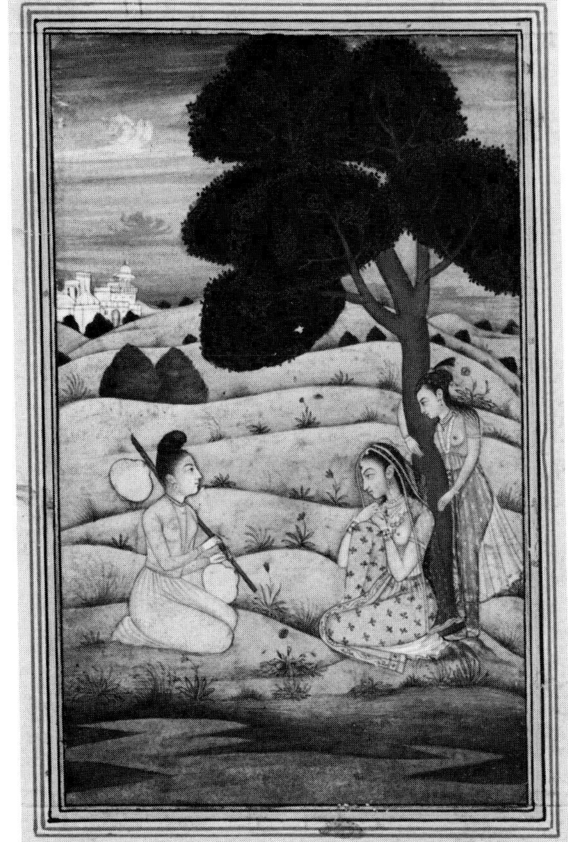

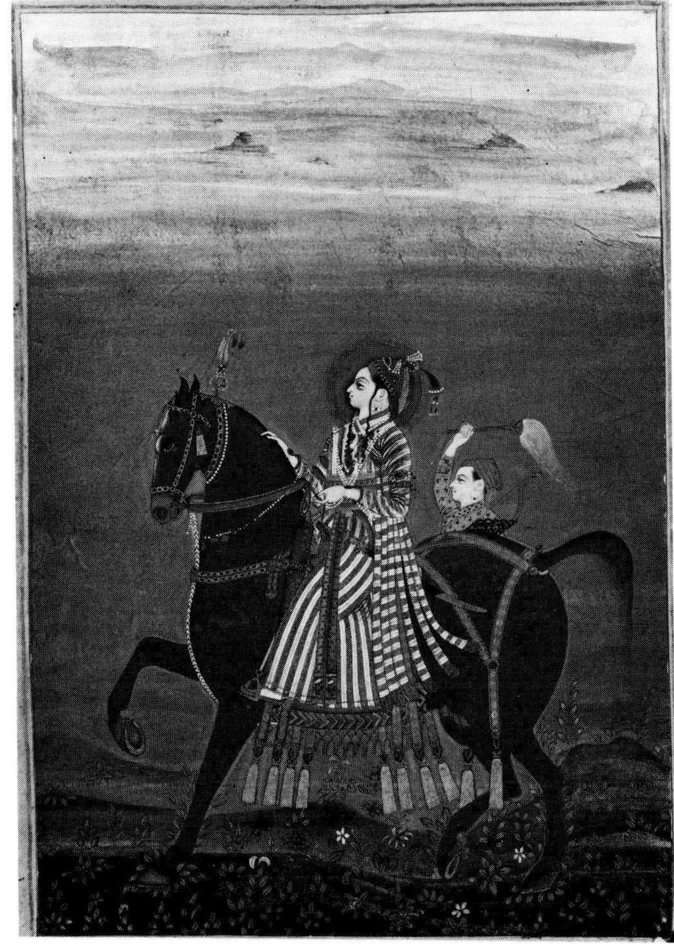

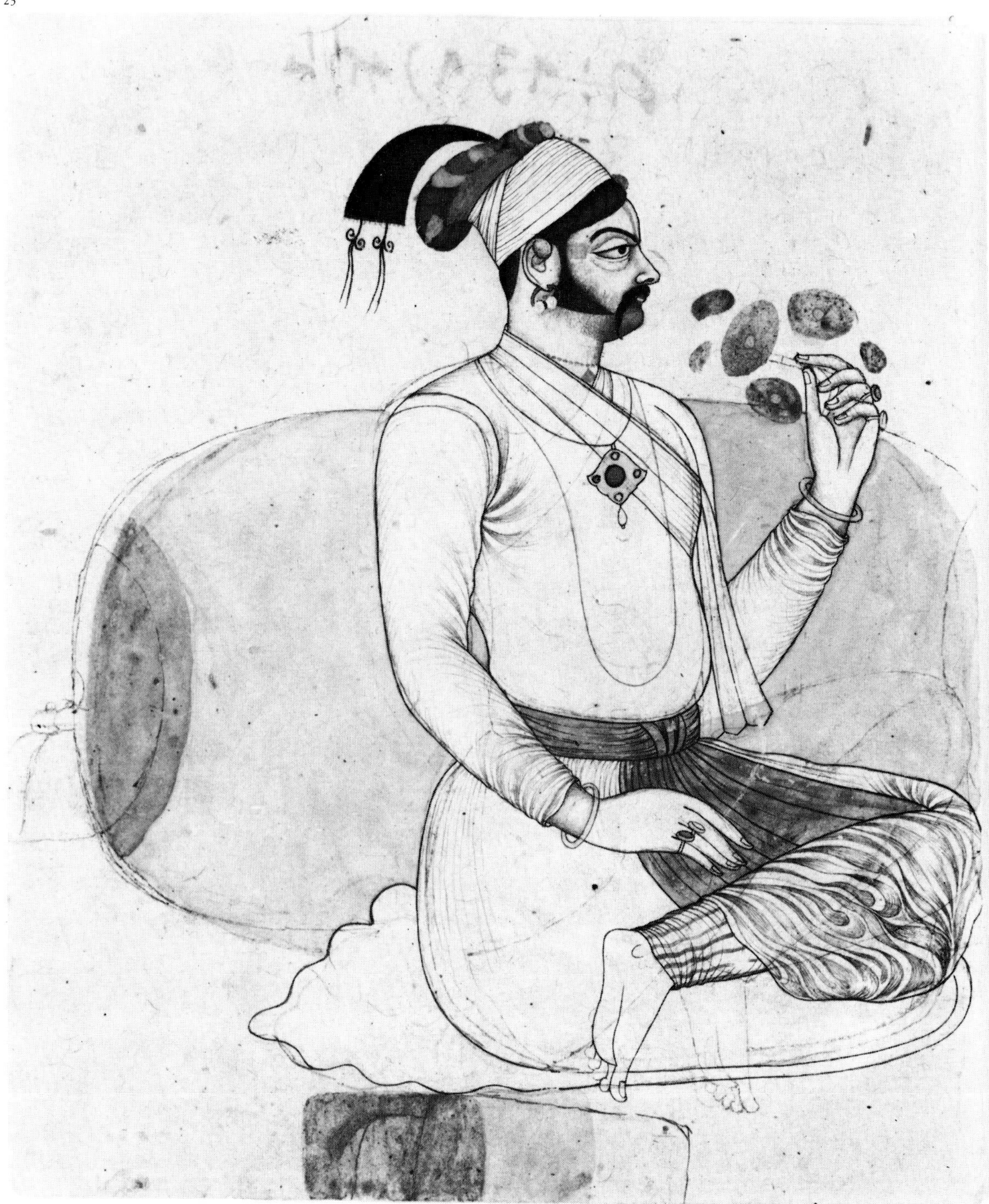

22

A Lady Worshipping the *Tulsi* Plant
Bikaner, early 18th century
15.7 x 9.7 cm

A bare-breasted lady stands holding a water-vessel and a rosary in front of a sacred *tulsi* plant shrine; a plantain tree stands to her right. Pale green background with red and gold streaks of cloud. Buff border with sparse silver flecks, numbered 112.

Inscribed on the back: *pāno tulachī ko? mātā āge devaka na..? ubhī mālā kare cha.*

Another version of this subject is in the British Museum.

23

A Seated Nobleman
Bikaner or Nagaur?, mid-18th century
13.9 x 11.2 cm

A lightly coloured, unfinished sketch of a Rathor nobleman seated holding a flower against a large yellow bolster. An earlier, rejected rendering of his folded leg can be seen.

24

Krishna and Radha

Kishangarh, c. 1800 or later

18.6 x 13.3 cm

Krishna stands with his arm round Radha's neck on a
garden terrace beside a *chattri* containing a bed with
pillows and garlands. A pool with fountains in the
foreground; orange railings and thickly clustered trees
behind. No border. Preliminary sketch marks of two
similar figures on the back.

25

A Prince with a Lady

Rajasthan, possibly Mewar, 18th century

17.7 x 12.3 cm

A somewhat crude, partially coloured sketch of a Rajput
prince holding a flower and a sword, standing with a
lady holding a long fan. Red border.

26

A Lady with a Monkey

Rajasthan, late 18th century

15 x 10.8 cm

A lady in red and gold striped sari stands holding a
branch of a spindly tree while she offers a branch with
mangoes(?) to a pet monkey. Uncoloured background
with grey-blue sky above. Buff border with sparse silver
flecks. Some rubbing and discolouration.

27

Maharaja Madho Singh of Jaipur

Jaipur, c. 1760. By Ramji

24.1 x 19.6 cm, 41.6 x 32.5 cm with border

The Maharaja, with nimbus, wearing a dark olive-green
pagri and *jama,* stands on a terrace holding a sword and
a rosary, facing a nobleman in white who also holds a
rosary. Mauve-grey background with blue cloud above.
Black margin with gold floral meander; pink border with
gold floral decoration, inscribed: *śrī manmaharajadhiraja
raja rajendra śrī savai madhava sinhaji.*

Inscribed at the foot of the picture: *sabi banai ramji
catera ki.*

Inscribed on the back: *pano babat jepur thi avyo so ori
jama samat 1822 ra savan sud 14 budhe jama pancoli
giradhar lal le o avyo.*

Ramji (also known as Ramji Das) was one of the more
prolific of Madho Singh's artists. A similar standing
portrait of him, signed by Ramji, was formerly in the
collection of Kumar Sangram Singh of Nawalgarh.
Cf. also O. P. Sharma, *Indian Miniature Painting,*
pl. 58, and Cat. nos. 28 and 183 below.

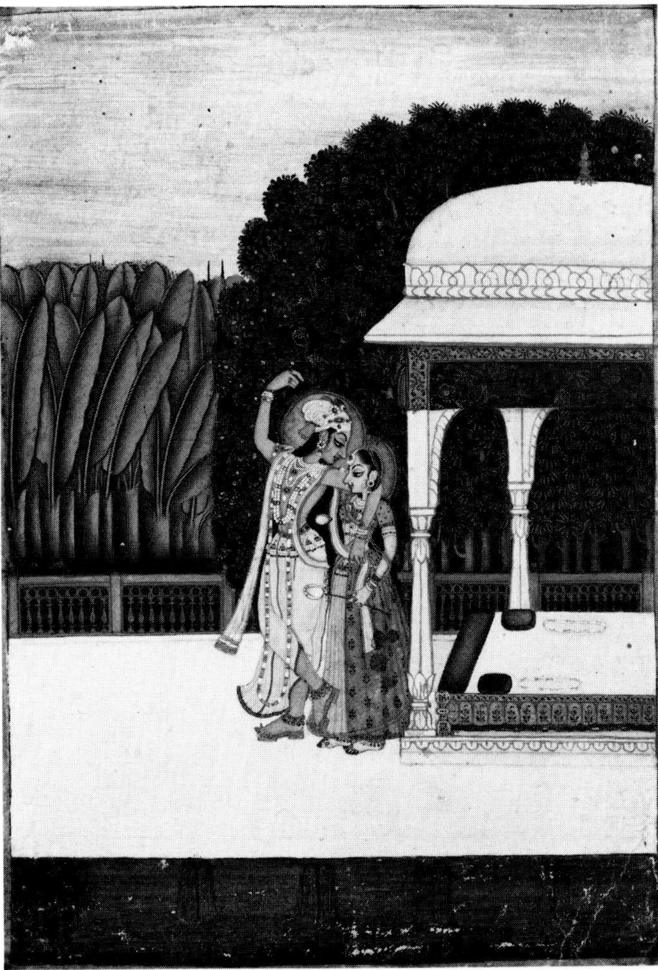

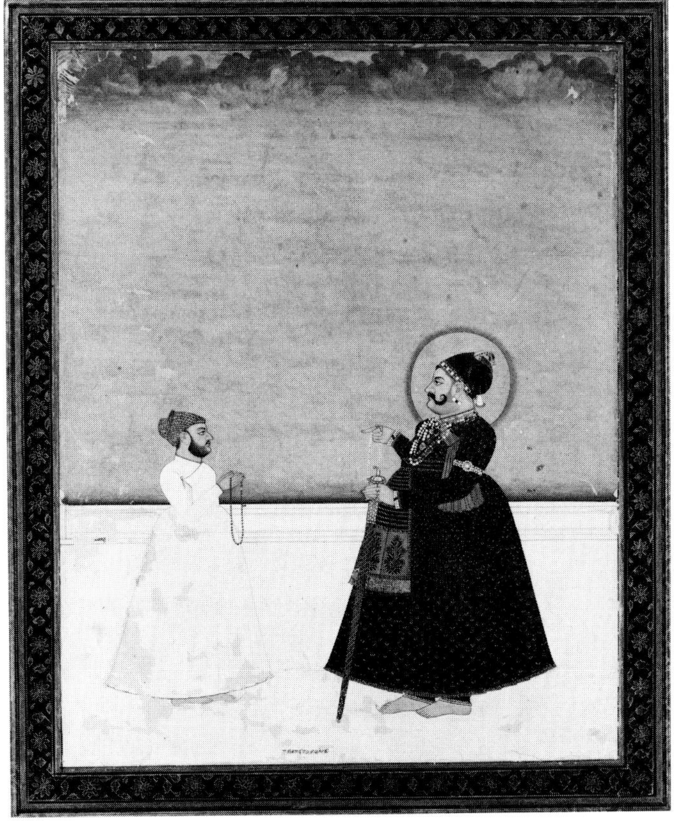

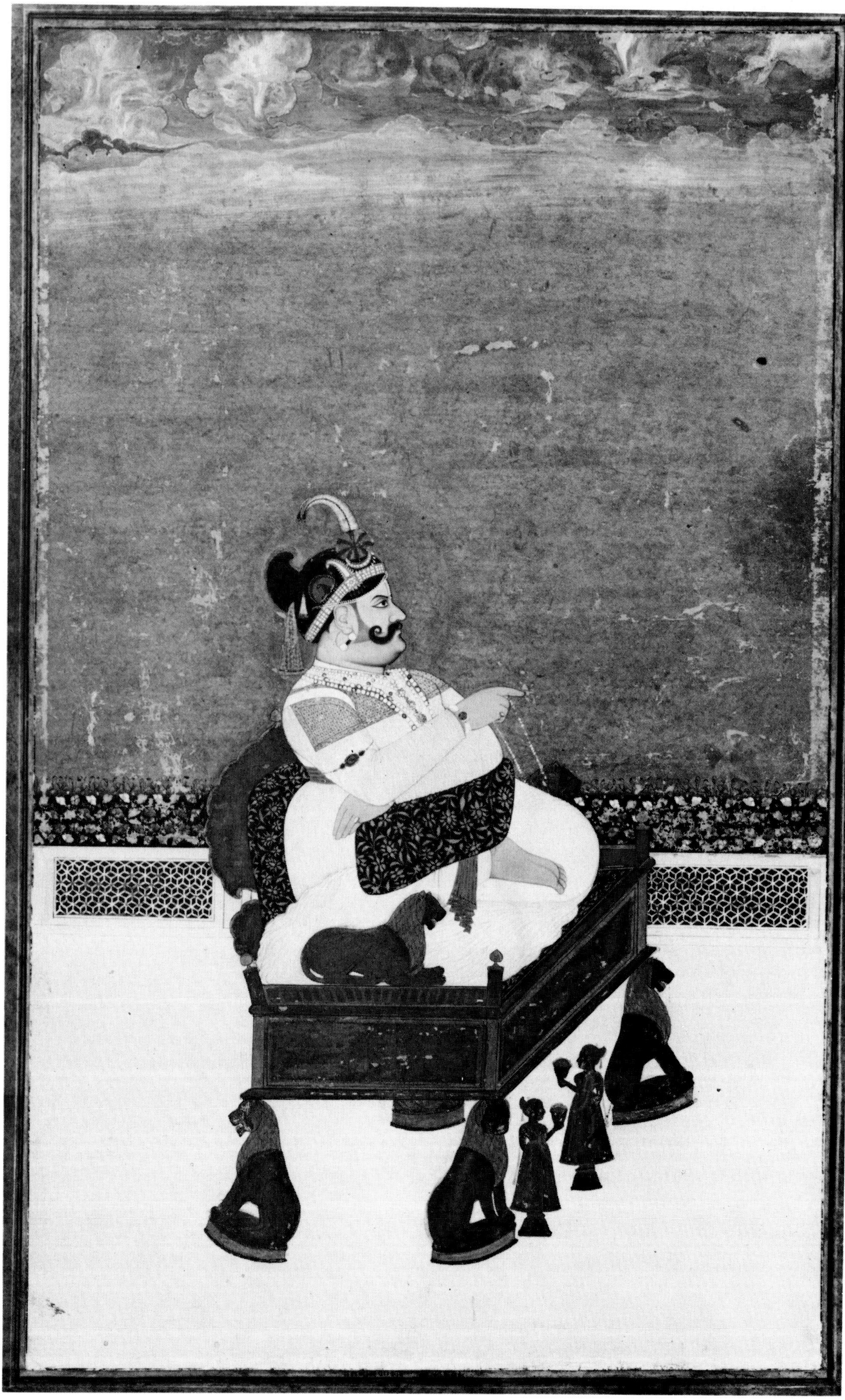

28

Maharaja Madho Singh of Jaipur
Jaipur, c. 1760. Attributed to Ramji
31.5 x 19.3 cm

The Maharaja, in black *pagri* and white *jama*, sits
clasping a cushion on a silver and gold throne, with lion
supports, on a terrace. Grey background with cloud
above. Discoloured cerise border.

Inscribed on the back: *śrī śrī maharajādhirāja śrī svai
mādho syanghjī kī*, together with faint preliminary
sketch marks for a similar subject.

A very similar painting, signed by Ramji, was formerly
in the collection of Kumar Sangram Singh of Nawalgarh.
See cat. no. 27.

29

Prince Jagat Singh of Jaipur
Jaipur, c. 1793-95
20.7 x 12.7 cm, 51.6 x 40 cm with border

The young prince (b. 1786, r. 1803-18) wears an orange
jama edged with gold and stands clasping the hilt of his
sword. Green background with cloud above. Dark blue,
turquoise, pale yellow and salmon-pink borders, all
flecked with gold.

Inscribed above: *śrī maharāja kumar śrī jagat sinhajī ko
citra,* and below, in Persian script: *srī maharāja kumar
srī jagat singh hu.*
Inscribed on the back: *jepar.*

Of Jagat Singh's later career Tod wrote that he had 'the
disgraceful distinction of being the most dissolute prince
of his race or of his age... His life discloses not one
redeeming virtue amidst a cluster of effeminate vices,
including the rankest, in the opinion of a Rajput –
cowardice.' (*Annals and Antiquities of Rajasthan,* vol.
III, p. 1364).

30

Maharaja Pratap Singh of Jaipur
Jaipur, c. 1800
25.2 x 15.1 cm

The Maharaja (r. 1779-1803) stands facing right, with a
nimbus, black and gold *pagri,* orange shirt and white
skirt over a magenta *paijama.* Pale blue background.
Yellow margin; no border.

Inscribed on the back: *rajā pratāp sihajī savai jepur.*

Cf. Skelton, *Indian Miniatures,* pl. 23.

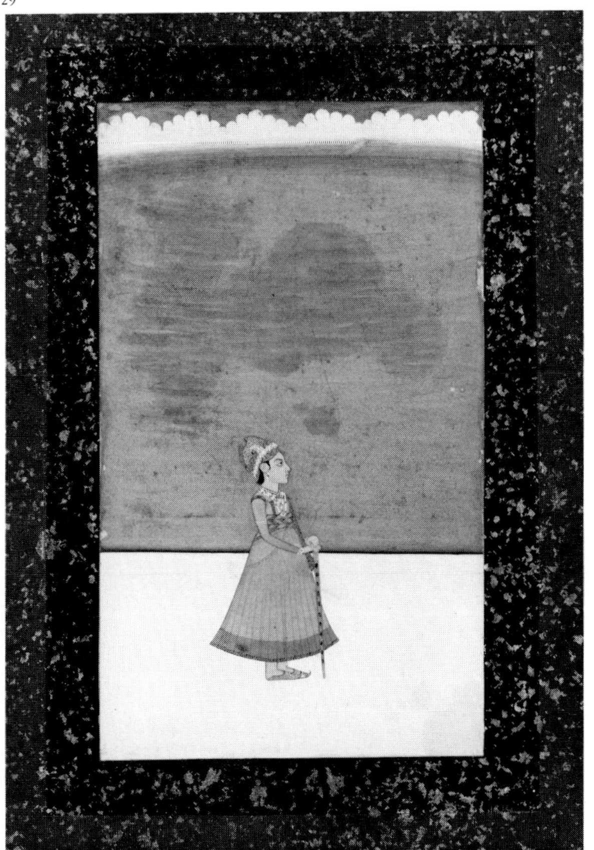

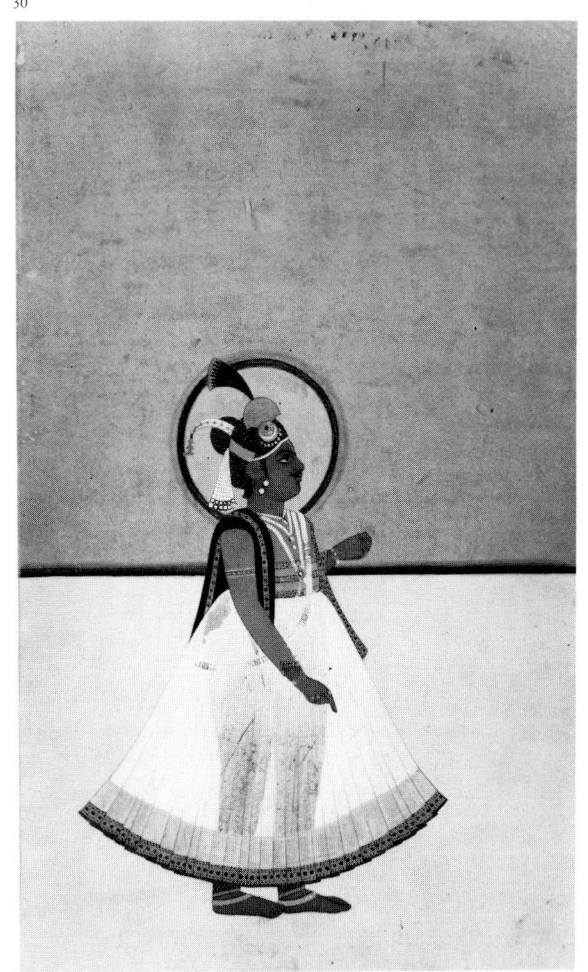

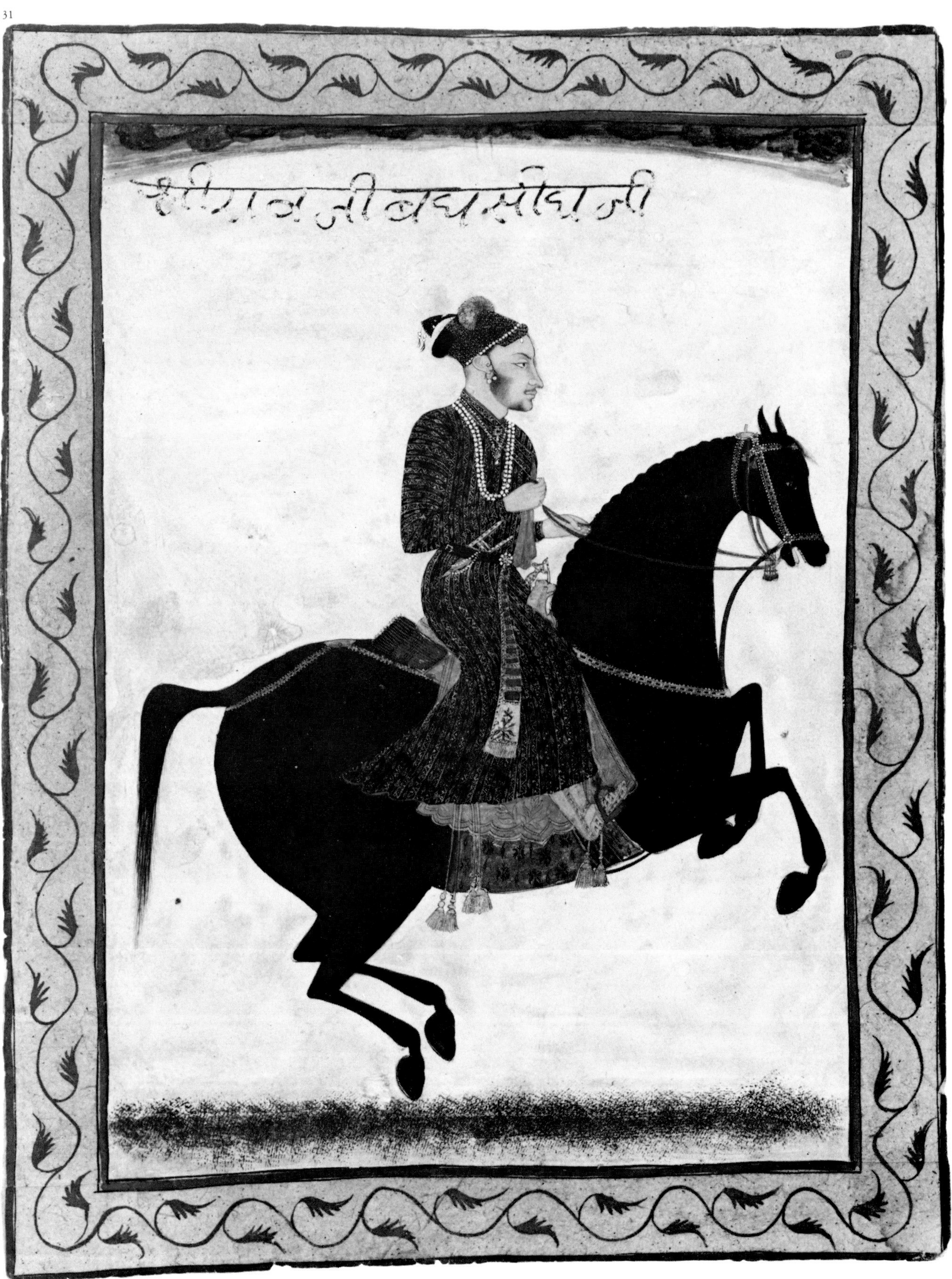

44

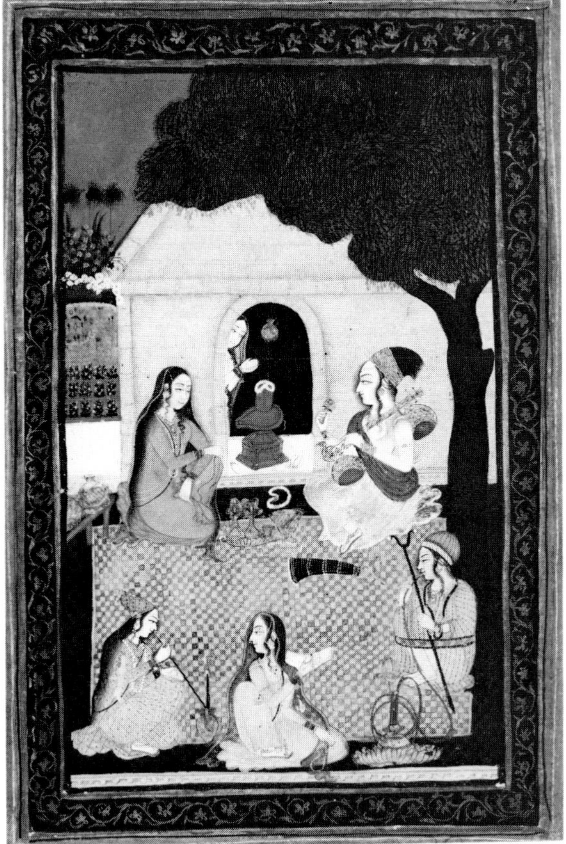

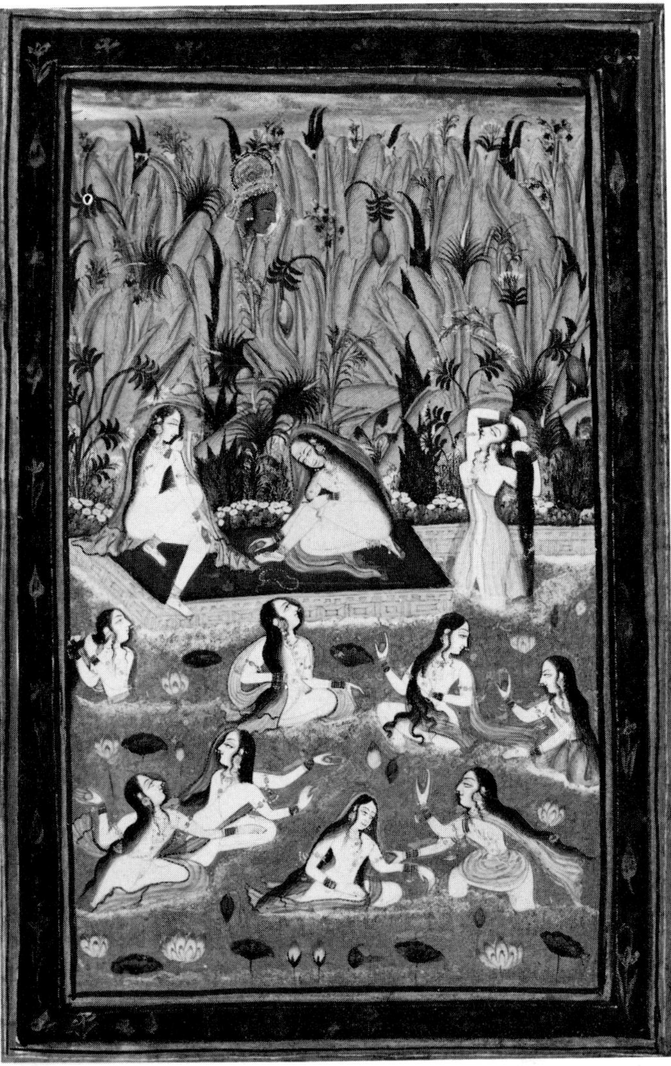

31
Rao Budh Singh Riding
Bundi?, early 18th century
17.6 x 13.2 cm

Rao Budh Singh (or Bagh Singh?), wearing a green and
gold *jama,* rides a chestnut horse. Grey background.
Green cloth-pad blotches in the foreground. Buff border
with silver meander pattern.

Inscribed above: *śrī rāvajī badh? sīghjī.*

32
Ladies at a Shiva Shrine
Bundi or Uniara, late 18th century
24.5 x 15 cm

Noble ladies and a *yogini* take their ease together under
a tree beside a yellow thatched hut containing a *lingam.*
Black margin with silver rules and floral meander; red
border with large silver floral motifs

Inscribed on the back: *śrī* [del.] *śrī mahadevajī
līlakanthajī ri pujā ?idra pasa pujā kare he 6?*

The same composition is found in two late 17th century
Mughal pictures in the Victoria and Albert Museum (I.S.
132-1885/14 and 22).

33
Krishna Spying on the Gopis
Bundi, late 18th century
23.3 x 14.2 cm

Krishna hides behind a screen of plantains and cypresses
to watch the scantily clad gopis bathing in the river
Jumna. Black margin with silver rules and gold floral
motifs; red border with silver floral decoration. A short
inscription on the back describes the scene.

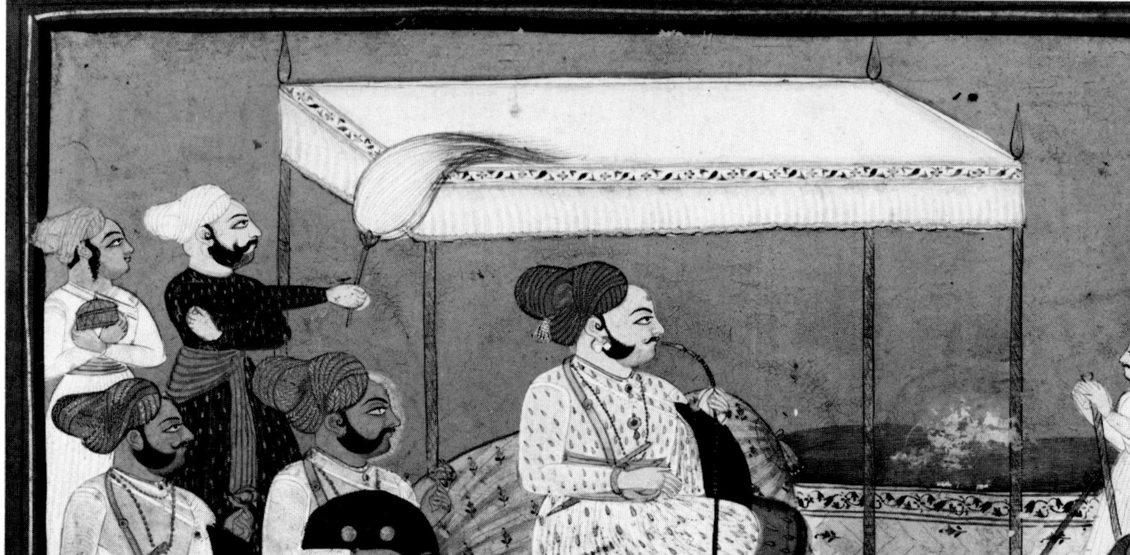

34

Thakur Bharat Singh Listening to Music
Bundi, late 18th century
19.1 x 25.5 cm

The Thakur sits under a canopy smoking a *huqqa* while a male singer holding a *tanpura* performs for him. Four sardars with shields sit on the left and servants stand in attendance. Pale green background. Red border.

Inscribed on the back: *thakurā śrī bharat saṅghjī ?camaru choṭa bhaī dhirat saghjī suratan saṅghja ?cana saghja salem saṅghjī pacu bhay..? kī sabhī narukā.*

35

Maharao Ram Singh II of Kotah and Companions Playing Holi on Elephants in a Street
Kotah, 1844. By Kisan Das
48.7 x 64 cm
(Colour Plate No. 7)

The Maharao and his courtiers, seated in elephant howdahs, fling powder and squirt coloured water at one another. Women fling powder from the roof-tops, while the Maharao retaliates with a hose-pipe connected to the palace fire-engine, pumped by four servants. Other townspeople join in the rejoicings in the foreground. Gold margin; red border with white rules. Many of the courtiers are identified by inscriptions on the painting.

Inscribed on the back: *māharajādhiraja mharaje mharavajī śrī ram sigh holī kī savarī hathī gomah? gaj..............? sam 1901 kalam kasan das kī.*

The Maharao was not the first to use mechanical aids when playing Holi. Sir John Malcolm, when going to join in the Holi celebrations at the court of Sindhia in 1804, wrote in a private letter: 'Scindiah is furnished with an engine of great power by which he can play upon a fellow fifty yards distance. He has, besides, a magazine of syringes, so I expect to be well squirted.' (Quoted in E. Thompson, *The Making of the Indian Princes,* London, 1943, p. 93).

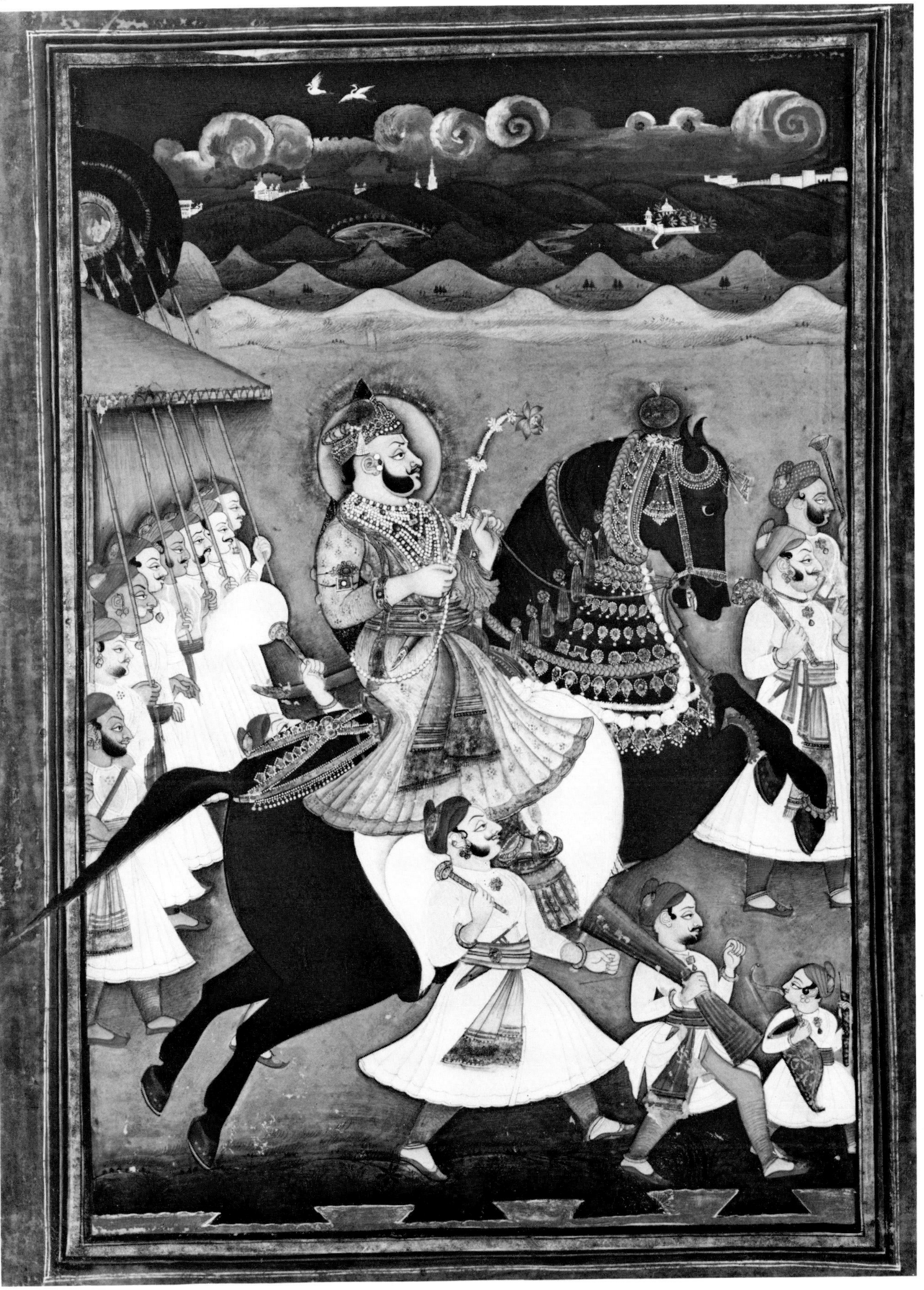

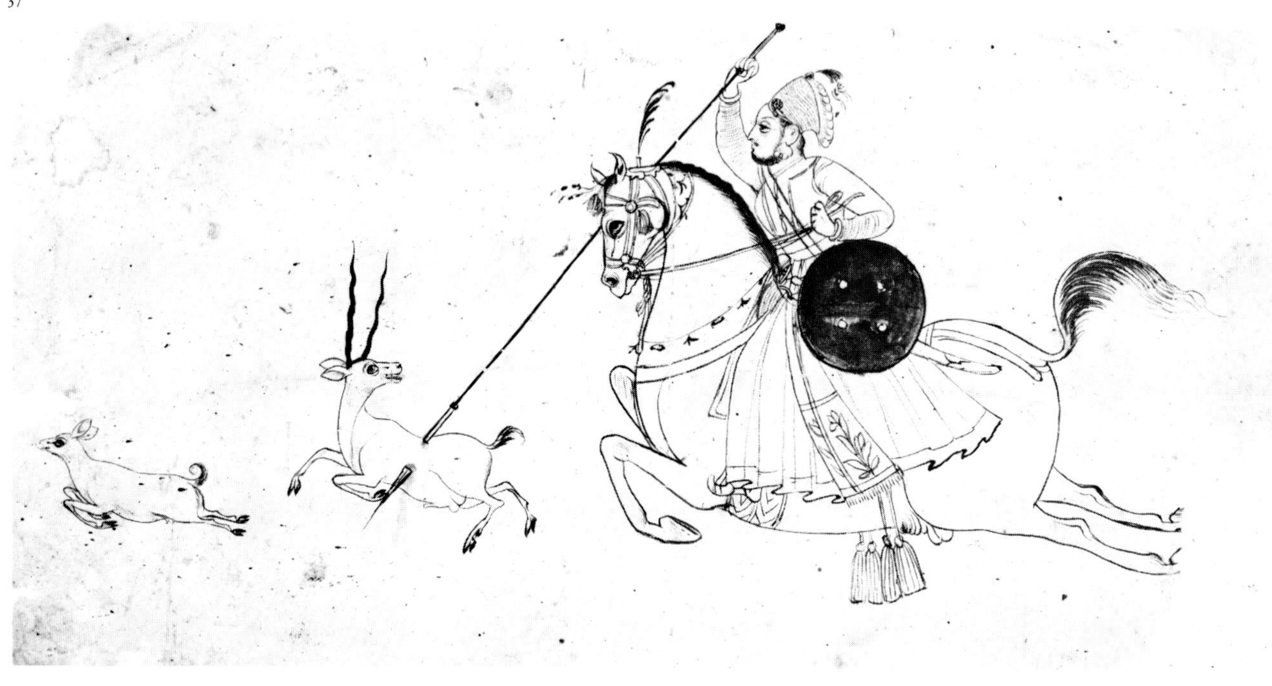

36

Maharao Ram Singh II of Kotah Riding
Kotah, c. 1840
31.6 x 21.6 cm

The Maharao, with nimbus, wearing a pink *jama* and holding a floral wand, rides a chestnut stallion, accompanied by attendants on foot with spears and regalia. A hilly landscape in the background under a dark blue sky with spiral clouds and flying cranes. Gold and blue margins; red border with white rules. Inscribed above: *śrī.*

Inscribed on the back: *mhorajadhīraja mharaja mharavajī śrī ram sīghjī ganagor ?kā ?ghata ragho ?do dīvan vagas udepur .....? asavar ...?vatī ?kī tasvir.*

Cf. Beach, *Rajput Painting at Bundi and Kota,* fig. 101.

37

A Rathor Nobleman Spearing a Blackbuck
Kotah, early 19th century
15.8 x 31 cm

A drawing depicting a mounted nobleman with a tall Rathor pagri spearing a male blackbuck.

38

Maharana Bhim Singh of Udaipur Riding
Jodhpur, c. 1830
34.3 x 22.6 cm

The Maharana, with nimbus, rides a dark brown stallion accompanied by a *huqqa*-bearer and two chowry-bearers. Pale green background. Red border with white rules.

Inscribed below: *aj khānajad kī mālam ho ?samaha nacoda cakarī kartā ho ?sagamā cha ?arī ?suraj cha khānajāda kī.*
Inscribed on the back: *mahāranaji śrī bhim sīnghjī.*

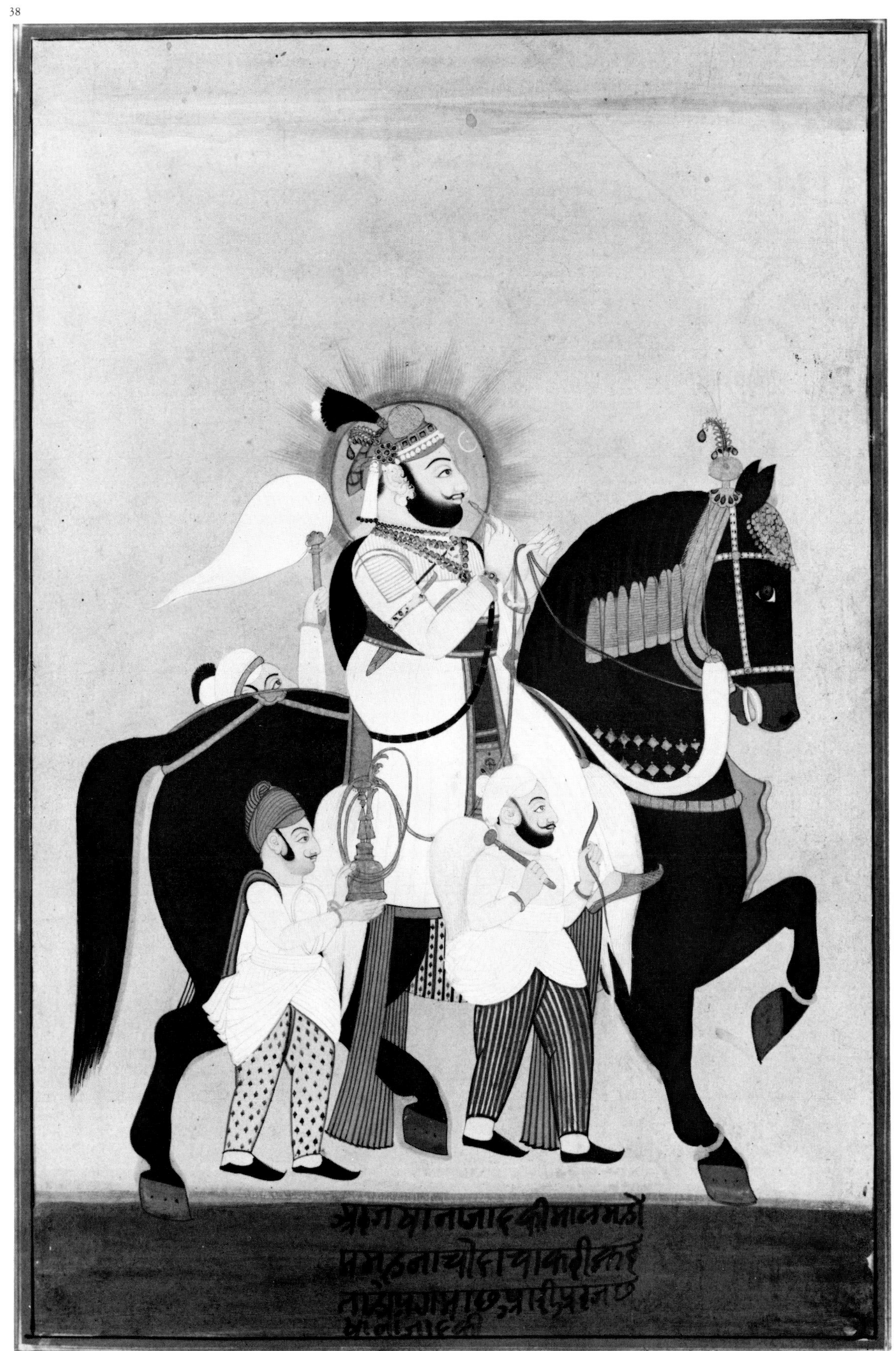

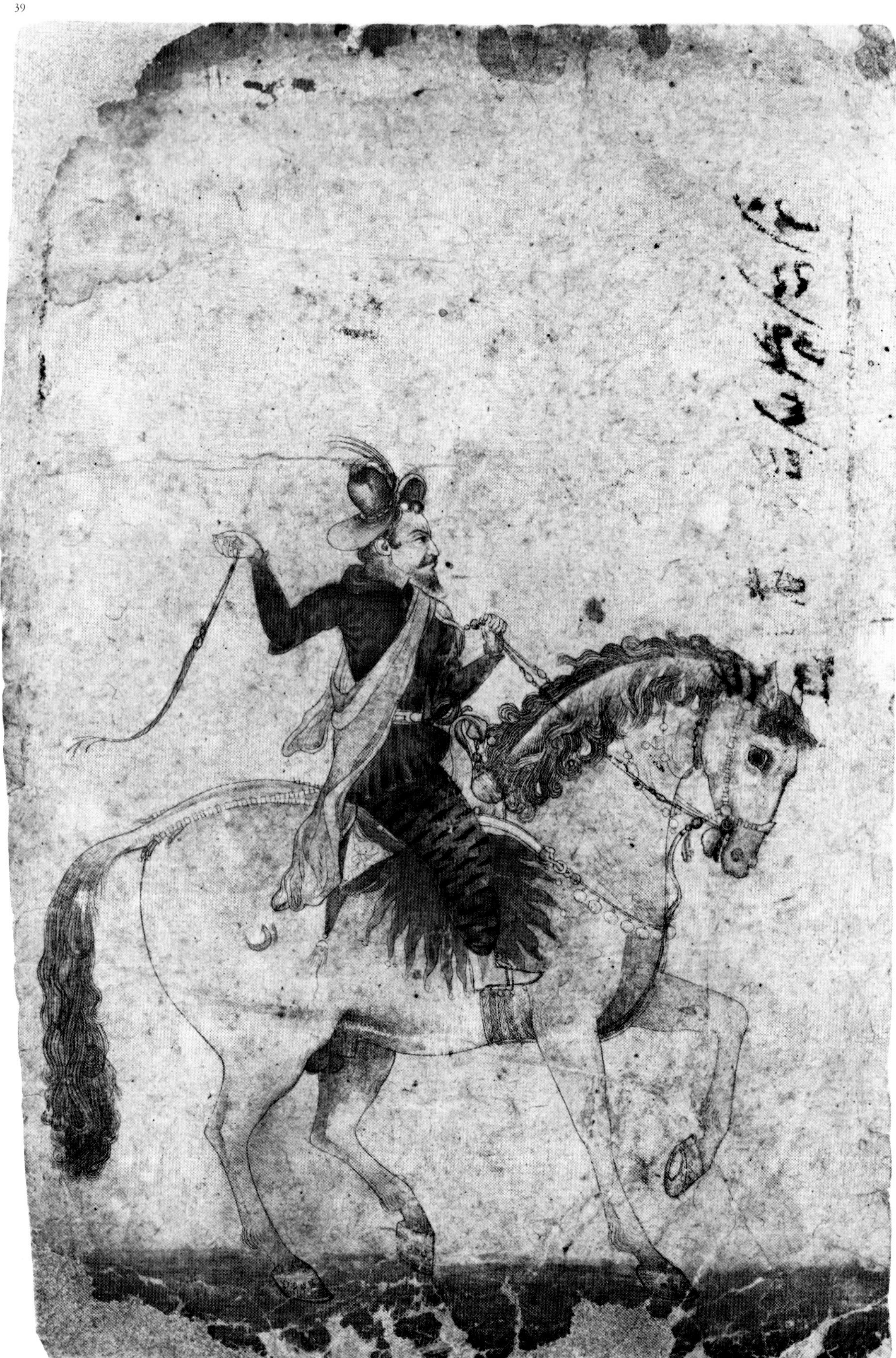

39

A European Cavalier
Rajasthan, after a European print, early 18th century
20.8 x 14 cm

Lightly coloured drawing of a bearded, Don Quixote-like
cavalier in 16th century costume tinted pink, pale
orange and green, riding a stallion. Damaged.

Inscribed on the back: *firaṅgī ghoḍai asavār.*

40

A Lady
Southern Rajasthan, early 18th century
By Incha Ram
20.2 x 12 cm

A lady wearing a magenta *choli,* pale green *ghaghra*
with floral pattern and a yellow *patka* stands facing right
on a knoll with coarsely painted grass tufts. Pale
turquoise background. Narrow red border,
numbered 73.

Inscribed on the back: *nagar īncha rām nijar kī do/
sovaṇī ko pāno,* together with a preliminary sketch, in
two superimposed versions, of a similar lady.

By the same hand as a related painting of a lady with a
parrot, in the Victoria and Albert Museum (see *Marg,*
XXIX, 4, 1976, p. 2), which also has a similar
preliminary sketch on the back. Another painting by
Incha Ram is in the Prince of Wales Museum, Bombay
(acc. no. 53.78), and four more are known in private
collections. Mr. R. Skelton reports having seen two
further pictures by him on the London art market in
1974, one of them inscribed as having been painted at
Dungarpur (to the south of Mewar). An artist of the
same name is briefly noticed by R. K. Vashishth,
'Mewad ki citrakala parampara aur pramukh citrakar',
Majjhamika, Pratap Shodha Pratishthan, Udaipur,
V.S. 2030, p. 34.

41

Raja Rai Singh
Rajasthan, late 17th century
17.7 x 11.9 cm

Probably the Sisodia Raja Rai Singh who took possession
of Toda (in the south-west of Jaipur state, adjacent to
Tonk) in the mid-17th century. He is seen holding a
flower, behind a ledge draped with a mauve and pink
textile. Pale green background. Tan border,
numbered 59.

Inscribed on the back: *rajā rai sigh rī* [in another hand:]
toda.

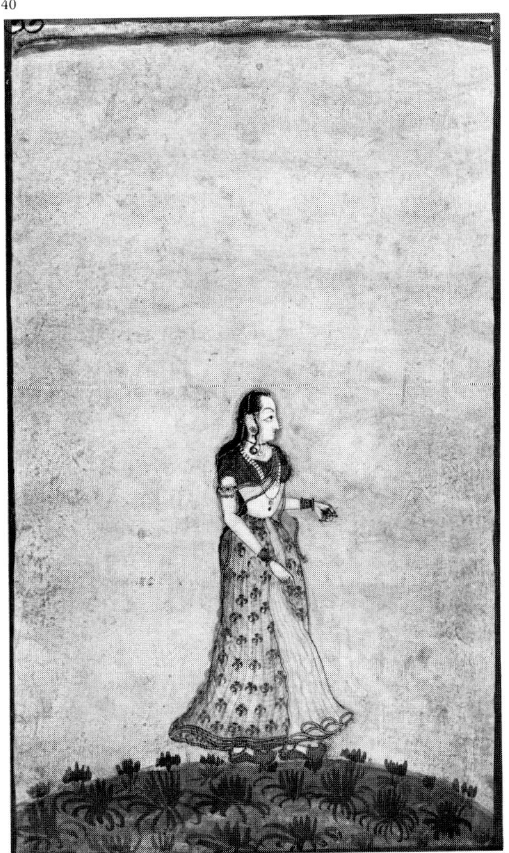

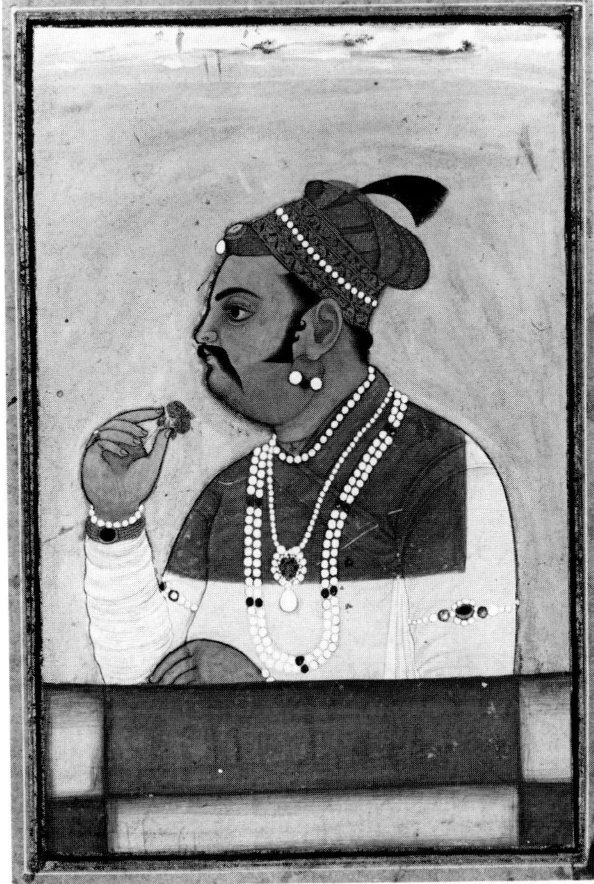

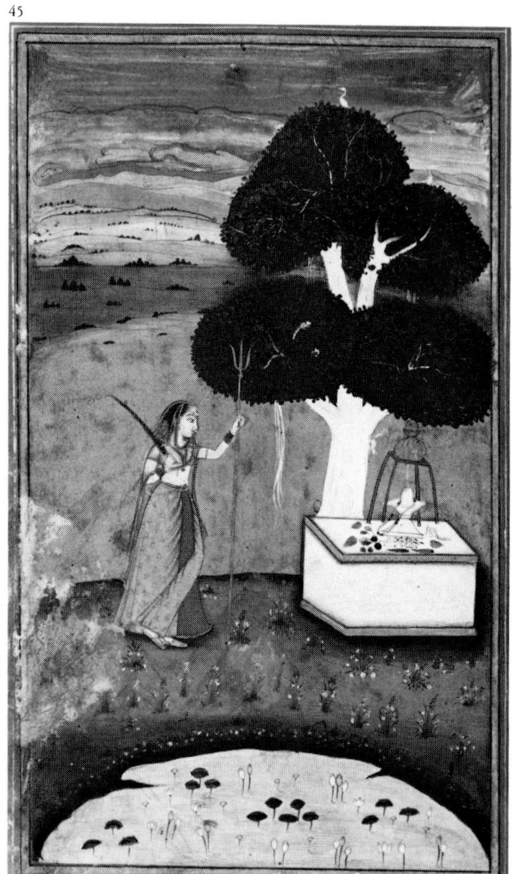

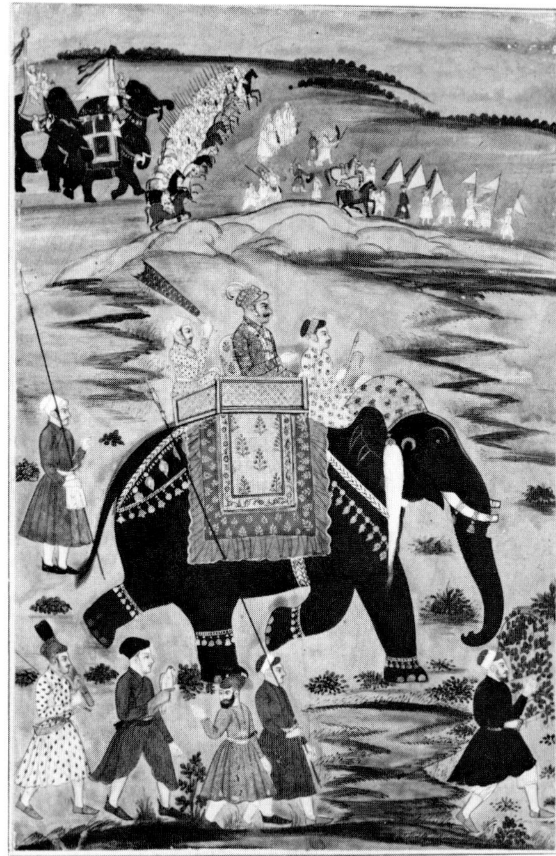

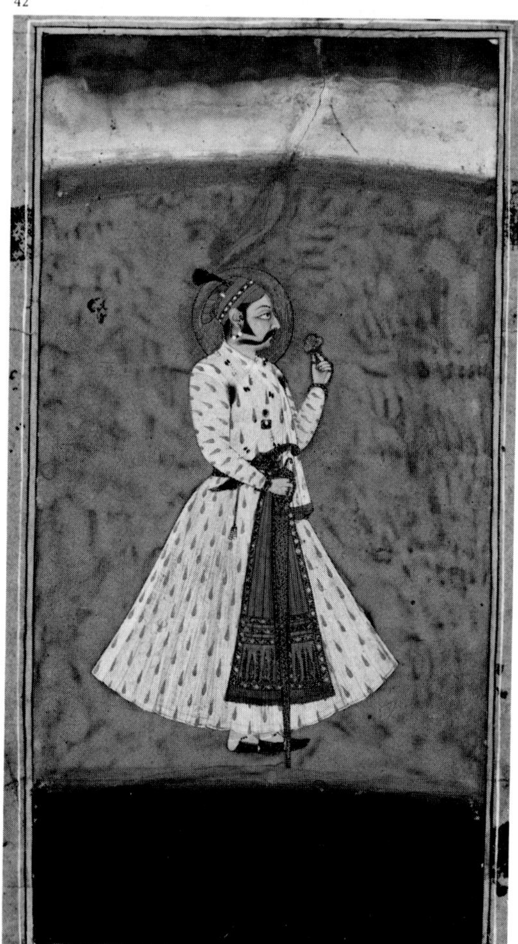

42

Maharana Amar Singh II of Udaipur
Rajasthan, possibly Mewar, early 18th century
23 x 12 cm

A ruler with nimbus, probably Maharana Amar Singh of Udaipur (r. 1698-1710), stands facing right holding the hilt of his sword and a flower. Dark indigo foreground; green background with cloud above, behind which a gold sun appears. Tan border with white ruling and large silver flecks.

Cf. cat. nos. 54-58.

43

A Prince Smoking on a Terrace
Mughal style in Rajasthan, early 18th century
19.9 x 16.4 cm

A Muslim prince reclines on a bed on a terrace, attended by five maids, one holding a *morchal,* another a flask, another his *huqqa,* while the other two play a *tanpura* and grind sandal-paste on a slab. A boat on a river appears in the background. No border.

Inscribed on the back: *tasbīr sultān bādasā rī.*

A late 18th century Mughal *charba* impression of the same composition is in the Chester Beatty Library, Dublin (MS 55.18).

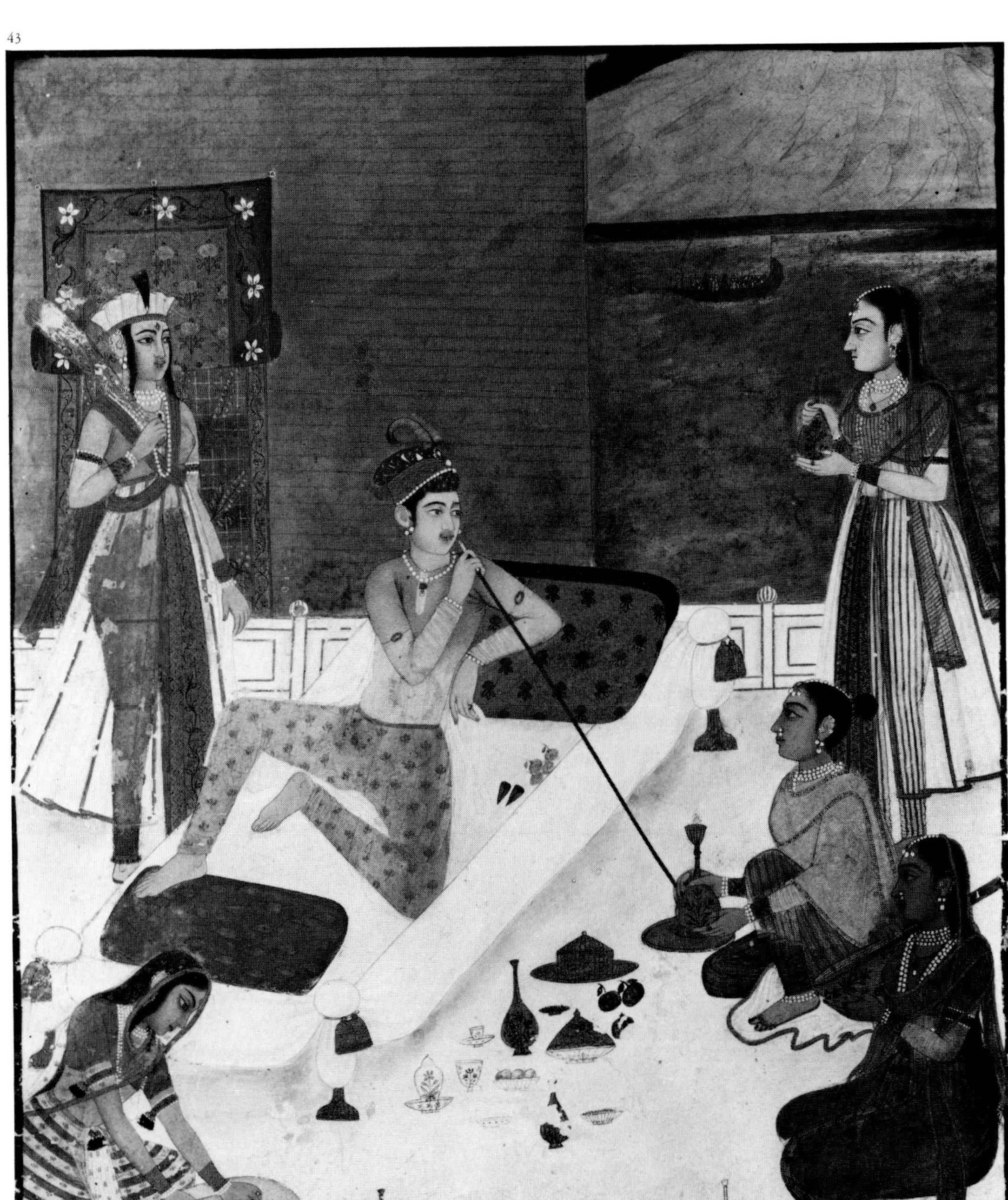

44

Maharaja Sawai Jai Singh of Jaipur Riding an Elephant
Probably a later Mewar version of an early 18th century
Amber original
24.5 x 16.4 cm

The Maharaja, riding in the howdah of an elephant
accompanied by attendants, proceeds through a marshy
landscape; elephants and mounted troops accompany
him in the distance. Buff border with black and white
rules, inscribed: *jepur rājā je sīgjī*. A largely
unintelligible inscription on the back appears to give the
value of the picture as ten rupees.

45

Parvati at a Shiva Shrine
Rajasthan, possibly Mewar, mid-18th century
24.5 x 14.2 cm

Parvati, dressed as a court lady, stands holding a floral
wand and a gold trident in front of a *lingam* shrine
under a *pipal* tree in which squirrels are playing. A pool
with lotuses in the foreground, and a landscape in the
background with multi-coloured cloud above. Gold
margin; red border.

Inscribed on the back: *śrī. śrī mahādevajī kelās me bethā
thakā parabatījī darasaṇ kara vāpa dāsa hāt me tarasul.*

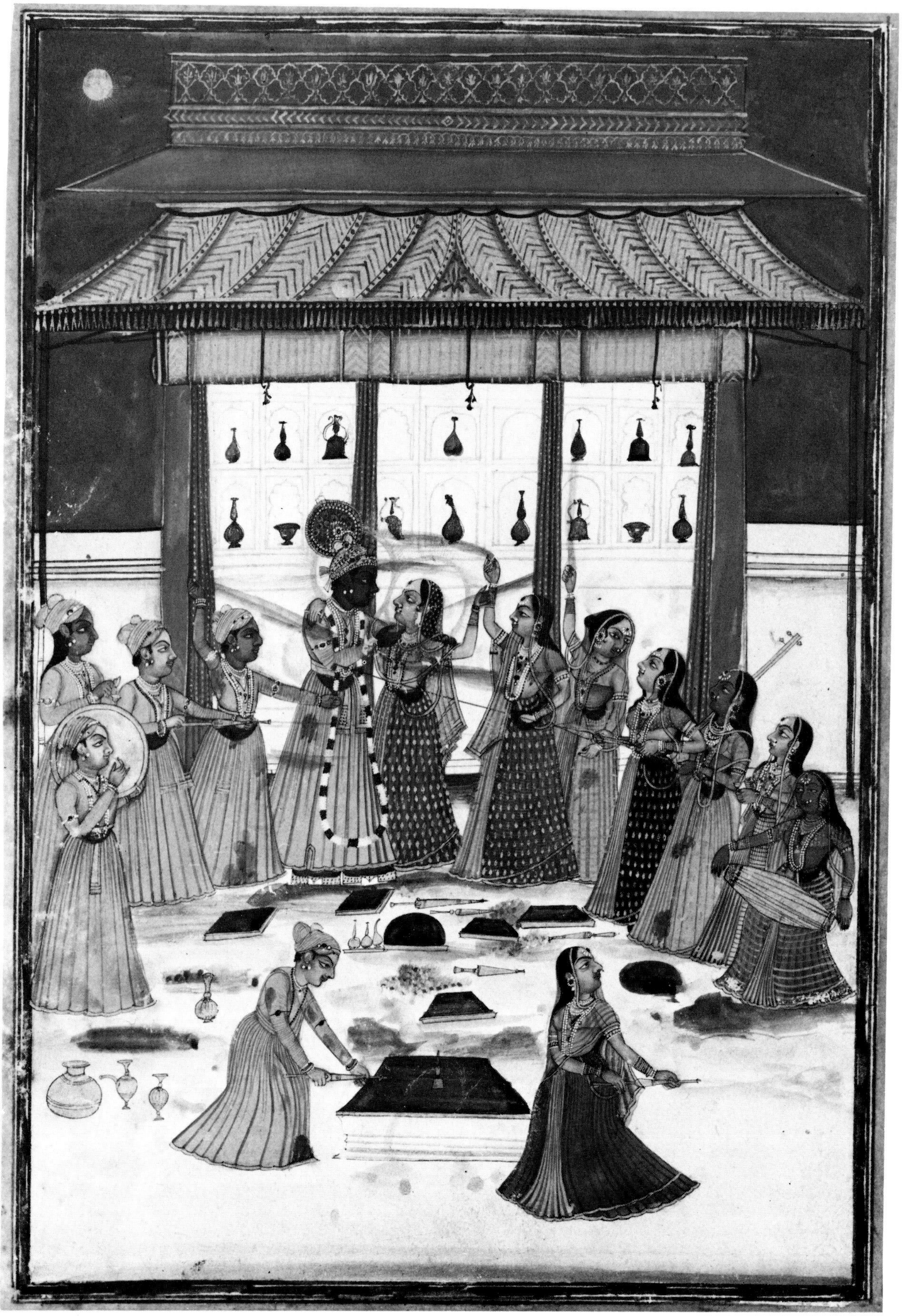

46

Laila Visiting Majnun

Rajasthan, perhaps Bikaner, after an earlier Deccani
model, 18th century

20.4 x 15.5 cm

Laila, accompanied by three maids, has come by camel
to visit the emaciated Majnun in the wilderness; he sits
against a sleeping tiger with a parakeet on his shoulder
and dogs, deer, hares and a squirrel in front of him. A
rocky hillside in the background. No border.

Inscribed on the back: *kāc rī būrj me su pāno kāḍyo jī
ṭhīkāne mhāraja śrī 108 śrī ser siṅghjī rī
tasbīr ko pāno jaḍyo moyo jotadān me melyo.*

47

Krishna Playing Holi in a Palace

Eastern Rajasthan, late 18th century

22.5 x 15.5 cm

Krishna, in a peacock crown, and noblemen dressed in
orange play Holi with a group of ladies, one of whom is
embraced by Krishna, in a courtyard in front of a
pavilion with ornamental wine-flasks in niches. Blue sky
behind. Orange border, inscribed: *śrī* and numbered
31(?). An inscription on the back briefly describes the
scene.

48

Varaha Avatara

Bikaner?, c. 1725

24.2 x 16.5 cm

The blue-skinned Varaha, or boar incarnation of Vishnu,
raises the earth from the primordial waters on his tusks,
while gods and celestial beings look on. Pale green
background with red-streaked sky with grey clouds
above. Tan border speckled with grey.

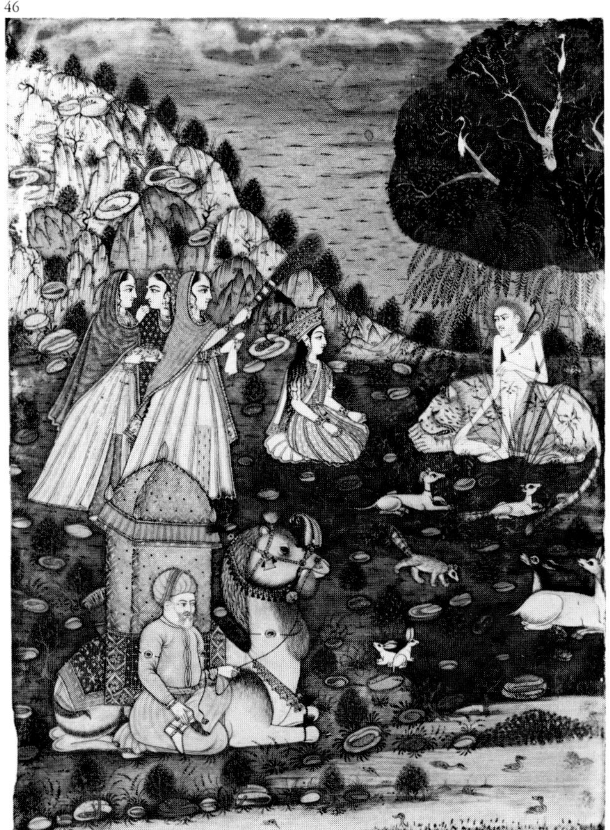

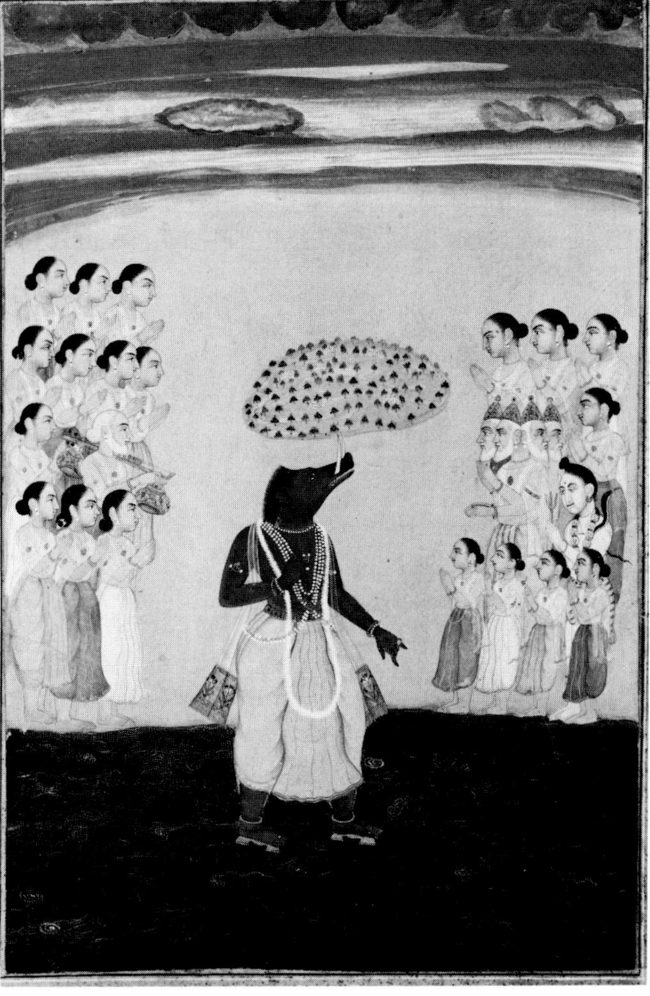

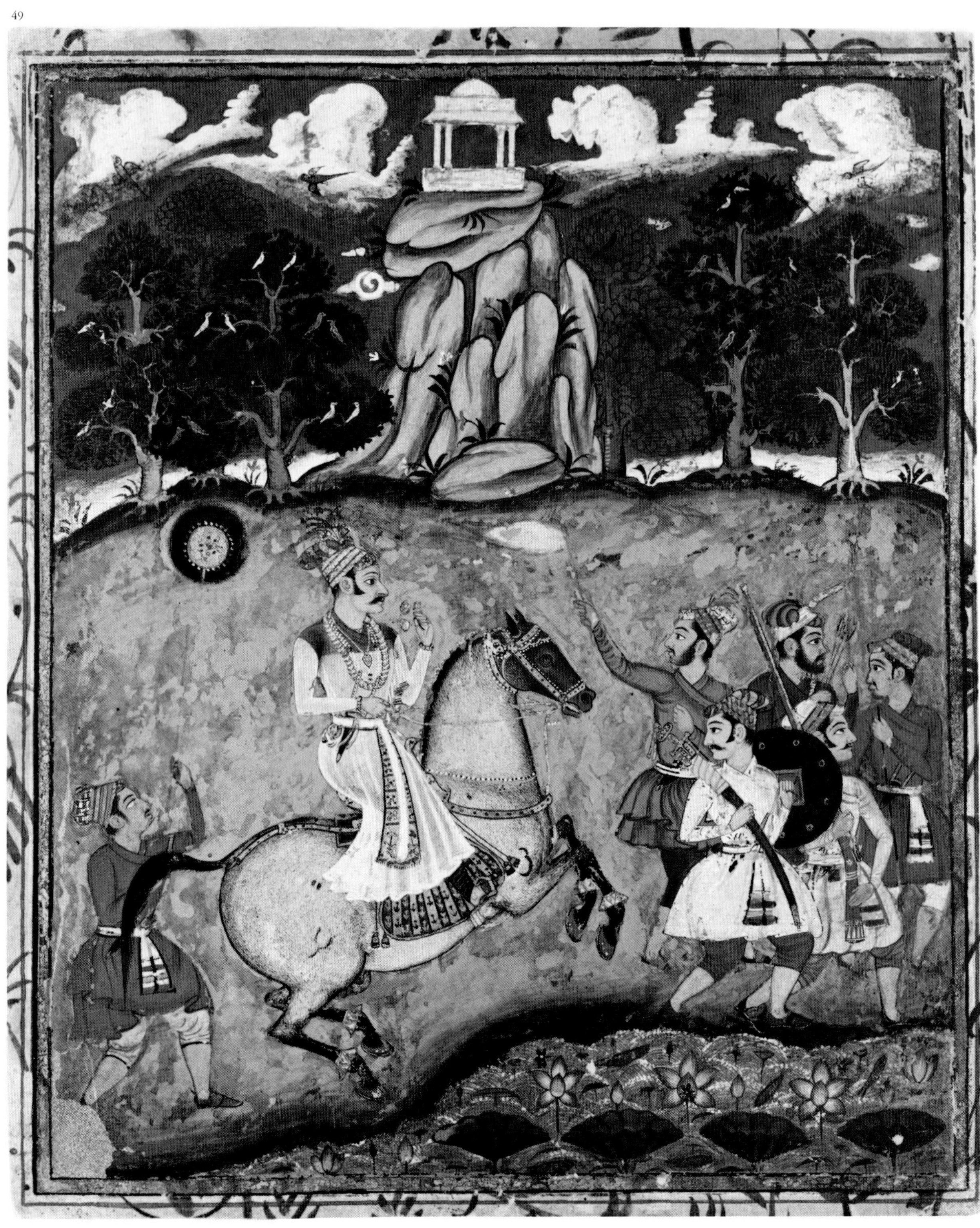

49

A Ruler on Horseback
Mewar or Bundi, mid 17th century
21.8 x 18.3 cm

An unidentified ruler rides a heavily stippled stallion,
accompanied by six attendants on foot. Flaked pale
green background with trees and pinkish-mauve rocks
crowned by a *chattri*. A pool with bee-frequented lotuses
in the foreground. Gold margin; plain border with grey
ruling and bold brush-marks, severely cropped.

The subject is possibly Maharana Jagat Singh I
(1628-52), of whom however no reliably inscribed
portraits are known. Given a later dating of c. 1680, the
ruler might be Maharana Jai Singh (1680-98).

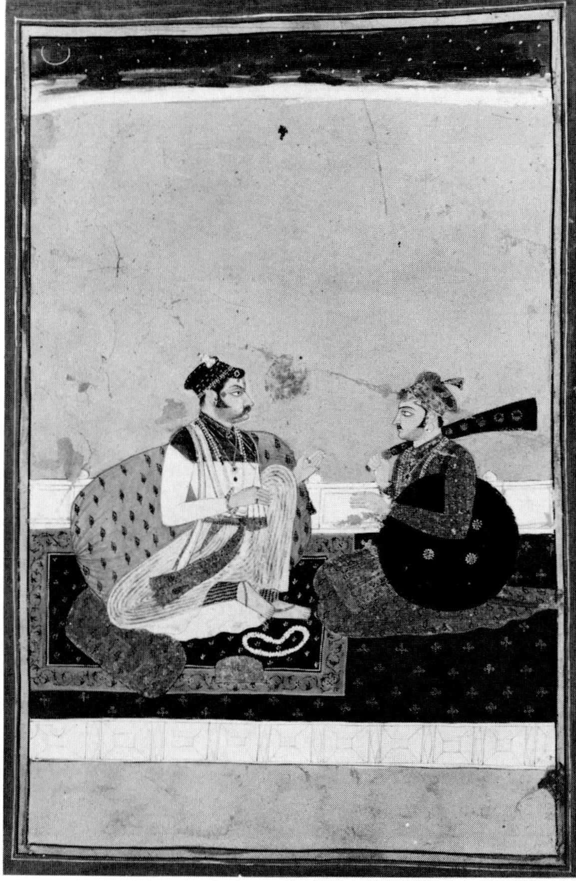

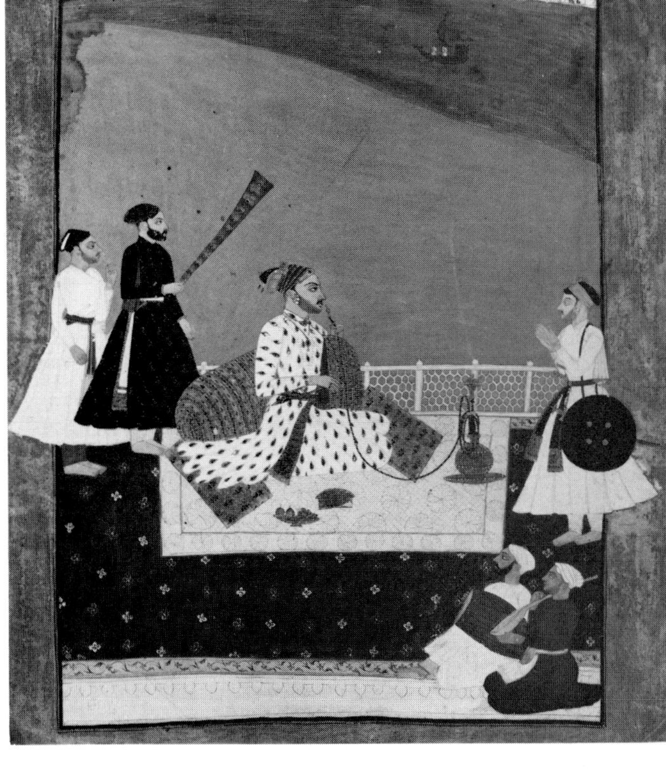

50

A Prince Receiving an Officer
Bundi or Mewar, late 17th century
28 x 18.5 cm

A (Bundi?) prince (cf. cat. no. 31) sits on a terrace smoking a *huqqa,* attended by two servants and two musicians; an officer with sword and shield stands respectfully before him. Pale green background with a crudely painted river landscape under moonlight. Trimmed red border.

51

Rao Chattar Sal of Bundi with his Son Bhao Singh
Mewar, c. 1680
27 x 17.8 cm

Rao Chattar Sal sits against an orange bolster on a terrace covered with a brown carpet with silver trefoil pattern, while his son Bhao Singh, holding a *morchal* and a shield, sits in front of him. Pale green foreground and background with starry night sky above. Yellow margin; red border.

Evidently based on a Bundi original; cf. Archer and Binney, *Rajput Miniatures from the Collection of Edwin Binney 3rd,* no. 12. Another comparable portrait, inscribed as Rao Chattar Sal, is in the G. K. Kanoria collection.

52

Diwali Celebrations at Kotah
Udaipur, c. 1690
48.5 x 43.4 cm
(Colour Plate No. 8)

A Kotah ruler (possibly Ram Singh I?) sits with his ladies at night in a courtyard in the *zenana* quarters of a palace on the occasion of Diwali, or the festival of lights, celebrated in the winter month of Karttika. The Rao, with gold nimbus, sits on a throne while a maid massages his foot. Lamps burn round the pool in the centre of the courtyard. Smaller figures of ladies are seen wandering in adjacent walled gardens and *zenana* courtyards. Outside in the palace courtyard, shown with a pale green ground, courtiers celebrate the festival with music, fireworks, acrobatics and animal fights. Low hills in the background, with scattered trees and temples, a tethered elephant and the moon and stars. Red border.

Inscribed on the back: *kota ro* [in another hand:] *kota ra mela ro bhava.*

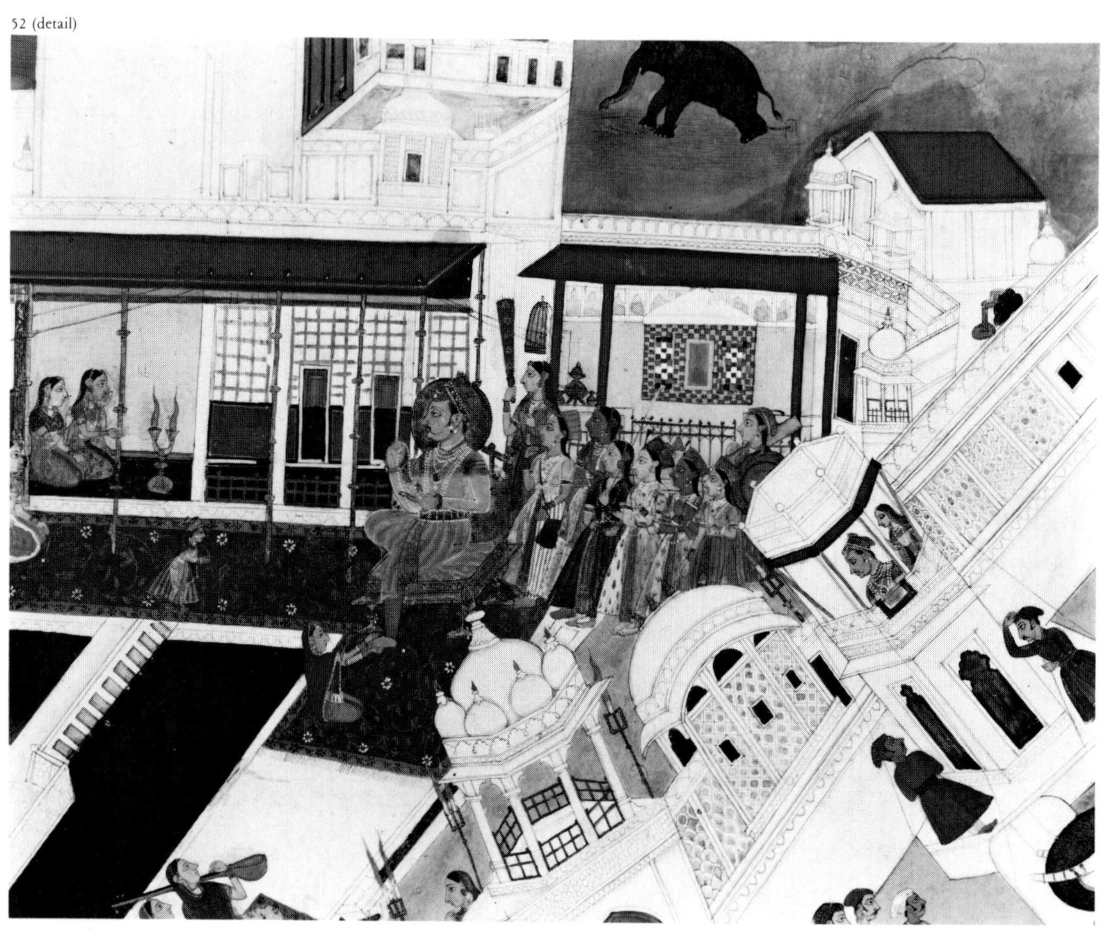

52 (detail)

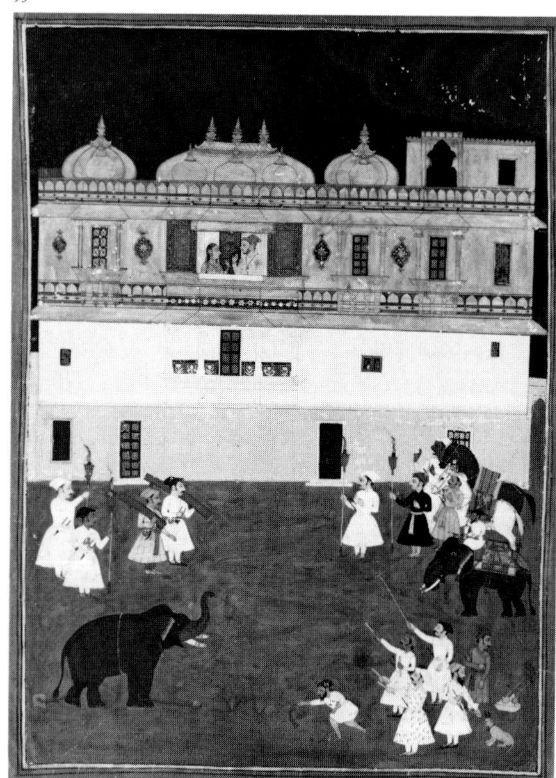

53

53
A Prince and a Lady at a Palace Window
Udaipur, c. 1690
37 x 27 cm

An unidentified prince (perhaps the young Amar
Singh?) stands with a lady in a palace window at night.
In the courtyard below fireworks are being let off, while
other servants stand in attendance with torches, horses,
elephants and a tame lynx. Yellow margin; red border
with black ruling.

54
Prince Amar Singh with Two Sardars
Udaipur, c. 1695-1700
23.5 x 16 cm

Amar Singh, in a yellow *pagri* and transparent white
jama, sits smoking a *huqqa* on a bed on a terrace,
attended by a servant who fans him, two sardars and a
dog. Blue-grey background. Yellow margin; red border,
inscribed: *mavatandanu k [unv] ar śrī amar sīghjī*
[underneath, in another hand: *je sighot*] *doḍī?ya ?hathī
sīghjī cahaṇ nāthjī.*

This picture was evidently painted in the last years of
Maharana Jai Singh, when his son Amar Singh, who had
revolted against him in 1691, held separate court at
Rajnagar to the north of Udaipur. There is good
evidence that Amar Singh was by this time a more active
patron of painting than his father.

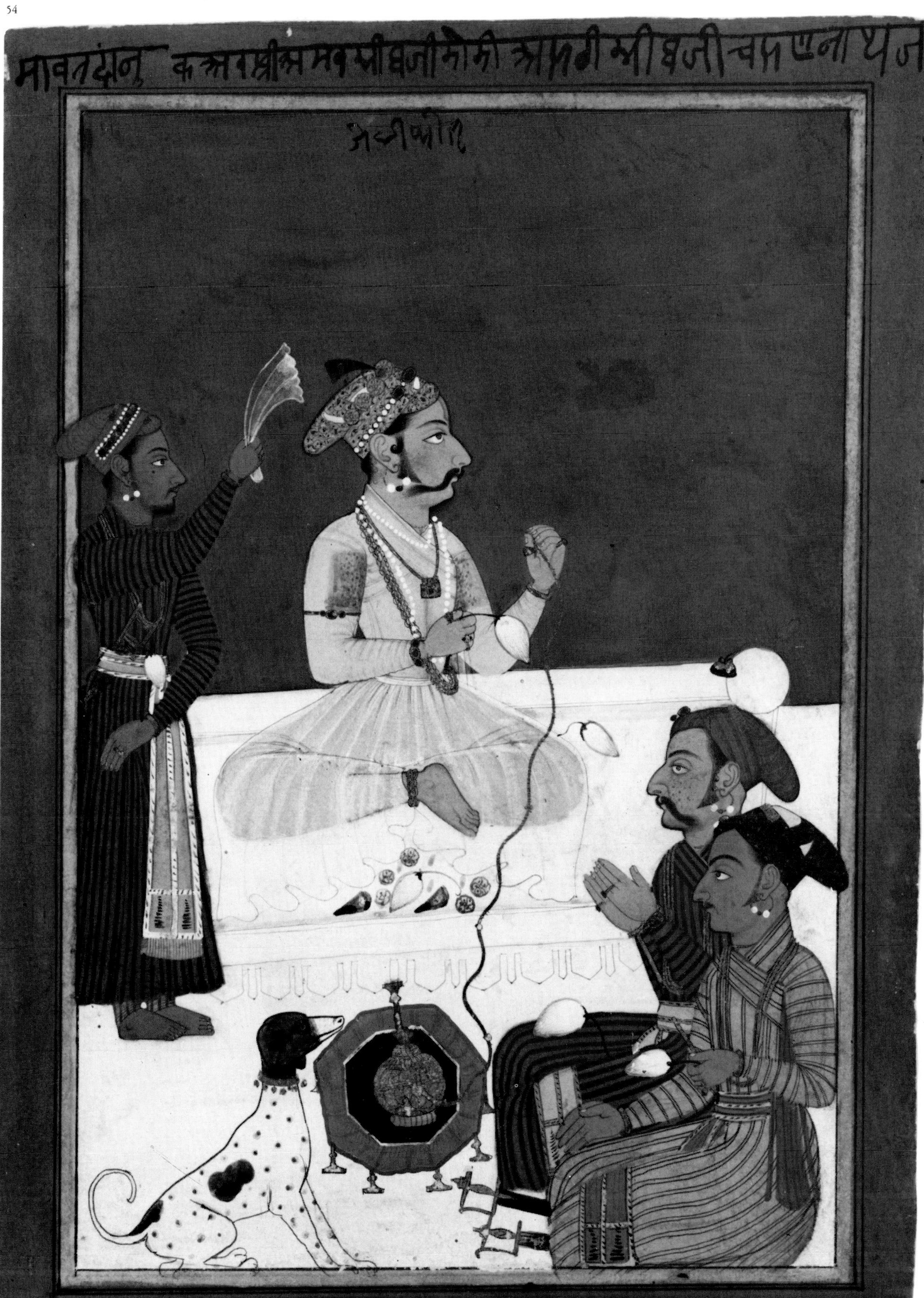
सावतसेन क आरा श्री अम सव पीबजी मेरी आदमी श्री बजी चप एन था जी
अवकोर

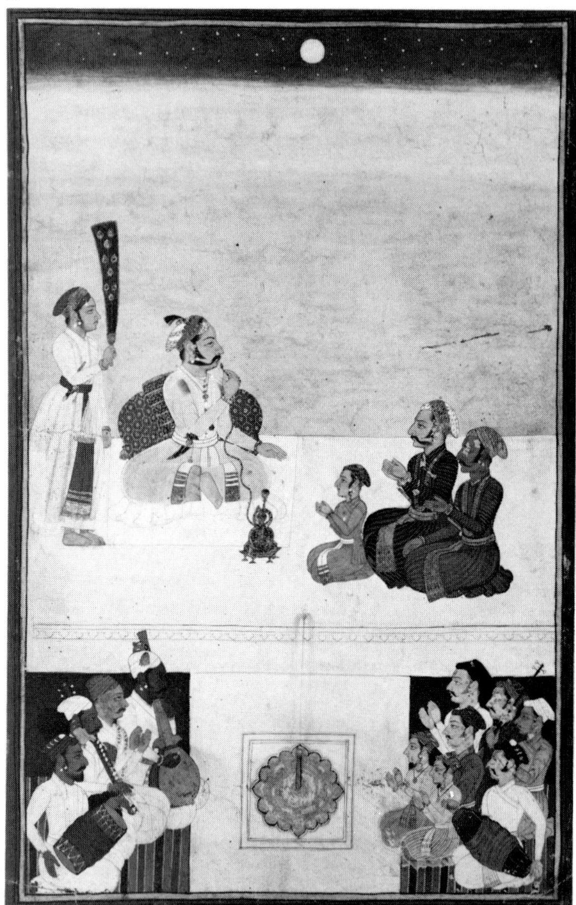

55

Maharana Amar Singh Listening to Music at Night
Udaipur, c. 1700
36.5 x 23.3 cm

The Maharana sits smoking a *huqqa* on a terrace at night, attended by a servant with a *morchal,* two sardars and a child, while two groups of musicians perform on either side of a fountain in the foreground. Pale blue-green sky with moon and stars above. Yellow margin; red border.

Inscribed on the back: *raja dali prathirajaji cuvana drikhane varajya chai mura age kuvar renasiji pache kaka kana pache pamari raye morachala khavas raye cada kare chai nala chute che dave hata musalamana kalamat gave cha jimane hata hidu kalamata gave cha canani rata veri cha tara ? dhavai riya? cha.*

The sense of this is: 'Prithviraj Chauhan, king of Delhi, is seated in his summerhouse. In front of him ?to one side is Prince Renasi (Ratnasimha); behind him is (Prithviraj's) paternal uncle Kanha; behind him is Pamari Rai; the attendant Rai Chand is fanning him; a fountain is playing; on the left-hand side Muslim musicians are singing; on the right-hand side Hindu musicians are singing; a moonlit night is ?spread out; stars are ?shining.' The identification of Maharana Amar Singh with the 12th century warrior king Prithviraj is both fanciful and unusual. The two sardars are evidently the same as those depicted in cat. no. 54).

57

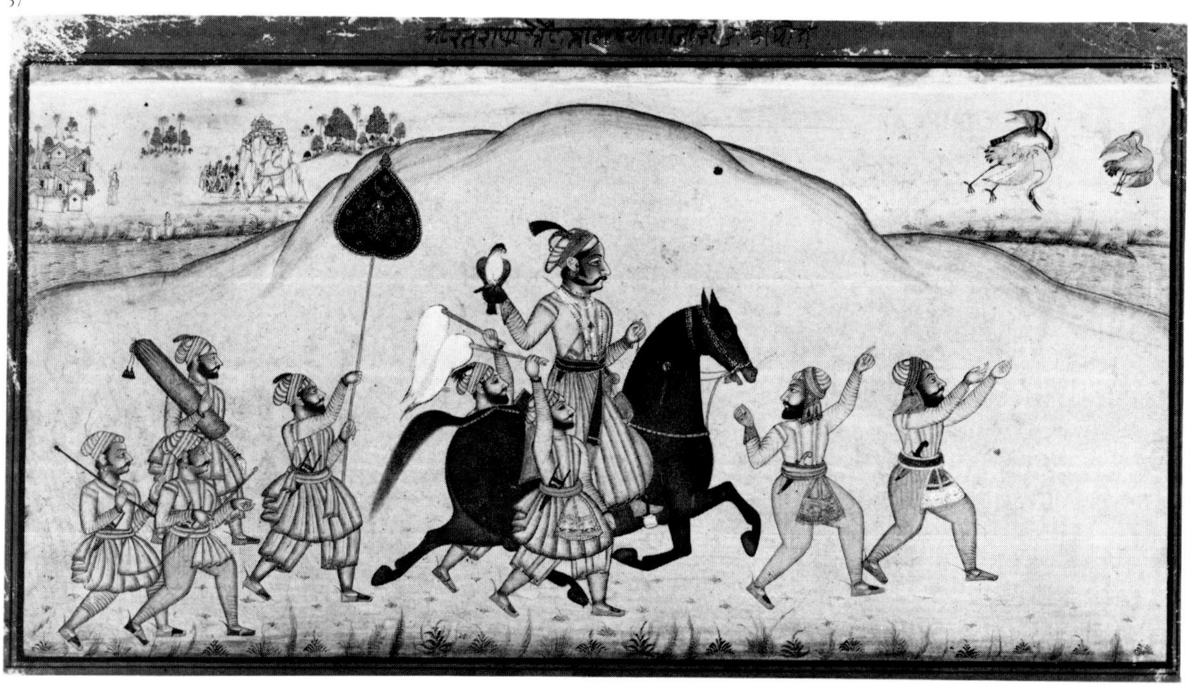

56

Maharana Amar Singh with his Son Sangram Singh

Udaipur, c. 1705

38 x 26 cm

A lightly coloured painting in the stippled style. The
Maharana, with nimbus, sits smoking a *huqqa* on a
terrace, conversing with a nobleman, perhaps his son
Sangram Singh; a chowry-bearer stands in attendance. In
the foreground are a fountain, flower-beds and lotus
pools; in the background a row of cypresses and sky with
a pale wash and (oxidised) silver moon and stars.
Severely trimmed buff border with crudely painted gold
vegetal motifs, inscribed: *mharaṇā śrī amr sīghjī* [in
another hand:] *je sīnghot.*

Other published portraits of Maharana Amar Singh in
the stippled, grisaille style current in his reign include:
Khandalavala *et al., Miniature Paintings from the Shri
Motichand Khajanchi Collection,* fig. 35; Skelton,
Indian Miniatures, pls. 10 and 11 (the latter incorrectly
described as Maharana Sangram Singh); Welch and
Beach, *Gods, Thrones and Peacocks,* pl. 28; Archer and
Binney, *Rajput Miniatures from the Collection of Edwin
Binney 3rd,* no. 6; Dahmen-Dallapiccola, *Indische
Miniaturen,* pl. 23; see also cat. no. 57 below. Portraits
of Amar Singh in the more conventional style include:
Gray, 'Painting', *The Art of India and Pakistan,*
nos. 415 and 417; Czuma, *Indian Art from the George
P. Bickford Collection,* no. 64; Welch, *Indian Drawings
and Painted Sketches,* no. 39. Further examples of both
types are dispersed in private and public collections.

57

Maharana Amar Singh Hawking

Udaipur, c. 1705

22 x 43.7 cm

A lightly coloured painting in the stippled style. The
Maharana rides a dark, highly stippled stallion and
carries a hawk on his right hand. He is accompanied by
six attendants on foot and by two *shikaris* who run
ahead, pointing to where a hawk has taken a crane in
flight. A riverside village appears in the background.
Red border, inscribed: *sirat raṇā śrī amar? sīgjī rī* [in
another hand:] *je sīghot.*

Two related paintings are in the collection of Mr Howard
Hodgkin.

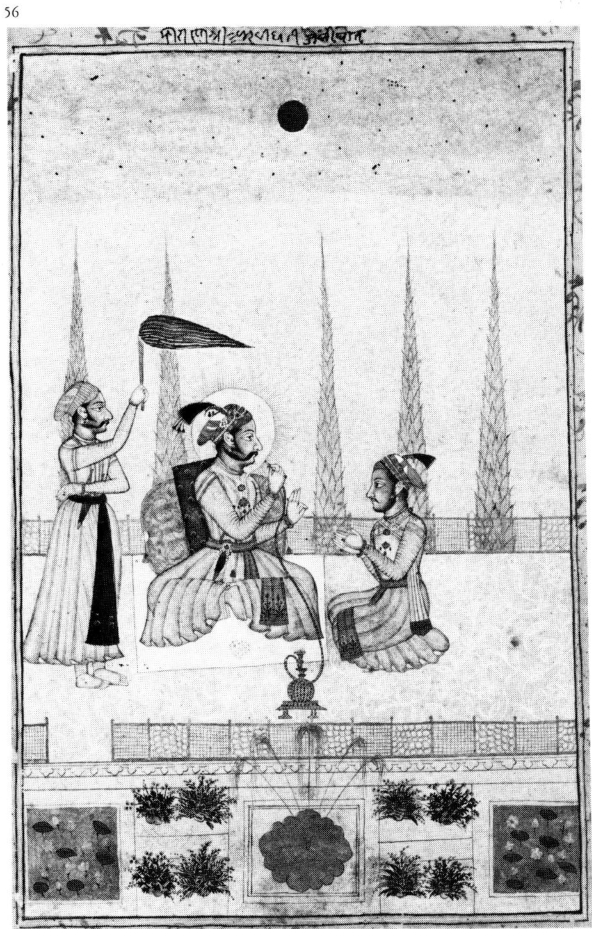

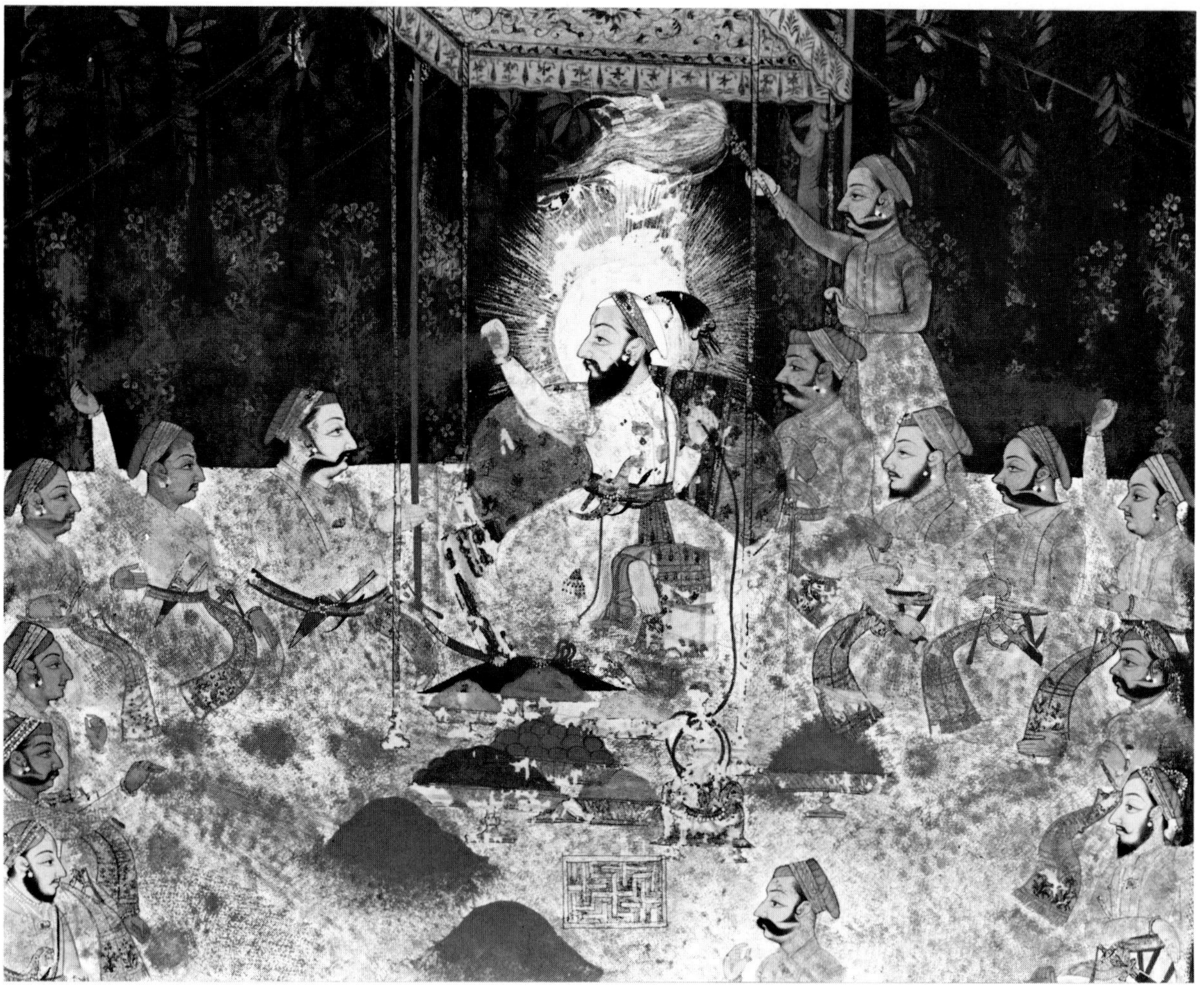

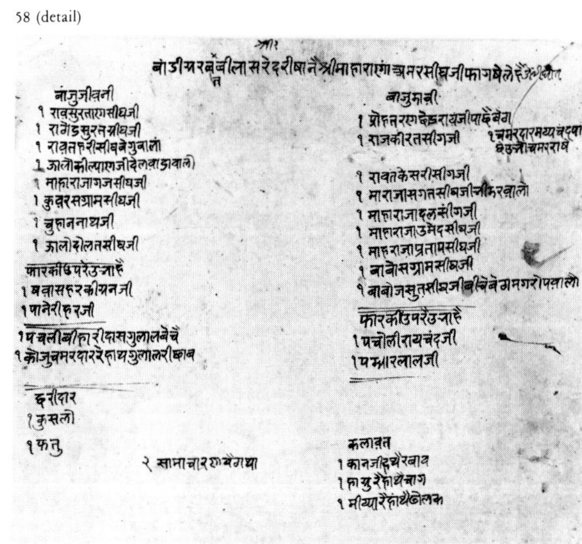

58

Maharana Amar Singh Playing Holi with his Sardars
Udaipur, c. 1708-10
47 x 40.5 cm
(Colour Plate No. 12)

The Maharana, with nimbus, and his sardars play Holi,
flinging coloured powder at one another as they sit in
formal durbar on a terrace in the Sabrat Vilas garden.
Courtiers stand in attendance, while three musicians play
in the lush flower-beds fringed by water-courses and
rows of cypresses. Yellow margin; red border. Some
flaking.

An inscription on the back, beginning: *śrī. bādī sarabat*
bilās re darīkhanai śrī maharaṇa amar sīghjī
phag khele hai [in another hand: *je sīghot*] , gives a full
list of names from the Maharana down to the musicians,
as follows; [on the left] *bāju jīvanī/ rāva suratan sīghjī/*
rāthod surat sīghjī/ rāvat harī sīgh beguvala/ jhālo
kilyanjī delavadavalo/ maharaja gaj
sīghjī/ kunvar sagrām sīghjī/ cuhan nāthjī/ jhālo dolat
sīghjī; phārakī upare ubha hai/ khavās hara kisanjī/
pane rī harajī/ pacalī biharī das gulal becaī/ koju
camardār re hāth gulal rī chāba; charidar/ kusalo/
*phatu/ 2 sāmācaran baitha thā; [on the right] *bāju dāvī/*
prohat ranachod rayajī pāchai bethā/ rāja kīrat sīgjī/

camardār ma?ya cand pāche ubho camar rākhe/ [name
del.] /rāvat kesarī sīgjī/ maraja sagat sīghjī*
bhindaravalo/ maharaja dala sīngjī/
maharaja umed sīghjī/ maharaja pratap
sīghjī/ babo sagram sīghjī/ babo jasut sīghjī bice
betha magaropavalau; pharakī upare ubha hai/ pacolī
raya candjī/ padyar? laljī; kalavat/ kanajī hathai rabav/
hasu rai hāthai caga/ mithya? rai hāthai dholaka.

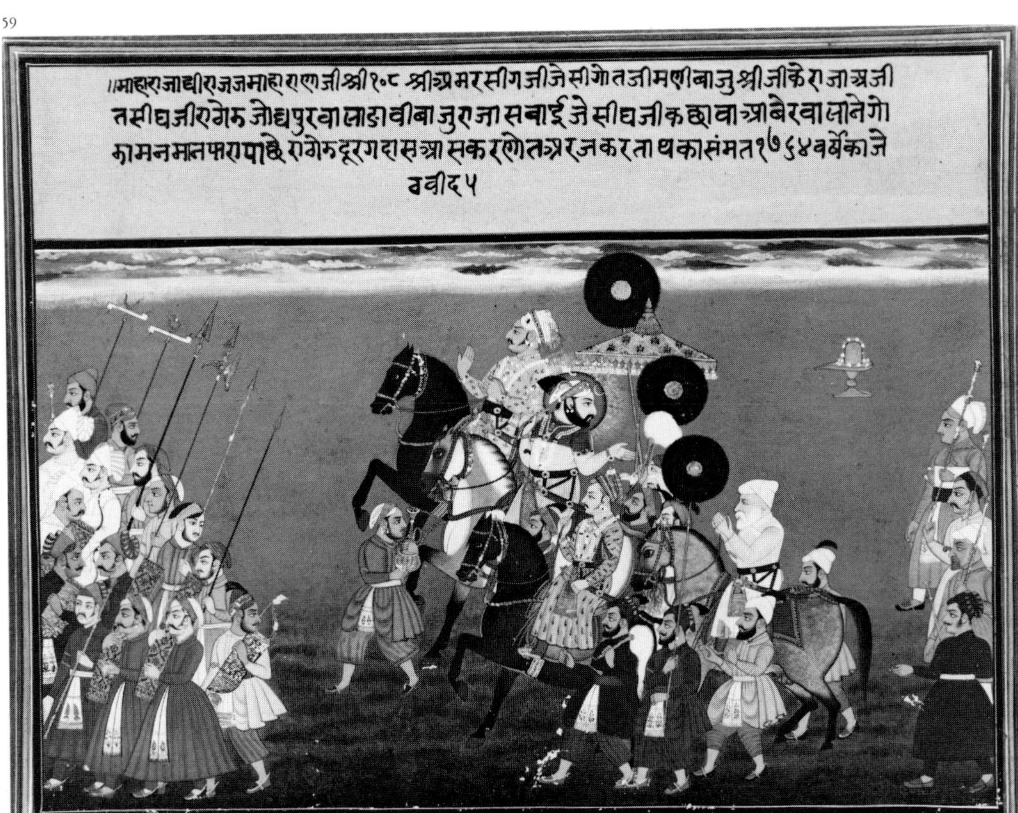

59

Maharana Amar Singh with Ajit Singh of Jodhpur and Sawai Jai Singh of Jaipur

Udaipur, 1867, probably after an original of c. 1708
29.8 x 39.3 cm

The Maharana, bearded and with nimbus, rides in procession with Maharaja Ajit Singh of Jodhpur and Maharaja Sawai Jai Singh of Jaipur (on the near side), accompanied by numerous attendants on foot. The Maharana turns to speak to Rathor Durgadas, riding behind, who folds his hands in respect. Turquoise-grey background with streaky cloud above and a *lingam* and *yoni* to the right. Red border with black, white and yellow rules.

Inscribed in the yellow text panel: *maharajadhirajaja maharanaji śrī 108 śrī amar sīgji je sīgot jimani baju śriji ke raja ajit sīghji rathod jodhapuravala davi baju raja savai je sīghji kachava abervala negoda mana mana ?...ra pache rathod durgadas asakaranot arj karta thaka samat 1764 varse ka jeth vid 5.*

A 19th century version of an untraced painting recording the visit to Udaipur by Maharaja Ajit Singh and Maharaja Sawai Jai Singh in 1708, when, with the help of Rathor Durgadas, an alliance was made between the three rulers against the Mughal power. A long inscription on the back, dated in Magha of V.S.1923 = 1867 A.D., discusses the historical background of these events.

A painting in a private collection of Maharana Sangram Singh (1710-34) riding with two sardars also derives from the composition on which this picture is based.

60

A Mughal Officer

Mewar, mid-18th century
18.3 x 11 cm

Lightly coloured study of a Mughal officer standing holding a flower in one hand and his sword-hilt in the other; possibly a version of a late 17th century Deccani portrait. Silver margin; red border. Some discolouration. Brief inscriptions on the back have been deleted and another (mutilated) inscription added, which includes the name Raja Jaswant Singh and a date (??V.S.1816 = 1759 A.D.) Below this is a folkish sketch of a woman dancing.

61

A Rathor Prince

Udaipur, early 18th century
25.7 x 19 cm

A youthful prince of the Rathor clan, possibly Maharaja Ajit Singh of Jodhpur, with a pock-marked face and a large nose, wearing a white *jama*, chocolate and gold *pagri* and orange and gold *patka*, stands facing left against a green background with a blue band above. Yellow margin; trimmed red border.

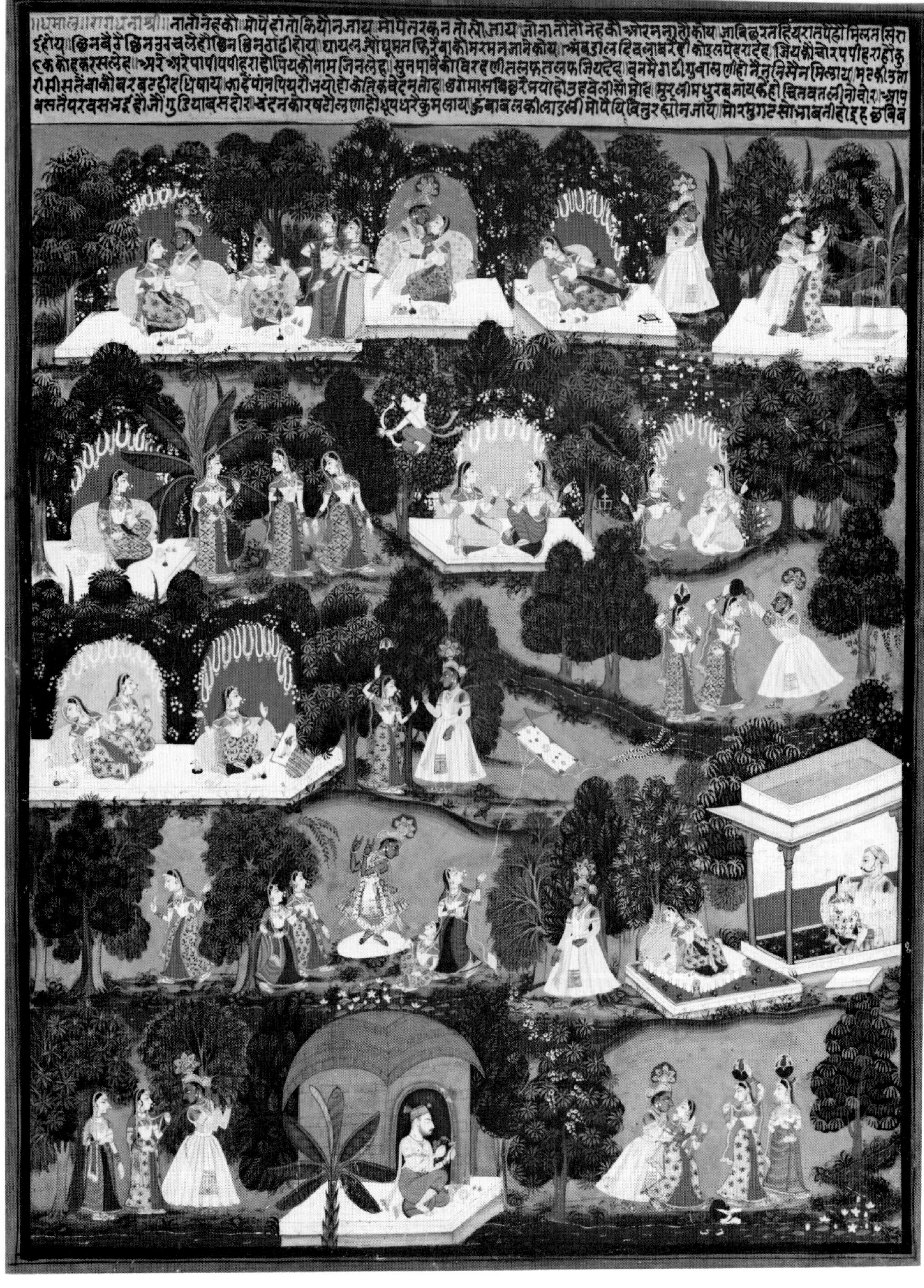

62

A Page from a Series of the *Sur Sagar*
Udaipur, c. 1700-10
46.3 x 34 cm

The composition comprises some twenty separate scenes
in five tacit registers, unified by the forest landscape.
Scenes of Krishna and Radha's love in union and in
separation are enacted in bowers hung with garlands.
Below, Krishna's games with the gopis by the Jumna,
including the taking of toll *(danalila),* are shown, while
the blind poet Sur Das himself sits singing outside his
house in the foreground. Yellow text panel with verses
from the *Sur Sagar;* red border.

Three inscriptions on the back, one of which reads:
?babat pancolī ?visan dās ?najar karayyo?

63

Shiva and Parvati
Udaipur, early 18th century
16.6 x 11.4 cm

Shiva, holding a flower, stands conversing with Parvati
on a flowery river-bank. Green background with streaky
cloud above. Red border. Some rubbing and flaking.

64

Ladies Listening to Music
Udaipur, c. 1710
21.5 x 16 cm

Two ladies, one of them smoking a *huqqa,* sit against
bolsters on a palace terrace, while female musicians
perform for them and maids attend to their needs. In
the foreground kebabs are being prepared. Behind,
there is a wooded garden with a Persian wheel and a
canopy suspended artificially over the terrace. Trimmed
red border. Some staining and flaking. Inscribed on the
back: *babat śrī gusaīji.*

Another version of this subject in the stippled style,
popular at Udaipur at this period, is in a private
collection. The composition has many features in
common with the 17th century Jodhpur painting of
Maharaja Jaswant Singh (cat. no. 12). There was a brief
vogue for this type of subject, influenced by Mughal and
Deccani example, at Udaipur under Amar Singh
(cf. Khandalavala *et al., Miniature Paintings from the
Sri Motichand Khajanchi Collection,* fig. 108, which can
be attributed to Udaipur).

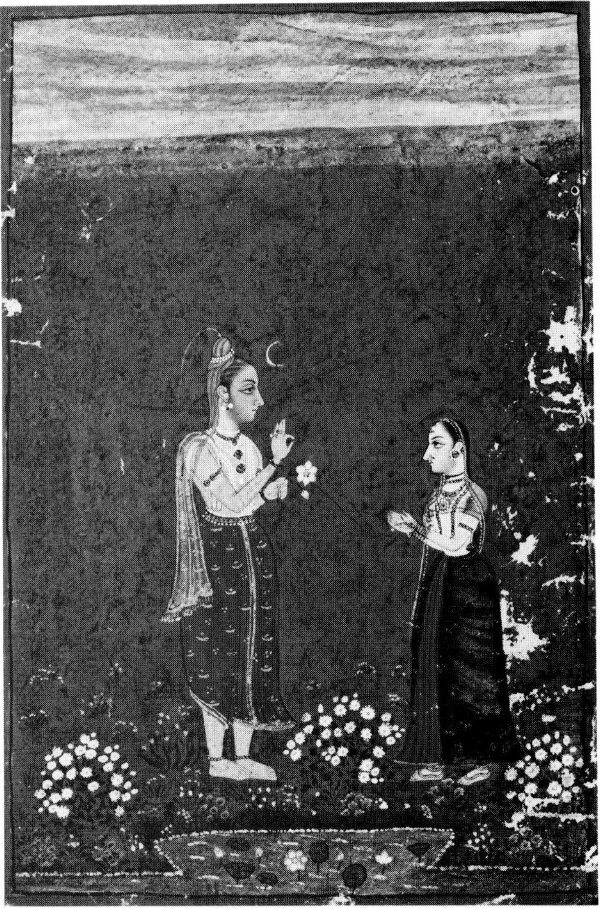

63

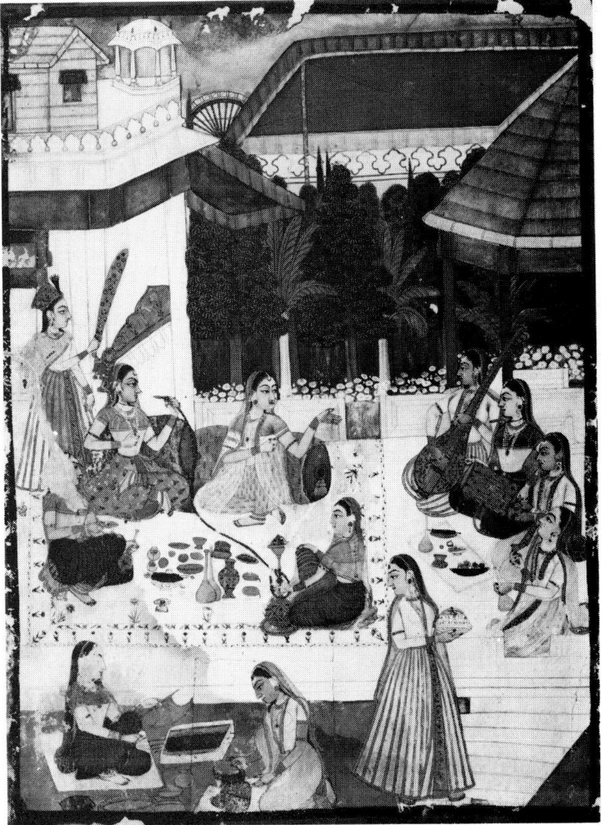

64

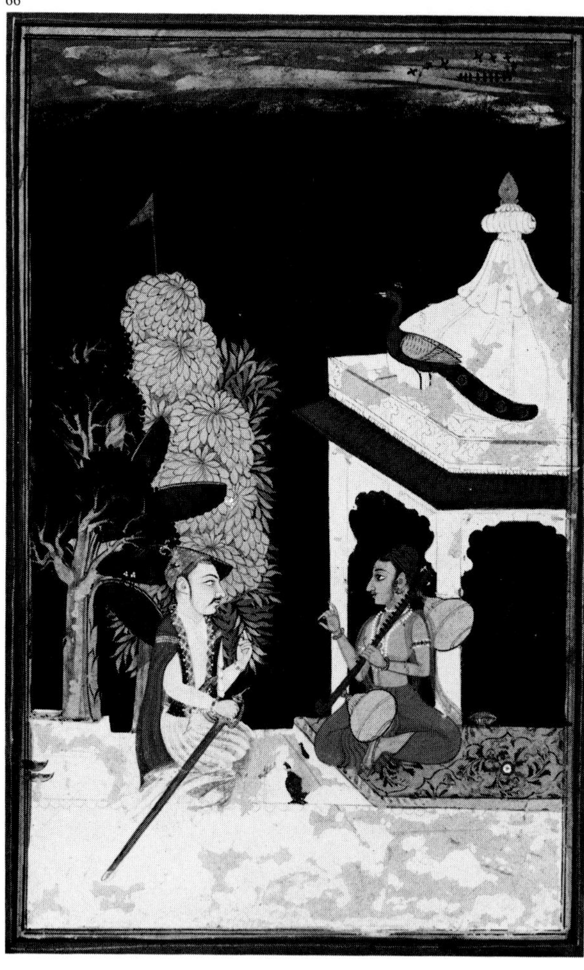

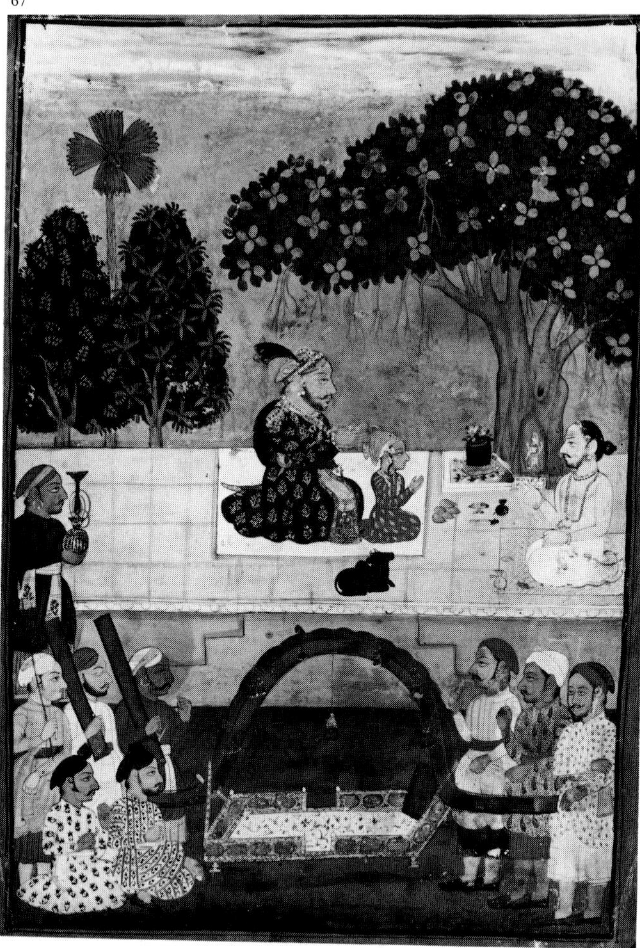

65

The Goddess
Udaipur, early 18th century
17.8 x 14.9 cm

Devi, seen in three-quarter face, with a nimbus and
lotus crown, sits on a lotus throne holding the attributes
of a conch, trident, lotus and discus in her four hands.
Her lion *vahana* sleeps in front of her. Pale green
background with a line of trees sketched in. Trimmed
red border. Numbered 31(?).

66

Kedara Ragini(?)
Udaipur, early 18th century
26 x 16.4 cm

A Muslim prince visits a *yogi* holding a *vina* on a terrace
in front of a *chattri*. Dark chocolate background with
cloud above. Yellow margin; red border. Much flaking.
Inscribed: *tanāsah rī surat ro pāno mudā? aj pātasā
akbar betho che.*

Although the figures are fancifully identified as the
Emperor Akbar and Tana Shah (Tansen??), the
composition is based on the standard iconography for
Kedara in Bundi *ragamala* series, whose origins are
discussed by Skelton, 'Shaykh Phul and the Origins of
Bundi Painting', *Chhavi 2*.

Cf. Skelton, *op. cit.,* where two Bundi versions of
Kedara are reproduced; also Pal, *The Classical Tradition
in Rajput Painting,* no. 14, and Ebeling, *Ragamala
Painting,* fig. 294.

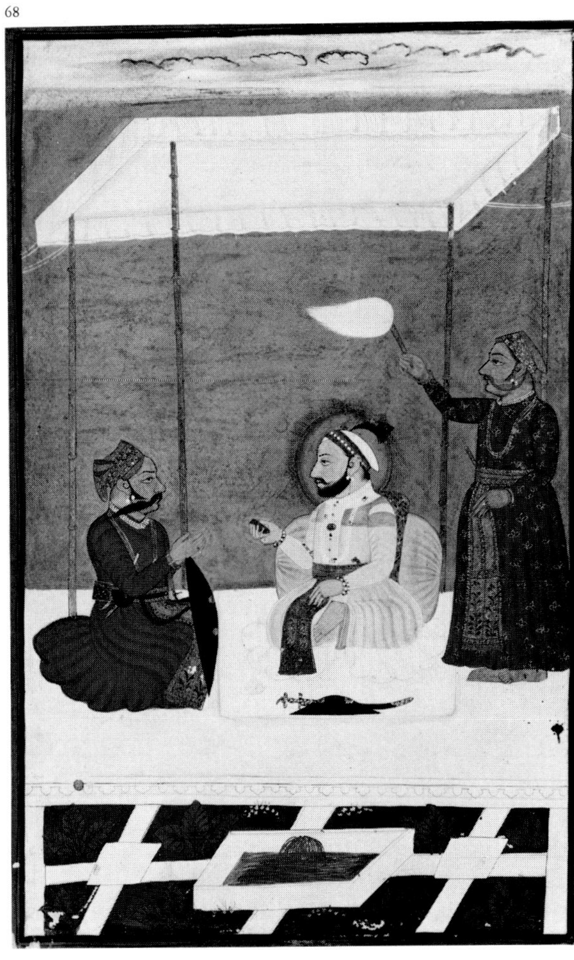

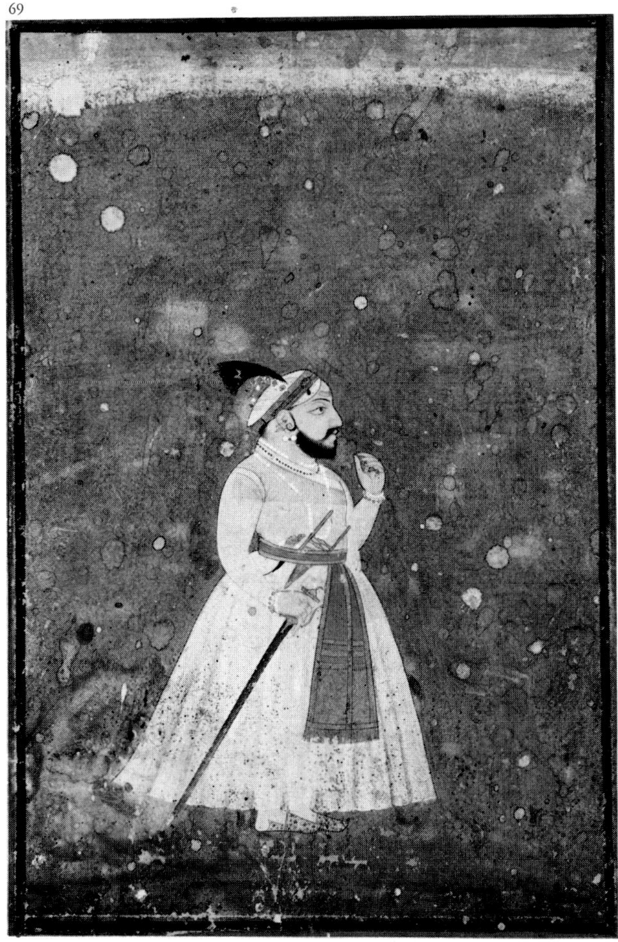

67

Maharana Sangram Singh and his Son at a Shiva Shrine
Udaipur, c. 1715
31 x 21 cm

The Maharana and his son, probably Jagat Singh
(b. 1709), sit facing a priest holding a manuscript leaf
by a *lingam* shrine under a pipal tree. Attendants and
palanquin-bearers wait in the foreground. Some rubbing
and discolouration. Red border.

Inscribed on the back: *maharajadhiraja
maharanaji śri sagaram sighji śri siva ro
darasan karta ri sabi ro pano.*

A similar composition in the stippled grisaille style exists
in a private collection.

68

Maharana Sangram Singh and a Sardar
Udaipur, c. 1720-25
35.9 x 22.2 cm

The Maharana, with nimbus, sits under a canopy on a
terrace, attended by a sardar in a red *jama* and a
chowry-bearer. Pale violet background. Red border,
numbered 97.

Inscribed on the back: *maharano śri sangram saghji ri
sabi.* Another inscription identifies the sardar as Pratap
Singh and the servant as Tulsi Das.

69

Maharana Sangram Singh
Udaipur, c. 1720
21.8 x 14.5 cm

The Maharana, in white *pagri* and *jama,* stands facing
right with one hand on his sword-hilt and the other
raised in front of him. Pale blue-green background,
much spotted and discoloured by water. Red border.

Inscribed on the back: *pano maharana śri sangaram
sighji ri surat ro.*

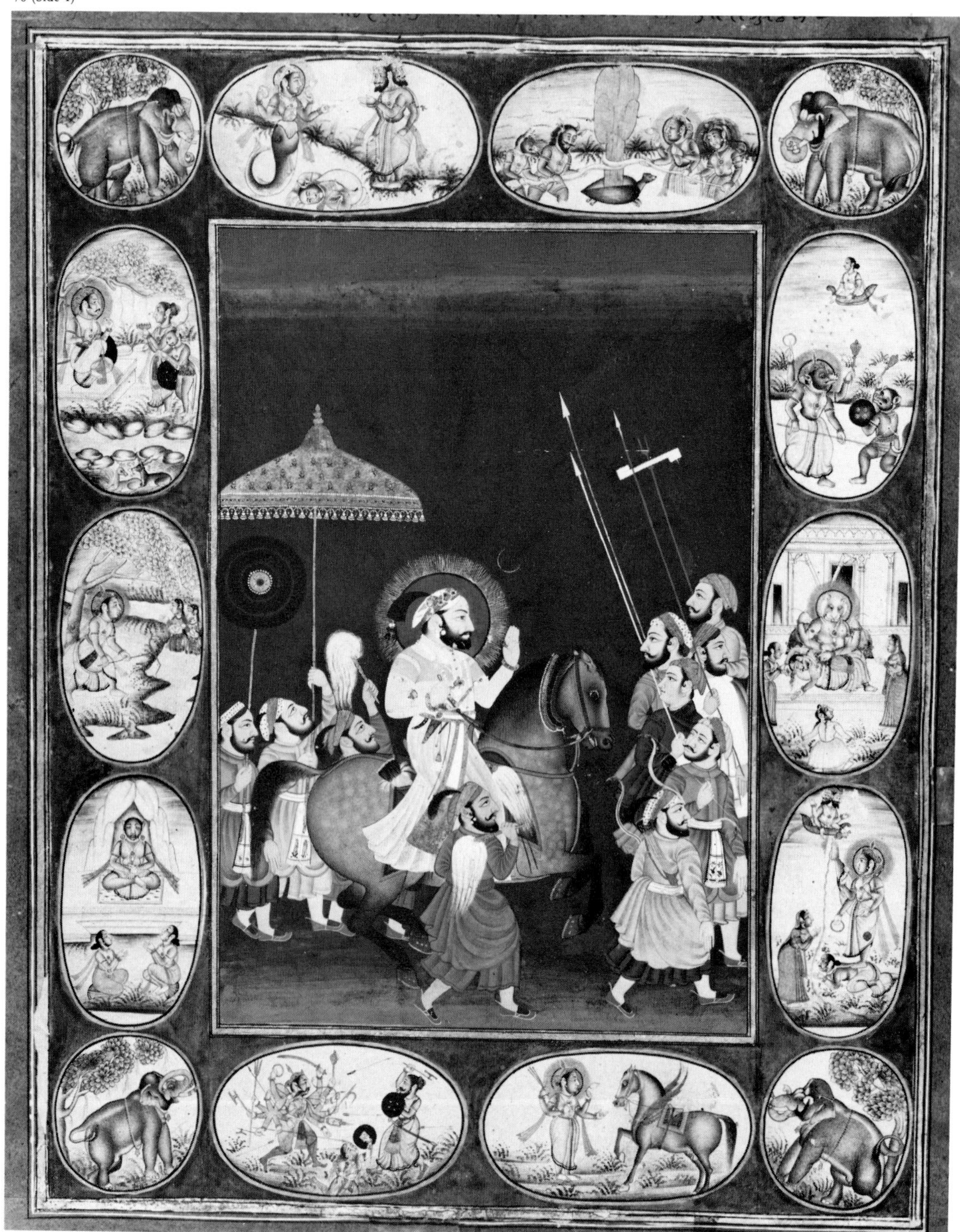

70
Double-sided Painting:
Maharana Sangram Singh II Riding and a Foppish Dutchman
Udaipur, c. 1715-20

Side 1:
Maharana Sangram Singh, with nimbus, rides a brown stallion accompanied by attendants on foot. Dark olive-green background. Cerise border with black and gold rules, containing fourteen grisaille studies within cartouches of the ten incarnations of Vishnu, with an elephant at each corner. Turquoise outer border, with a modern inscription dated V.S.1931.
41 x 31.7 cm

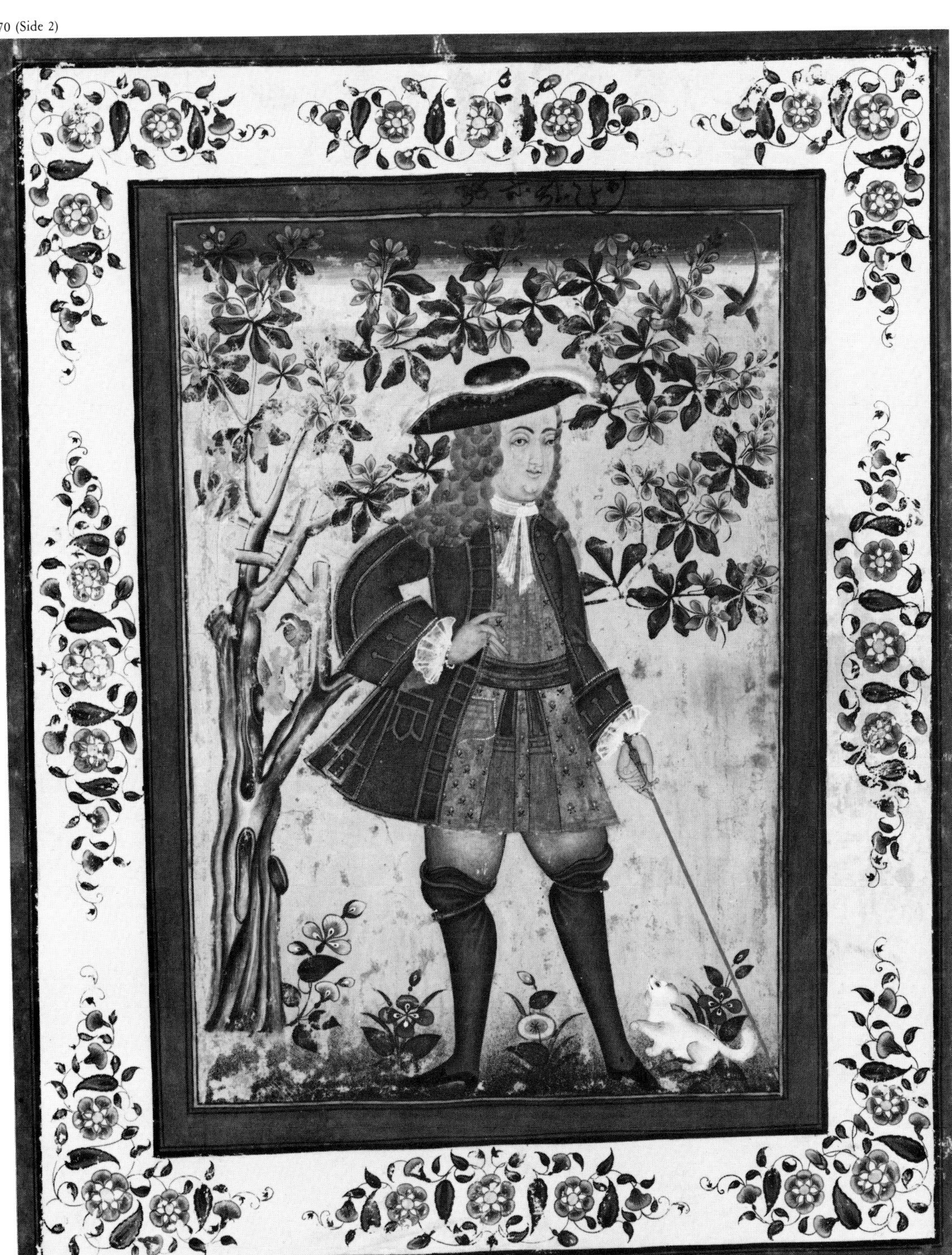

Side 2:
An elegant European gentleman stands holding a sword
with a small dog at his feet in front of a flowering tree.
Yellow and red margins; cream inner border with floral
decoration showing European influence; red outer
border. Inscribed in a modern hand: *farāsīs* (a
Frenchman)
40.2 x 30.5 cm with inner border
Although this gallant's posture is possibly borrowed
from a 17th century French fashion print (related
Udaipur versions of such prints are in the British
Museum and other collections), his general appearance is
based on that of the Dutch East India Company officers
led by J. J. Ketelaar who visited Udaipur in 1711 on
their way to the Mughal court, an event recorded in two
contemporary Udaipur paintings on cloth in the Victoria
and Albert Museum. A further exotic element is added
to this picture by the chinoiserie background. A similar
but less attractive double-sided picture, probably
deriving from the present example, is in the National
Museum, New Delhi (acc. no. 54. 61/17).

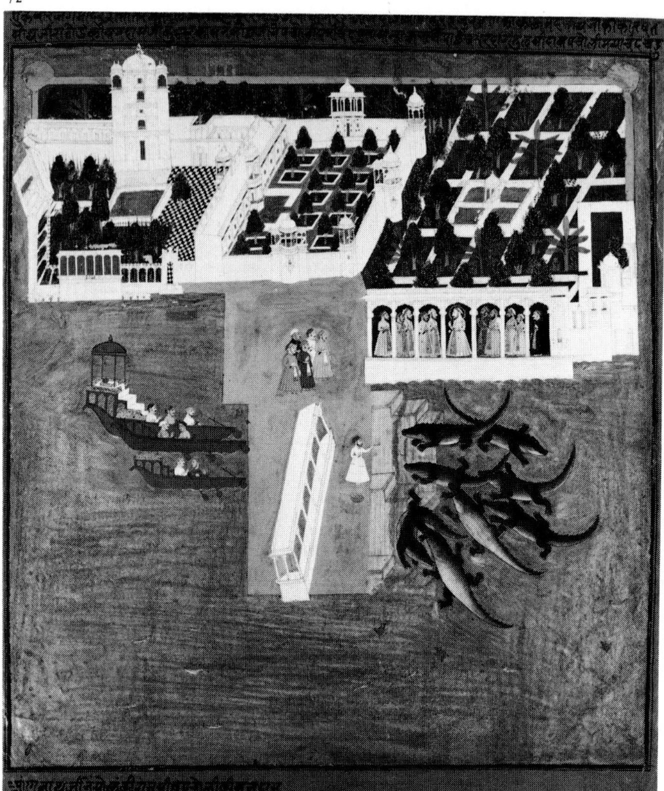

71

Maharana Sangram Singh Riding
Udaipur, c. 1720
41 x 25.8 cm

The Maharana, with nimbus, wearing a transparent white *jama* over orange, rides a grey stallion accompanied by attendants on foot. Green foreground and blue-green background with cloud above. Trimmed red border.

Inscribed on the back: *mhārano śrī sangram sīnghjī ghode jag jeṭh.*

72

Maharana Sangram Singh Watching the Feeding of Crocodiles at Jagmandir
Udaipur, c. 1720
50 x 46.2 cm

The Maharana, with nimbus, stands with his sardars in a water-side pavilion on the lake island of Jagmandir; on the left stand Umed Singh, Takhat Singh, Rathor Kisan Das, Kunvar Kisan Singh and Pancholi Devi Chand; on the right (behind the Maharana) Tulsi Das, Pancholi Maya Chand, Chauhan Nathji, Solanki Ram Singh and Pancholi Kisan Das. In front of them enormous crocodiles fight for hunks of meat thrown by a servant. Three royal barges await the party nearby. (Oxidised) silver water with fish and turtles.

Red border, inscribed: *eka vāra jagamandira ?ra sātare magara ladyā ko hajur rakho?de ubhā najar?u ajadī ītrā ṭhakura hajur* [del.] *kākā umed sīghjī kākā takhat sīghjī rāthod kīsan dāsjī kuar kīsan sīghjī ne pancolī devī cand eto samahā ubhā ne pache camardar tulasī das pacolī mayā cad cahuana nathjī ne solankī rām sīgh pacolī kisan das.*

Tod records (c. 1820) that 'there are two of these alligators quite familiar to the inhabitants of Udaipur, who come when called 'from the vasty deep' for food; and I have often exasperated them by throwing an inflated bladder, which the monsters greedily received, only to dive away in angry disappointment.' (*Annals and Antiquities of Rajasthan,* vol. II, pp. 753-4). The French traveller Rousselet, who was at Udaipur in 1866, describes the crocodiles as still numerous but increasingly wary 'since the English Residency has been established at Oudeypour, and the Rana, overcoming the ridiculous religious prejudices which protect these reptiles, has allowed Europeans to hunt them down' (*India and its Native Princes,* p. 162). Their numbers continued to dwindle in the present century and the last of them is thought to have perished as a result of a drought in the early 1970s which dried out the Pichola Lake.

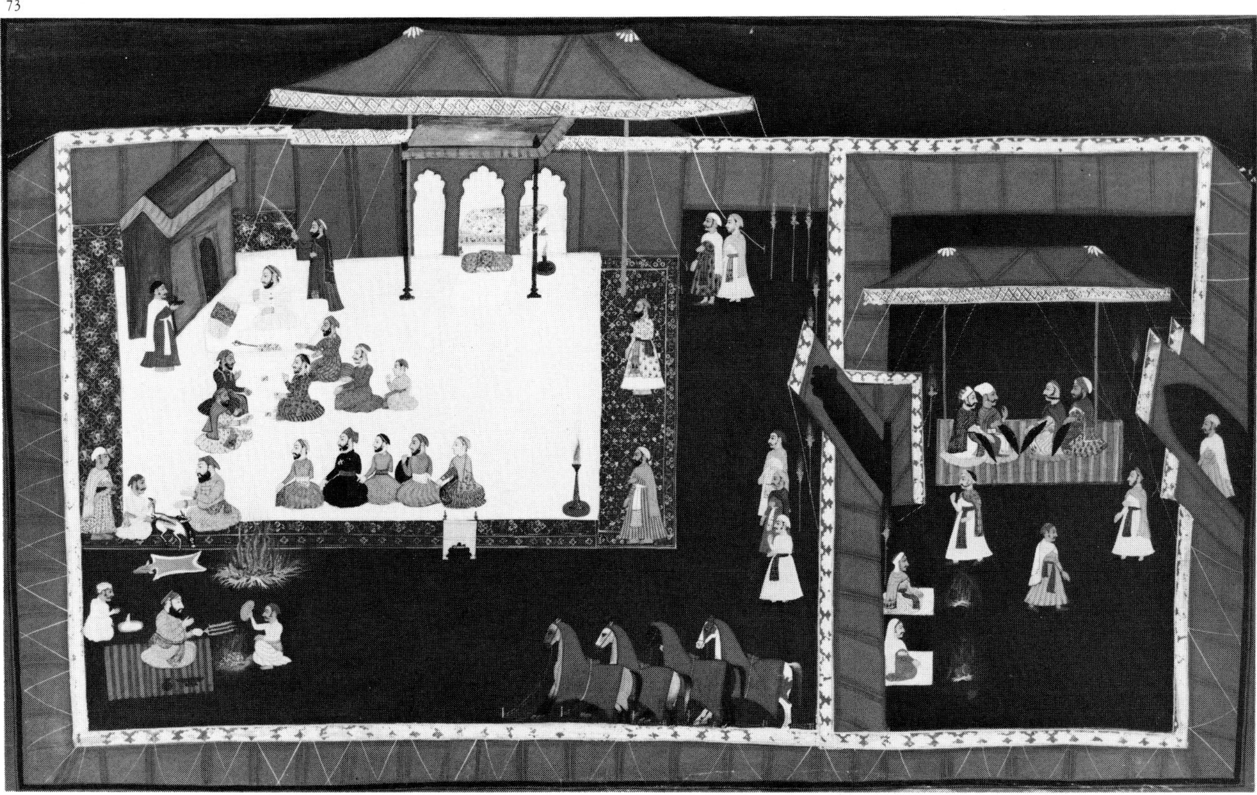

73

Maharana Sangram Singh Playing Cards in Camp at Night
Udaipur, c. 1720-25
42.3 x 69 cm

The Maharana and sardars sit playing cards on a white floor-spread within a red tented enclosure. The sardars taking part in the game are (on the left) Takhat Singh and Kisan Singh, (on the right) Nagaji and Ram Singh, behind whom sits Pancholi Kisan Das. Umed Singh, Rathor Kisan Das, Chauhan Gopal Singh and Chauhan Zoravar Singh sit in a row. Venison is being cooked, and servants stand in attendance and keep watch in the antechamber of the encampment to the right. Red border.

Inscribed on the back: *śrī mahārājadhirāja mahāranoji śri saṅgrām sīghji ?derā mahe birājya thaka gaṅjafo khele jathe age mahārāja takhat sīghji kisan sigh tuar jana pache dhaabhai nagaji dhi..? ram sīghji jana pache pancoli kisan dasji betha nicali katar mhe mahārāja umed sīghji rathod kisan dasji cuhan gopal sīghji cuhan joravar sīghji betha haran ukhele jathe cuhan kitoji betha nice kitoji sulase ke hajur pache tira vai vasadeva cavo rakhe ?derana re maṅgare.*

According to Dr R. von Leyden, the authority on Indian playing-cards, this is one of only two known miniature paintings showing a card-game in progress *(detail);* the other, a mid-18th century Udaipur picture showing Maharana Raj Singh II, is in a Pasadena private collection.

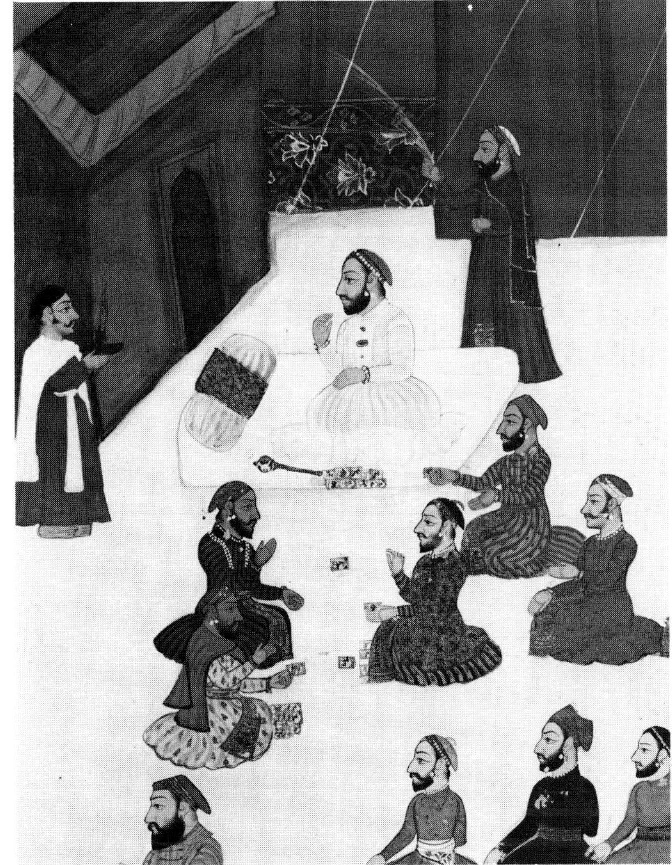

73 (detail)

74

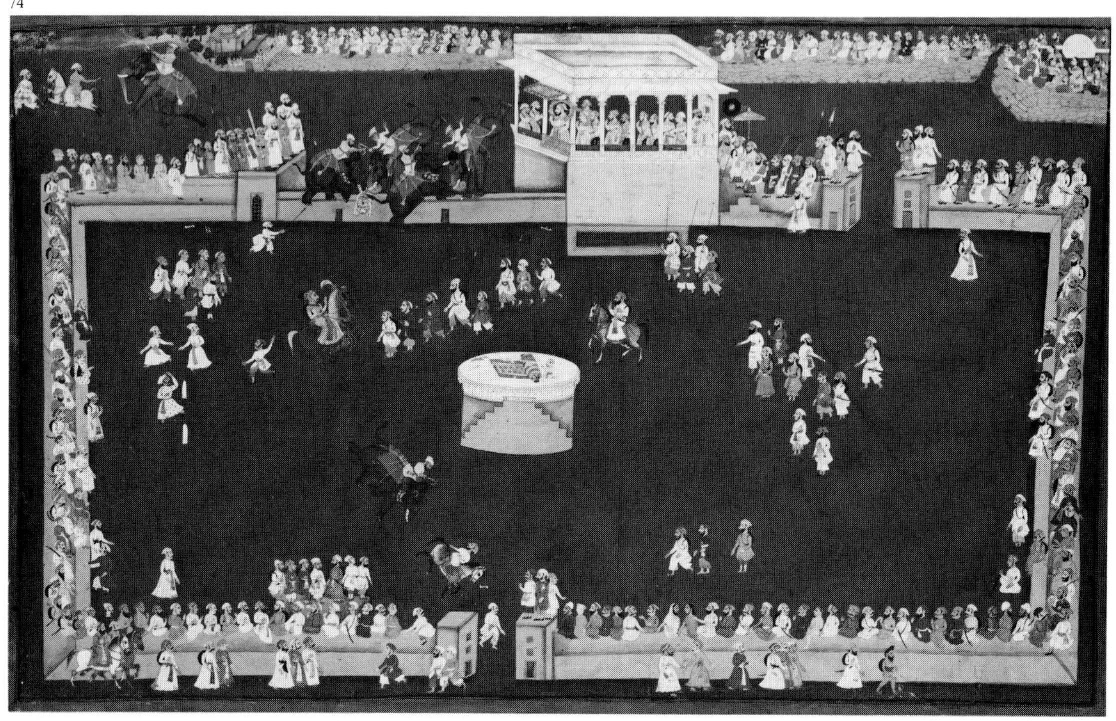

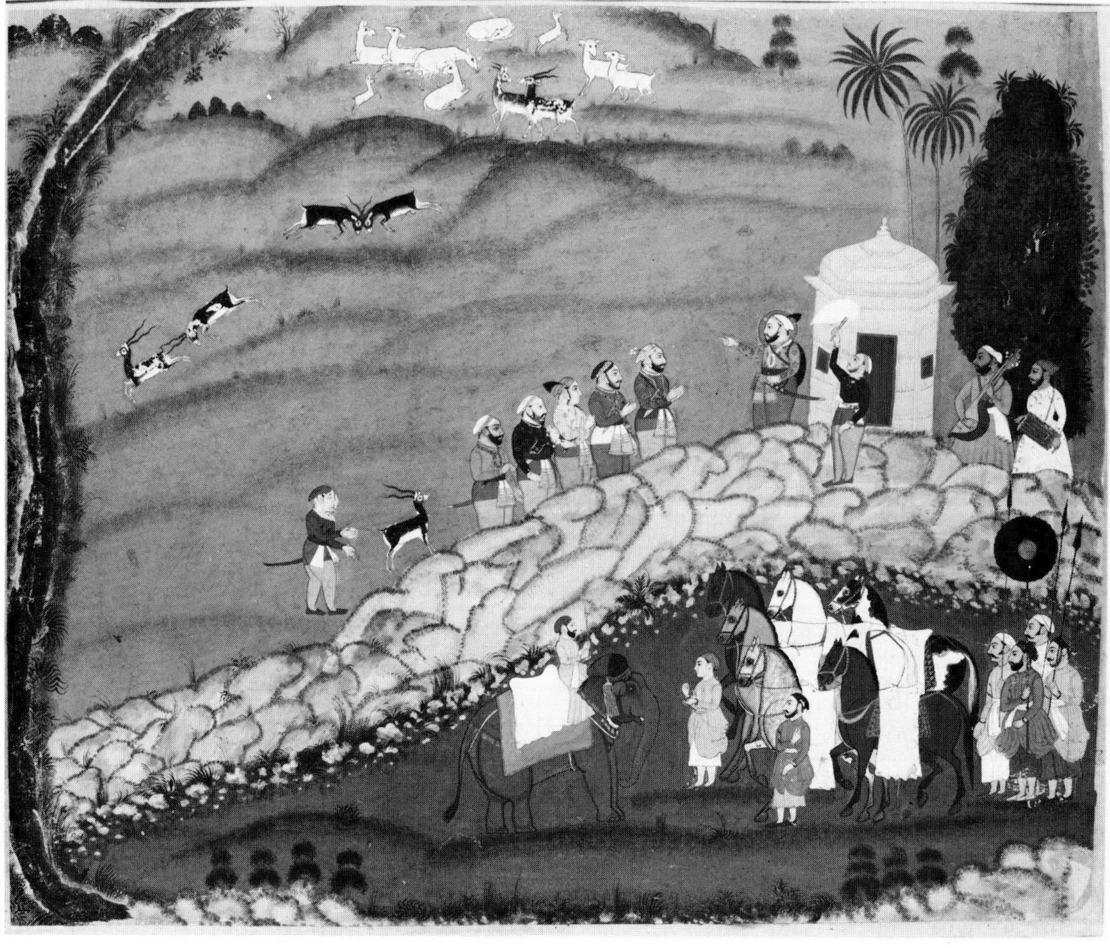

72

74

Maharana Sangram Singh Watching an Elephant Fight
Udaipur, c. 1725
44.4 x 73.5 cm

The Maharana, with nimbus, stands with his sardars and
ministers in the pavilion at the Chaugan. In front of
him two elephants are seen fighting together and also
finishing off a tiger which is slumped over a wall.
Bakhat Singh and Takhat Singh stand in front of the
Maharana, behind him Bihari Das Pancholi, Pratap
Singh, Kisan Das Pancholi and others. Courtiers,
townspeople and sadhus line the walls of the arena,
which is shown with a greyish-umber ground. Red
border.

Inscribed on the back: *śri maharajadhiraja maharanoji śri
sangram sighji cogan re darikhane ubha
sama rav bakhat sighji ubha maharaja takhat
sighji ubha hajur pache itra thakur ubha
pancoli bihari dasji maharaja
pratap sighji pancoli kisan dasji tuar kisan
sighji cuhan joravar sighji sagtavat sam sighji
dhaabhai nagaji khavas rugo camardar tulsi dasji camar
rakhto thako hathi rajagaj hathi sighadal angada
ladta thaka kota ?kharane rajagaj mahe sighadal ladai
hua pache nahar nakh?e agad upre so nahar he muda
doi hathi karta thaka cogan mahe ram sigh dhikad?e
ghore patasa prasanga upre ca..? ubha.*

75

Maharana Sangram Singh and Sardars Before a Hunt
Udaipur, c. 1720-25
52.2 x 63.7 cm

The Maharana, with nimbus, stands by a yellow hut
next to a rocky outcrop, attended by a chowry-bearer
and musicians, addressing five sardars (Pratap Singh,
Takhat Singh, Prince Jagat Singh, Daulat Singh and
Saktavat Surat Singh) before a hunt. Blackbuck are seen
playing and at rest in the distance. An elephant with
mahout, horses and attendants stand in the foreground.
Buff border.

Inscribed on the back: *śri. śri mharajadharaja mharanoji
śri sangram sighji hirana ri sikar padarya? so
ubha he: śriji hajur sama ubha: mahaja pratap
sighji: maraja takhat sighji: kuvar śri jagat sighji: dolat
sighji: sagatavat surat sighji: śriji pachai camardar ubho:
kalavant cad: kalavat piro.*

76

**Maharana Sangram Singh Visits Gosain Nilakanthaji
after a Tiger Hunt**
Udaipur, c. 1725-30
66 x 48 cm

The Maharana, with nimbus, is seen in the middle of a
procession returning from a hunt with a dead tiger,
which had been lured to a clearing by the use of a
buffalo as bait. The procession is shown travelling down
from the hills as it were at right angles to the picture
plane. Further below, the Maharana visits the residence
of Gosain Nilakanthaji, where the Gosain is seated on a
tiger-skin. The Maharana, who presents the dead tiger
with his respects, is shown both standing upright and
bowing before the Gosain. His retinue meanwhile wait
on the further bank of a stream. Red border.

Inscribed on the back: *3 khado? nahar marye tiri sikar ro
bhava pana 4 pano tijo* [further below:] *śri
maharajadhiraja maharanoji śri sangaram
sighji nahar ri sikar padharya ne nahar mare ne lade ...?
khede savi ne gusai nilakanthagaraji re ?page laga ne
naharavata o* [in another hand:] *khadau nahar.*
Nilakanthaji also appears in cat. nos. 81 and 92.

77

**Maharana Sangram Singh Hunting Blackbuck with a
Cheetah at Nahar Magra**
Udaipur, c. 1725-30
42.5 x 47.5 cm

The Maharana, with nimbus, is seen four times, riding
alongside his hunting cheetah in its covered bullock-cart,
riding in pursuit as the cheetah is released and springs
on a blackbuck, and inspecting the kill, while the second
of the two blackbuck that had been fighting together
runs away. A long procession of attendants appears in
the background, while a group of sardars riding in the
foreground express their admiration. Red border.

Inscribed on the back: *śri. śriji nara magara su pacha
padarata tha mharanoji śri sagram sighji jadi
hiran ladato dakhya? jadi cita chodi hiran bhaga
citi doraine hiran pakadye jadi śriji ghodo dodabainai
citi nakhai ga?ya: hiran ro? pag śriji pakade rakhya?:
nakhai ram sighji baitha: camardar ubha: nilai ghode
kunvar śri jagat sighji: dhabhai nagaji: sagtavat syam
sighji: tuvar kisan sighji: rav bakhat sighji ghode
doravene hajur jata: mharaja takhatsighji: ghodo
dorabene hajur jata: tulisi dasji cavaki ghodai.*

Prince Jagat Singh (b. 1709), wearing a red *pagri* and
riding a grey and white horse at lower left, appears here
to be in his late teens.
Cf. a later sketch of a cheetah taking a deer, attributed
by Welch to Bakhta (S. C. Welch, *Indian Drawings and
Painted Sketches*, no. 58).

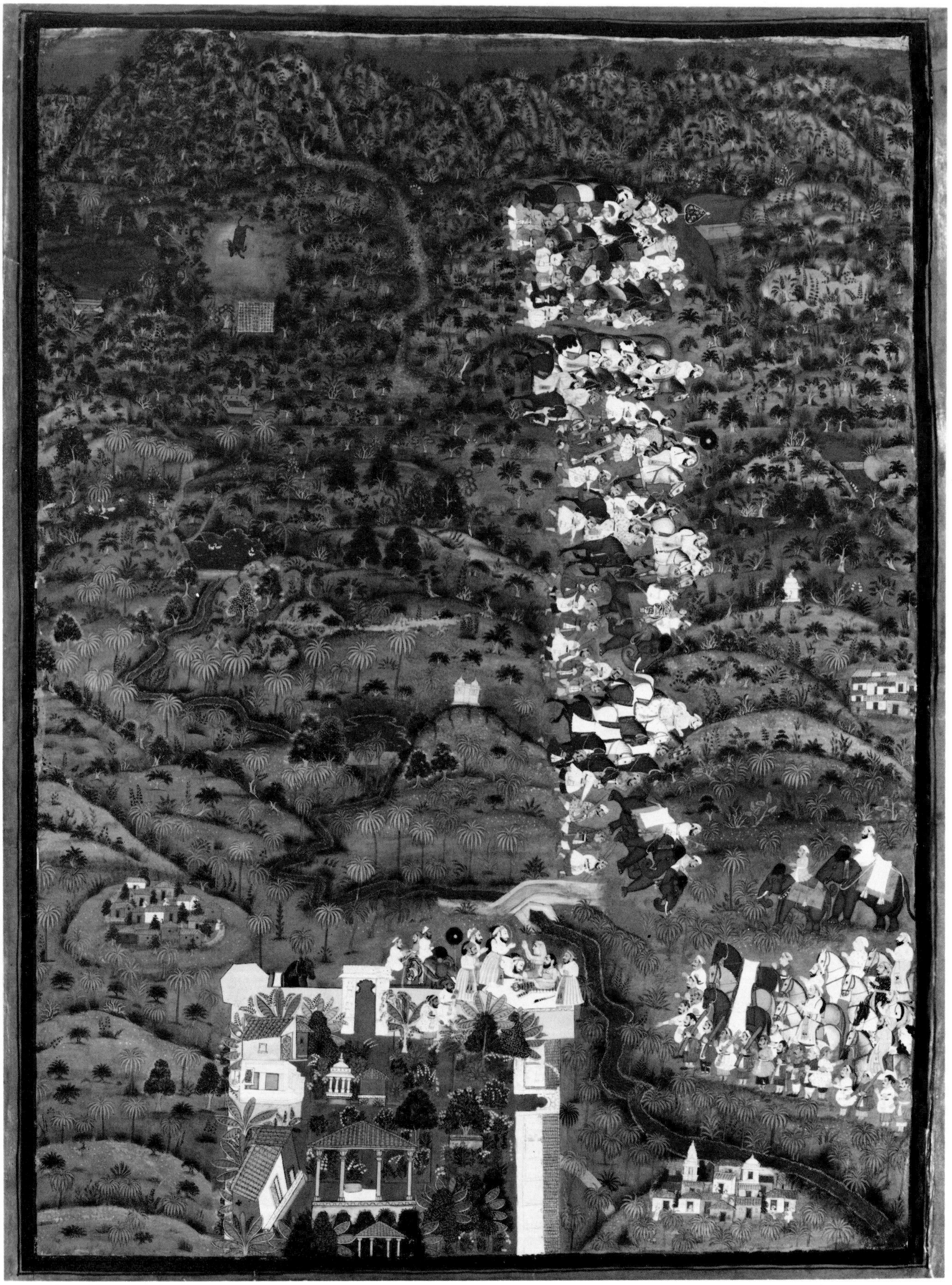

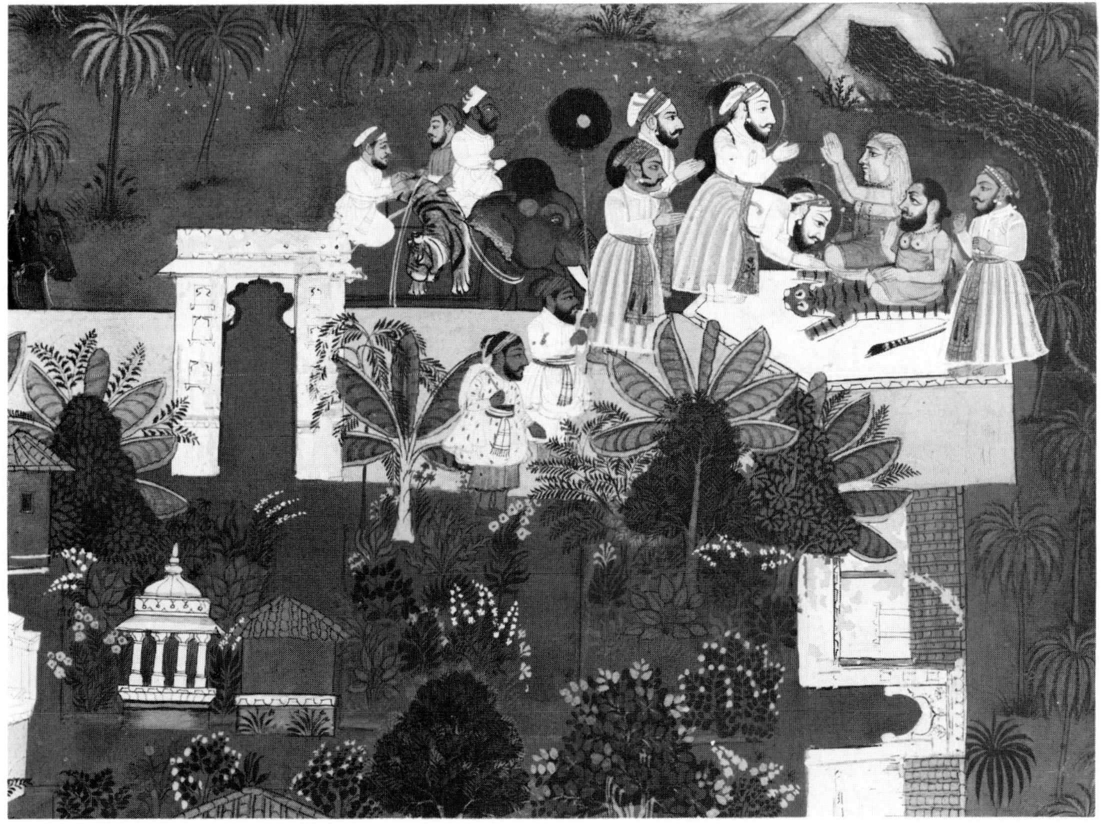

77

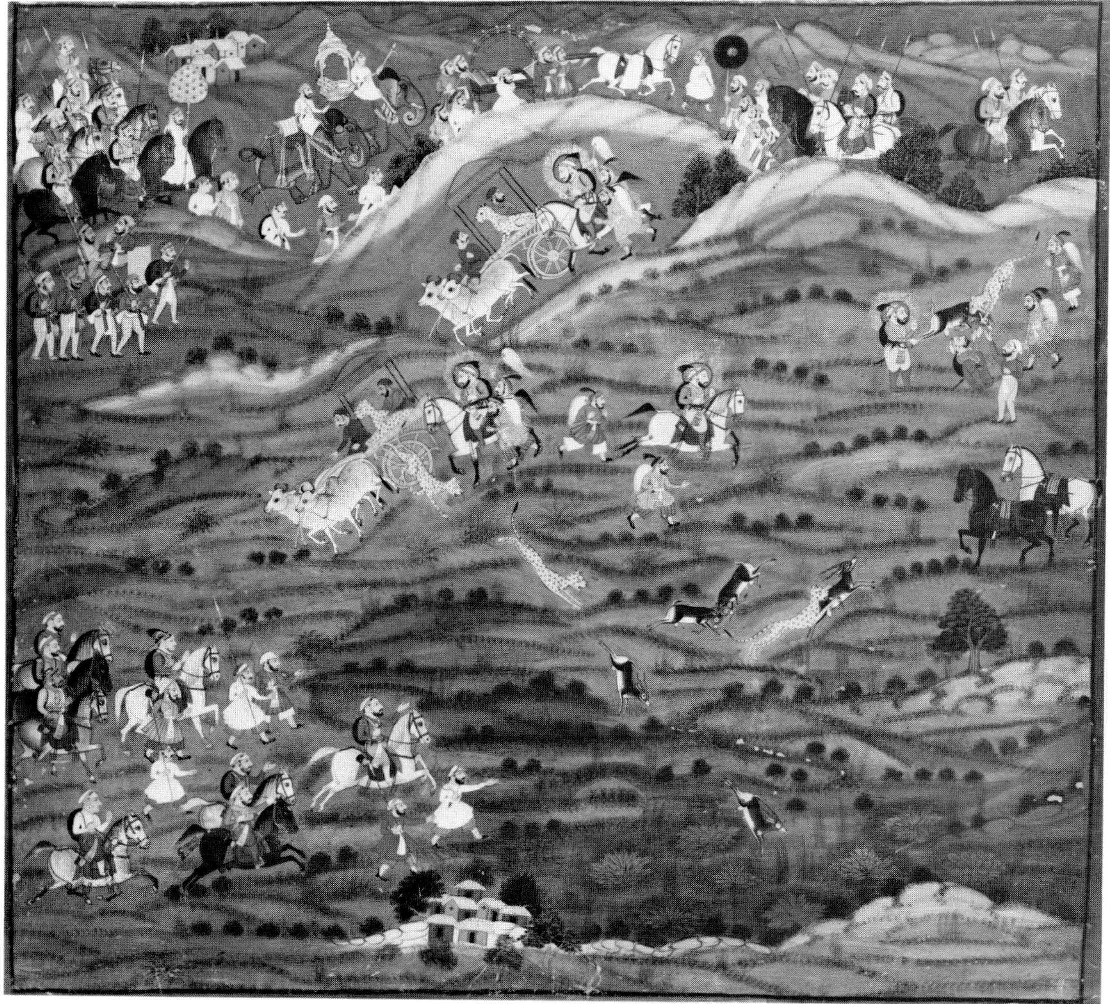

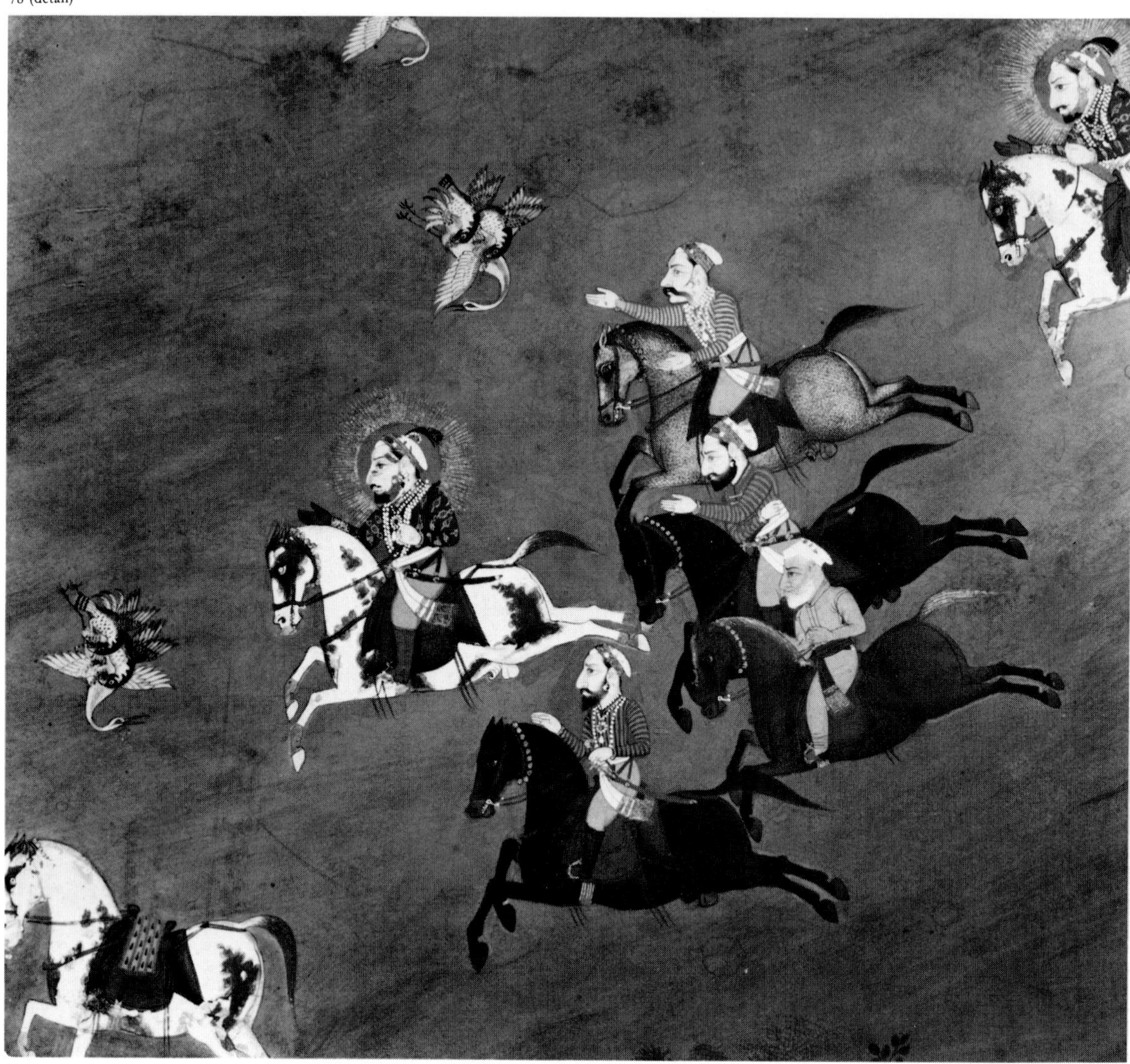

78

Maharana Sangram Singh Hunting Crane at Nahar Magra

Udaipur, c. 1720

47 x 82 cm

(Colour Plate No. 10)

The Maharana, with nimbus, is seen seven times. From bottom centre to the right, he leads the hunting party, which also includes Maharaja Umed Singh, Pancholi Bihari Das, Rathor Kisan Das and the *shikari* Murad Bakhsh. In the centre of the picture they disturb cranes in a field; the Maharana and *shikari* release their hawks, and the Maharana gallops in pursuit followed by his companions. A crane is brought down and the kill is examined by the *shikari* amid general congratulations. Other sardars watch from a hilltop. A procession and a temple are seen in the distance, while the sun sets behind the hills. Yellow margin; red border with black ruling.

Inscribed on the back: *śrī. śrī mharajadhiraja śrī mharanaji śrī sagram sighji: nare magre padarya kulang ri sikar khailya: bira dholya: bice: palana bicai kulang ri sikar khelya: ghode he citra sobha śriji asvar: hath mahe beri: pache mharaja umed sighji ghode kumet asvar: ghode nile pacoli bhari dasji: ghode bhamar rathod kisan dasji: mir sikari murad bagas: khuda bagas: śrī hajur thi kulang upare beri chodi: kulang jae? nai mari: pache thi śriji ghode dodavene: kulang padi jathe padarya ne ghoda su utara ne śriji ubha: ora sarai umarava peli magari upare ubha asvar huva thaka: mir sikari: haiyyat? kha re hath me kulang ri gardan pakad..? thaka: hajur bethyo? he rathod kisan dasji: su śriji banta kare he:* [in another hand:] *kulang ki sikar.*

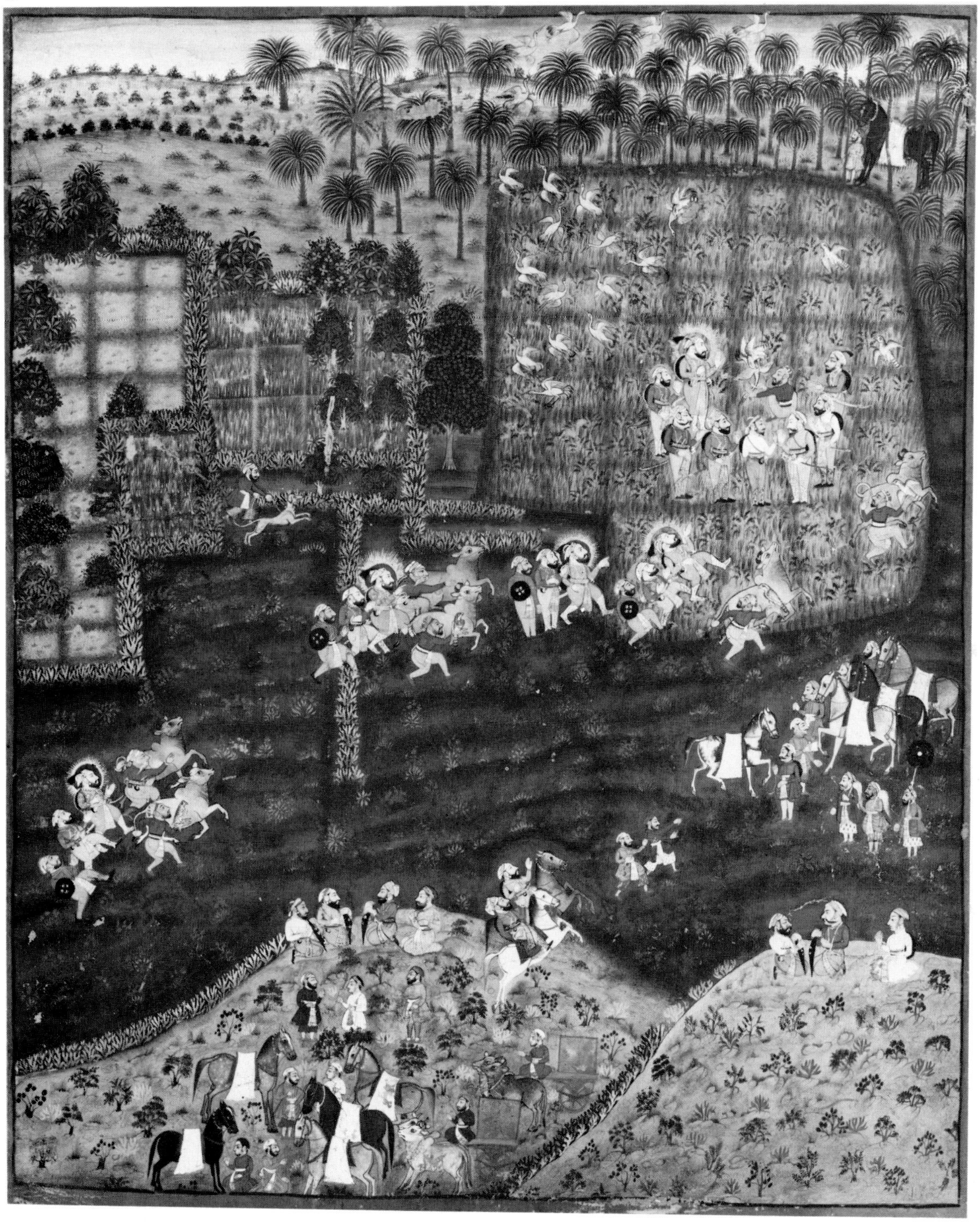

79

Maharana Sangram Singh Hunting Crane

Udaipur, c. 1725

41.7 x 35 cm

The Maharana, with nimbus, accompanied by sardars and *shikaris,* is seen five times, stalking cranes in a field, releasing a hawk which takes a crane and finally inspecting the kill. Attendants wait with horses and bullock-carts on a hillock in the foreground. Red border, somewhat trimmed.

Inscribed on the back: *śrī. śrī mhārājadhārājā mhārāṇājī śrī sagrām sīghjī: kulaṅg rī sīkār pādāryā āgai balad pāchai jhālo saikhjī balad ekā..? thākā jī pāchai śrījī kulag batāvatā pāchai pāṅcolī devacaṅdjī pāchai jīvo mithyā?: ḍhāl hajur kī pakaḍyā thāko: dujā valada pāṅche khīlāvār khāju: hāth me behārī thī jyā choḍī: kulag mārī pāchai śrījī jāya ubhā rahnā? jaṭhe ītarā ṭhākur: mhārājā takhat sīghjī: jhālo dolat sīghjī: rāṭhoḍ kīsan dāsjī: ?idra bhāṇjī: camardār tulsī dāsjī: pācolī devacandjī: rām sīghjī: kulaṅg māryā pelī: ṭhākurā ro sāth beṭhā thā so hajur āyā: kulaṅg pakaḍyā pache.*

80

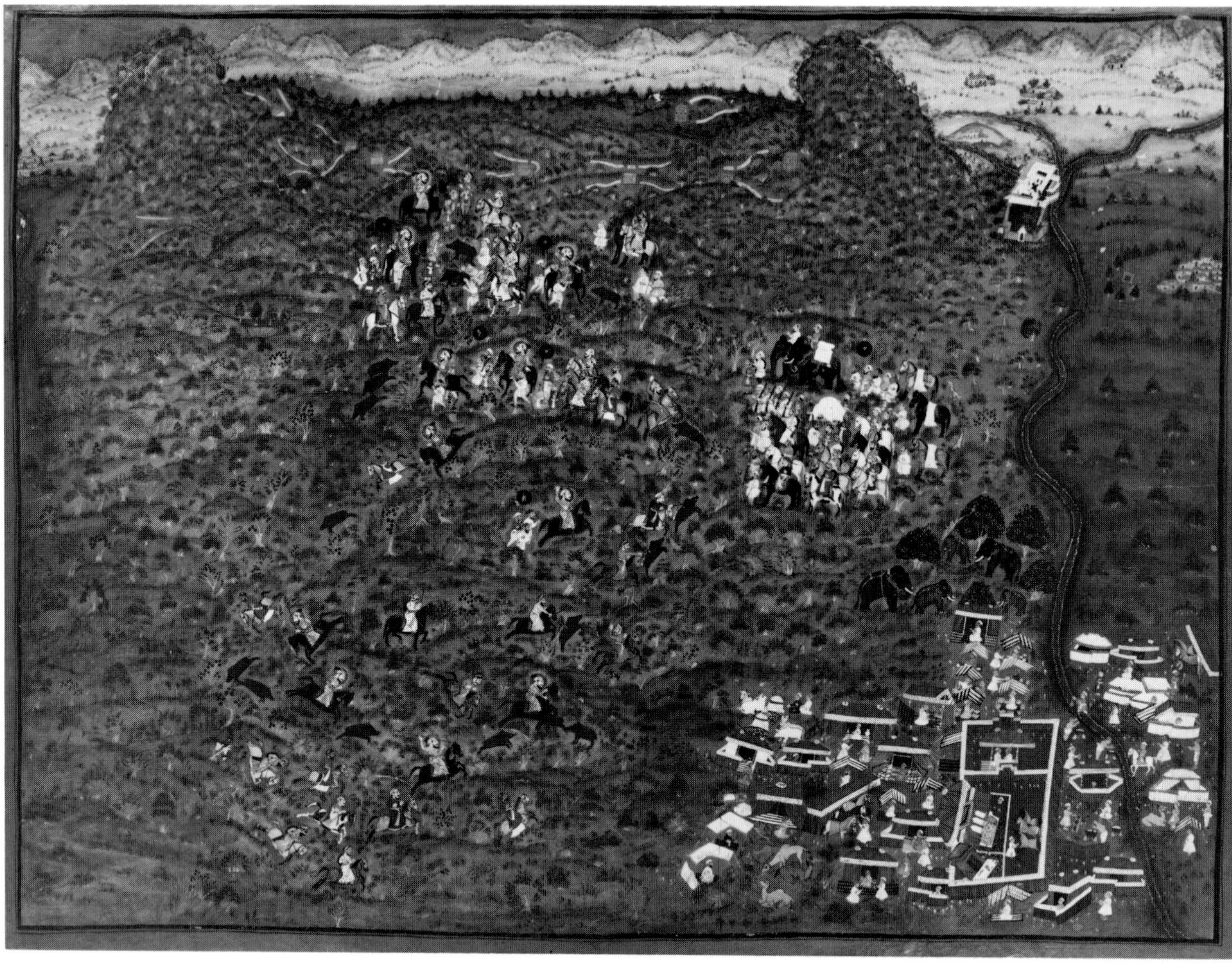

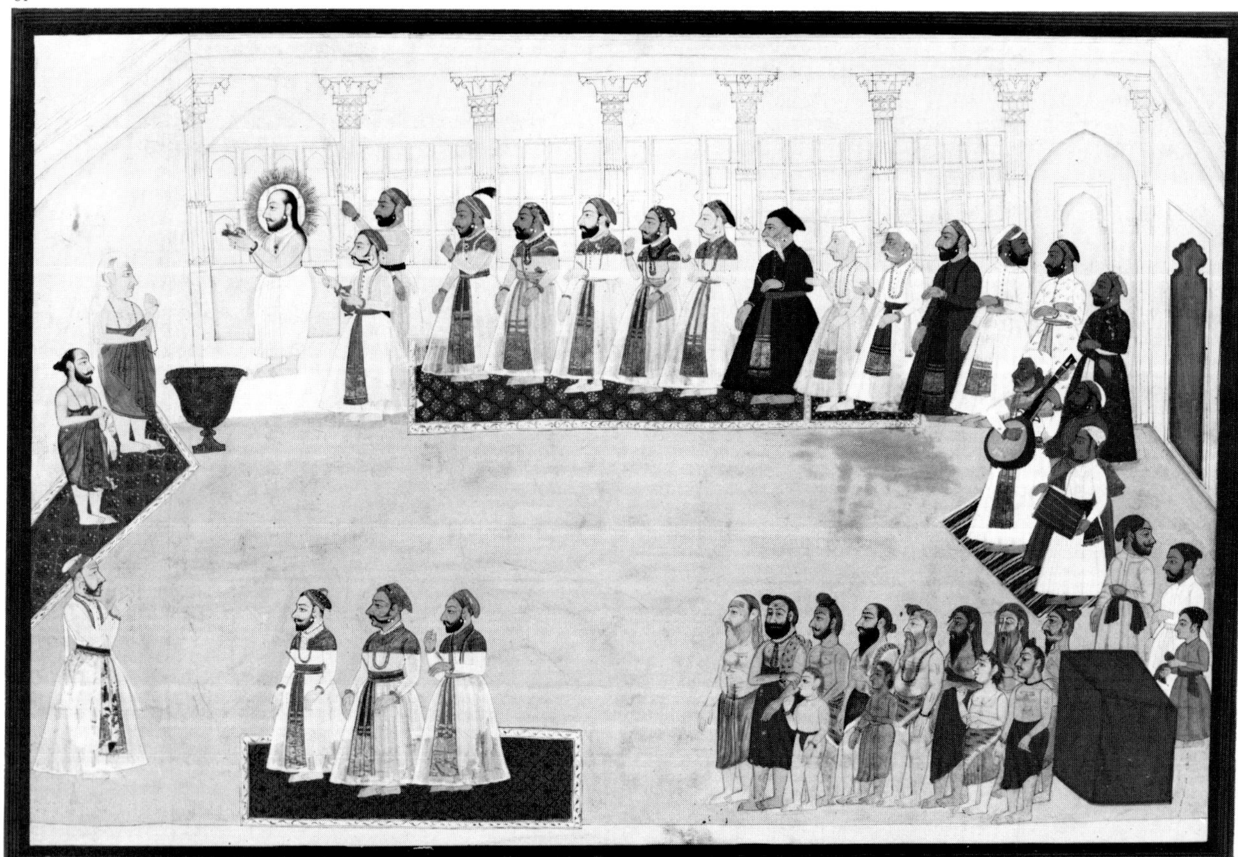

81

80

Maharana Sangram Singh Hunting Boar at Nahar Magra
Udaipur, c. 1720-30
45.3 x 61.2 cm

The Maharana, with nimbus, is seen ten times in all
sticking pigs at Nahar Magra, accompanied by numerous
sardars and attendants. A camp has been pitched on the
banks of a stream; in the distance a palatial building
appears in jumbled perspective. Red border.

Inscribed on the back: *śrī. śrī mharajadharaja mharanaji
śrī sagram sighji: nare magare padarya ugamani baju
sikar padarya: ghodo dodavene: sura rebar chiri dighi:
barachi tuta gai: sura ubho re gayo: pachai sura re saraki
cota kari: sura mudhyo?* [in another hand:] *naro magri
ro bhava.*

81

Maharana Sangram Singh II and Gosain Nilakanthaji
Udaipur, c. 1725-30
35.3 x 53.2 cm

The Maharana, with nimbus, bare-headed and bare-
chested, offers flowers to Gosain Nilakanthaji in a
ceremony in the Dilkhush Mahal, attended by sardars,
ministers, *bhats,* musicians and a group of sadhus. Red
border.

Inscribed on the back: *śrī. śrī mharajadharaja mharanaji
śrī sagram sighji: dilkhusmal re padachane suraj he
aragade he: samu ubha gusai nilakanthaji: gusai kisan
girji ubha bhata devaramji: śriji pache: prohat sathok
ramji: ?travadi vasadevaji: hajur chavo rakhe: mharaja
takhat sighji: tuvar kisan sighji: dhayabhai nagaji:
ram singhji: masani lakhmanji: ?jhalo saikhji: bhata
ram: bhata sukhanandji: dhikadna? ubha sama ubha:
pacoli kisan dasji: camardar tulasi dasji: sagatavat surat
sighji: ange jegera? ubha: kalavat: kanji: cad: piryo
dholakyo:* [further below:] *dilakhusmal rai padachanai.*

See also cat. nos. 76 and 92.

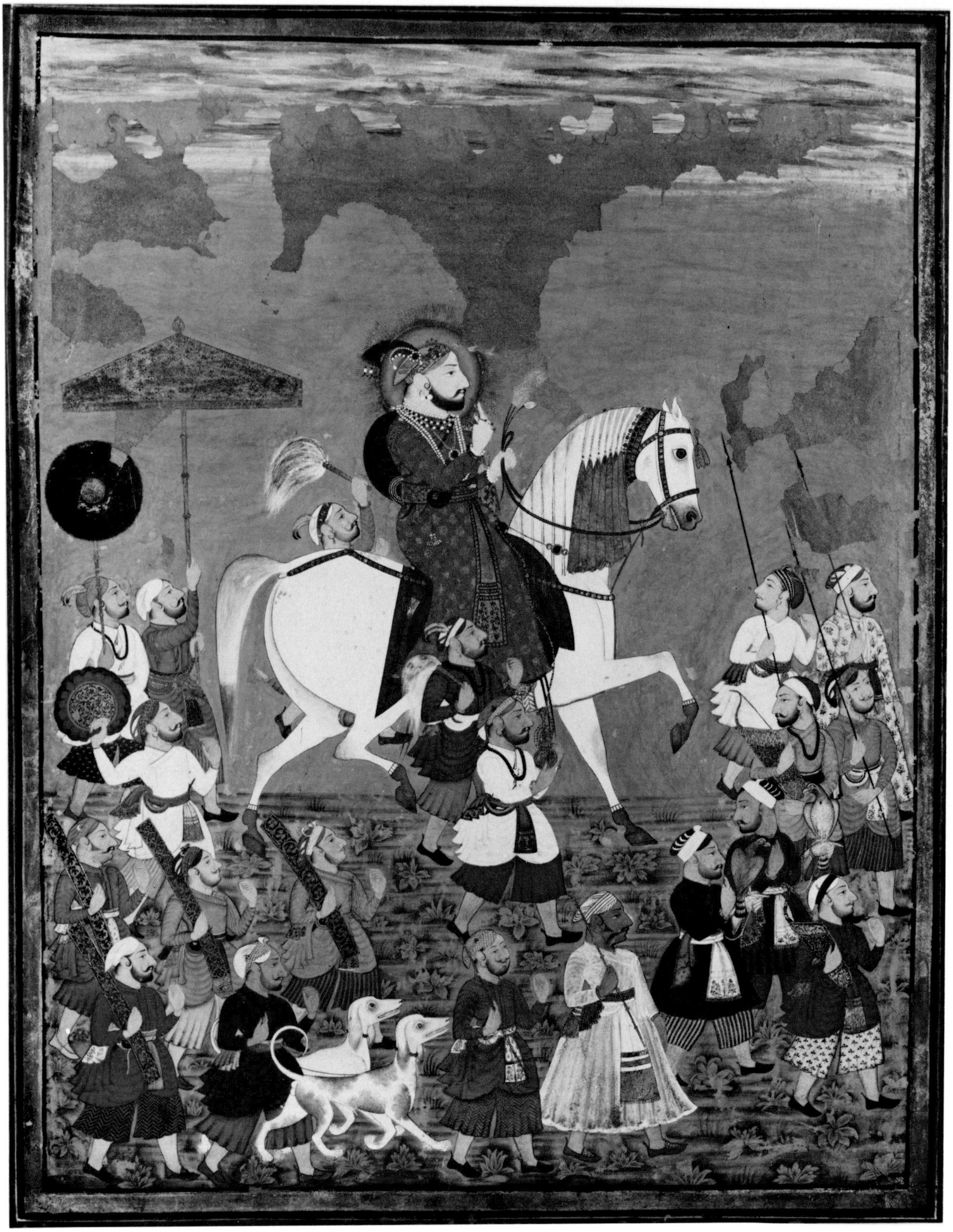

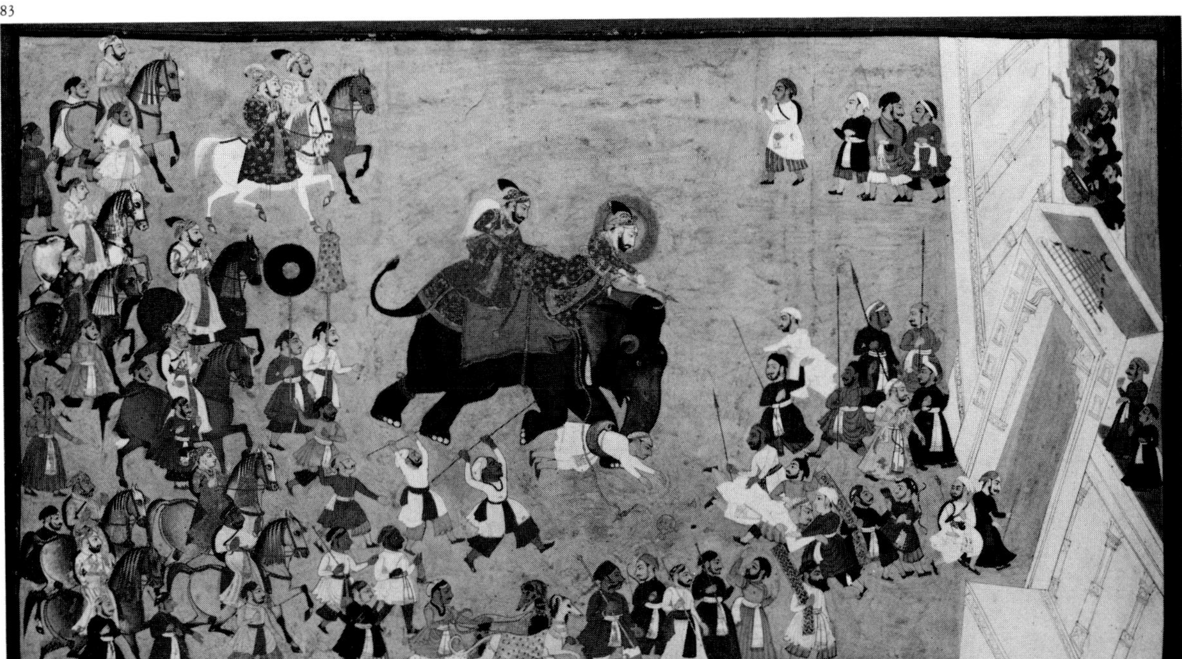

84

**Maharana Sangram Singh Receiving Maharaja Sawai Jai
Singh in Camp**
Udaipur, c. 1730-34. Attributed to Jai Ram
40.5 x 46.5 cm
(Colour Plate No. 13)

The Maharana, with nimbus, and Maharaja Sawai Jai
Singh of Jaipur, together with five sardars, sit on a white
floor-spread in the royal quarters of an encampment,
drinking liquor and eating a meal. Within the outer
circle of chintz-lined red *qanats,* cooks prepare kebabs
(detail), horses are tethered and courtiers stand in two
groups. In smaller tents outside, other members of the
royal entourages cook, eat, sleep, smoke or converse,
while four musicians play shehnais and naqqaras. Red
border.

Inscribed on the back: *kherādāre dera mahe maharaṇa
śrī sagaram sīghjī rajā savaī śrī je sīghjī
barājya thakā ro pāno* [in another hand:] *kherodāre dere
?bīrajya.*

The subject is probably one of several meetings between
the two rulers at which they discussed the growing threat
from the Marathas, who were soon to engulf both their
kingdoms from the south. One such meeting occurred in
1732, towards the end of Sangram Singh's reign
(Somani, *History of Mewar,* vol. 1, p. 332).
The red colour of the royal *qanats* was considered by the
Mughals to be an imperial prerogative (F. Bernier,
Travels in the Mogul Empire, ed. V. A. Smith, London,
1934, p. 366). It had been adopted by the Maharanas

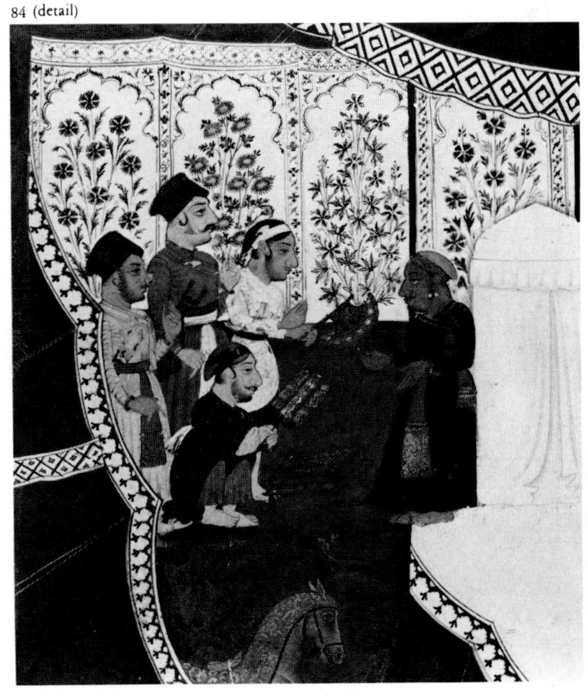

84 (detail)

after the capture of such tents from Babur's vanguard in
1527 (Erskine, *Rajputana Gazetteers: The Mewar
Residency,* p. 115) and was retained by them in spite of
imperial displeasure (Tod, *Annals and Antiquities of
Rajasthan,* vol. I, p. 457).

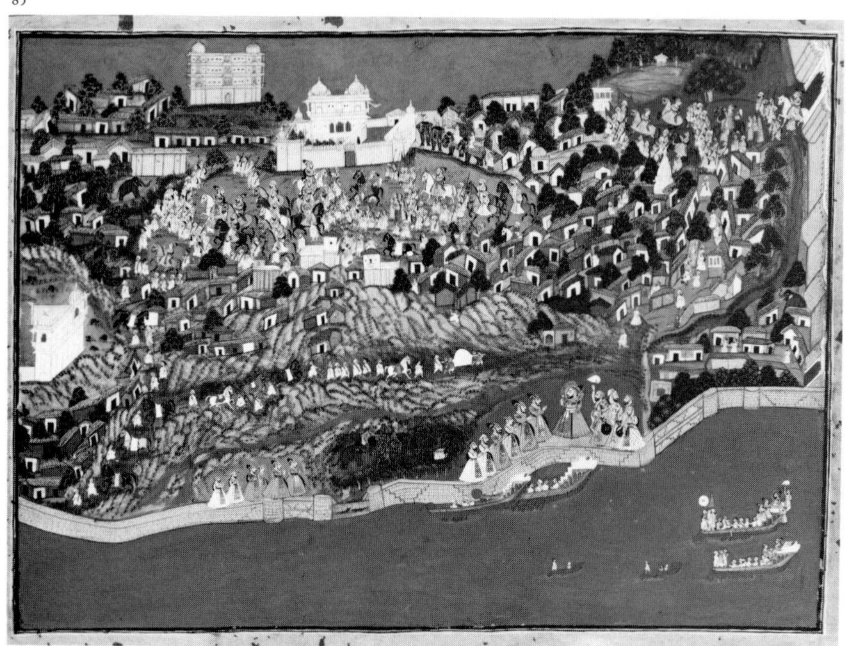

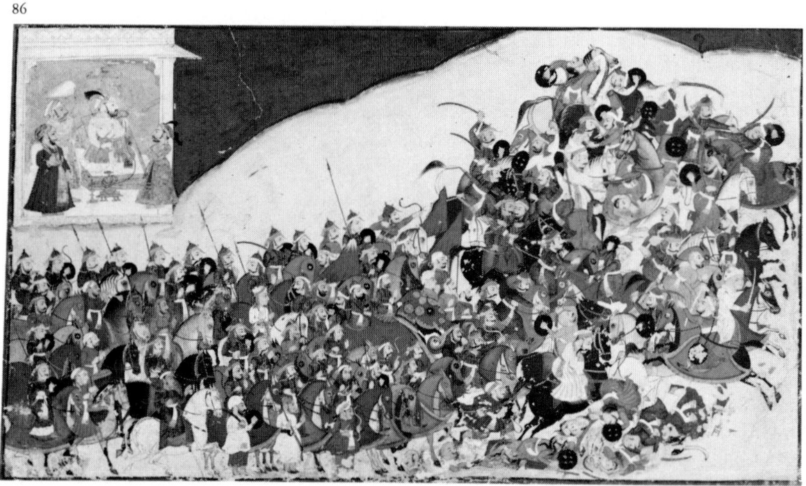

85
Maharana Sangram Singh Receiving his Sons in Procession near the Rang Sagar Lake
Udaipur, c. 1730
42 x 58.5 cm

The Maharana, accompanied by mounted sardars, receives his sons Nathji and Jagat Singh, who advance from a gateway to the right; the meeting takes place in front of the *haveli* of Rawat Sangram Singh on an isthmus adjoining the Rang Sagar lake. The Maharana and sardars are seen again standing on the embankment, where they embark in two royal barges. Pinkish-buff border with silver patches; pale turquoise outer margin.

Inscribed on the back: *śrī mhārājadharāja mharāṇojī śrī sāgram sighjī raṅga sāgara pāla upare śrījī ubhā* [below:] *rāvat saṅgram sighjī rī havailī kuvar nāthjī paraṇya?*

86
A Battle Scene
Udaipur, c. 1730
23.5 x 42 cm

The Mewar cavalry, advancing from the left, is shown engaging and defeating a smaller force in battle. The news is related to Maharana Sangram Singh, who sits smoking a *huqqa* in a pavilion in the upper left corner. Cream background with blue sky above. Red border, inscribed: *māharāṇa śrī sagrām sighjī* [in another hand:] *28* [in another hand:] *mevātā bābāt*.

The subject is perhaps a successful action in 1711, when Ranabaz Khan Mewati was granted the contested *parganas* of Pur, Mandal and Badnor in northern Mewar by the Emperor Bahadur Shah; when he went to take possession of them he was defeated and slain by a strong Mewar force at Bandhanwara.

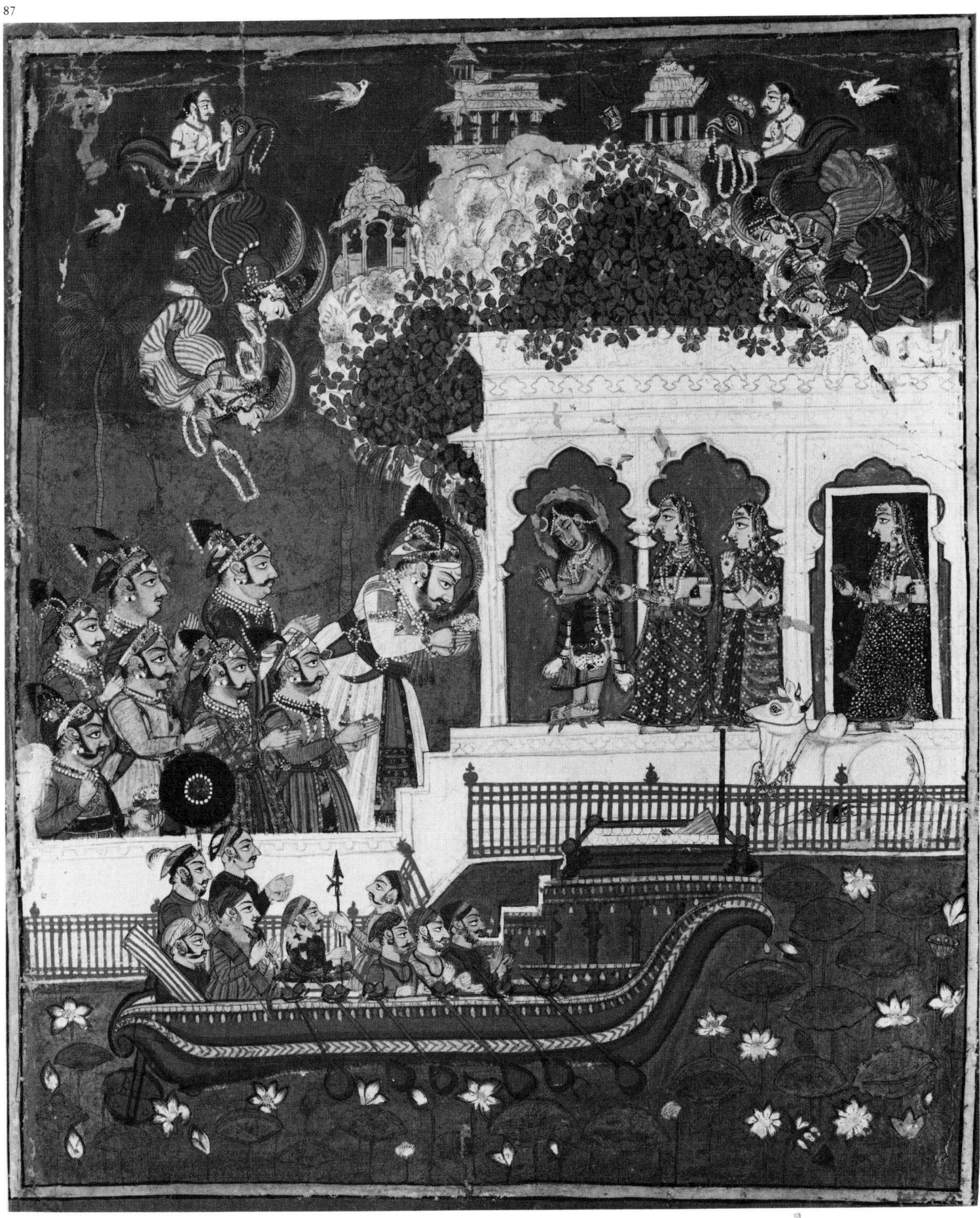

87

Maharana Sangram Singh (?) Worshipping Shiva
Udaipur, c. 1730-40
33.5 x 28.7 cm

The Maharana, with nimbus, and his sardars have
arrived at a lakeside Shiva temple, shown with Mt.
Kailasa behind it, in the royal barge. The Maharana
offers a garland to Shiva, who is dressed as an ascetic
and attended by three maids and the bull Nandi.
Celestial figures fly above holding garlands. Yellow
margin and severely trimmed red border.

Inscribed above: *mharana śri sagaram sighji.*
Inscribed on the back: *maharana śri sagaram sighji ri
surat siva ro drasan karata thaka.*

The Vaidyanath temple on the southern edge of the
Pichola lake at Udaipur was constructed by Maharana
Sangram Singh's mother and inaugurated in 1715
(Ojha, *Rajputane ka Itihas*, p. 332); it is uncertain
whether this is the temple shown in the painting, which
is of later date and may even represent Maharana Jagat
Singh rather than his father Sangram Singh.

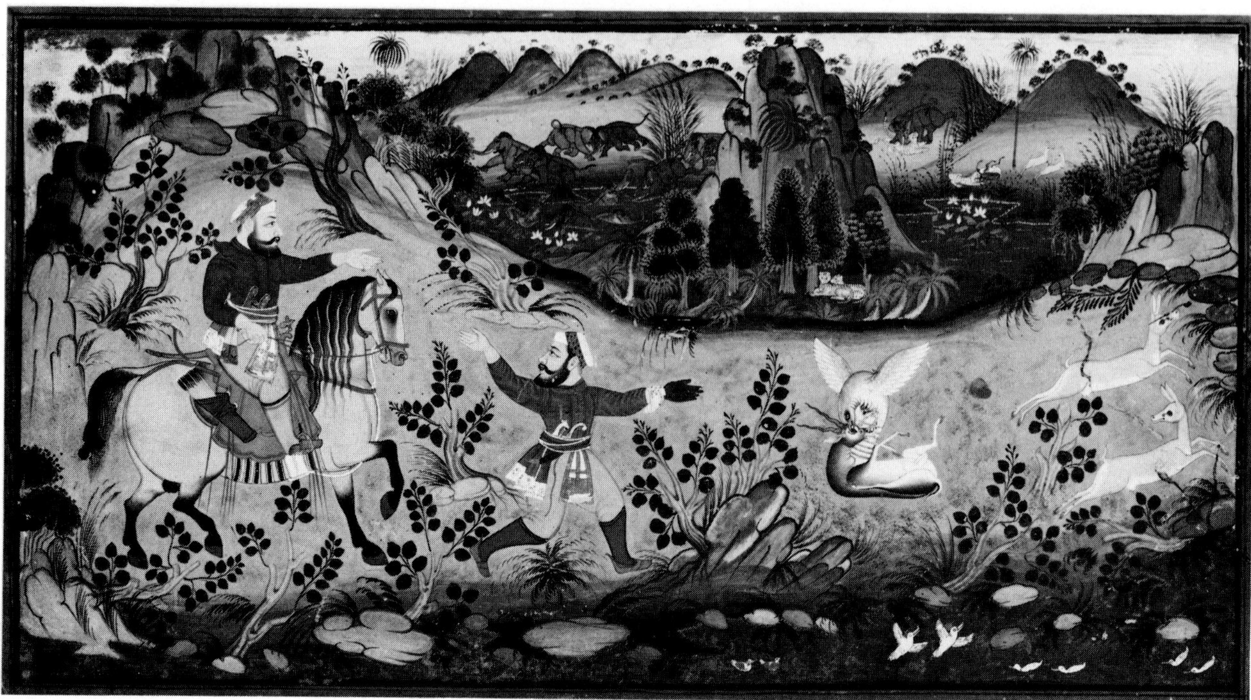

88

Maharana Sangram Singh Riding
Udaipur, c. 1730
32.5 x 21 cm

The Maharana, in gold *pagri* and *jama,* rides a dappled
horse, smoking a *huqqa* carried by an attendant; seven
other attendants on foot accompany him. Dark green
foreground; blue-green background. Indifferent quality.
Buff border.

Inscribed on the back: *maharajadhiraja*
maharanaji śri sagram sighji ri sabi
ro pano ghode asavari ro.

89

A Mughal Ruler, Possibly Shah Jahan
Udaipur, c. 1720
20.2 x 13 cm

Possibly based on a Mughal portrait of Shah Jahan. The
Emperor, with a faint gold nimbus, wearing a white
pagri and *jama* and a flowered gold *patka,* stands facing
right holding a fly-whisk. Yellow-green background.
Buff border.

90

A Mughal Officer Hunting
Udaipur, c. 1710-20, perhaps based on a Mughal
original
23 x 43.5 cm

A mounted Mughal officer watches as his similarly
attired attendant points to where his hawk has brought
down a blackbuck. Hilly landscape with frolicking
elephants, a pair of tigers and a leopard hunting
blackbuck. Red border.

A difficult inscription on the back begins: *nakhale uko*
nakha khakhanakhan sakar khele re.....

91

A Mughal Officer
Udaipur, c. 1720-30
25.5 x 14.8 cm

The officer, in white *pagri* and transparent *jama* over
striped *paijama,* sits on a carpeted garden terrace with
his arms folded over his shield. A sword, *pandan* and
spittoon lie beside him. Green background with cloud
above. Red border.

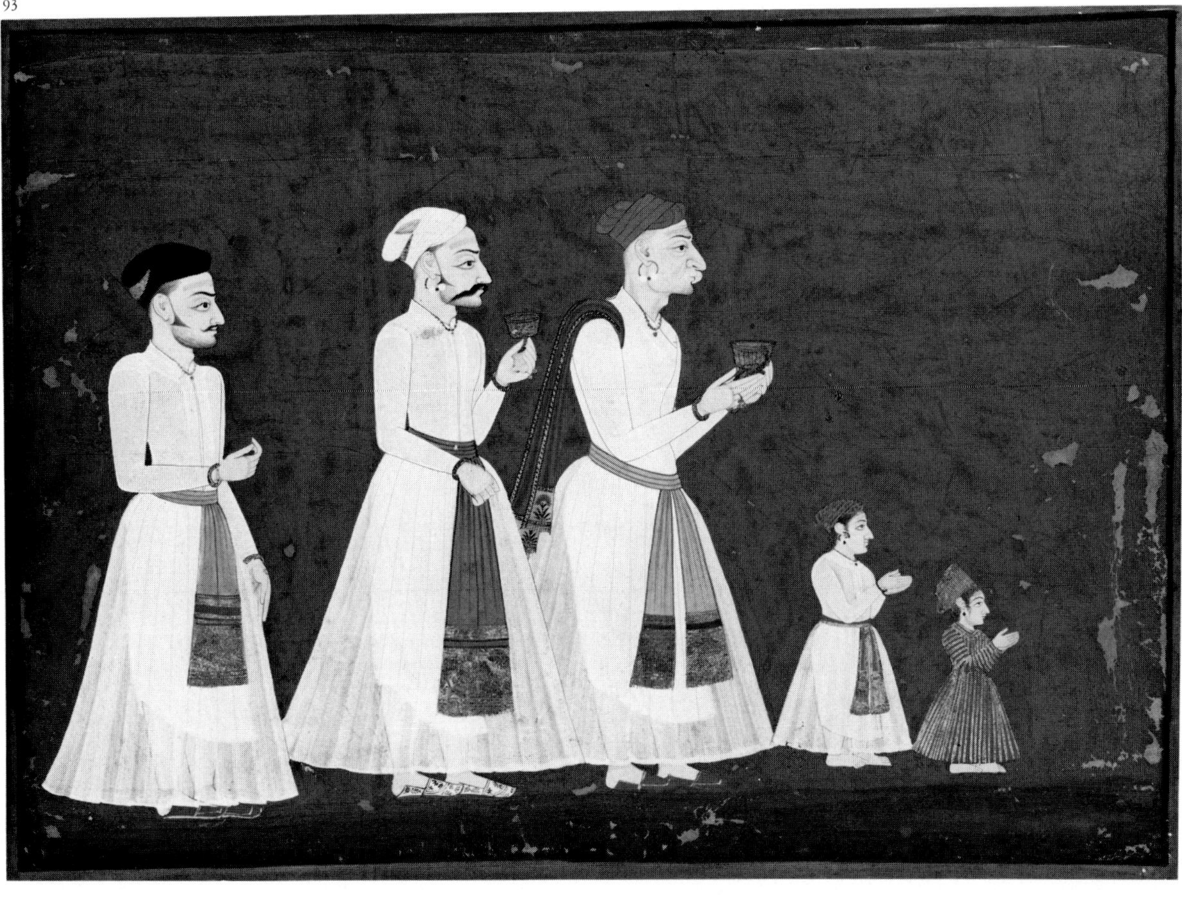

92
Nilakanthaji and Other *Yogis* at an Ashram
Udaipur, c. 1720
22.5 x 15.9 cm

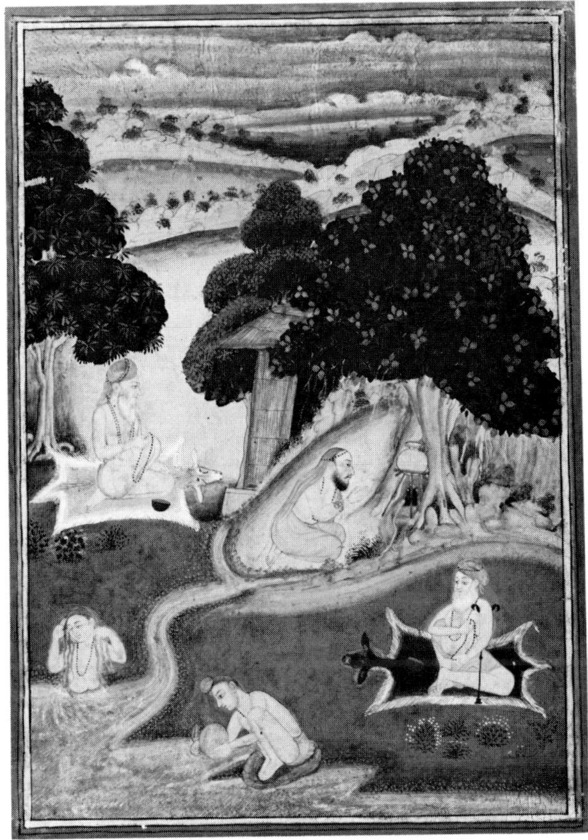

92

The *yogi* Nilakanthaji is seen kneeling before a *lingam* shrine under a pipal tree by the Gobind Sagar lake. His companions, who perform ablutions or sit meditating on deer-skins, are Baba Garib Das, Baba Tulsi Das, Bansadhari Das and another. Landscape background with cloudy blue sky above. Pale yellow margin; red border.

Inscribed on the back: *mahādevajī śrī nīlakanthajī ri chabī bāboji gobīda sāgarajī drasan kare chai bābaji garīb dāsji kālī mragachala pe bethā che bāba tulachi dāsji supet mragachala pe beta chai ?vyā bānsadharī dāsji jala bhare che aba..? taṇi ?..mau sagara sāpaḍe chai.*

Nilakanthaji is seen honoured by Maharana Sangram Singh in cat. nos. 76 and 81.

93
Devotees
Udaipur, c. 1725
22 x 30.7 cm

Three men and two boys, evidently devotees, stand facing right in a reverential attitude. Green background. Red border.

Inscribed on the back: *vyāsa mangala valabha kaṇho chagana rughanātha nagara vīsalanagarā vaida.*

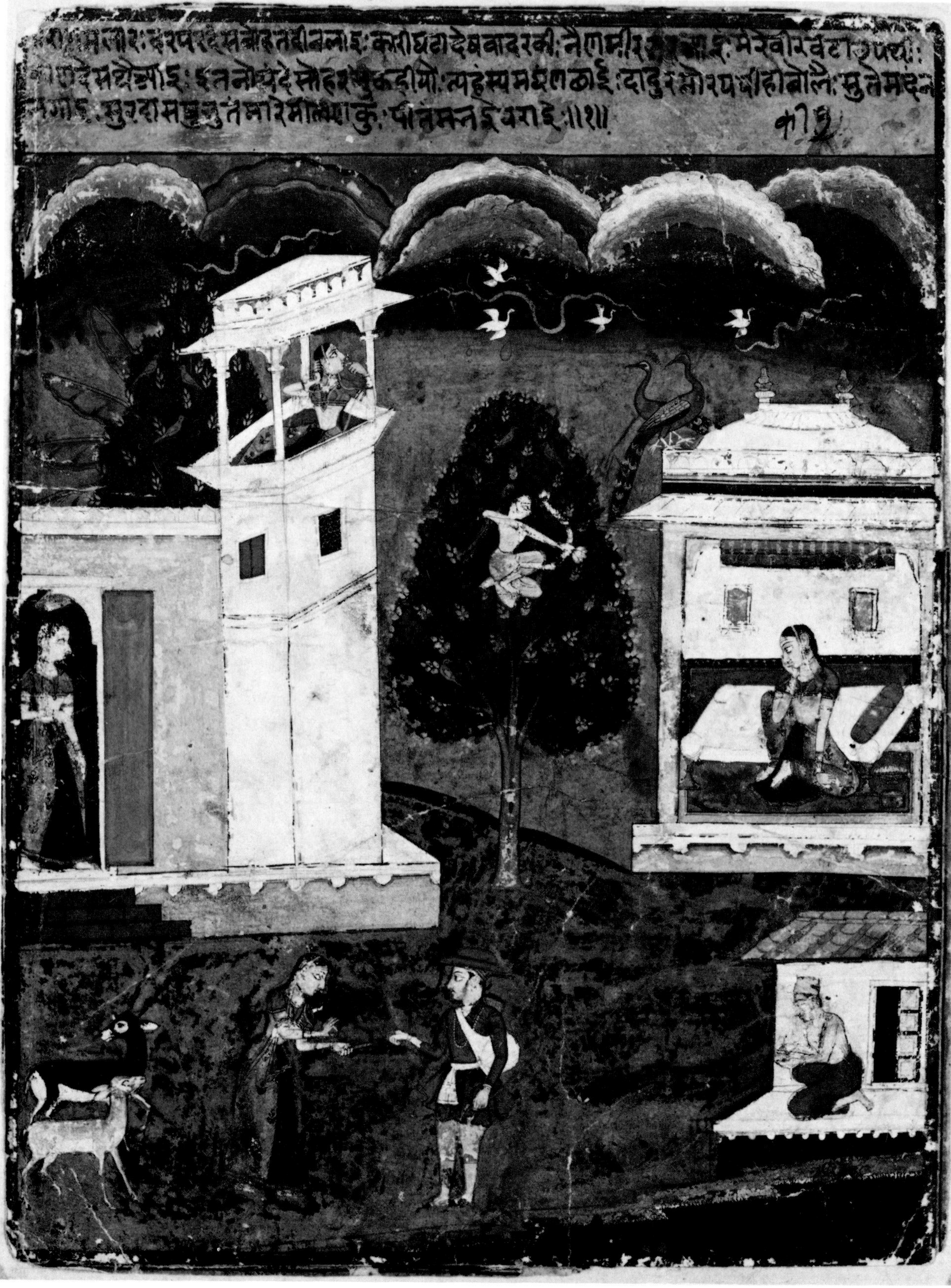
रामगौरी: हरवर दे सनबार तबीबलइ: करीघटादेववादरकी नैलगौर ... सार: मेरवीरवटा रुपधा:
देमदवेगोइ: इतनोयदे सोहर सुकुरदीयो त्यहस्यमधेलठाई: दादुरमोरवधीहोबोले: सुतेमदन
गोइ: सुग्दासमधुतेमारेमोलिधाकु: पीतमननइवराइ: ॥श॥

94

Chandangir
Udaipur, c. 1720-30
15.8 x 10.6 cm

The Gosain (?) Chandangir, wearing a white robe and
circular orange *pagri*, stands holding a staff and a *pan*.
Mauve-grey background, with the sun and silver clouds
in blue sky above. Gold margin; silver-flecked salmon-
pink and pale turquoise borders. Inscribed above, twice:
candanagir.

95

Solanki Ram Singh Riding
Udaipur, c. 1730
33.3 x 22.5 cm

Solanki Ram Singh was a contemporary of Maharana
Sangram Singh (cf. cat. no. 72). He rides a prancing
piebald horse, preceded by four attendants. Turquoise-
grey background with cloud above. Red border,
inscribed: *solanki ram singhji*.

96

A Page from a Series of the *Sur Sagar*
Udaipur, c. 1730
26.7 x 20.5 cm

The text describes the pain of separation *(viraha)*
experienced by the gopis in Krishna's absence during the
rainy season, with its dark skies and cries of peacocks;
they ask a traveller to take a letter to Krishna for them
(*Surasagara*, ed. A. Upadhyay *et al.*, 5th ed., Varanasi,
V.S. 2033, no. 4000). The gopis sit forlornly in a palace
setting; in the foreground the message is handed to a
traveller and the poet Sur Das himself is seen singing
outside a house. Border severely trimmed.

97

A Page from a Series of the *Sur Sagar*
Udaipur, c. 1710
28.5 x 31.8 cm

The text describes the splendour of Vrindaban in the
springtime. In the foreground the love-god Kama
perches in a tree, while Krishna and Radha sit in a
riverside bower. A contingent of soldiers moves through
the landscape. In the background a strong wind pulls at
the trees, while Shiva and Parvati sit together on a tiger-
skin and the blind poet Sur Das himself appears at the
right. (*Surasagara*, ed. A. Upadhyay *et al.*, 5th ed.,
Varanasi, V.S. 2033, no. 3465). Red border.

Inscribed on the back: *vasat pancami re din nijar huvai.*

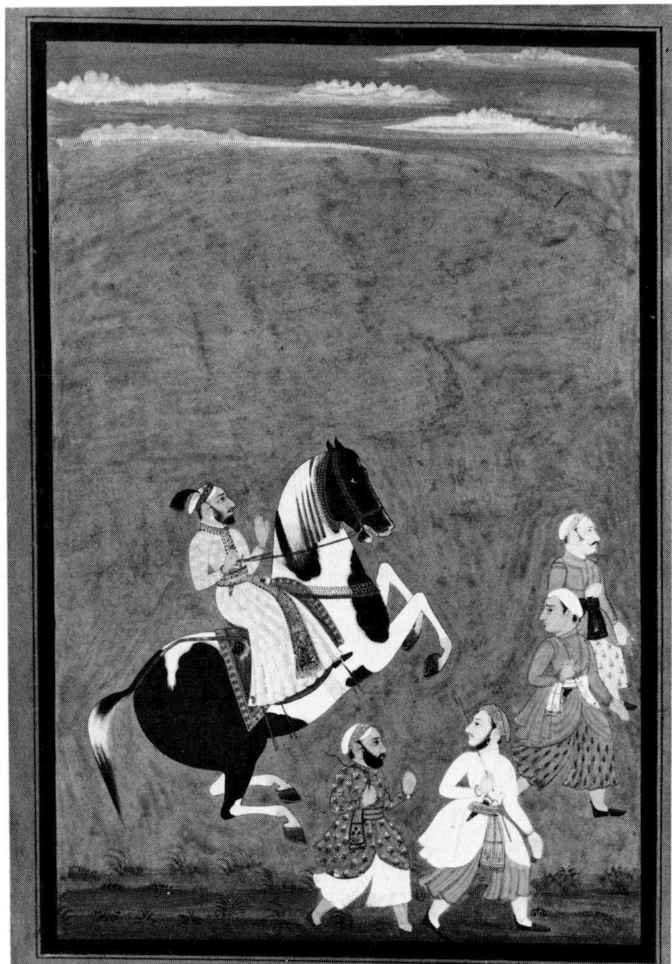

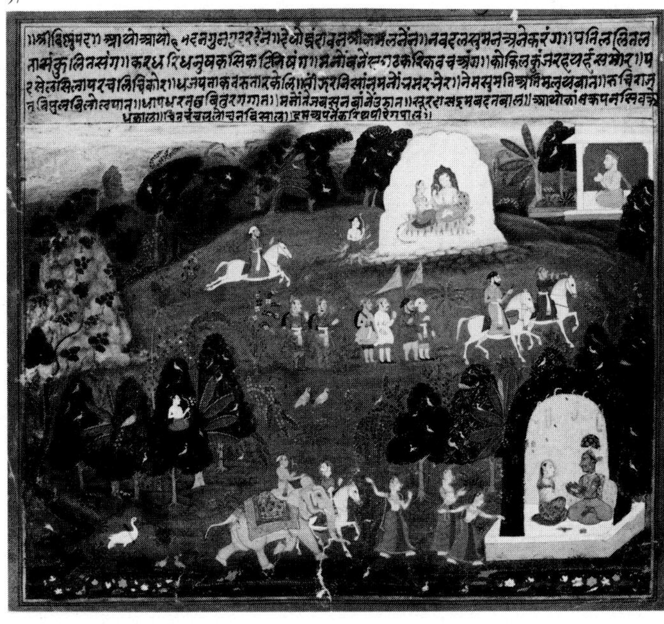

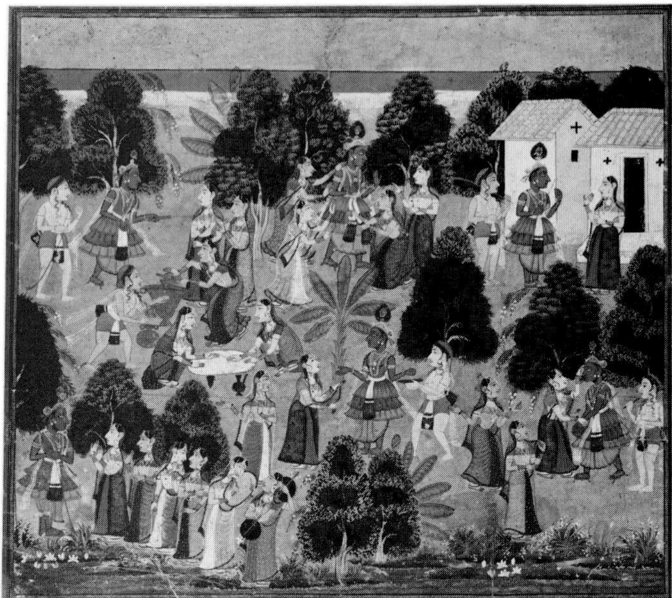

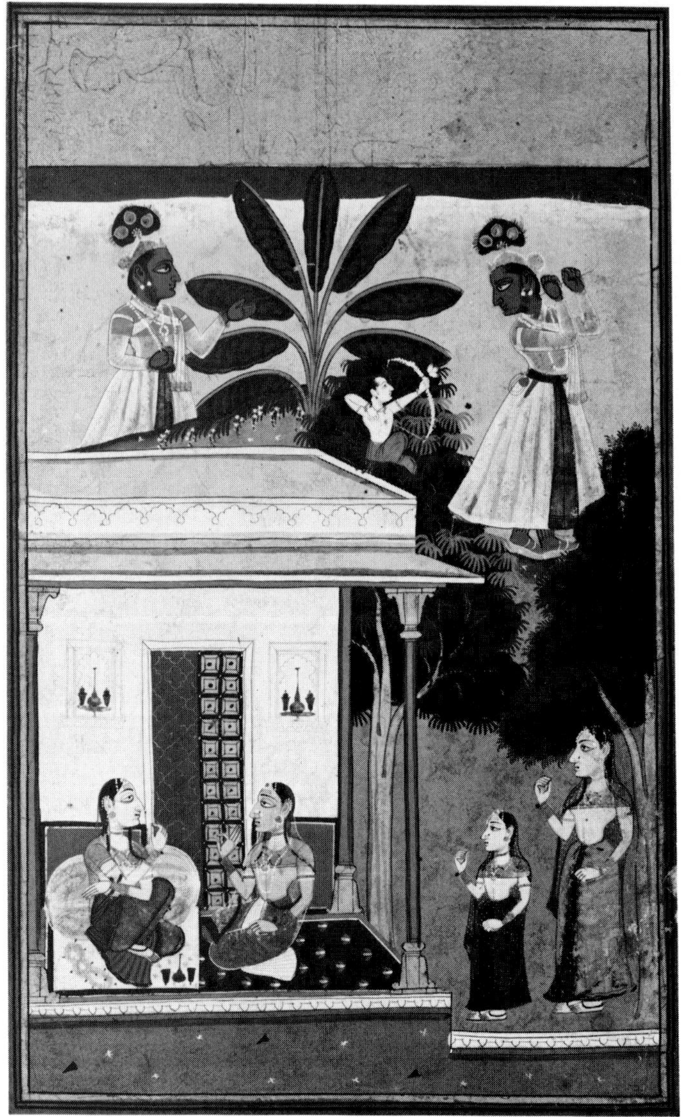

98

Krishna Playing Holi with the Gopis
Udaipur, c. 1730
35 x 40.5 cm

Krishna is seen in six scenes, playing Holi and sporting
with the gopis on the banks of the Jumna river. A page
from an unidentified series, similar in style to cat.
nos. 100-106. Vacant yellow text panel; silver margin;
red border, numbered 130. A short inscription on the
back describes the subject as the Krishnalila.

99

A Page from a Series of the *Rasikapriya* of Keshav Das
Udaipur, c. 1720-30
27.3 x 18 cm

The *nayaka,* or Krishna, in a peacock crown, sits beneath
a white *chattri,* attended by a maid, to receive the
nayika. In the foreground a garden with fountains;
behind, a palace courtyard in which a maid stands.
Yellow margin and text panel, inscribed with verses; red
border.

100-106

**Seven Pages from a Series of the *Rasikapriya* of Keshav
Das**
Udaipur, c. 1730
28 x 17 cm (average). Red borders

Although the yellow panels above the paintings have
been left textless and the rough prose inscriptions on
their backs merely summarize the subject matter, these
compositions are based quite closely on the original
Rasikapriya illustrations by the artist Sahibdin at
Udaipur in the 1630s, many of which are in the
Government Museum, Udaipur (see Topsfield,
'Sahibdin's *Gita Govinda* Illustrations' in *Chhavi 2,*
where the prototype of cat. no. 106 is reproduced). The
present series of about a century later is technically
cruder and harsher in effect. Further pages are in a
private collection.

100

Kama aims a flower-arrow at the fluting Krishna, while
below Radha and her *sakhi* converse in a chamber.
Numbered 31.

101

The *sakhi* addresses Radha outside a pavilion, while
Krishna spies on them from behind a plantain tree.
Numbered 84. Five compartmented sketches on the
back, showing noblemen conversing, bazaar vendors and
an elephant fight.

102

The *sakhi* converses with Radha in a chamber, while
Krishna mounts a flight of steps adjacent to a plantain
tree on the right. Numbered 86.

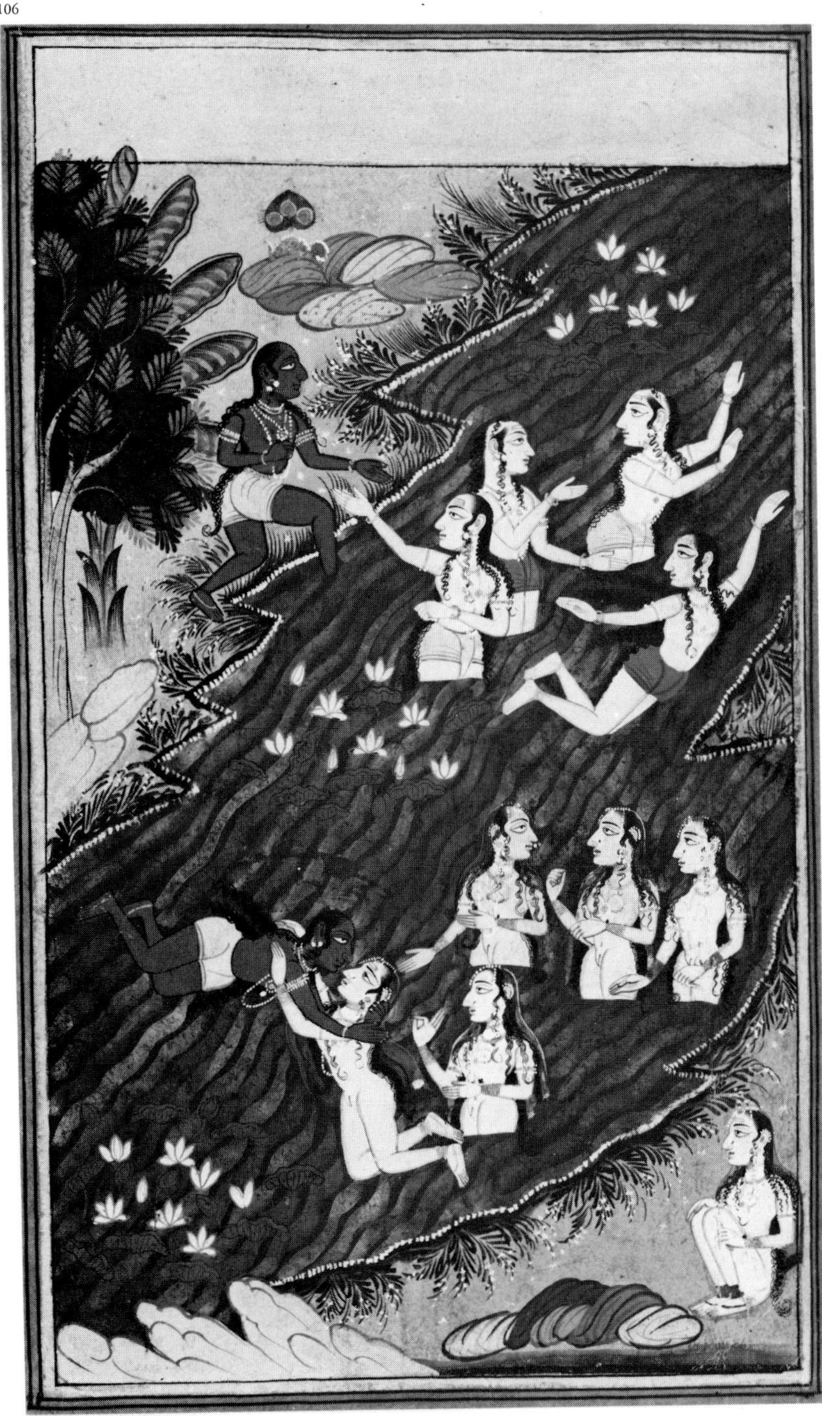

103
In the lower register, ladies are shown in a convivial
gathering, while Krishna stands in a doorway; in the
upper register he leads a lady to a bed-chamber at the
left, which has been excised (an erotic scene has
probably been removed). Numbered 114.

104
Two noblemen lead the youthful Krishna, accompanied
by gopas and gopis, away from a cattle-byre. In the
background a forest scene in the rainy season, partly
mutilated (an erotic scene in a bower has probably been
removed). Numbered 118.

105
In the upper register, Radha lies languishing in bed,
attended by maids who evince concern at her condition.
In a pavilion below the *sakhi* bears the news to Krishna.
Numbered 119.

106
Krishna enters the river Jumna to sport with the gopas;
below, he steals an underwater embrace with the nude
Radha while the other gopis look on. Numbered 138.

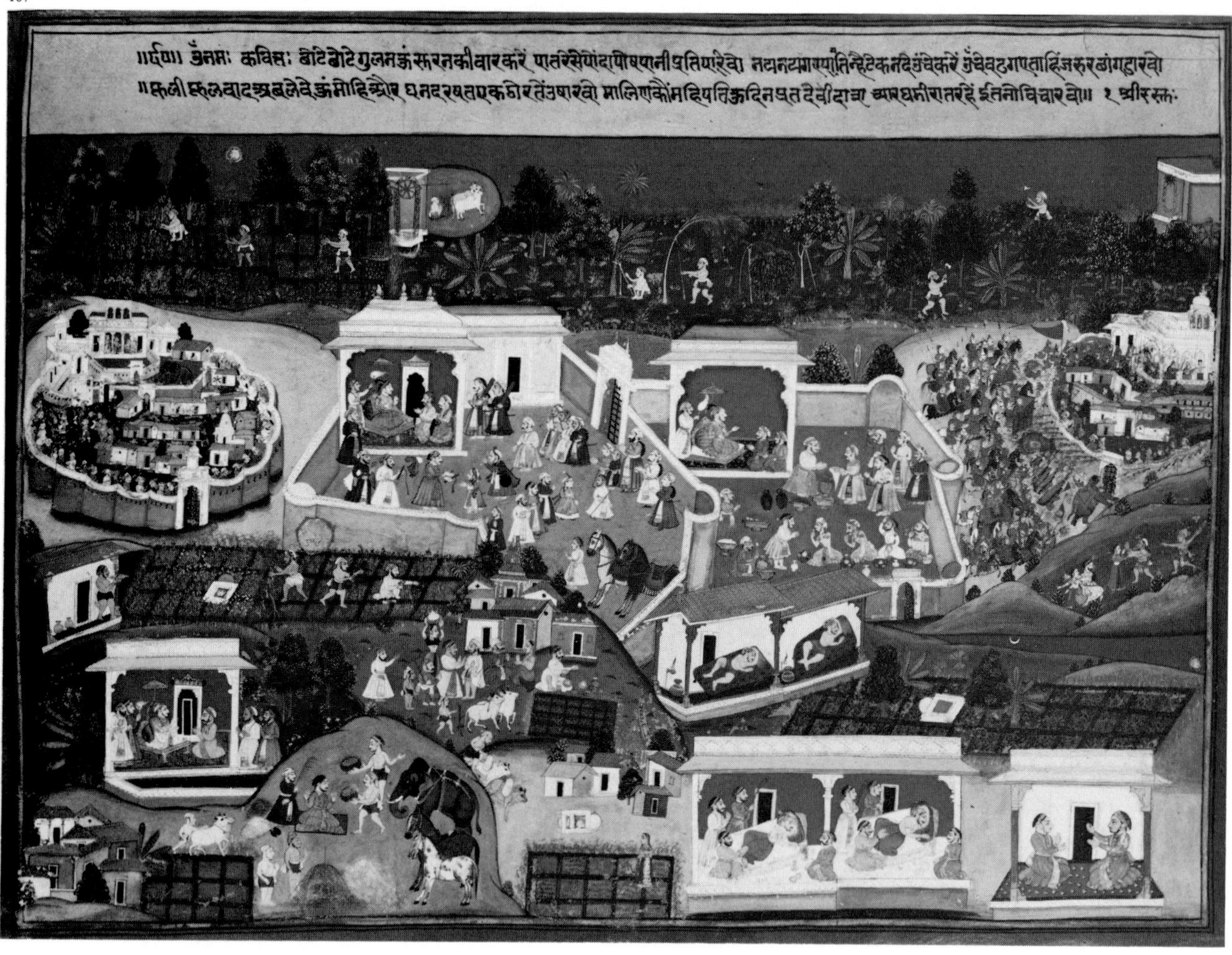

107

Hints on Arboriculture
Udaipur, c. 1715-20
45.2 x 62.5 cm

This large composition is filled with incident, much of it of uncertain relevance to the unidentified Braj Bhasha text above (numbered 90), which gives detailed directions as to the pruning, watering, supporting and thinning out of growing trees; gardeners are engaged in these activities in the background and part of the middle ground. Two walled towns, one of them under siege, are also seen, as well as scenes of village life and several scenes of a raja conversing with his courtiers and sleeping in a chamber. A narrator in a chamber at bottom right is perhaps relating these incidents to his companion. Yellow margin; red border.

Inscribed on the back: *pancolī vīsan dās ro karo o pānau.*

108

Krishna Slays Dhenuka
Udaipur, c. 1730
20 x 39.5 cm

Krishna, Balarama and the gopas set out above to find pasturage for their cows; they come to the riverside, where Krishna confronts the ass-demon Dhenuka, who sought to prevent Krishna and Balarama taking fruit from a grove belonging to him. From an unidentified series, possibly of the *Bhagavata Purana*. Yellow margin; red border.

109

Krishna and Radha in a Bower
Udaipur, c. 1730-40?
23.4 x 19 cm

Probably an illustration to the *Gita Govinda* of Jayadeva, perhaps to the penultimate song describing the tryst of Krishna and Radha in the forest (see Topsfield, 'Sahibdin's *Gita Govinda* Illustrations', *Chhavi 2*). Krishna and Radha sit in a red bower hung with garlands, while two maids wait outside. Yellow margin; trimmed red border.

108

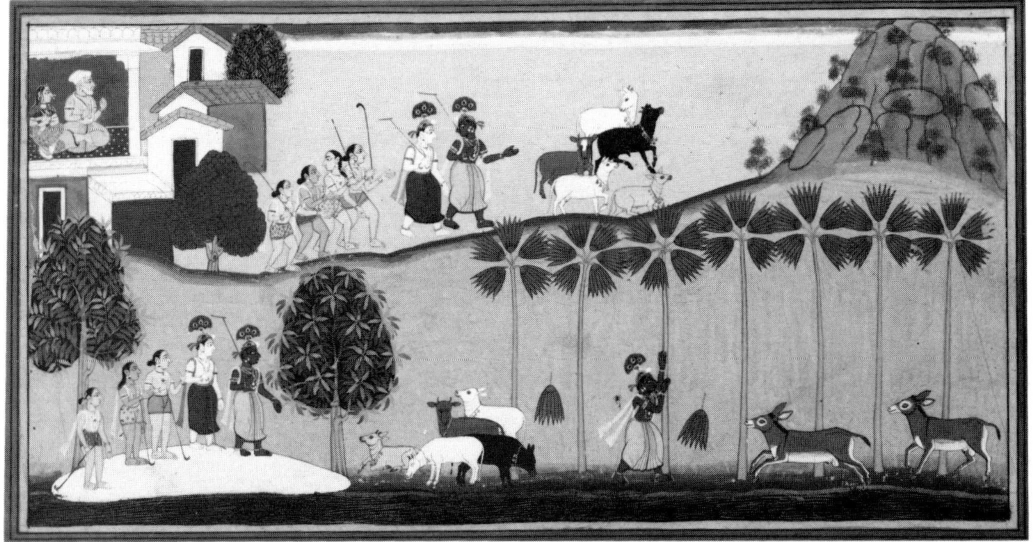

109

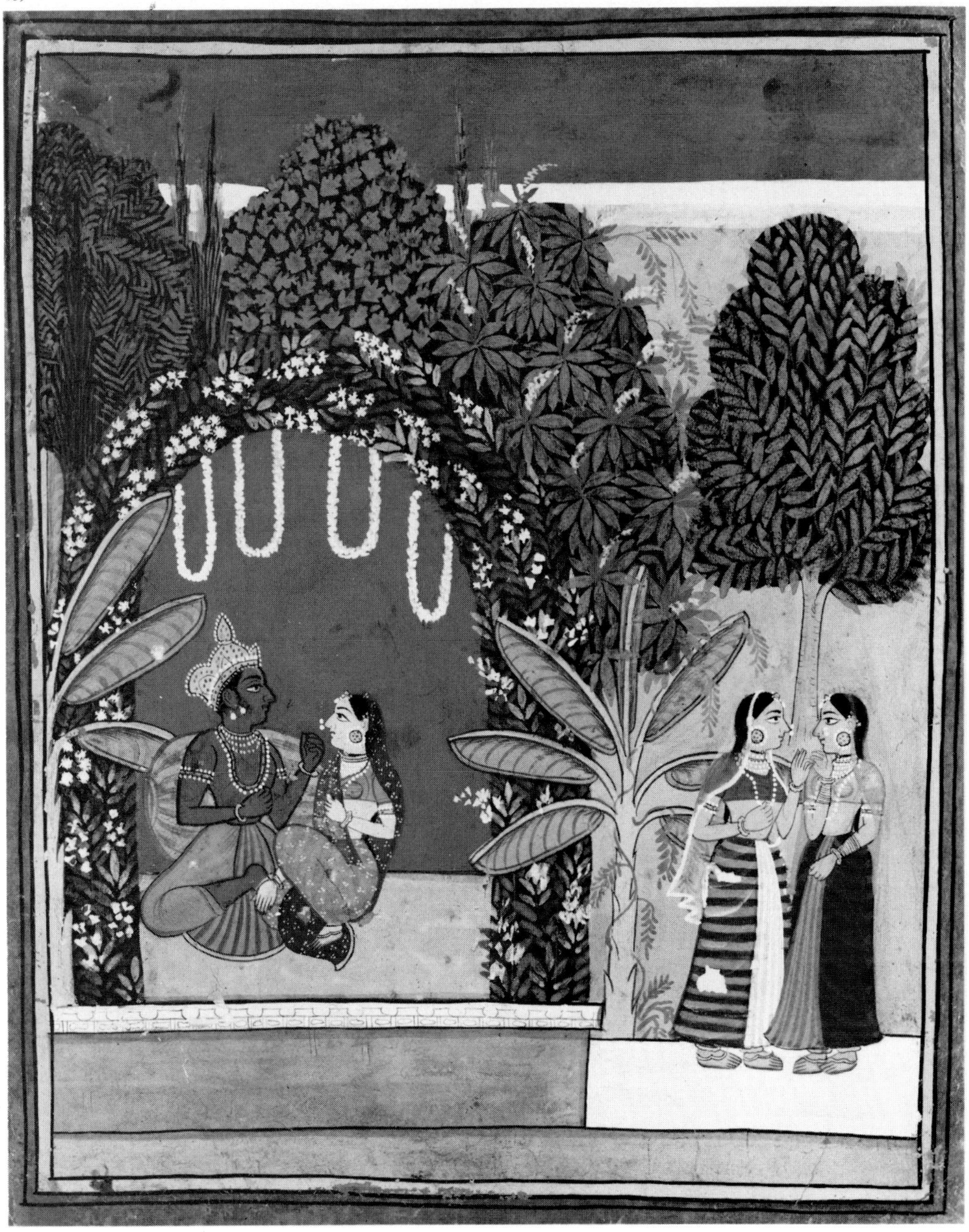

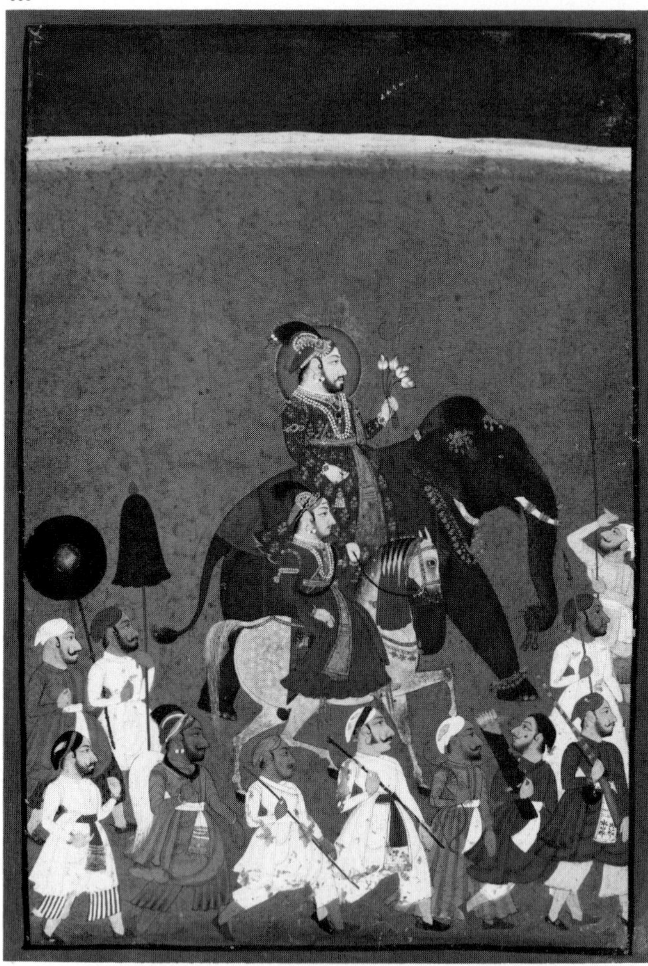

111

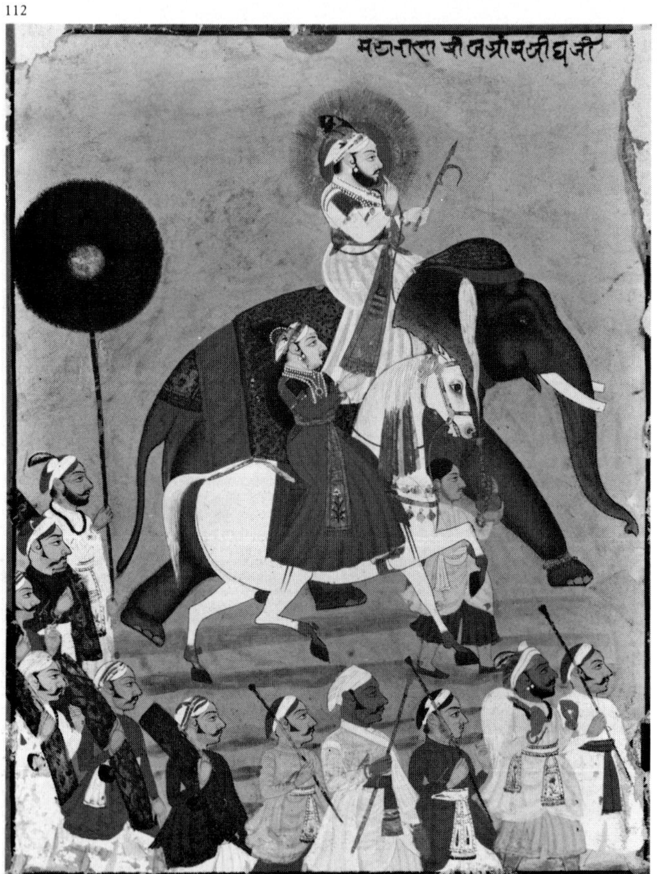

112

110

A Page from a Series, possibly of the *Sur Sagar*
Udaipur, c. 1730-40
24.8 x 40 cm

Radha leaves her solitary bower and, impelled by Kamadeva's flower-arrow, goes to join Krishna playing Holi with the gopis by the river Jumna. To the right an attendant halts a running elephant with a goad. Yellow margin and text panel with unidentified verses written in a coarse hand; red border, numbered 69.

Inscribed on the back: *can?am hī naro same.*

111

Maharana Jagat Singh Riding with his Brother Nathji
Udaipur, 1735. By Naga, son of Bhagvan
32.8 x 22.2 cm

The Maharana, with nimbus, in a gold-printed blue *jama,* rides an elephant, holding flowers and an ankus in one hand. His younger brother Nathji, in a red *jama,* rides alongside on a grey stallion. Attendants accompany them on foot. Green background, with a blue band above. Red border.

Inscribed on the back: *śrī ramji. samvat 1792 āsoj vid 10 some re dīn śrijī re janam ūchava re dīn pāno nijar hu citare nage bhagavān re nijar ki do 15* [in another hand:] *hati gada? ro* [in still another hand:] *māharaṇa śrī jagat saghji nathji māharaja.*

Cat. no. 176 is ascribed to the same artist. For other works by him, see Gangoly, *Critical Catalogue of the Miniature Paintings in the Baroda Museum,* pl. XXVI, p. 93; there is also a small portrait of Maharana Raj Singh II, ascribed to him and dated 1754, in a private collection. See also Dwivedi, 'Some Inscribed and Dated Rajasthani Miniatures in the Collection of State Museum, Lucknow', *Journal of the Indian Society of Oriental Art,* n.s., VIII, 1976-77, pp. 49-50.

112

Maharana Jagat Singh Riding with his Brother Nathji (?)
Udaipur, c. 1735
26.5 x 21.6 cm

A similar subject to cat. no. 111, on which it is perhaps based. Pale green background. Trimmed red border. Some damage and repainting. Incorrectly inscribed above: *māharaṇa śrī saṅgrām sīghji.*

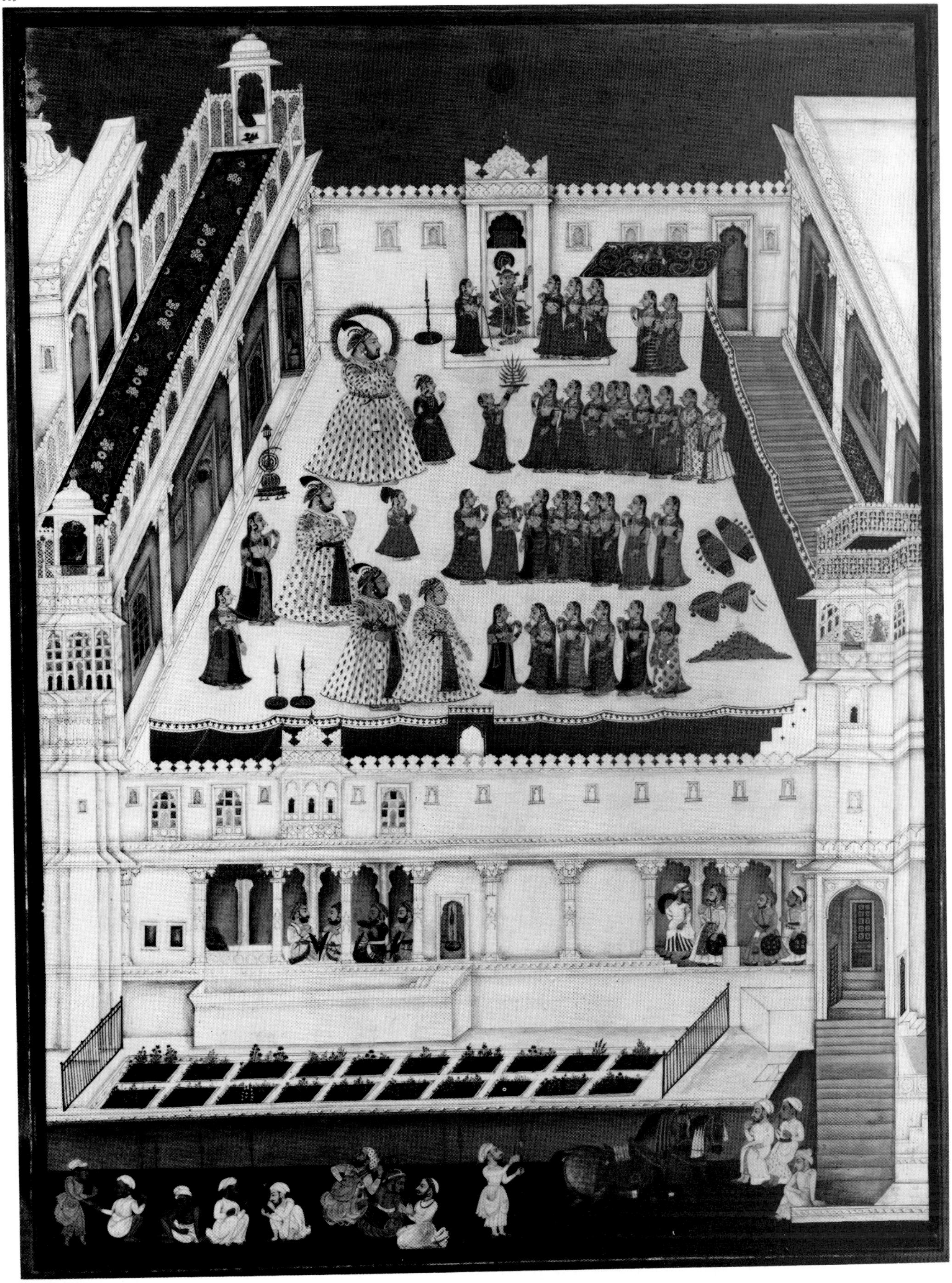

113

Maharana Jagat Singh Attending the *Rasalila*
Udaipur, 1736. By Jai Ram
59.8 x 44.8 cm

The Maharana, with nimbus, attends the preliminary
invocation with the *arati* lamp before a dancer in the
form of Shri Nathji at the beginning of a *rasalila* dance
performance in a palace courtyard by night. The
Maharana, his brother Nathji, his son Pratap Singh, his
brother Baghji and Nathji's son Bhim Singh stand on
the left, with the female players in four rows on the
right, in an area screened by red *qanats*. Drums and
stage properties, such as a canopy with the figure of
Indra among clouds and a small model of Mt.
Govardhana, stand ready for use in the performance.
Further below, sardars are seated and standing in an
open arcade, while in the courtyard in the foreground
syces wait with horses, and musicians and smoking
servants while away the night hours. Red border.

Inscribed on the back: *śrī. śrī mharajadharaja mharanaji
śrī jagat siṅghji: smat 1793 bīrasai kati sud 15 subha
dīne re dīn rāsa: bīra jaroka radho:* [in another hand]
atara sardar ubha thaka [name del. = *?śrī hajur...bhai
nathjī*] [in another hand:] *nojī śrī hajurī jimanī baju
bhaī nathjī kuvar pratap sīghjī bhai bagjī
bhaī nathjī ro beto bhim sigh. 1.* [further below:] *citaro
jai ram.*

See also cat. no. 114. These two paintings belong to a
series of large, near-identical compositions showing
different dramas, involving several deities, being danced
in front of Maharana Jagat Singh. At least eight other
examples are known in private collections. All are dated
in Karttika of 1736, as far as is known, and it is likely
that all may be by Jai Ram in part at least. The present
picture, which is the only one ascribed to him, is
probably the first in the series in that it depicts the
preliminary invocation before the performances. These
paintings afford a unique record of the dance dramas of
the period, of which only scant early 19th century
reports by Broughton and Tod otherwise remain (see N.
Hein, *The Miracle Plays of Mathura*, New Haven, 1972,
pp. 131 ff.). See also discussion of cat. no. 82.

114

Maharana Jagat Singh Attending the *Rasalila*
Udaipur, 1736. Attributed to Jai Ram
61 x 45 cm
(Colour Plate No. 1)

From the same series as cat. no. 113. Here the
Maharana, with nimbus and smoking a *huqqa* in the
form of a woman, has taken his seat to watch the dance
performance, together with a child and Raja Raghodev,
Takhat Singh, Prince Pratap Singh, Baghji, Sardar Singh
and Bharath Singh. A dancer playing the role of
Ganesha, accompanied by women dancers and
musicians, is seen three times, dancing, seated on a stool
and astride a wheeled rat *vahana*. A dancer posing as
Krishna, with maids, stands in the background. Red
border.

Inscribed on the back: *śrī. śrī mharajadharaja mharanaji
śrī jagat sighji: smat 1793 bīrasai: kati sud 15 subha dīne
re dīn rāsa: biran? ro karayo?: śrī hajur ra mudā age
camanoji gadi sama raja ragodevaji he ?the babo takhat
sighjī bhai nathjī kuar pratap sighjī
bhai bagjī kako bakhat sighjī ?do o saradar sighjī
baba bharath sighjī.*

See discussion of cat. no. 113.

115

Maharana Jagat Singh
Udaipur, c. 1740
20 x 13.8 cm

The Maharana, with nimbus, in an orange *pagri* and
dark green *jama* with pink floral decoration, stands
holding a flower in one hand and a gun in the other. A
bow and arrows hang from his shoulder; a dagger, *katar*,
wallet and powder-horn are attached to his *patka*. Red
border, inscribed above: *maharana śrī jagat sighji.*

116

Maharana Jagat Singh and a Sardar
Udaipur, c. 1740-45
30.3 x 19 cm

The Maharana, with nimbus, wearing a gold-printed
orange *jama*, stands holding a lotus-bud and conversing
with a sardar who folds his hands in respect. Green
background; small flowers in foreground; white and blue
bands above. Buff border with salmon-pink wash.
Inscribed above: *maharajadharaja maharanaji śrī jagat
sigji rī sabi.*

The Maharana's companion in this picture, and in cat.
no. 117, may be his minister, Bihari Das Pancholi (see
also cat. no. 121).

117

Maharana Jagat Singh with a Sardar
Udaipur, 1747. By Raghunath, son of Maluk Chand
28.5 x 20.4 cm

The Maharana, with nimbus, wearing an orange *jama*,
presents a *pan* to a sardar in a dark pink *jama*.
Turquoise-grey background; white sky above with
curiously shaped blue and red clouds. Red border.

Inscribed on the back: *śrī. sighī śrī maharajadhiraja
maharanaji śrī jagat sighji rī surat ro pano sam
1804 virase jeth sud 11 sukare nīraja la..?ra sare dīn
pano nijar huo kalamī citaro ruganath maluk cand ro.*
Compare cat. no. 116, of which this is probably a
version.

114 (detail)

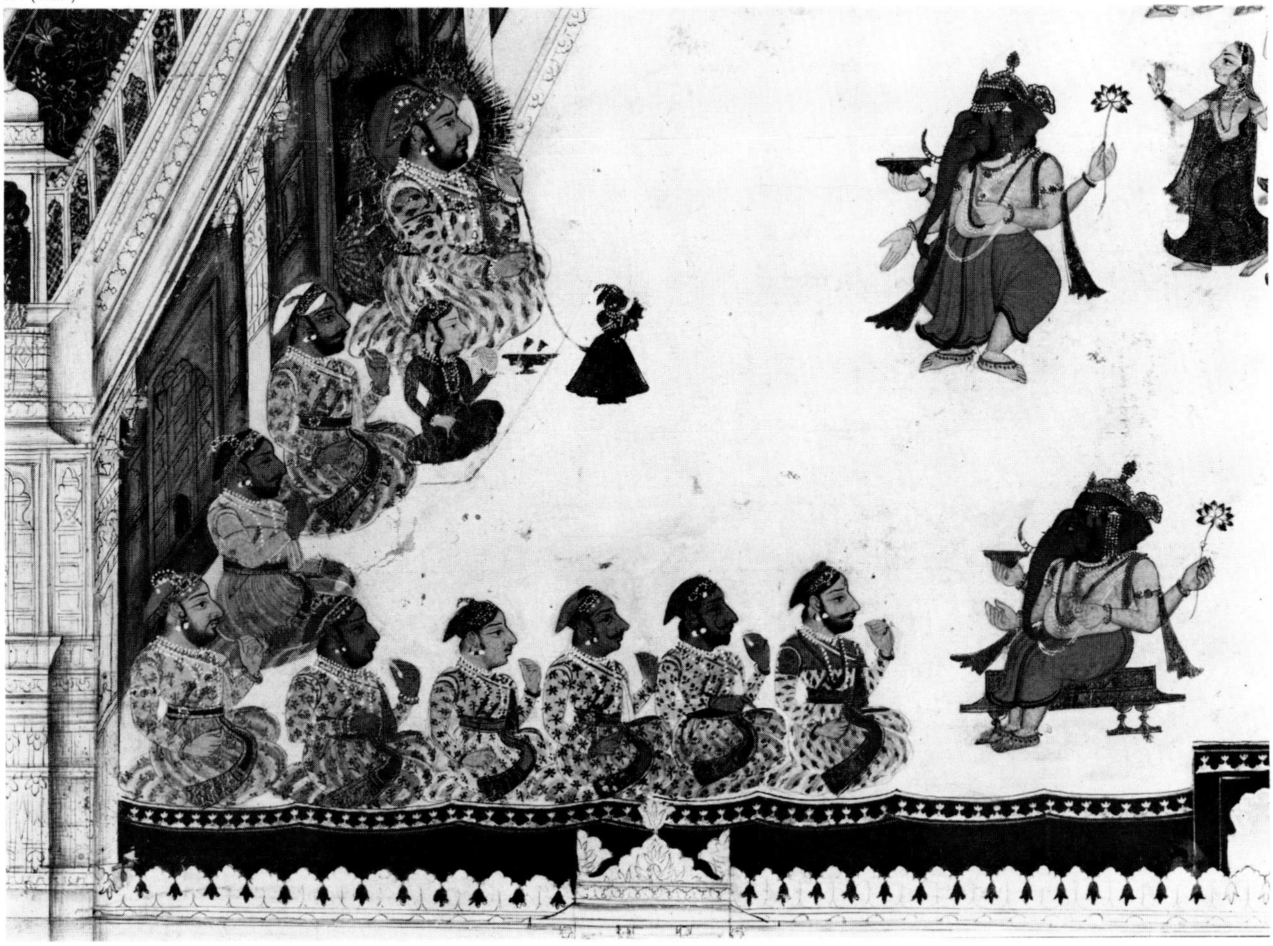

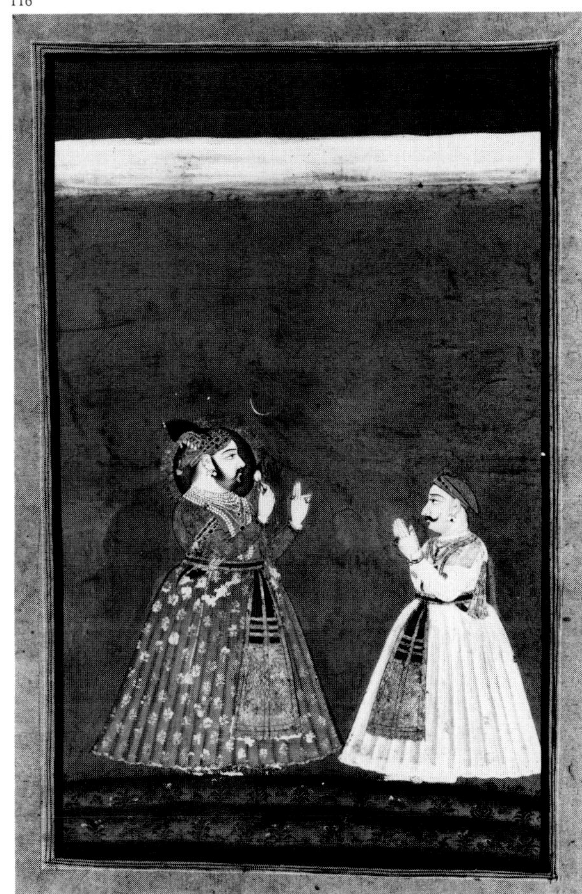

116

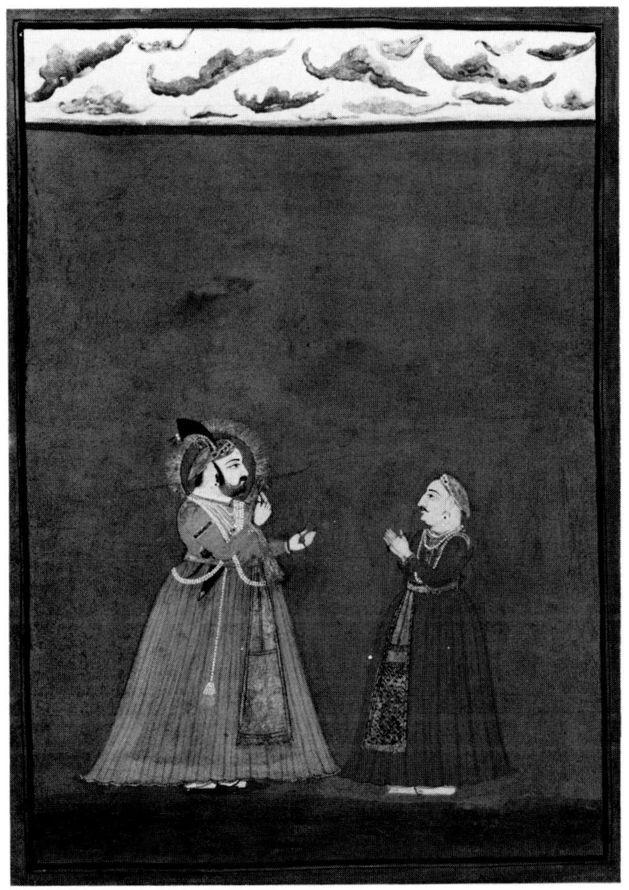

117

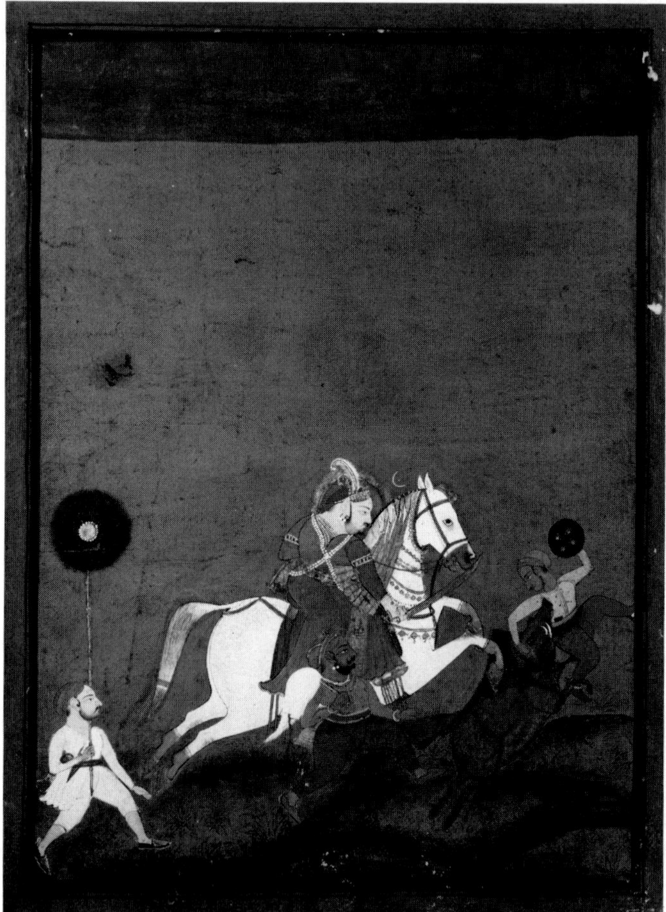

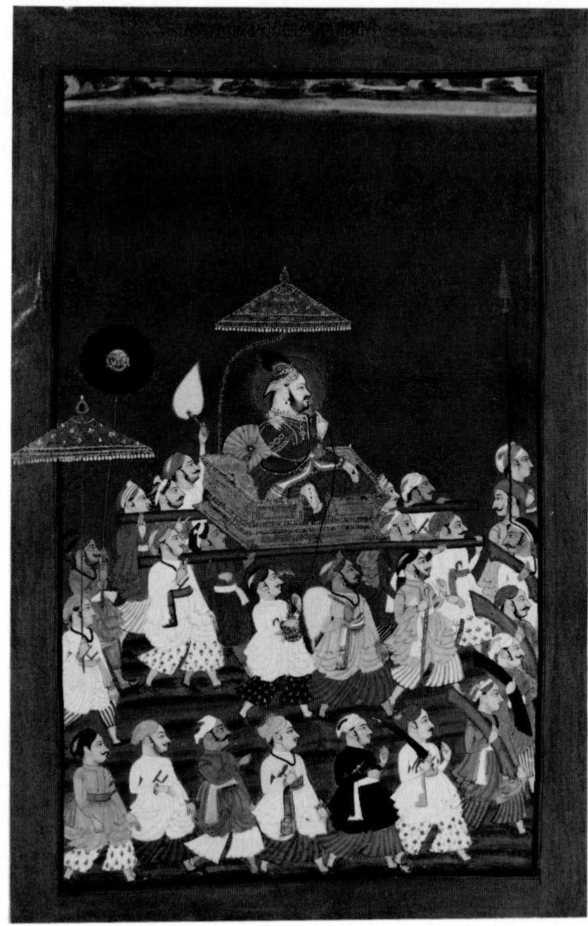

118
Maharana Jagat Singh Hunting Boar
Udaipur, 1747. By Raghunath, son of Maluk Chand
32.5 x 24 cm

The Maharana, with nimbus, wearing a green *jama,* rides a white stallion and slashes with a *talwar* at a boar which is attacking one of the three attendants accompanying him on foot. Turquoise-grey background with a blue band above. Red border, slightly trimmed.

Inscribed on the back: *mharanaji śri jagat sigji* [in another hand:] *kalami citaro maluk cand ro beto vaisakh sud 4 samvat 1804 varse.*

The slightly mutilated inscription names the artist as the son of Maluk Chand, who on the evidence of cat. nos. 117 and 128 can be identified as Raghunath.

119
Maharana Jagat Singh in a Palanquin
Udaipur, c. 1745-50
39 x 23.2 cm

The Maharana, with nimbus, wearing a red *jama,* rides in a gold palanquin holding a *pan* in one hand and the mouthpiece of his *huqqa* in the other. He is accompanied by numerous attendants on foot, with *huqqa*, chowry, regalia etc. Azure background. Red border.
Inscribed above: *mharajadhiraja mharana śri jagat sghiji.*

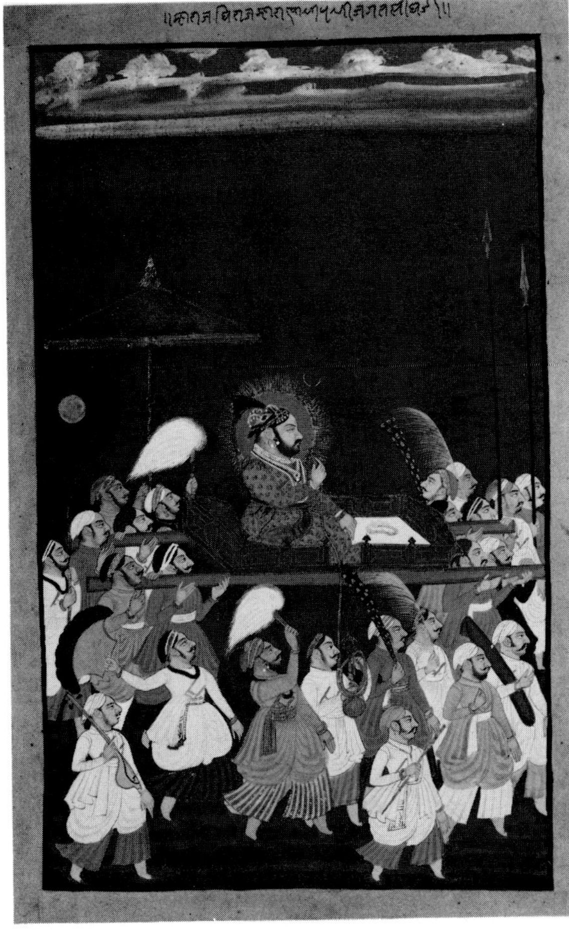

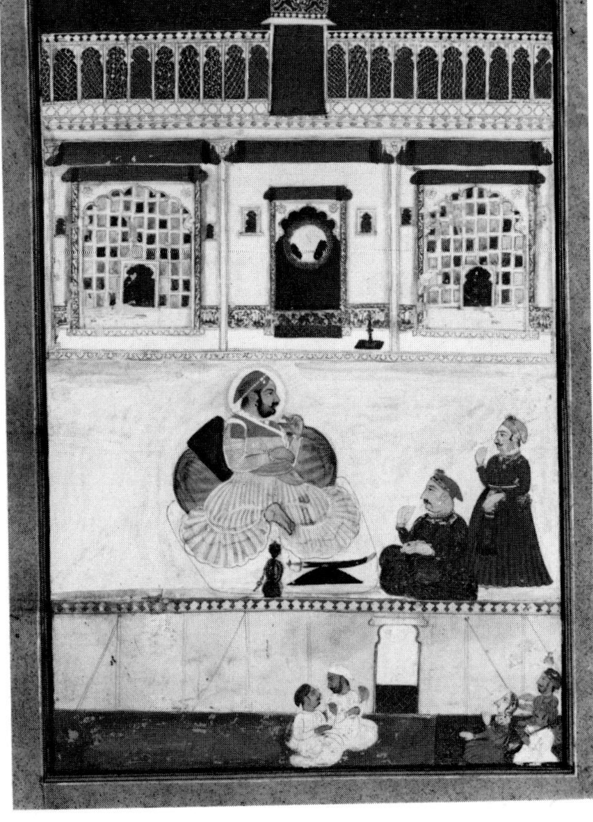

120
Maharana Jagat Singh in a Palanquin
Udaipur, c. 1745-50
40 x 24.8 cm

The Maharana, with nimbus, wearing an orange *jama*
printed with blue flowers, rides in a palanquin smoking
a *huqqa,* accompanied by numerous attendants with
chowries, regalia etc. Dark green background with clouds
above. Buff border with yellow edging.
Inscribed above: *mhārājadhirāja mhāraṇa śrī 5 śrī jagat
sīghjī.*

121
Maharana Jagat Singh Receiving Two Ministers
Udaipur, c. 1745-50
37.3 x 23.5 cm

The Maharana, with nimbus, sits in a palace courtyard at
night with a sword, shield and *huqqa* in front of him,
attended by two courtiers, probably ministers (the seated
figure may be Pancholi Bihari Das). The sun-window in
the palace appears behind the Maharana, with bays
filled with stained glass panels at either side. In the
foreground servants and musicians sit in attendance
behind a screen. Repaired at the left side. Tan border
speckled with grey.

Inscribed on the back: *mharaṇa śrī jagat sīghjī.*

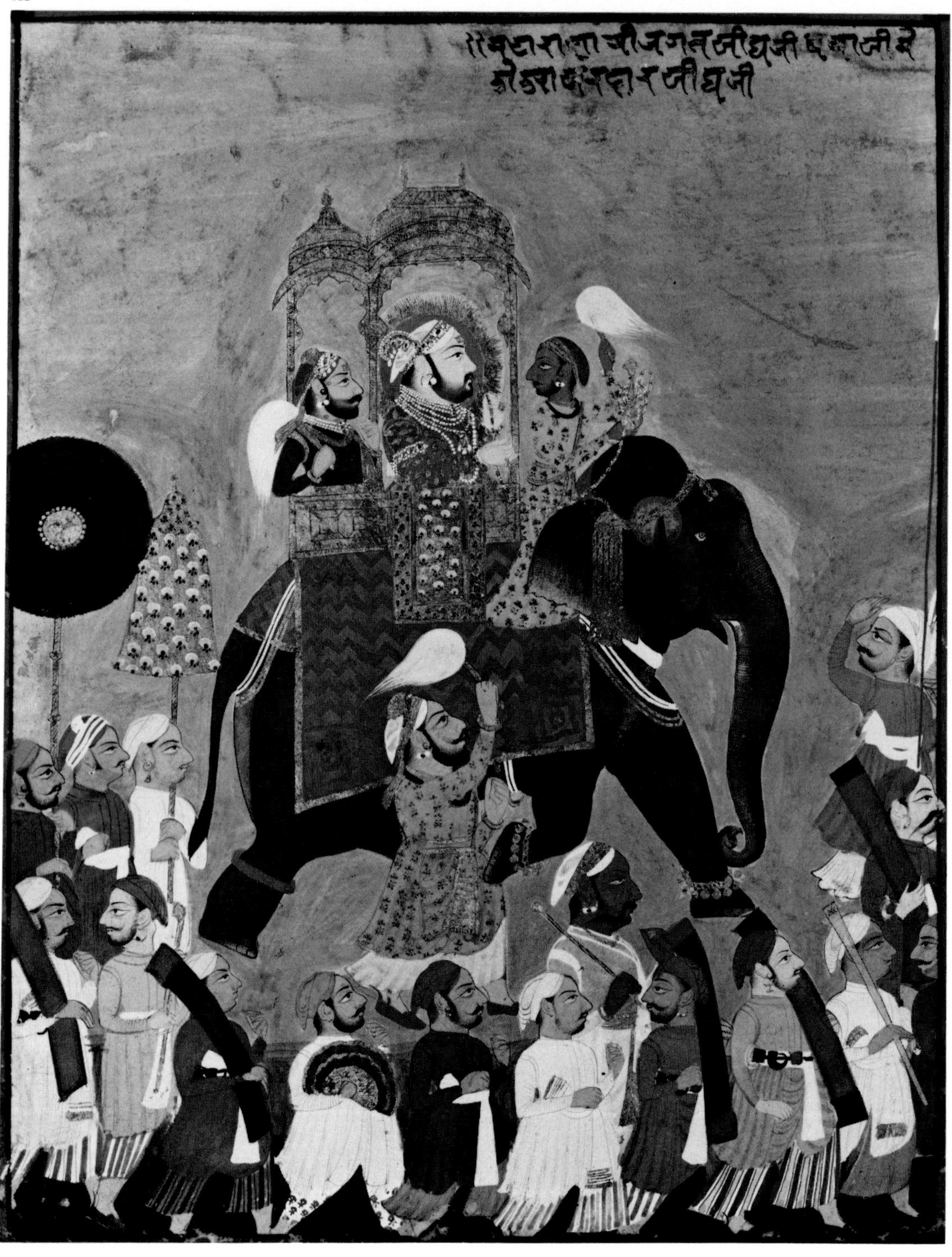

122

Maharana Jagat Singh on an Elephant
Udaipur, c. 1740-50
26.5 x 20.6 cm

The Maharana, with nimbus, sits in a gilded elephant
howdah smoking a *huqqa* held by the mahout; Sardar
Singh rides behind him holding a chowry. Attendants
on foot carry regalia and swords wrapped in coverings.
Pale green background. Severely trimmed red border.
Inscribed above: *maharanaji jagat sighji khawasi me
dodara? sardar sighji.*

123

Maharana Jagat Singh
Udaipur, c. 1740-45
22 x 14.1 cm

A half-length portrait of the Maharana appearing within
an arched window-frame, wearing a black *bandhana
pagri* and a gold-printed *jama,* holding a *pan* and
smoking from a silver *huqqa* in the form of a woman.
Pale blue-grey background. Yellow margin; buff inner
border with silver flecks, inscribed: *rano śri jagat sighji;*
pale turquoise outer border.

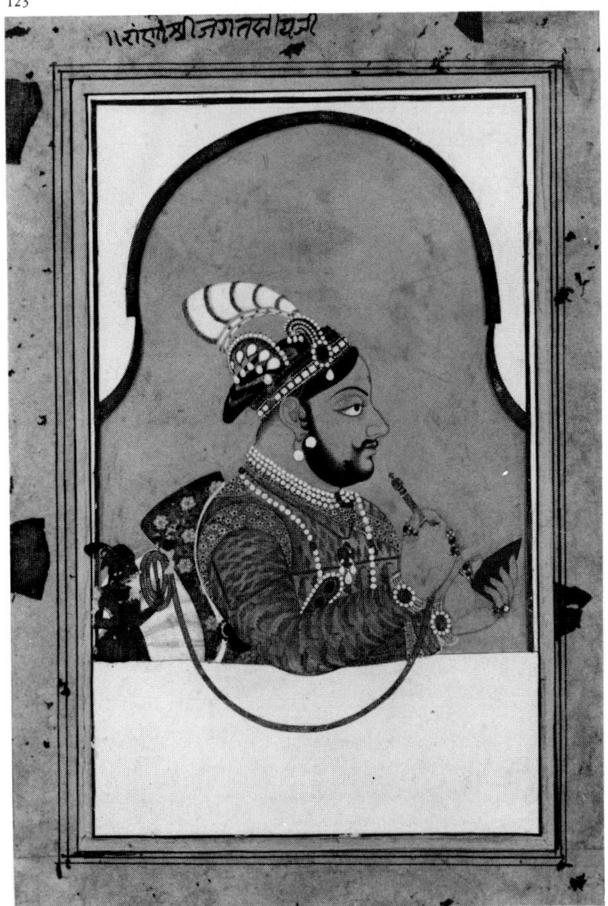

124
Maharana Jagat Singh Playing Holi
Udaipur, c. 1745
42 x 61 cm

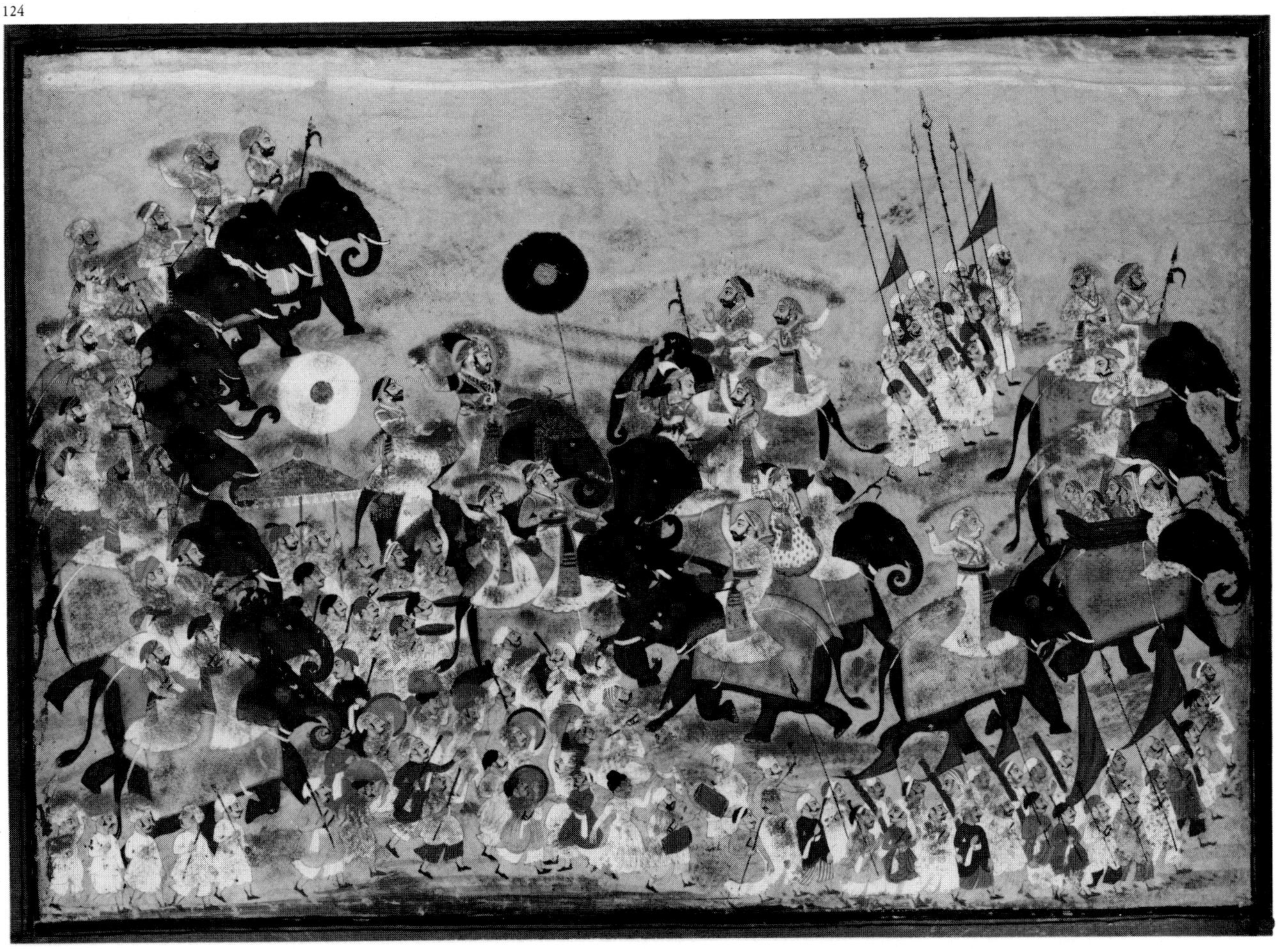

The Maharana, with nimbus, orange *pagri* and yellow *jama,* his sardars and male members of his family all mounted on elephants fling red powder *(gulal)* at one another. Ram Singh is seated behind the Maharana; also participating in the mêlée are Nathji with Pancholi Kubera Chand behind him, Raja Raghodev with Sirdar Singh behind him, Maharaja Bakhat Singh with Baba Bharath Singh behind him, and Nagaji, who all ride on the four elephants immediately beside and facing that of the Maharana. There are nineteen elephants in all, and numerous attendants on foot, all splashed with red colour. Pale green background. Red border.

Inscribed on the back: *śrī. śrī mharanojī śrī jagat sīghjī hathya rī asavarī ro phag hajur ra hathī nīce bhaī nāthjī ro hāthī nāthjī pache pacolī kubair cadjī: raja rāgodejī ro hāthī sāmu āvato pāchai sīrdar sīghjī baithā thakā mahārajā bakhat sīghjī ro hāthī sāmai modai? pachai babo bharath sīghjī bethā: dhayabhāī nagajī ro hāthī nāthjī ra hāthī sāmu: māhā* (the inscription is apparently unfinished).

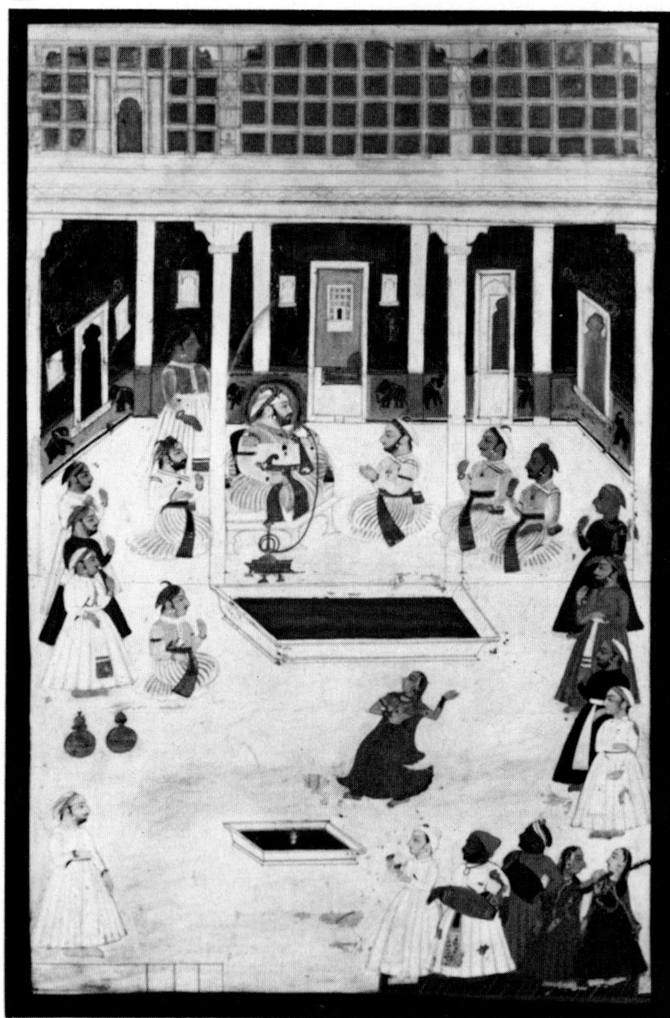

125

Maharana Jagat Singh Pursuing an Escaped Elephant
Udaipur, 1746. By Deva, son of Nathu
23.8 x 40 cm

The Maharana, with nimbus, riding a dappled stallion,
accompanied by a mounted sardar and attendants on
foot, pursues an escaped elephant, whose keepers run
before and after it with whips and prodders loaded with
fire-crackers. Olive-green background with blue sky
above. Speckled buff border with black rules.
Inscribed above: *maharajadhiraja maharanaji
sri jagat sighji ri sabi che.*

Inscribed on the back: *sambat 1803 jeth sud budhe
pano 1 hathi dela? vadal choda ojani tare ro nijar huo
kalami citaro devo nathu ro.*
Cat. no. 127 is by the same artist.

126

**Maharana Jagat Singh and his Sardars Watching a
Nautch**
Udaipur, 1748(?)
47 x 32 cm

The Maharana, with nimbus, sits on a low throne
smoking a *huqqa*, attended by sardars and servants, in
the Kachari Mahal. A tank filled with orange water
stands in front of him. An elephant frieze is painted on
the lower part of the wall behind. In the foreground a
nautch girl performs, accompanied by a group of
musicians standing on a durree. Red border.

Inscribed on the back: *sri. maharajadhiraja
maharanaji sri jagat singhji ri surat ro pano:
kaceri mel ri? tare: kati sud 1 some sam 1805?*

127

Maharana Jagat Singh Watching an Elephant Fight
Udaipur, 1750. By Deva, son of Nathu, (Sutar)
39.3 x 54 cm

The Maharana, with nimbus, and his sardars watch an
elephant fight at the Chaugan, which is shown with a
green ground. In front of their pavilion the elephant
Kalikunvar mounts a wall to close with its opponent; it
is also shown running round the arena, pursued by its
keepers and sardars on horseback. A group of sadhus
watch the spectacle on the right. Buff border with fine
silver flecks.

Inscribed on the back: *mharajadhiraja maharana sri jagat
singhji cogan re darikhane barajya thaka hathi
kalinkunvar ne hathi moti ganj agada lada a
hathi kalinkunvar cogan mhe hathi moti ganj cogan
barane hathi kalikunvar agada upre ?cadyo kalami citaro
sutar devo nathu re nijar ki dho pos sud 15 sam 1807.*

The artist Deva, son of Nathu, is identified as belonging
to the *sutar* or wood-working caste. See also cat. no. 125.

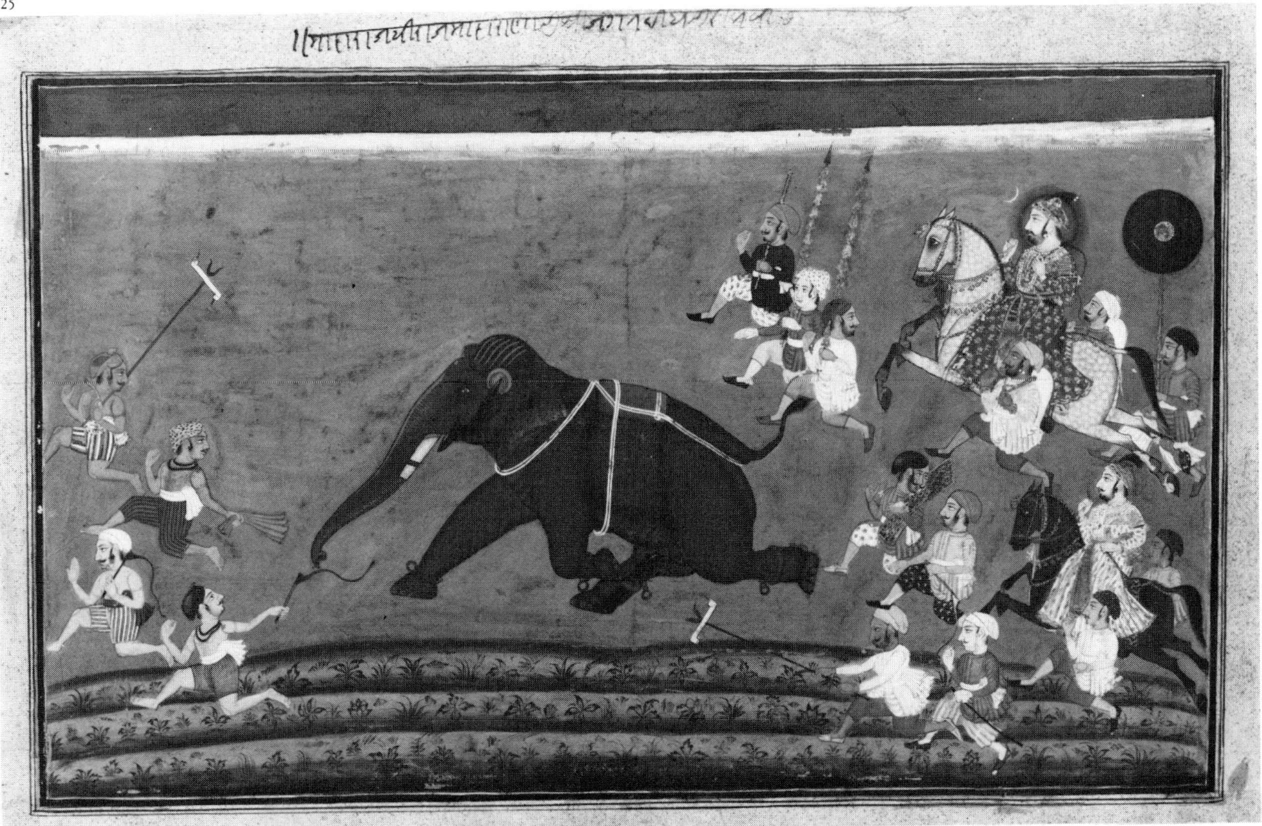

127

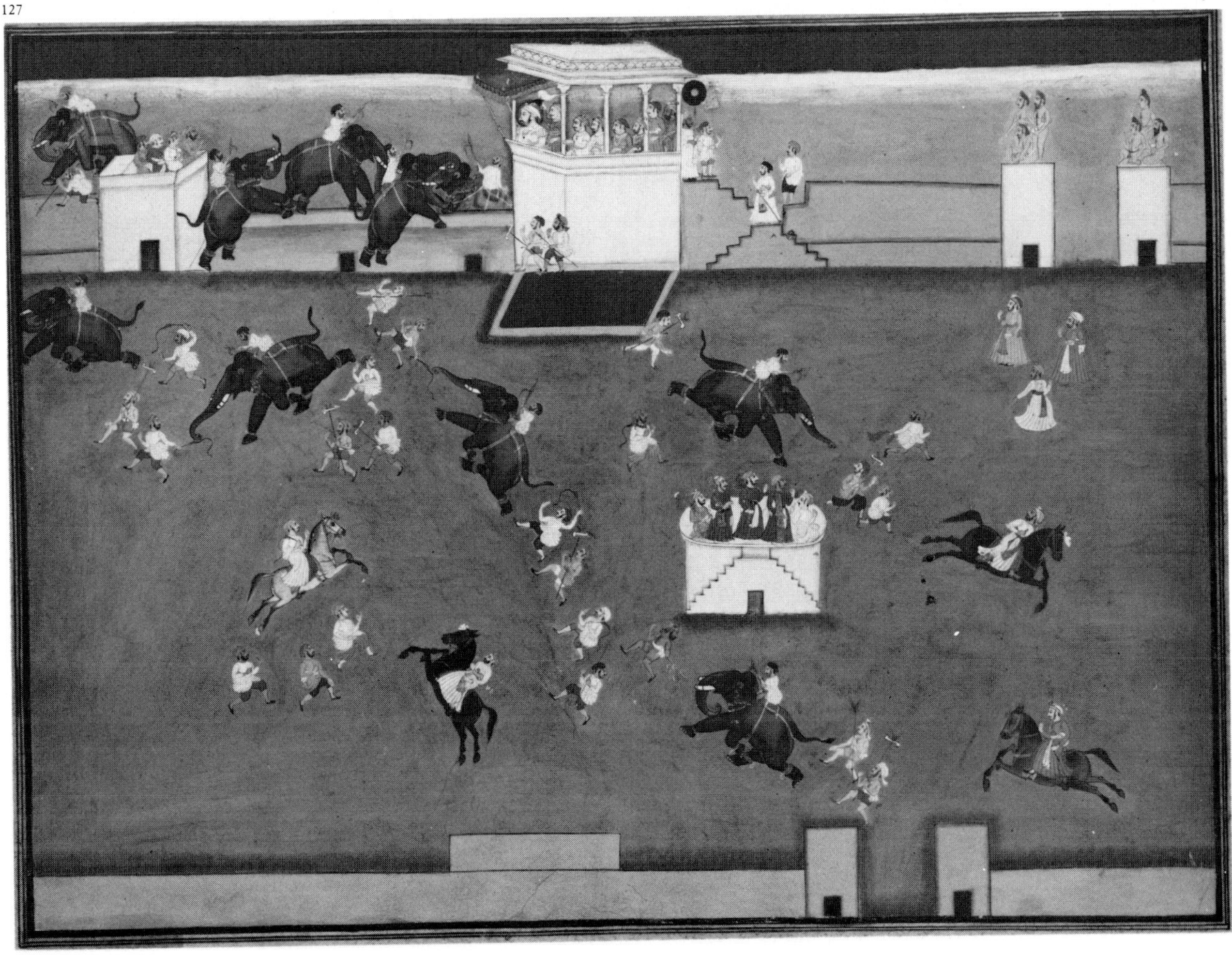

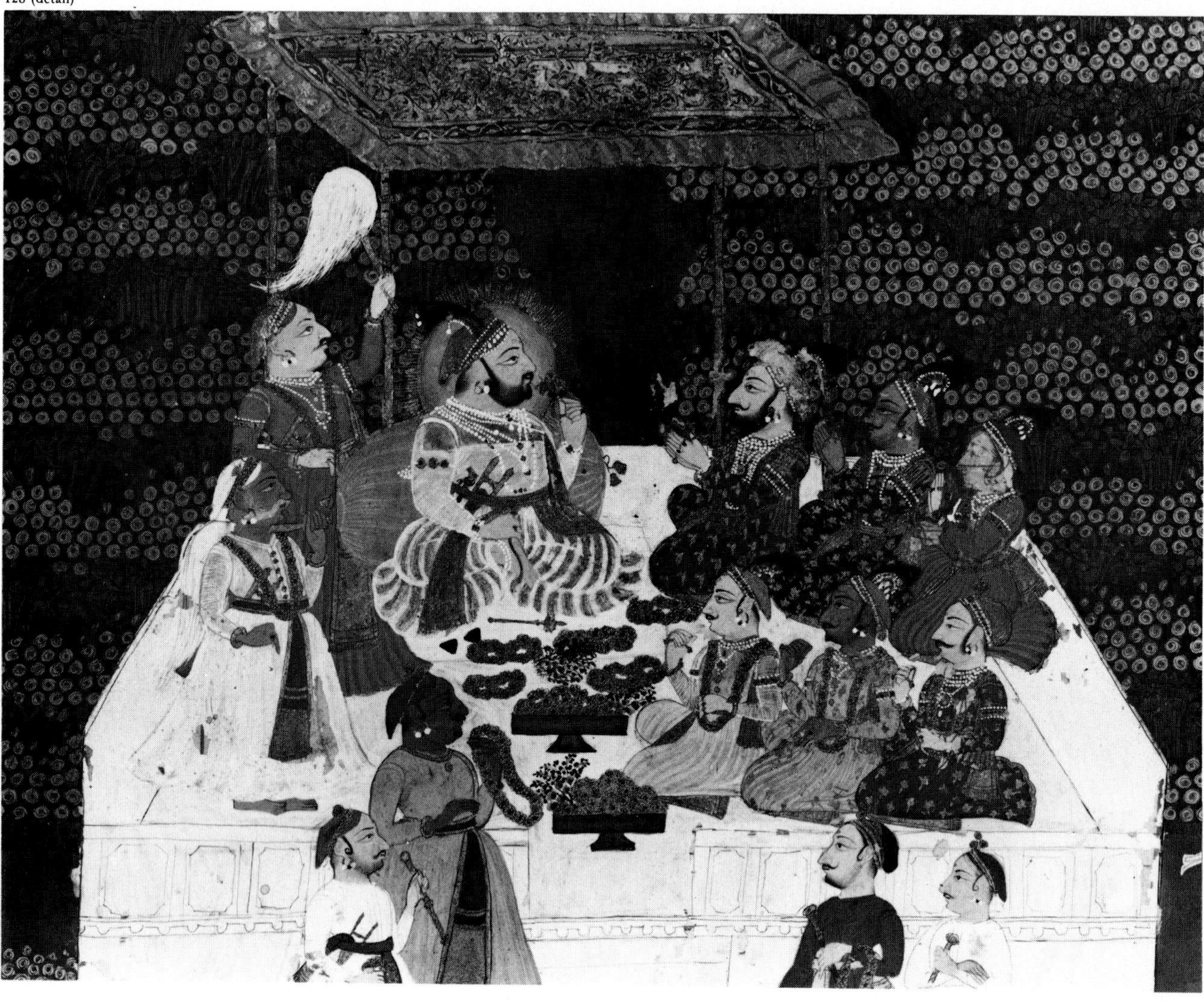

128

Maharana Jagat Singh Celebrating the Festival of Flowers in the Gulab Bari Garden
Udaipur, 1750. By Raghunath, son of Maluk Chand
49.7 x 41.1 cm
(Colour Plate No. 11)

The New Year, which falls in the spring month of Chaitra, was celebrated at Udaipur by worship of the sword and by the flower festival, when 'all the fair of the capital, as well as the other sex, repair to the gardens and groves, where parties assemble, regale, and swing, adorned with chaplets of roses, jessamine, or oleander, when the Naulakha gardens may vie with the Tivoli of Paris' (Tod, *Annals and Antiquities of Rajasthan*, vol. II, p. 665). Here Maharana Jagat Singh, with nimbus, is seated with his sardars in the Gulab Bari rose-garden, screened by a line of red *qanats.* On the right musicians and dancers dressed as Shiva and Parvati perform. All wear garlands. Attendants wait outside the *qanats,* where shrines to Shiva and Ganesha stand. In the foreground, the Maharana is borne home on a palanquin, accompanied by his son Pratap Singh riding beside him and sardars, attendants and musicians; all wear roses in their *pagris.* Red border.

Inscribed on the back: *śrī. śrī mahārājādhirāja mahārānāji śrī jagat siṅghji rī surat ro pano gulāb vari padaryā: hajur bhaī betā ro sāth ?tha camardār hajur: ?tha asavari ro loka kalami citaro ruganātho maluk cand ro: o pano śriji aṅgolo ki do jani din uchava huo jadi nijar ki do: rija śri hajur thi devani sam 1807 virase pos sudi 5 sinu.*

129

Maharana Jagat Singh Shooting a Buffalo in a River near the Udai Sagar

Udaipur, 1750. By Nath (son of Mitha?)

43.2 x 40.6 cm

The Maharana, with nimbus, attended by sardars, attendants and palanquin-bearers, kneels beside a stream flowing from the Udai Sagar lake and aims an arrow at a buffalo. A camp has been pitched by the lake in the middle distance. The hills in the background have been coloured with a dabbed cloth-pad. Red border.

Inscribed on the back: *śri. śri mahārajādhirāja mahāranaji śri jagat singhji ri surat ro pano: talav ude sāgar ri pal ri joka me bhe so nankhyo tira ri cota pure he: hajur pasavan ro sāth: kalami citaro nātho mithā ro o pano śriji angoli ki do uchava huo jani din nijar huo: pos sudi 5 sinu sam 1807 virase ri ja śri hajur thi devani.*

A finer treatment of this subject, in the National Museum, New Delhi, had been painted a few months earlier in the same year by Nuruddin (O. P. Sharma, *Indian Miniature Painting*, fig. 35). The prototype for both versions is a painting dated 1720 showing Maharana Sangram Singh practising archery at the same spot (private collection).

130

Maharana Jagat Singh Slaying a Boar at Khas Odi

Udaipur, 1761 (?). By Bakhta

41.3 x 33.8 cm

(Colour Plate No. 9)

The Maharana, with nimbus, wearing an orange and gold *jama*, stands with four sardars, Nathji, Bakhat Singh, Bharat Singh and Sardar Singh, inside a pink shooting-box at Khas Odi, on the southern shore of the Pichola lake at Udaipur. He holds a *talwar* with both hands behind his head, poised to strike at a boar, which is also shown hewn in half after the event. Other boar and hares bound away in the thinly wooded rocky landscape; white sky above, streaked with reddish cloud. Two red barges in the foreground wait to take the Maharana home. Red border.

Inscribed on the back: *śri. pano 1 maharanaji śri jagat sighji ri surat ro khās odi sur upare jatako karta thaka odi me itra sardār ubhā thaka bhai nathji kāko bakhat sighji ubhā thaka bāboji bharat sighji ubhā thaka thakur sardār sighji ubhā thaka kalami citara bakhata ro ki do thako vila prohet anop rām re sambat 1818 rā pos sudi 8 ri vau* [in another hand:] *pano ori jamā pos sud 8 ri vau samat 1818 varse mhe jma.*

This picture and cat. no. 167 invalidate the assumption of earlier writers that the artist, Bakhta, worked exclusively at Deogarh, a *thikana* to the north-east of Udaipur (e.g. Beach, 'Painting at Devgarh', *Archives of Asian Art,* XXIV, 1970-71, and Andhare and Singh, *Deogarh Painting*). Bakhta appears in fact to have worked as an Udaipur court artist for some years as a

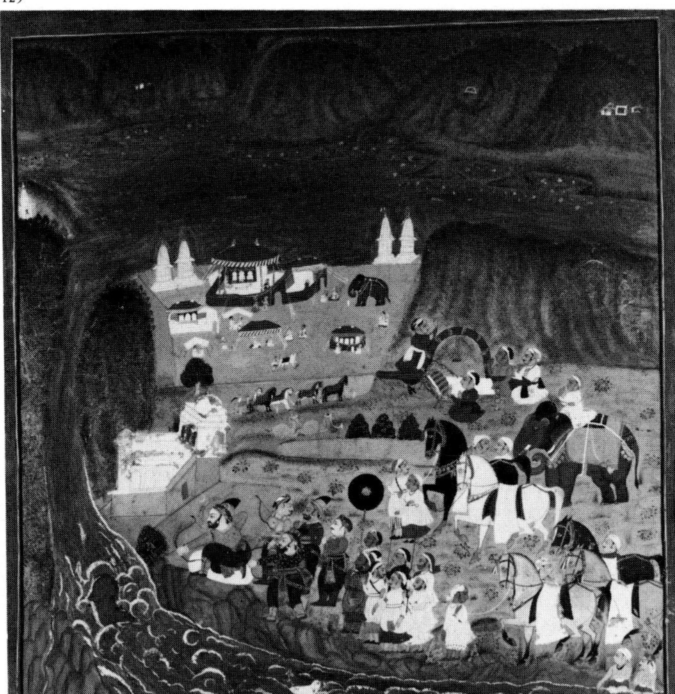

young man (cf. his self-portrait, cat. no. 167); the name of his father, or mentor, is unknown. His move to Deogarh must have occurred, probably as a result of the increasing political and economic breakdown under Maharana Ari Singh in the late 1760s, at some point after the painting of his durbar scene (cat. no. 167) in early 1765. His next dated work is a study of a Deogarh prince dated 1769 (Andhare and Singh, *op. cit.,* pl. 2); he remained active at Deogarh at least until 1811 (see Andhare, 'Painting from the Thikana of Deogarh', *Prince of Wales Museum Bulletin,* 10, 1967, fig. 50).

Besides these two paintings, both of excellent quality, in the National Gallery of Victoria, at least two other pictures of Udaipur Maharanas, ascribed to Bakhta and dated V.S.1818 (1761-2 A.D.), are known in a private collection and await further study. These are studies of Maharana Ari Singh hunting boar and riding accompanied by attendants on foot; a similar painting of Maharana Raj Singh II riding with attendants on foot dated V.S.1813 (1756-7 A.D.) is possibly also by Bakhta. These three pictures are however less well-finished and comparatively flat and uninspired, lacking Bakhta's peculiar stylistic mannerisms, such as the nervous vitality of his tightly bunched rock-forms and the pale sky suffused with red in the present example.

It remains puzzling that Bakhta should have presented a study of Maharana Jagat Singh, who had died in 1751, to his son Ari Singh after his accession ten years later. It would be unusual for such a forceful and vivid representation of a Maharana, far above the level of tediously conventional official portraiture, to have been painted posthumously at Udaipur.

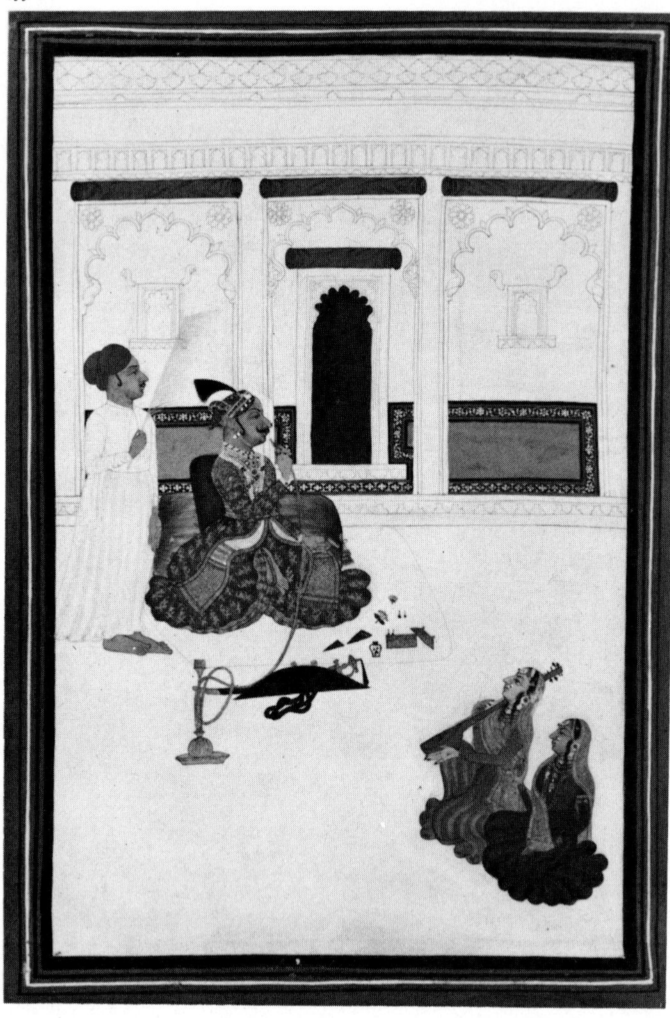

133

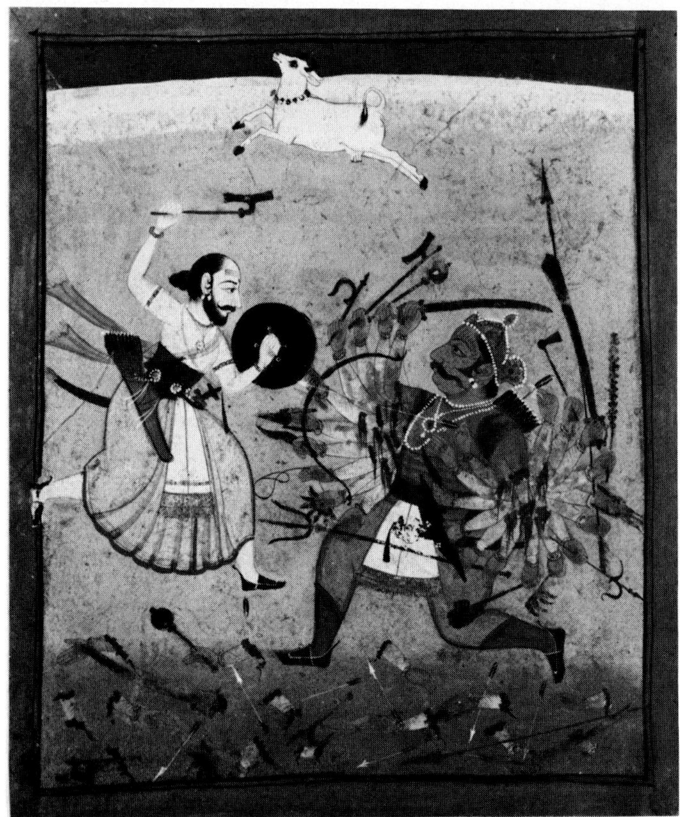

134

131

Rathor Padam Singh
Udaipur, c. 1730-40
22 x 12.2 cm

Padam Singh, in tall Rathor *pagri*, white *jama* and gold *patka*, stands facing left holding a flower. Pale blue-green background. Much rubbed and creased. Yellow margin; red border, numbered 78 and inscribed: *rathod padam sīghjī.*

Probably from a series of portrait studies. The subject may be Padam Singh of Ghanerao, on the borders of Mewar and Marwar, of whom other portraits are known (see Archer, *Indian Miniatures,* pl. 57; O. P. Sharma, *Indian Miniature Painting,* pl. 70; and the collections of the Victoria and Albert Museum, and Kumar Sangram Singh of Nawalgarh).

132

Maharaja Nathji, Younger Brother of Maharana Jagat Singh
Udaipur, 1737(?)
12.6 x 8.2 cm

The youthful prince stands facing right in a gold-printed blue *jama* holding a flower-bud. A pool in the foreground with a strip of flowery meadow. Pale green background. Buff border with silver flecks, numbered 64.

Inscribed on the back: *māha nata māha tara? ro* [in another hand:] *pano gurajī babat besakh vad 9 sa 94* [= V.S. 1794?] [in Persian script:] *mahārāja nathjī* [in yet another hand:] *mharajādhīraja mharana śrī raj saghjī.*

This portrait resembles a picture of Nathji with a lady in the G. K. Kanoria collection. See also cat. no. 111. The inscription identifying the subject as the youthful Maharana Raj Singh (1754-61) is later and incorrect.

133

Baba Bakhat Singh Listening to Music
Udaipur, c. 1750
25.9 x 17.3 cm

Baba Bakhat Singh, son of Takhat Singh (one of the brothers of Maharana Amar Singh), wearing a gold-printed crimson *jama*, sits in a palace room smoking a gold *huqqa*, attended by a servant with a fan and two female musicians. Red border with black and white rules.

Inscribed on the back: *bābā bakhat sīgh taggat sīghot.*

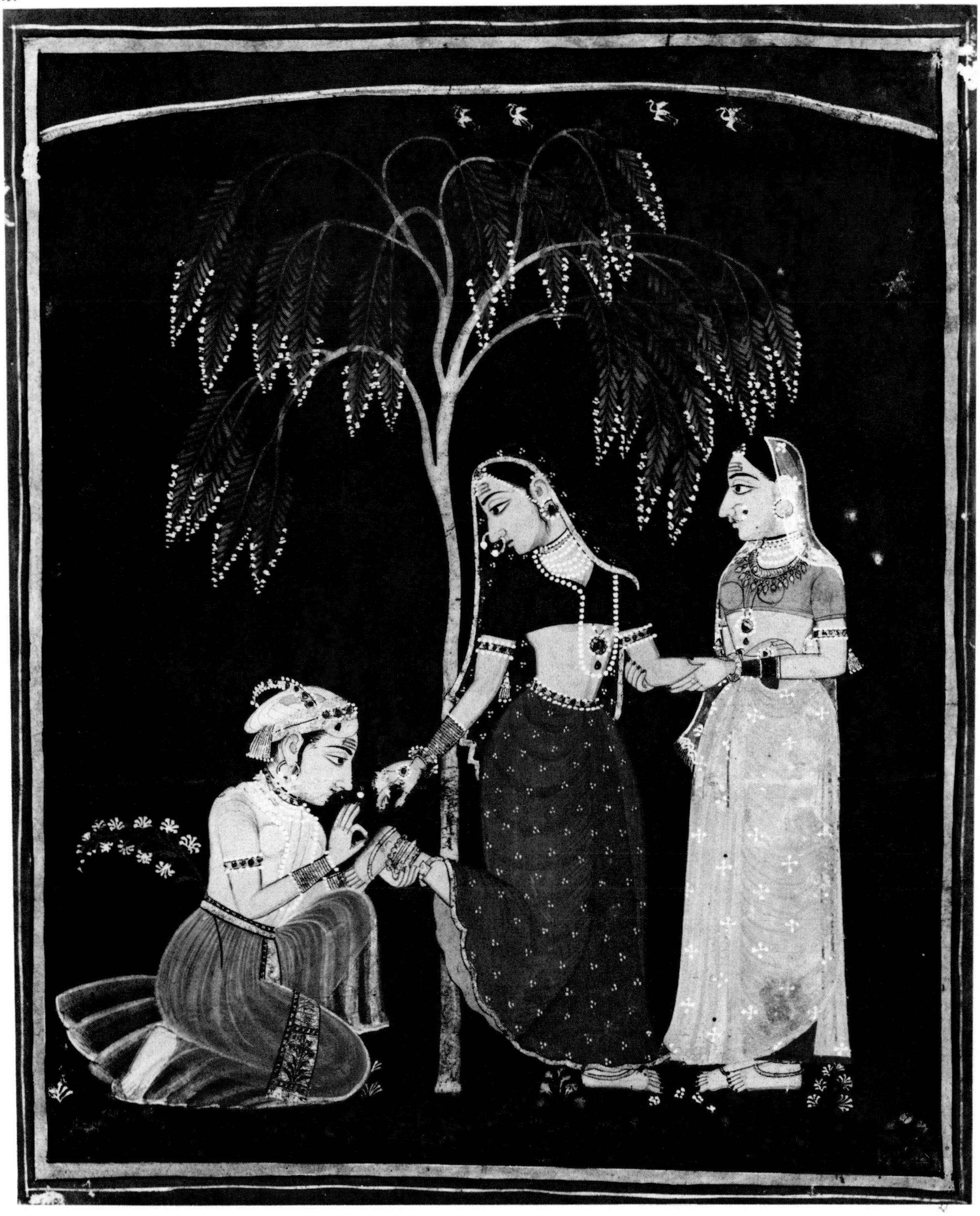

134
Parasurama Avatara
Udaipur, mid-18th century
16.7 x 14 cm

Parasurama, or 'Rama with the battle-axe', an
incarnation of Vishnu, fights with Kartavirya, the
thousand-armed king of the Haihayas, who had carried
off a calf (seen above) belonging to the sage Jamadagnio
Severed arms lie in the foreground. Pale green
background. Red border.

135
A Lady with a Thorn in her Foot
Udaipur, mid-18th century
20.5 x 17.2 cm

A lady in a blue *choli* and orange *ghaghra* stands under
a tree, supported by a maid, while a female companion
dressed in nobleman's costume removes a foreign body
from her foot. Chocolate background. Yellow margin;
red border with white ruling.

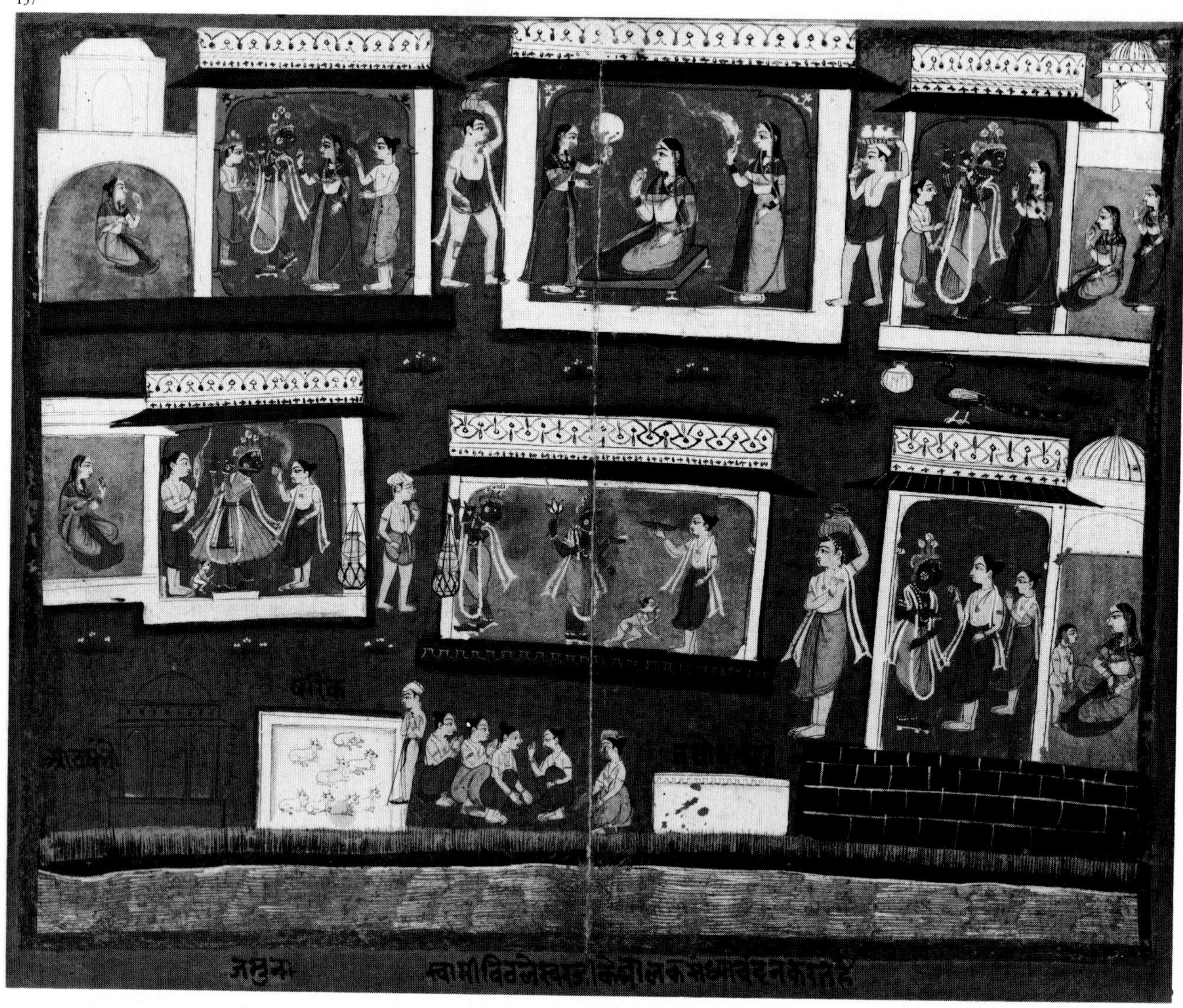

136

Krishna and Radha Embracing
Udaipur, c. 1750 or later
29 x 18.5 cm

Krishna and Radha sit embracing against a bolster in a palace courtyard, attended by two maids and two female musicians. *Pans* and wine-vessels stand nearby. A fountain plays in the foreground. Coarsely executed. Some flaking and discolouration. Yellow margin; red border. On the back a fragmentary sketch of an elephant's head with an invocation to Ganesha.

137

Krishna at Gokula
Eastern Rajasthan or Mathura, 18th century
25.2 x 32.5 cm

Several scenes of Krishna playing his flute in the houses of Gokula, while the inhabitants venerate him; from an otherwise unknown series. Silver margin; red border, numbered 106.

Inscribed: *śrī gokulajī ke mandir/ kharika/ āth khambo/ jasodhā ghāta/ jamunā/ svāmī viṭhalesvarajī ke bālaka sandhyā candana karata hai.*

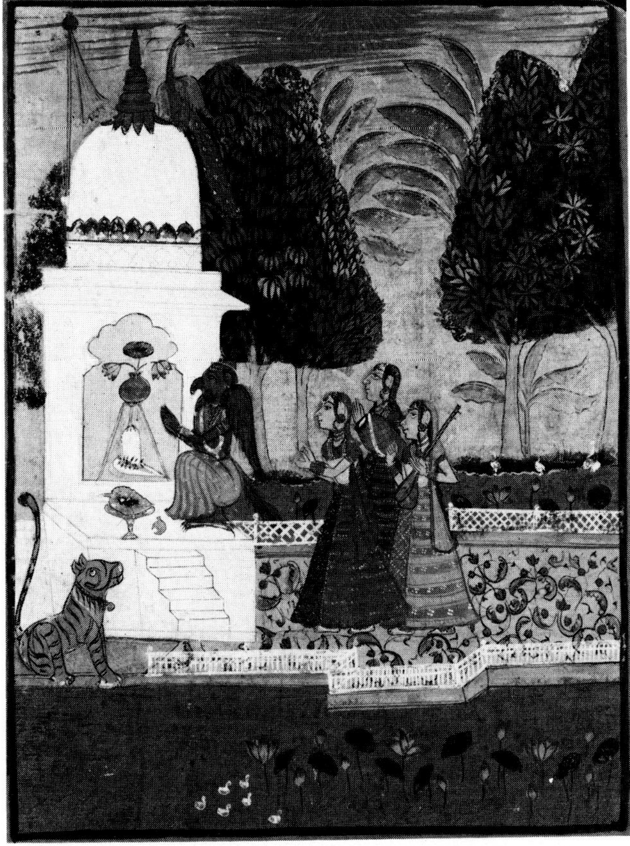

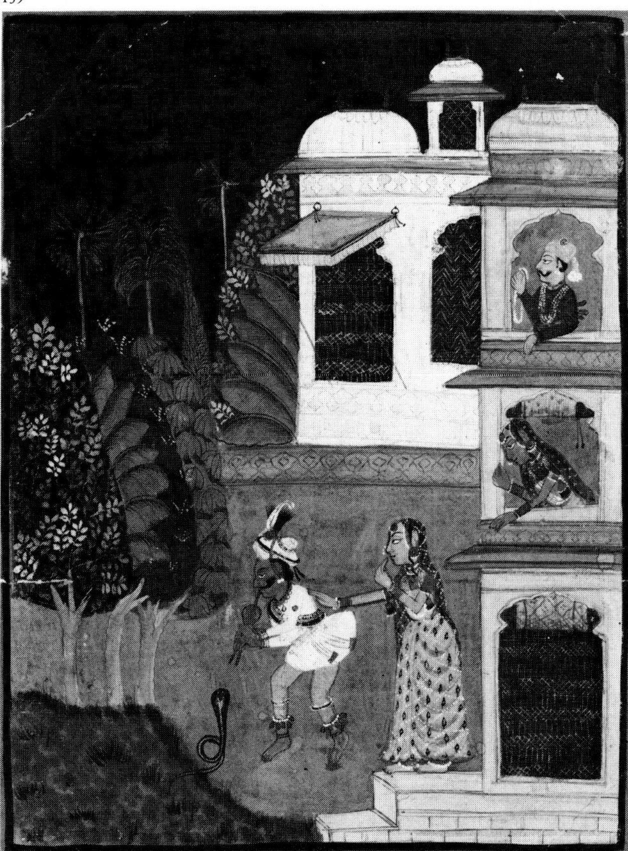

138-49
Twelve Pages from a *Ragamala* Series
Mewar sub-style, mid-18th century
29 x 22 cm (average)

This series of *ragas* and *raginis,* or visualizations of
musical modes, would probably have comprised thirty-
six leaves originally. Its style belongs to southern
Rajasthan, with a number of features associated with
Mewar painting. Despite its roughness it does not lack
poetic feeling. Many of the *raga* iconographies are
unusual, and in some cases the conventional
identifications have been followed here in preference to
those given in the inscriptions on the paintings. The
leaves have red borders, and all have suffered damage in
varying degrees. Seven other leaves, illustrating
Madhumadhavi, Khambavati, Lalita, Patamanjari, Todi,
Malavi(?) and Bhairavi, are in a private collection.

138

Devagari Ragini(?)

The bird Garuda, with green feathers and orange *dhoti,*
worships at a Shiva shrine set in a lake, attended by
three female musicians. This iconography, a variant of
Bhairavi, also occurs in Pahari painting (cf. Ebeling,
Ragamala Painting, p. 284, fig. 339). Inscribed: *ragani
devagari ro pano.*

139
Unidentified *Raga*

A snake-charmer plays to a cobra in front of a palace at
night. A lady rests her hand on his shoulder, and
another lady and a nobleman holding a garland watch
from above. Inscribed: *raga nata vo? ro pano.*

140
Raga Bhairava

Shiva, blue-skinned, is seated inside a pavilion with
pillars and a yellow interior, at night, attended by four
maids with musical instruments, a *morchal* and a lamp;
the bull Nandi and a tiger sit at either side. Inscribed:
*raga bheru ko pano duha: bheru ki dhuna bheravi:
bangali berara: madhumadu hara sindhavi: panc ?brehe
nara nara.*

141
Megha Raga

A blue-skinned lord is seated with his arm round a lady
in front of a pavilion, attended by a maid with a
morchal. Four female musicians sit before them, with a
vase of flowers in between. Inscribed: *raga mega ko
pano duha: bhopali hara gujari: desakar malar: ?tanka
?bi..? gana kamani: mega raga ki nara.*

142
Desavarati Ragini

A lady sits on an hour-glass-shaped seat, stretching her
hands behind her head in love-longing and ignoring the
ministrations of her two maids. Pavilions on either side
and trees with perching peacocks in the background.
Inscribed: *ragaṇī saro..? ro pano.*

143
Asavari Ragini

A tribal woman sits on a rock in a clearing, surrounded
by snakes which coil round her body and round the tree-
trunks. She holds a snake in one hand and an ankus in
the other. A snake-charmer's reed instrument lies before
her. In the background a *chattri* on a rocky ridge
delineated in the 'Central Indian' manner; in the
foreground a pool with lotuses. Cf. Coomaraswamy,
*Catalogue of the Indian Collections in the Museum of
Fine Arts, Boston,* vol. 5, pl. XXIX. Inscribed: *ragaṇī
giranari sorath.*

144
Unidentified *Raga*

A lord and lady sit together on a bed in front of a
pavilion with a fountain and flower-beds in the
foreground. To the left two ladies embrace under an
awning. Inscribed: *raga kali gadi? ro pano.*

145
Malasri Ragini

A lady seated on a black chair, with white inlay,
plucking the petals of lotus-flowers picked for her by
two of her five maids from a pool in the foreground.
Pavilions, trees and dark khaki-green background.
Inscribed: *raga śrī duha: dhanasari asavari: madu? gora
basanta: śri raga ki ragaṇi: malasari he..? 4.*

146
Unidentified *Raga*

A lady seated against pillows with her head resting on
her hand, attended by a maid with *morchal* and three
female musicians. An open pavilion behind, with three
windows and trees in the background. Dark blue sky.
Inscribed: *raga hindola ko pano duha: ramakali
patamanjari: ora kahe devasakha: ?o nari hindola ki:
lalat vilaval raga: 5.*

147
Malkaus Raga

A lord and lady sit together in front of a garden
pavilion, attended by maids with *tanpuras* and a
morchal. A cat(?) sits nearby. Peacocks and cranes perch
on the roof and trees. Inscribed: *raga malakosa ro pano
duha: todi gori gunakali: kumava? chape chana: ora
kukaba? kuke tahe: malakosa ki jana: 3.*

148
Vibhasha Ragini

A lord, seated with a lady in a chamber, aims a flower-
arrow at the crowing cock. A maid stands on the roof,
while another fills a vessel in the pool in the foreground.
Inscribed: *raga kafi kanada? ro pano.*

149
Sri Raga

A lord with a lady on his lap sits in front of a pavilion
listening to the celestial musicians Narada and the horse-
headed Tumburu. A pool with ducks and lotuses in the
foreground. Upper portion mutilated. Inscribed: *ragaṇi
syam kalyaṇ ro pano.*

150

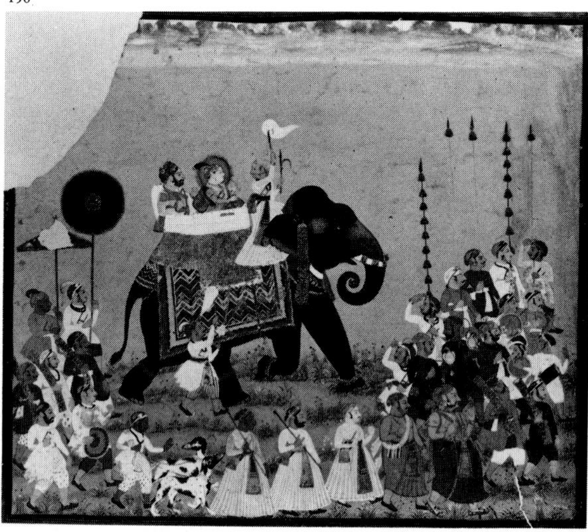

150
Maharana Raj Singh II Riding an Elephant
Udaipur, 1754. By Nuruddin
42 x 48.6 cm

The Maharana, with nimbus, sits in the howdah on the
elephant Eklinga Prasad, together with a sardar, Jodh
Singh, and a mahout holding chowries. Numerous
attendants accompany him with hawks, hounds and
regalia. Pale green background with cloud above. Red
border (damaged). The upper left corner of the picture
is missing.

Inscribed on the back: *śri. maharajadhiraja
maharanaji śri raj sighji ri
asavari ro pano hathi ekaliga prasad upare danta ro
hoda: [del.] mahe birajya thaka: śriji pachai joda sighji
camar rakhai phagan sud 2 smat 1810 ra varas ro [del.]
vaisakh sud 13 si nuredin najar huyo:*

The Maharana is here aged ten, shortly after his
accession. The picture shows some features associated
with the style of the slightly earlier painter, Jai Ram.
Another painting by Nuruddin, dated 1750, is in the
National Museum, New Delhi (see O. P. Sharma,
Indian Miniature Painting, fig. 35).

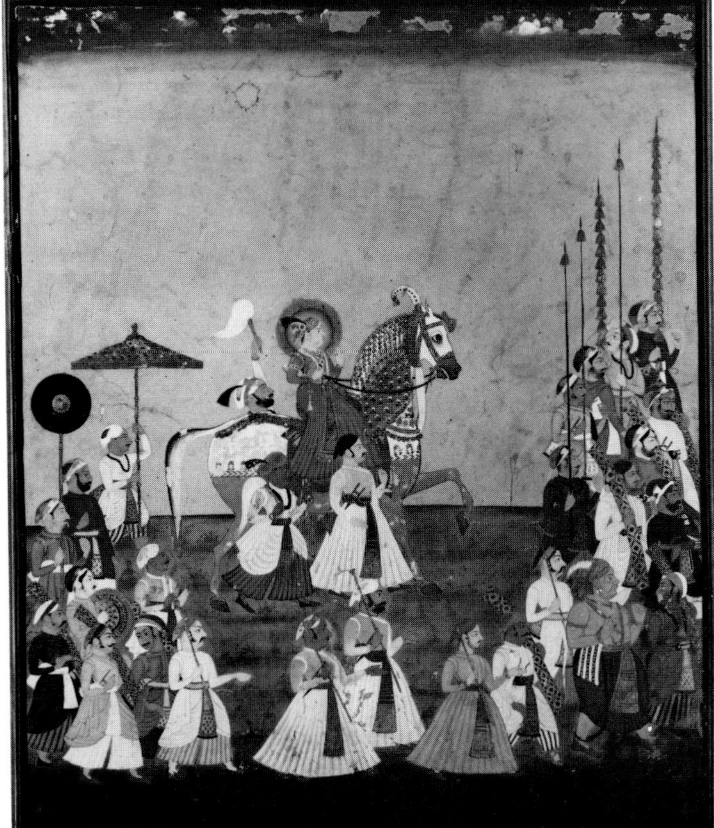

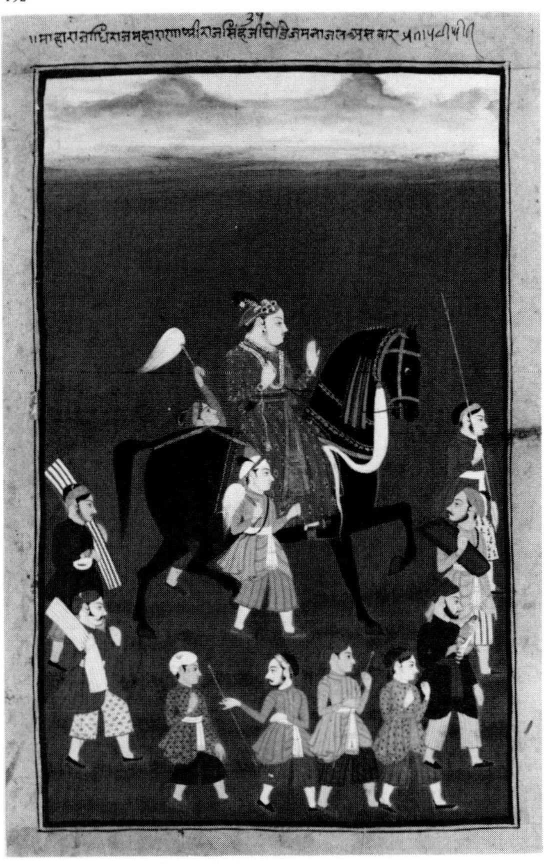

151

Maharana Raj Singh II Riding
Udaipur, 1755. By Ala Bagas
48 x 41 cm

The Maharana, with nimbus, in orange *jama* and *pagri*, rides a white horse, partly hennaed and hung with festoons and gold trappings, on the occasion of the 'Little Ganggor' festival (held on the 3rd of the dark half of Vaisakha and peculiar to Mewar; instituted, according to Shyamaldas, *Vir Vinod,* vol. I, p. 123, by Maharana Raj Singh I — see also Tod, *Annals and Antiquities of Rajasthan,* vol. II, p. 674). Numerous attendants accompany him. Pale green background with cloud above. Some flaking and repairs. Red border with black and white rules.

Inscribed on the back: *śrī. sigh śrī mahārajadhīrāja mahāranaji śrī raj sighji* [above: *chota*] *ri surat ro pano: samat 1810 ra vaisakh vadi 3 budhe gagangor ri din ro athamata ri asavari ra bhava ro pano: śriji ghode kohakalas asavar: samat 1811 ra phagan vadi 3 sukare re din: śri hajur nijar huyo: kalami citaro ala bagas ?pyanra ro: ri jari baja kare devani:*

152

Maharana Raj Singh II Riding
Udaipur, c. 1760
36.8 x 23.8 cm

The Maharana is depicted towards the end of his short life, riding a black stallion, accompanied by eleven attendants on foot. Khaki-green background with grey and white cloud above. Buff border, numbered 31 and inscribed: *maharajadhiraja maharana śri raj sinhaji ghode jamana jala asavar* [in another hand:] *pratap sighot.*

153

Maharana Raj Singh II Riding
Udaipur, late 18th century
27.5 x 22 cm

The Maharana, with nimbus, rides a partly hennaed grey stallion, accompanied by two chowry-bearers. Pale green background. Red border.

Inscribed on the back: *mharajadhiraja mharanoji śri raj sighji pratap sighot.*

Coarsely painted, with heavy green outline shadow round the Maharana's face.
Similar in style to cat. no. 209.

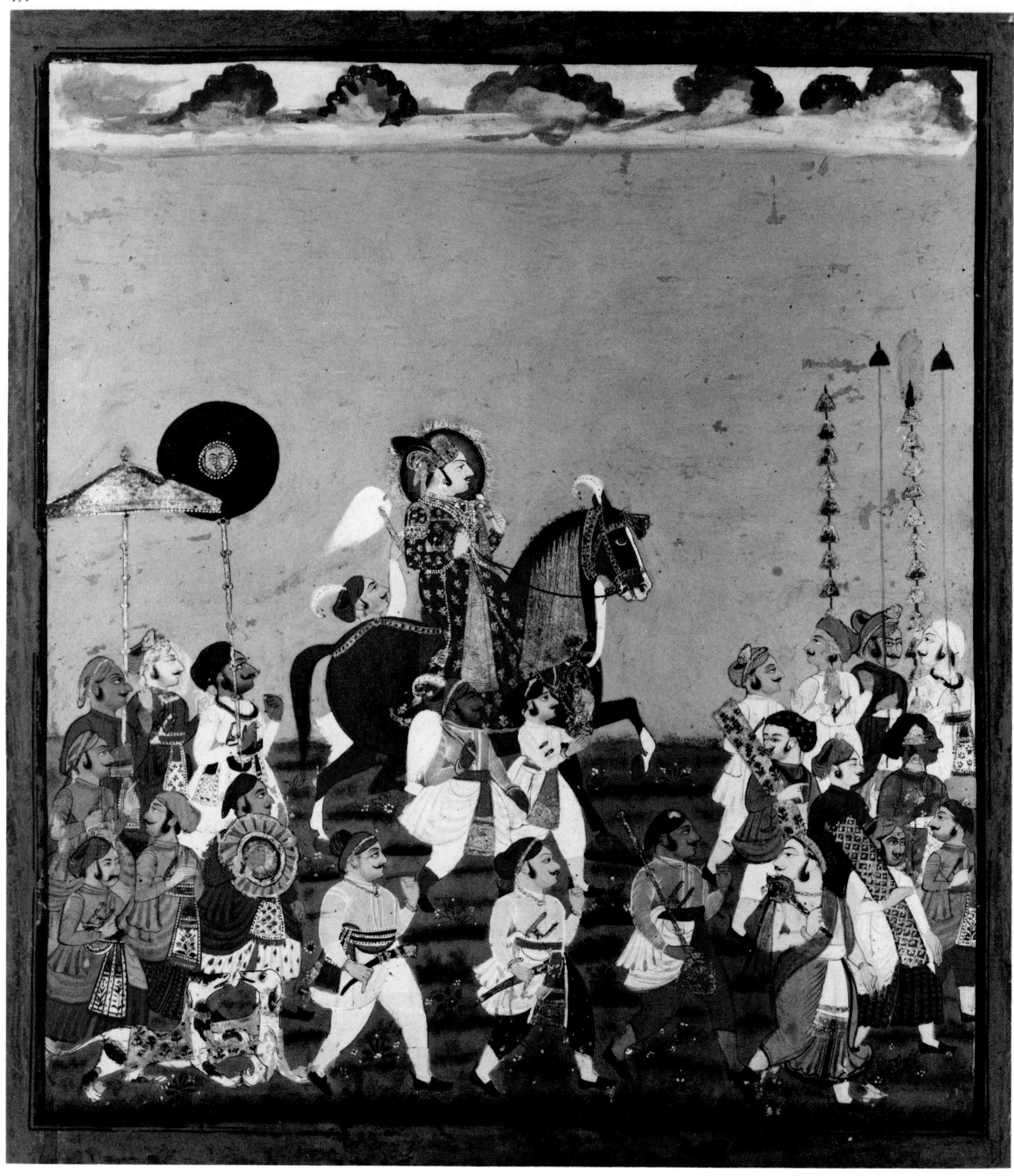

154

Maharana Ari Singh Riding
Udaipur, 1761. By Bhopa
40.2 x 36 cm

The Maharana, with nimbus, in gold *pagri* and *patka*
and crimson *jama* with gold floral pattern, rides a brown
stallion, accompanied by numerous attendants on foot
with regalia, dogs, etc. Grassy foreground with flowers,
pale green background with clouds above. Some flaking.
Red border.

Inscribed on the back: *śrī. pano 1 śrī maharajadhiraja
maharanaji śrī arasihaji ri surat ro ghode
pelavan asavar asavari ro pano kalami citaro bhopo nagā
ro* [in another hand:] *pano ori jmā asādh vid 4 samat
1818 varṣe.*

This inscription establishes that Bhopa (see also cat.
nos. 171, 172, 197) was the son of Naga, son of
Bhagvan (see cat. nos. 111 and 176). The picture is not
one of his best, however, being a coarse version of a by
now stereotyped composition.

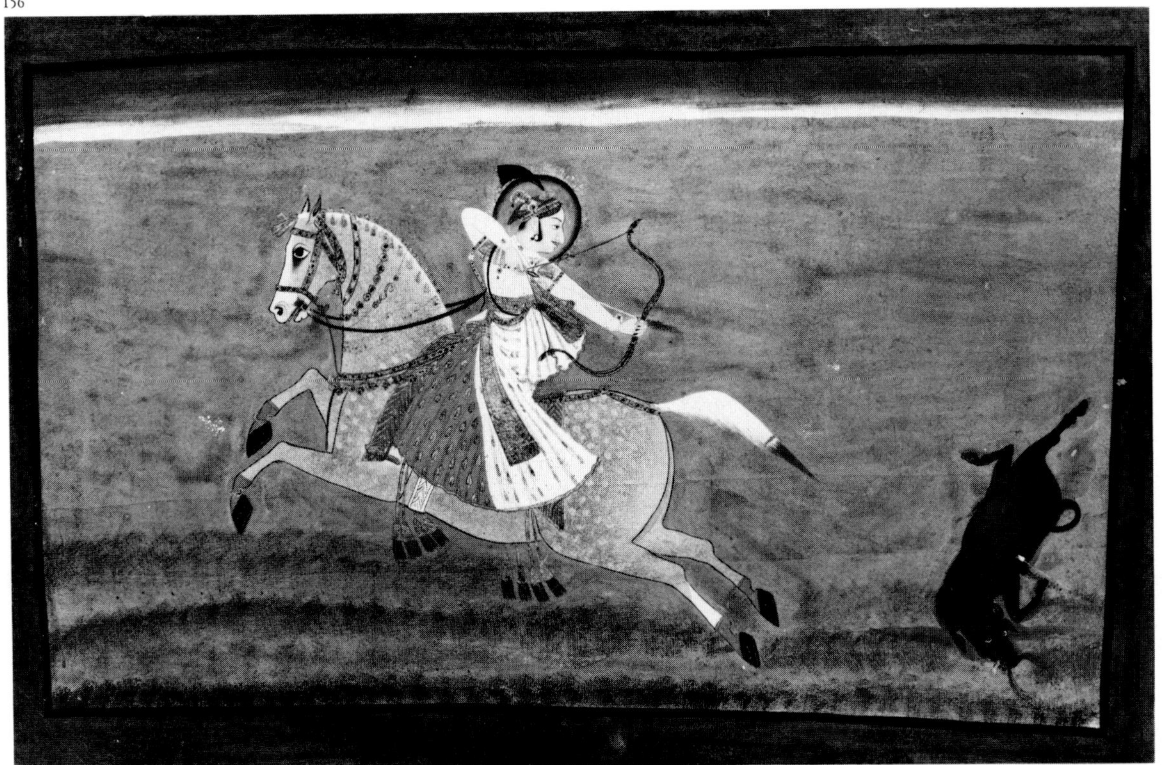

155

Maharana Ari Singh Riding
Udaipur, 1761. By Deva
46.5 x 39.7 cm

The Maharana, with nimbus, in gold-printed white
jama, rides a partially hennaed white horse,
accompanied by numerous attendants on foot with
regalia, dogs, etc. Turquoise-grey background with
clouds above. Some flaking. Red border with black and
white rules and an obscured inscription: *ghoro hara
bagas.*

Inscribed on the back: *ghore hara bagas asavar kati sudi
4 sam 1818 ayo cetare deve nijar ki ?dho* [in another
hand:] *maharajadhiraja maharaṇaji śri
arsiji ri sabi.*

156

Maharana Ari Singh Killing a Buffalo with an Arrow
Udaipur, 1761. By Jugarsi
23 x 38.5 cm

The Maharana, with nimbus, in white and orange
costume, rides a tan-coloured horse. He turns in the
saddle to dispatch a buffalo with an arrow, on the
occasion of the autumnal Navaratri festival (see cat.
no. 210). Pale green background, with cloth-pad
blotches in the foreground. Red border.

Inscribed on the back: *maharajadhinraja
maharanaji śri arasihiji ri surat ro
pano ghode diladirava asavar asoji norata mahe atham
tera? vela mhe ?pag... ari hathaṇi age bhesa upre
bhalaka thini ramadaji karta thaka ri sibi ro
kalami citra jugarasi ro ki do so ori jama pos sud 7 sinai
samat 1818 varse mahe jma.*

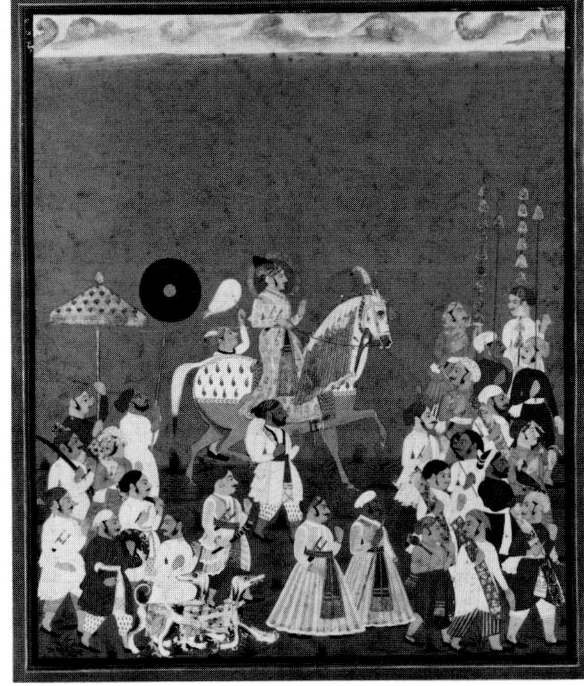

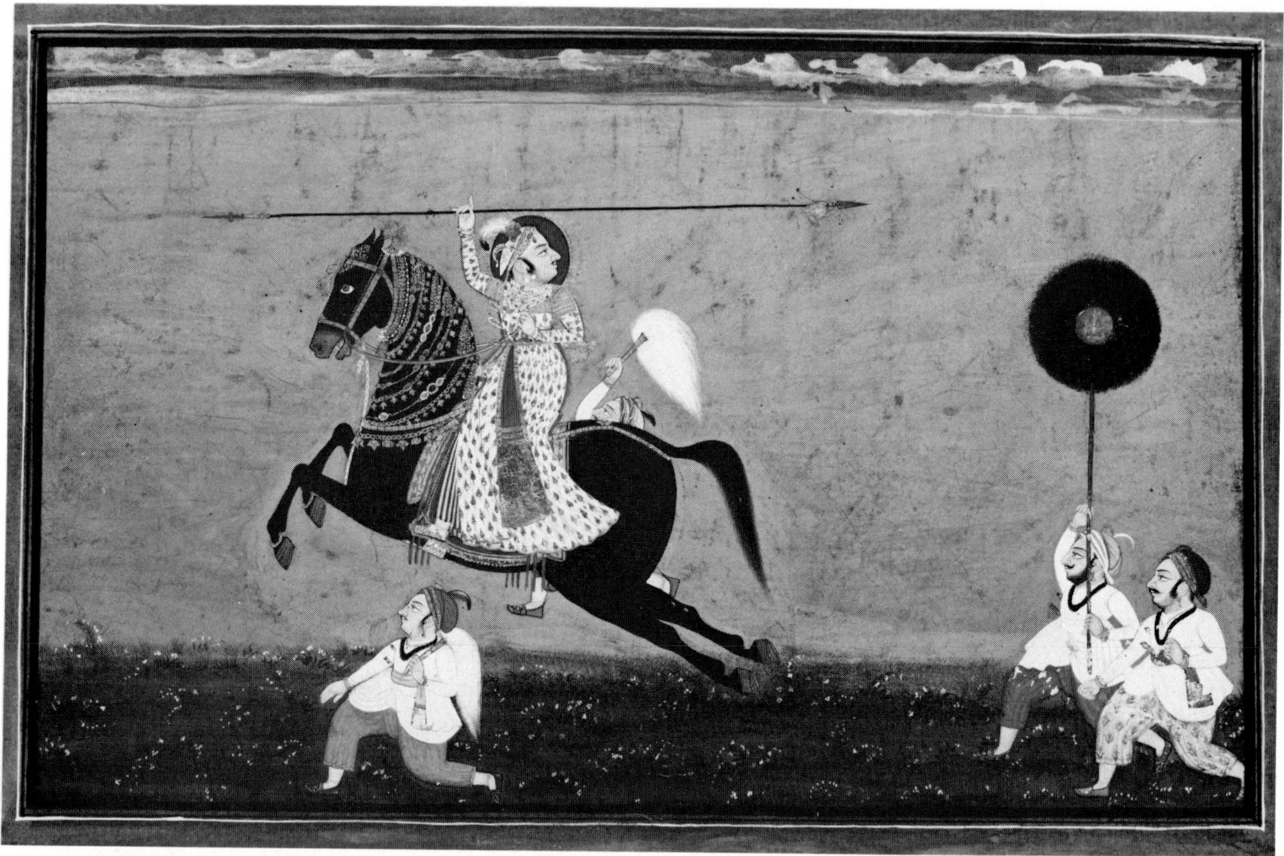

157

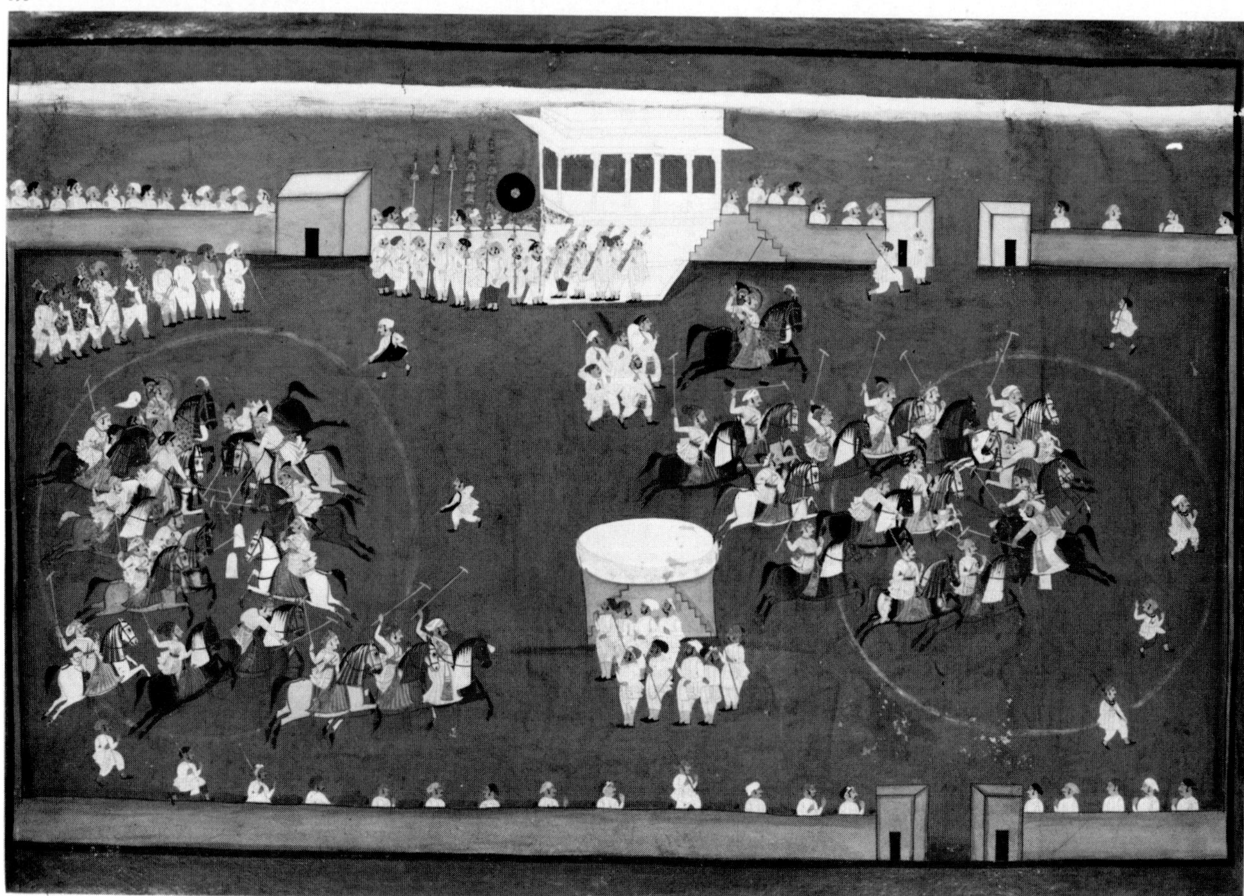

158

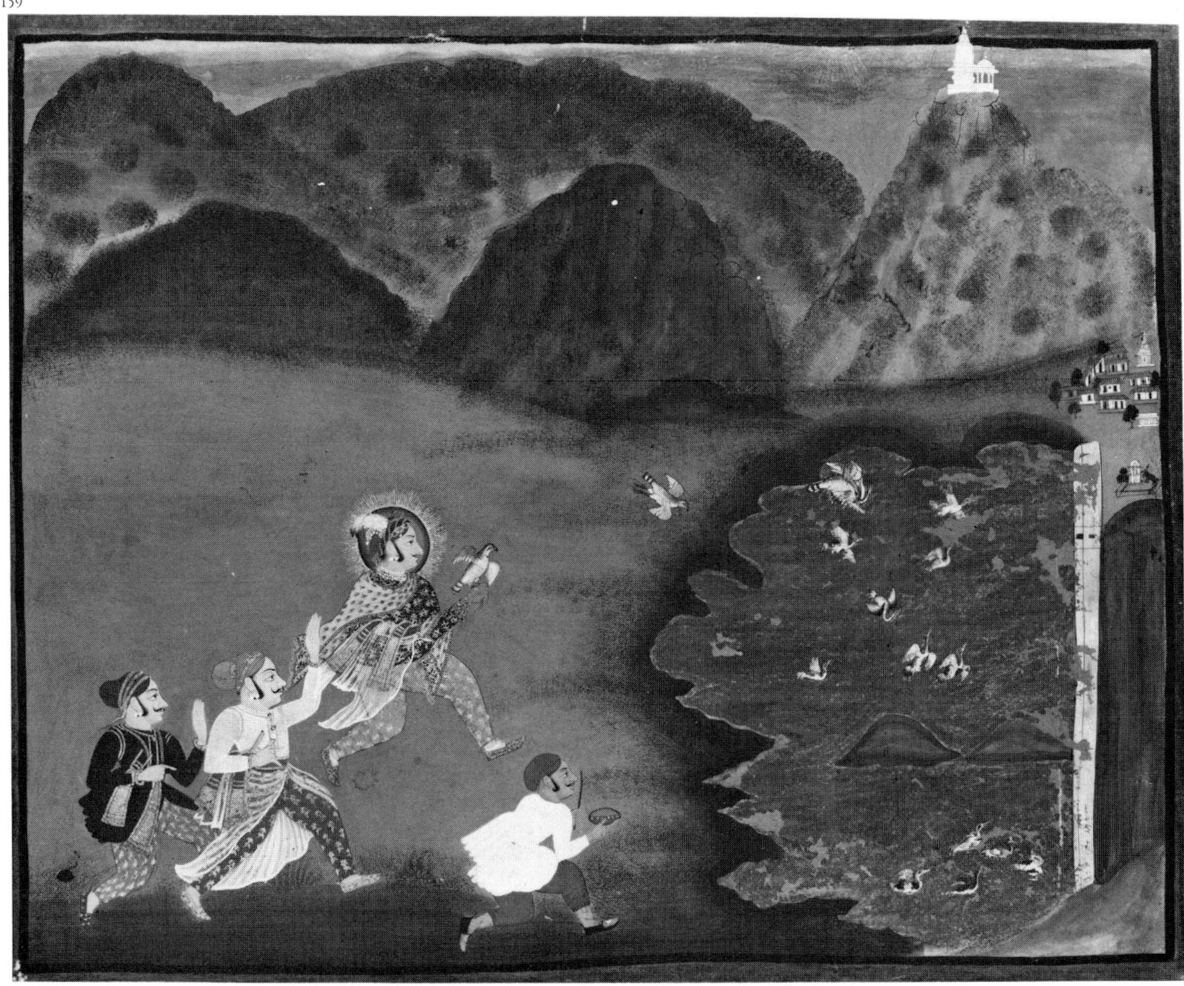

157
Maharana Ari Singh Riding
Udaipur, 1762
23.9 x 39 cm

The Maharana, with nimbus, rides a galloping dark chestnut stallion; he turns in the saddle and wields a spear in one hand. Four running attendants accompany him. Yellowish-green background with cloud above. Red border with black and white rules.

Inscribed on the back: *maharajadhiraja maharanaji śri arasihiji ri surat ro ghode he* [del.] *lala asavar bhalo pherata thaka pano asavari mhe nijar huvo so ori jama maha sud 8 sam 1818 vars.*

158
Maharana Ari Singh Playing Polo
Udaipur, 1761. By Bhima Sutar
39.5 x 63.2 cm

The Maharana, playing polo with his sardars in the Chaugan, appears twice, with nimbus, on the periphery of two mêlées. Numerous servants stand in attendance, some of them with regalia near the royal pavilion, and spectators line the walls of the arena. Two water-carriers *(bhistis)* sprinkle water on the ground from their bags. The arena is shown with a pale blue-green ground. Red border.

Inscribed on the back: *maharajadhiraja maharanaji śri arasihaji ri suṛat ro ghode mega popa(?) asavar cogan mhe cogan gata khelta thaka ri sibi ro kalami citra bhima sutar ro ki do so ori jama asoj vid 14 ri vai sam 1818 mhe jama huvo.*

159
Maharana Ari Singh Hawking
Udaipur, 1762. By Jugarsi
32.2 x 41 cm

The Maharana, with nimbus, accompanied by his *dhabhais*, Rupji and Kikaji, is seen on foot hunting waterfowl. He releases a hawk which takes a duck in flight above a lake. Green landscape background with a distant town and heavily outlined mauve-pink hills. Red border.

Inscribed on the back: *śri. pano 1 śri maharajadhiraja maharanaji śri arasihaji ri surat ro ?chadagama devali rat lava ri runa me murgabi ri sakar khelta thaka hath me jurabaja śri hajur pache dhaabhai rupaji ubha thaka dhaabhai kikoji ubha thaka pano kalami citara jugarasi ro ki do thako vile prohet anop ram re* [in another hand:] *pano ori jma phagan vid 11 sam 1818 mhe jma.*

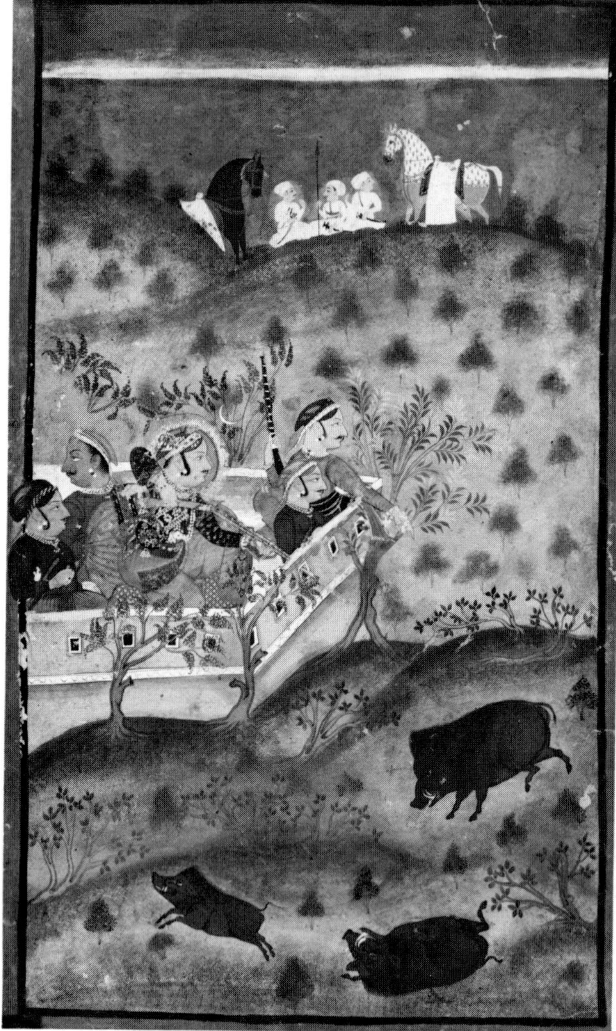

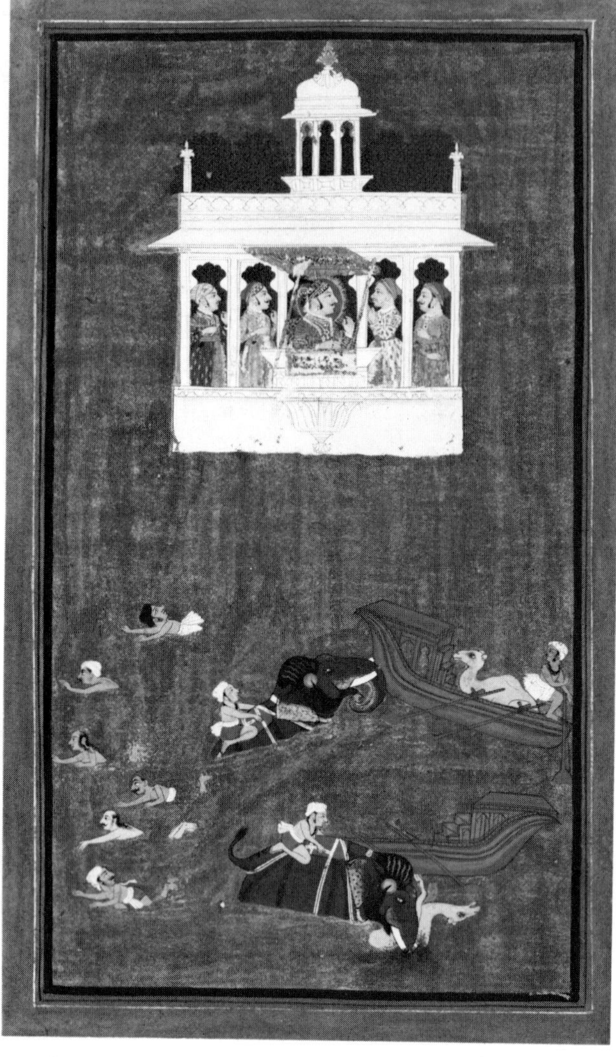

160
Maharana Ari Singh Shooting Boar
Udaipur, c. 1762
36.3 x 21.5 cm

The Maharana, with nimbus, shoots boar from a
hunting-box, accompanied by four sardars, Maharaja
Baghji (holding a gun) and Maharaja Durjan Singh, and
(behind the Maharana) Maharaja Bakhat Singh and Rao
Ram Chand. Three attendants wait with horses in the
distance. Red border, much trimmed.

Inscribed on the back: *marajadhiraja śrī arī sīghjī cīrjī
vīsur rī odī rata preta rī mudā age
maraja vāgjī vaduk hāth me varovari vāgjī rī
maraja ?darajan sīghjī dīvan pache
maraja bakhat sīghjī dīvan rī nimanī
vaju rava ram cadjī vedale vakhat sīgot.*

161
An Incident on the Pichola Lake
Udaipur, 1762
28.5 x 16.5 cm

Maharana Ari Singh, with nimbus, appears in the
balcony of a small lake-palace, flanked by two sardars on
each side. In the (oxidised) silver water in front of him
an accident has occurred. An elephant, Jasa Tilak,
swimming across in the water, has attacked and mortally
wounded a camel which was also being ferried across by
boatmen in a barge. Red border.

Inscribed on the back: *maharajadhiraja maharanajī
śrī arasīhajī rī surat śrījī jala midra birajyā
thaka hāthī jasa tilak pāni mhe chudavyo so uta marato
thako tīrī sībī ro citra* [artist's name omitted] *ro kī do
samat 1819 rā bhadava vid 4 rī vau mhe jama pāno
babat asavari mhe thī avyo.*

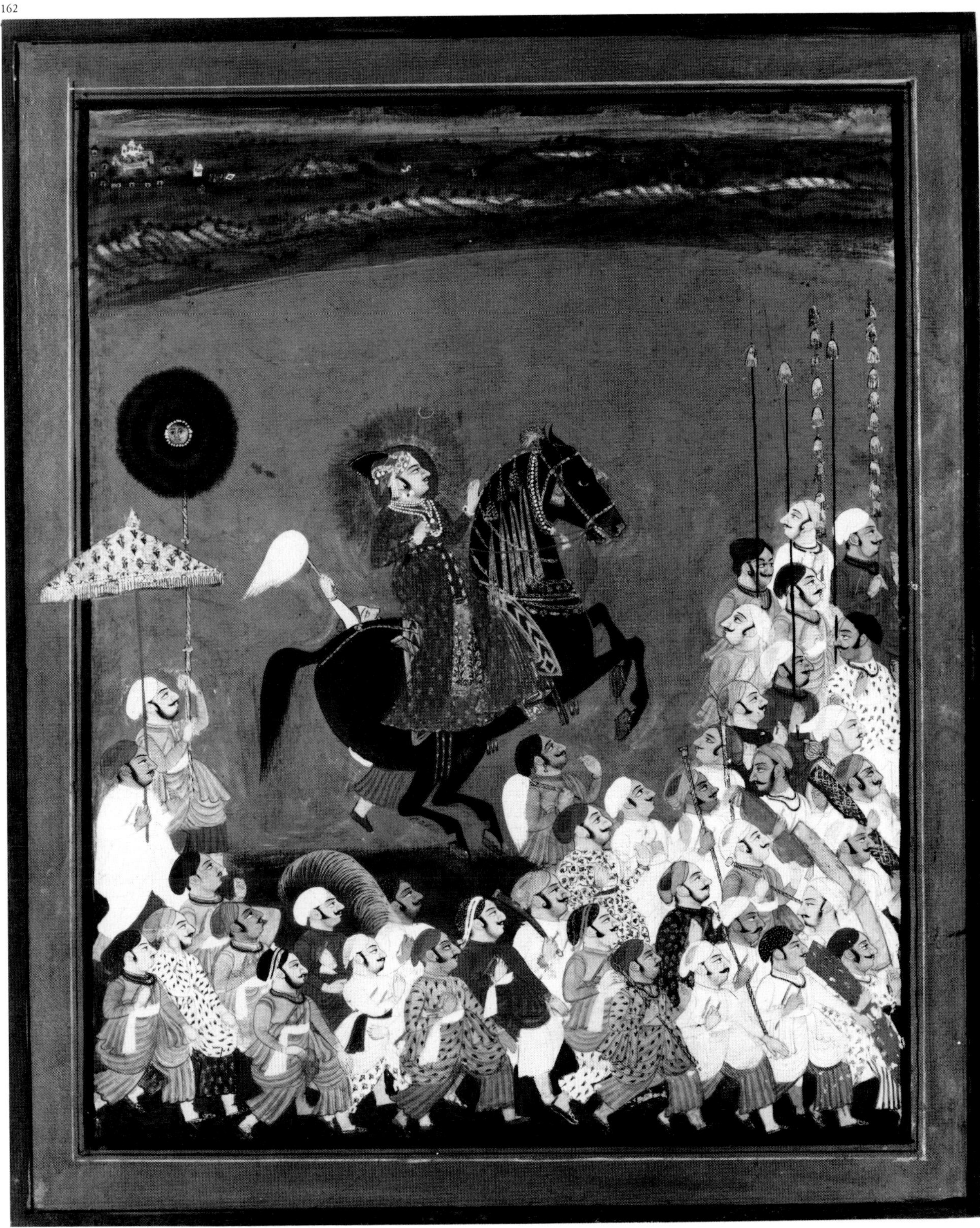

162

Maharana Ari Singh Riding
Udaipur, 1762
40 x 32.5 cm

The Maharana, with nimbus, in a gold-printed red *jama,* rides a chestnut stallion, accompanied by numerous attendants on foot with regalia, etc.

Yellowish-green background and distant landscape with diminutive huntsmen and village women. Red inner border with black and white rules; green outer border.

Inscribed on the back: *mahāranajī śrī arsījī* [in another hand:] *pāno orī jamā samat 1819 rā bhadavā sud 15 mhe asavārī mhe thī orī jmā.*

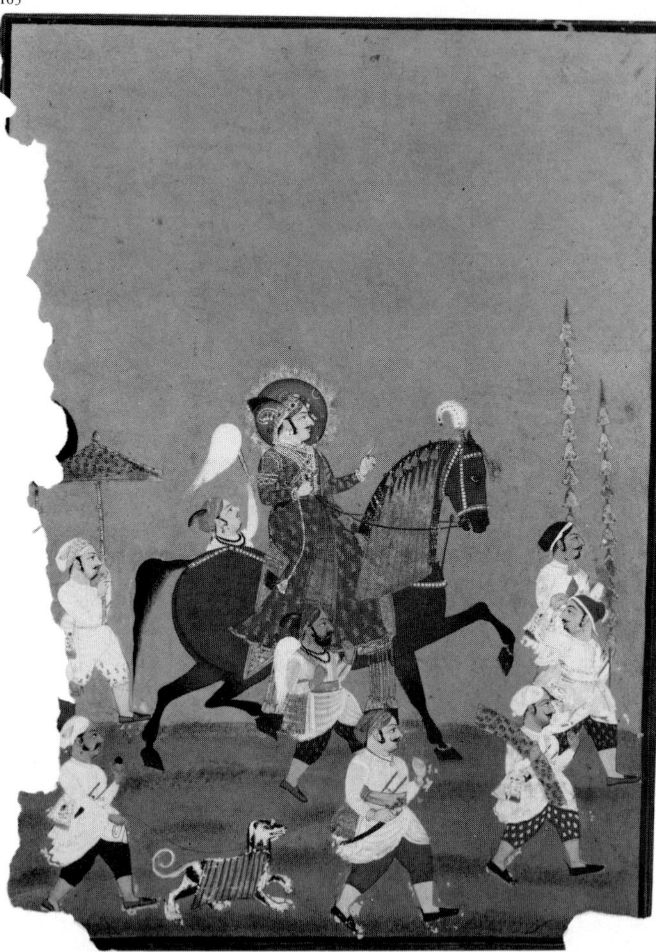

163

Maharana Ari Singh Riding
Udaipur, 1762. By Kesu Ram
39.5 x 29 cm

The Maharana, with nimbus, wearing a gold-printed crimson *jama,* rides a chestnut stallion, accompanied by attendants on foot with chowries, regalia and a hound. Pale green background. Severely damaged by rodents at the left hand and lower edges. Trimmed red border with black ruling.

Inscribed on the back: *śrī rāmjī. pano 1 śrī maharajadhirāja maharaṇajī śrī arasīhajī ri surat ro ghode arabī..?ara asavār huva thaka pano asavārī ro pano kalamī citāre keso rām nijar ki do vile prohat devanath re* [in another hand:] *pano orī jamā samat 1819 ra bhadava sud 11 mhe jma.*

164

Maharana Ari Singh with Two Sardars
Udaipur, 1762. By Kesu Ram
24.1 x 18.7 cm

The Maharana, with nimbus, is seated against a bolster beneath a canopy; before him, with their shields against their knees, sit Rawat Jaswant Singh, to whom the Maharana presents a *pan* as a token of dismissal, and Raja Raghodev. The Maharana's *dhabhai,* Rupji, sits on the right. Pale green background. Red border.

Inscribed above: *maharaṇajī śrī arasījī sama ravat jasut sighjī rāja raghodevajī pachādi dhabhai rupajī.*
Inscribed on the back: *śrī. pano 1 śrī maharajadhirāja maharaṇajī śrī arasīhajī ri surat ro birajya thaka sama ravat jasut sighjī rāja ragodejī betha thaka gadī pache dhaabhai rupajī betha thaka pano kalamī citara kesu rām ki do vile prohet anop rām re* [in another hand:] *pano orī jma ?ki [phagan?] vid 8 samat 1818 vars.*

165

Maharana Ari Singh Hunting Bear
Udaipur, 1763
48 x 31 cm

The Maharana, with nimbus, and three mounted sardars converge with their spears on a bear which is savaging a huntsman on foot. Other huntsmen and dogs join in the fray and servants stand in attendance. A lake appears in the distance with palaces and ghats. Red border.

Inscribed on the back: *mahaṇajī śrī arsījī* [in another hand:] *pano orī jama samat 1820 ra besak sud 8 mhe jma asavārī mhe thī jma.*

Another version of this subject, reportedly by Jiva and dated in Pausa of V.S.1820 = 1763-4 A.D., was sold at Sotheby's, 8 October 1979, lot 125.

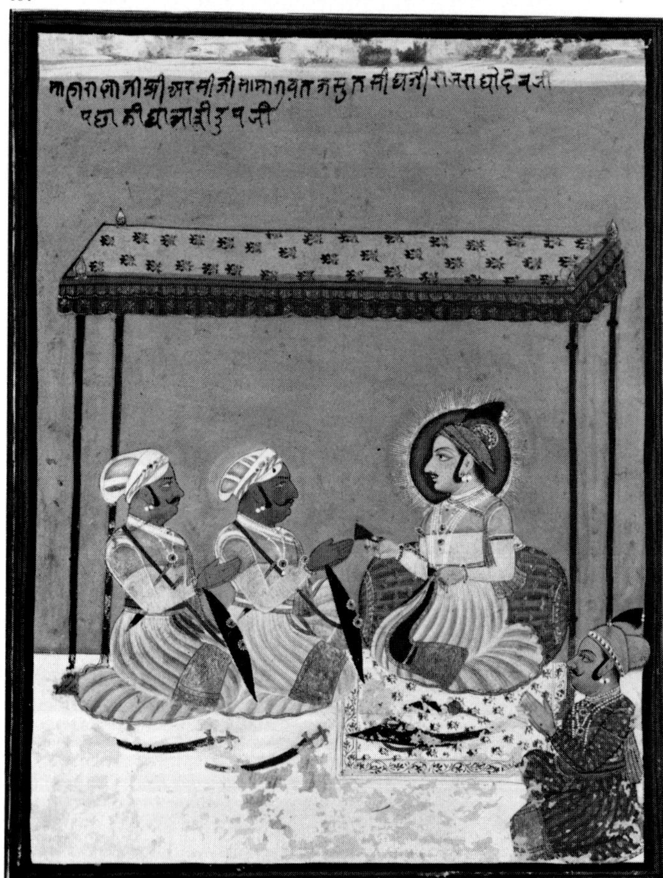

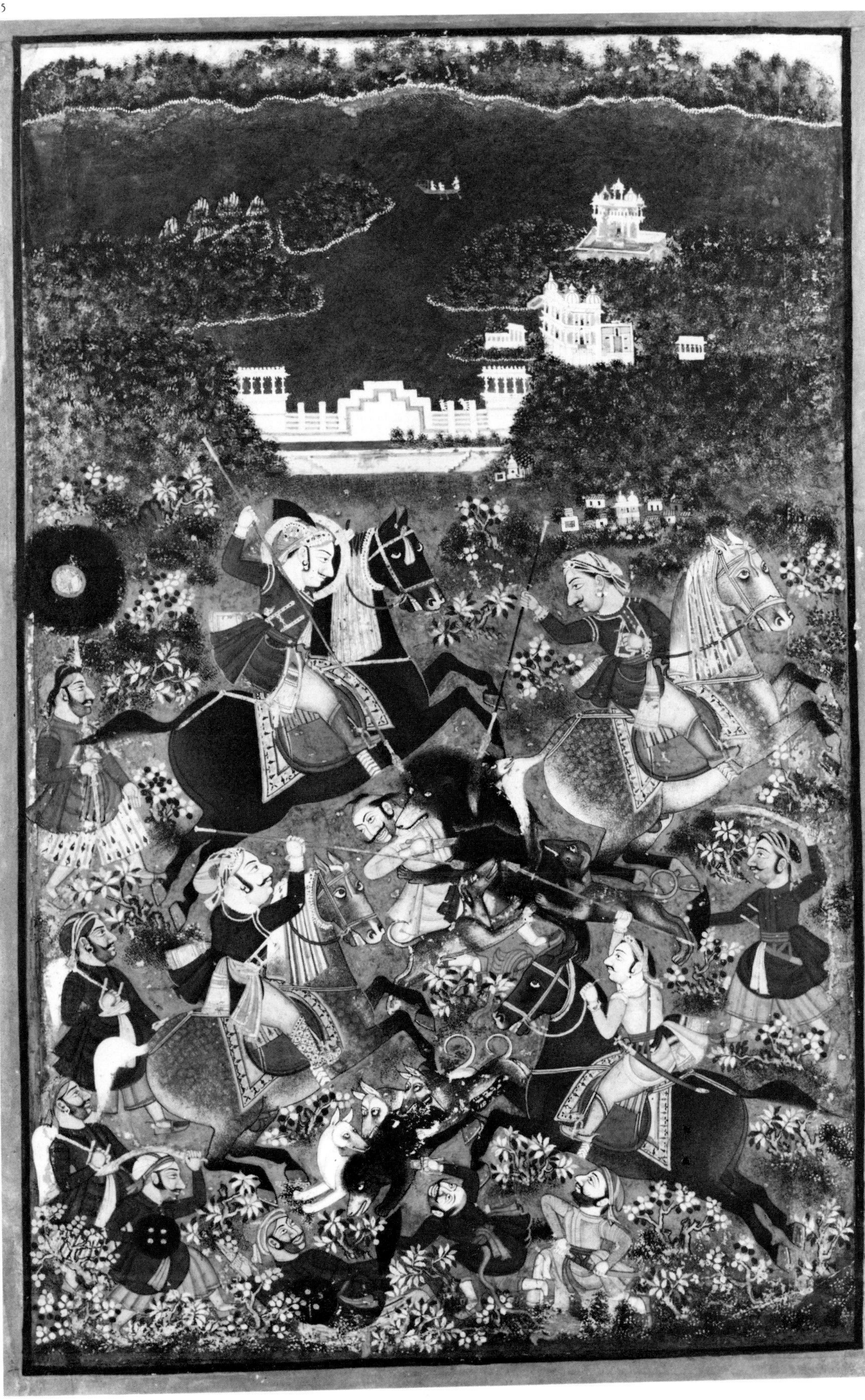

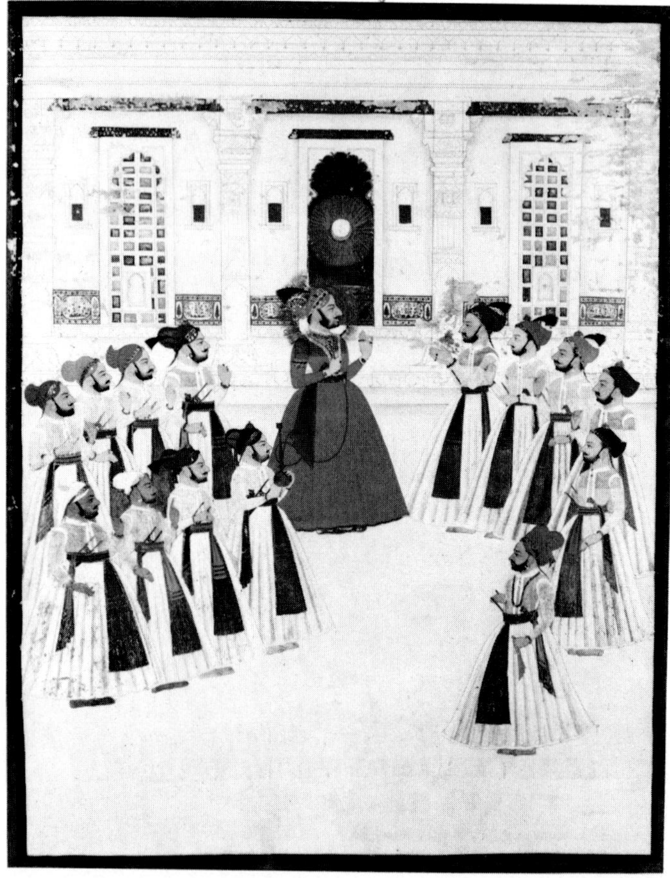

Maharana Ari Singh with his Sardars
Udaipur, 1764. By Bhima
47.3 x 37.6 cm

The Maharana, with nimbus, in orange *pagri* and *jama*,
stands in the lower *Chitrashala* in the palace, attended
by fourteen sardars and members of his family. Among
those on the right are the Maharana's uncles, Baghji and
Durjan Singh, Maharaja Sagat Singh, Chundavat Bhim
Singh and Rawat Durjan Singh. On the left are Rupji,
Baba Sagat Singh, Baba Surat Singh, Jhala Udai Singh,
Kikaji, Jodaji, Ranavat Durjan Singh and Amar Chand.
Behind the Maharana appears an image of the sun,
described by Tod as 'a huge painted sun of gypsum in
high relief, with gilded rays' (*Annals and Antiquities of
Rajasthan*, vol. II, p. 659) and symbolizing the
Maharanas' legendary solar ancestry. On each side of it
are bays containing panels of coloured glass. Red border.

Inscribed on the back: *śrī ramjī. pano 1 śrī
maharajadhīraja maharanajī śrī
arasihajī rī surat śrījī citrasālī hethalī
śrījī ubha thaka itra sardar śrī hajur ubha
thaka itra sirdar sma? kako bagjī pache kako durjan
sighjī maharaja sagat sighjī cudavat bhim
sighjī ravat durjan sighjī pano caran itra sardar
sama ubha pache dhaabhai rupajī ubha
baba sagat sighjī baba surat sighjī pache jalo ude
sighjī dhaabhai kikojī ubha thaka
dhaabhai jodojī śrī hajur huko arogavata thaka ranavat
durjan sighjī pat?ara amar candjī itra sardar pache ubha
thaka pano citare bhime śrī hajur nijar kī do* [in another
hand:] *pano orī jma samat 1821 ra bhadava sud 4 mhe
jma.*

167

Maharana Ari Singh in Durbar
Udaipur, 1765. By Bakhta
55.8 x 44 cm
(Colour Plate No. 14)

The Maharana, with nimbus, is seated with his sardars in
formal durbar at night in the upper palace courtyard
decorated with blue and white tiles. Seated in front of
him are his uncles, Baghji and Durjan Singh, Baba
Sagat Singh, Chauhan Nathji, Ranavat Visan Singh,
Baba Sagat Singh(?), Surat Singh and Ranavat Dhirat
Singh. Standing on the far left are Pancholi Gumani
Ram, Ajit Singh, Kisor Das, Lal, two others and,
wearing white and holding a scroll of paper, the artist
Bakhta himself *(detail)*. Seated on the right are
Chundavat Bhim Singh, Ravat Durjan Singh, Rupji,
Jhala Udai Singh, Kikaji, Jodaji and Amar Chand.
Below is the empty gallery known by Tod as 'the Surya
mahall, or "hall of the sun", so called from a medallion
of the orb in basso-rilievo which decorates the wall'
(*Annals and Antiquities of Rajasthan*, vol. I, p. 551; see
also cat. no. 166 above). Trimmed red border.

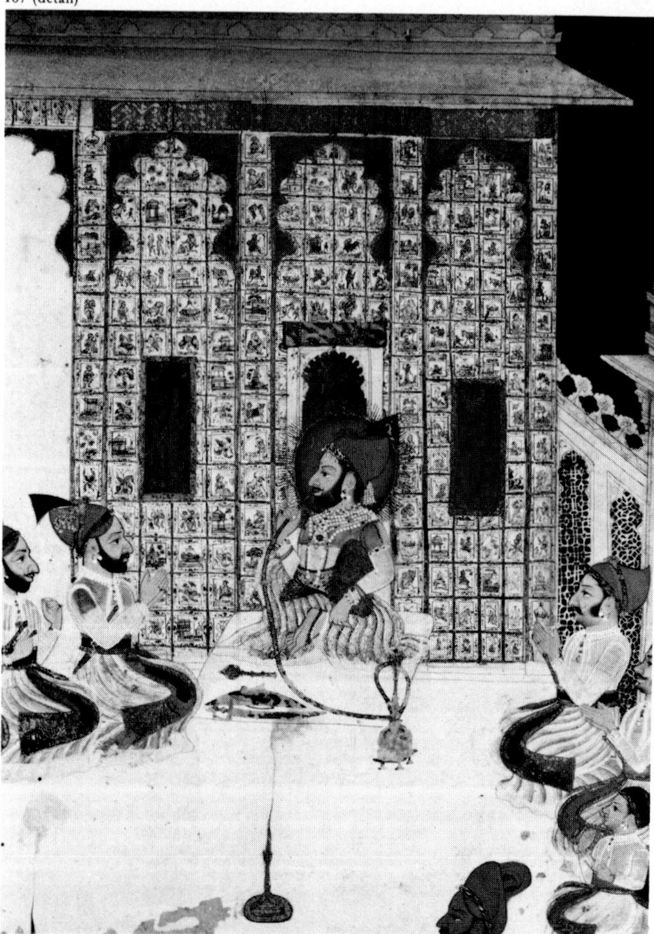

167 (detail)

Inscribed on the back: *śri ramji. pano 1 śri
maharajadhiraja maharanaji
śri arasihaji ri surat ro śriji ri janam gatha re din rate
śriji bhithi ri citrasali me śriji
cagatana? ro nacakara o? so itra siradar śri hajur betha
thaka jimani du?or me kako bagji kaka durjan
sighji babo sagat sighji cuhavan nathji ranavat
visan sighji baoba sagat sighji ba surat sighji
ranavat dhirat sighji sama pasavan ubha
thaka pancoli gumani ram ajet sigh saha kisor
das meto...? dhaabhai samo bhai lalo citaro bakhato
ubho davi baju cudavat bhim sighji ravat durjan
sighji dhaabhai rupaji mada age jalo ude
sighji dhaabhai kikoji dhaabhai jodoji
pidar? amar cadji samo betho thako caran pano pano
citare bakhate śri hajur nijar ki do* [in another hand:]
pano ori jama samat 1821 ra phagun vid 11.

This painting is the latest dated example so far known
from Bakhta's early period at the Udaipur court, before
he finally went to work at the *thikana* of Deogarh (see
discussion of cat. no. 130). He has included in it a self-
portrait holding a roll of paper which may be compared
with his son Chokha's portrait of him as an old man in
a picture dated 1811 (Andhare, 'Paintings from the
Thikana of Deogarh', *Prince of Wales Museum Bulletin*,
10, 1967, figs. 46-47). Bakhta's portrait studies here
show the beginnings of the great talent that he was to
display at Deogarh. He has playfully reinterpreted the
vegetal motifs and stock Dutch genre scenes on the blue
and white tiles, filling them with summary sketches of
boats, horsemen, various animals including elephants,
European and Indian figures smoking, Indian landscapes
and erotic scenes. These tiles, which are still to be seen
in situ in the palace, are of Dutch and Far Eastern origin
and were probably obtained from the Dutch East India
Company some time after J. J. Ketelaar's visit to
Udaipur in 1711 (see cat. no. 70); the courtyard in
which they are installed, sometimes called the Chini ki
Chitrasali, was completed in 1723 (Shyamaldas, *Vir
Vinod*, vol. II, p. 956; see also H. Goetz, 'Holländische
Wandfliesen in einem altindischen Königspalast', *Oud-
Holland*, LXVI, 1951, pp. 239-240, and R. Cameron,
Shadows from India, London, 1958, pp. 92-93).

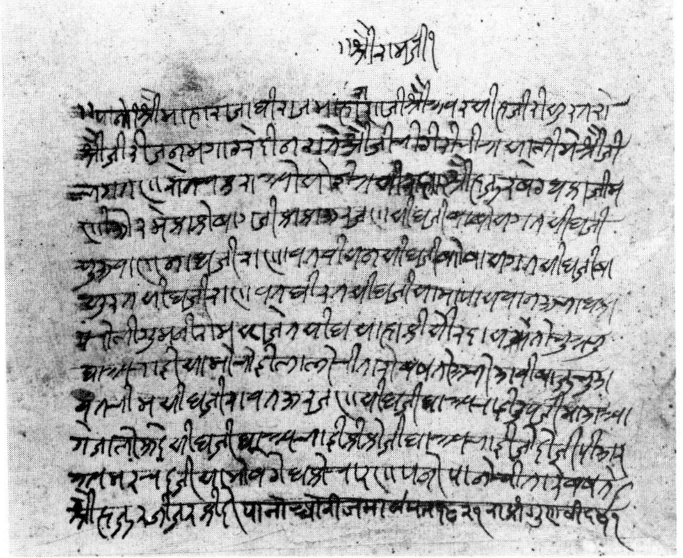

167 (detail)

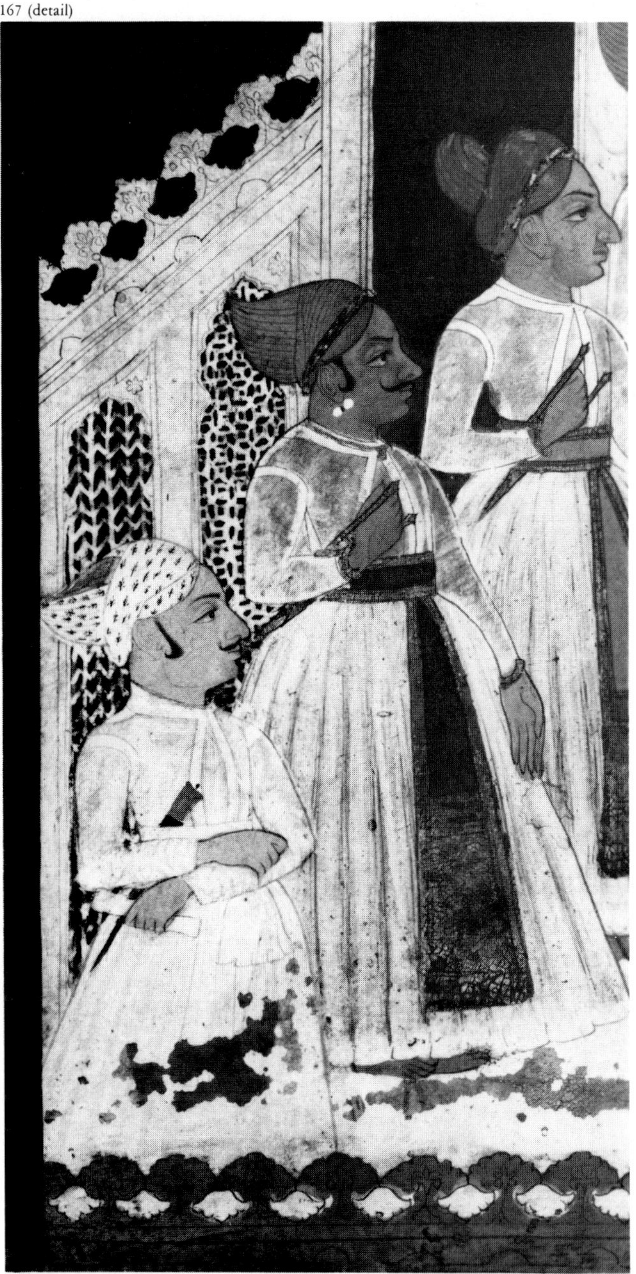

167 (detail)

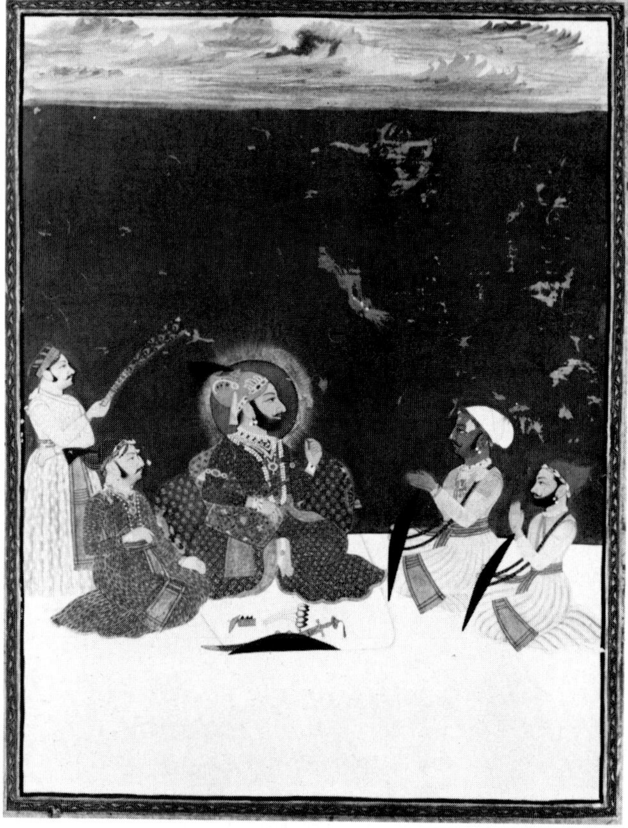

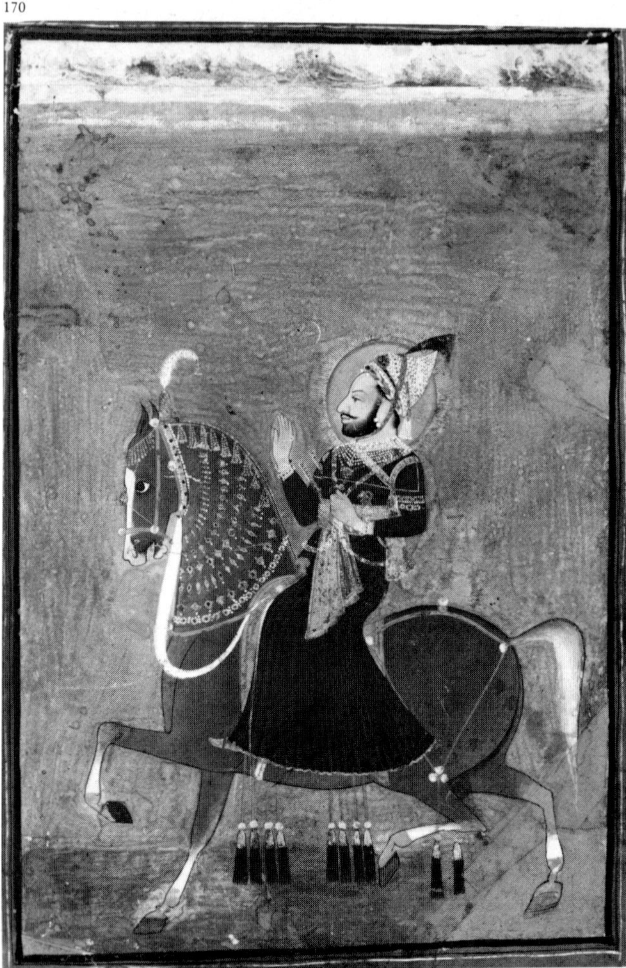

168

Maharana Ari Singh Hunting Boar
Udaipur, 1762. By Jugarsi
46 x 66 cm
(Colour Plate No. 15)

The Maharana, with nimbus, is pig-sticking, accompanied by Sagat Singh, Samat Singh and Rupji and a number of attendants on foot; the Maharana is seen four times in all. Blue and green landscape with a palm-fringed silver river and numerous stylized trees dabbed in with a cloth-pad. Red border.

Inscribed on the back: *śrī. pano 1 śrī maharajadhiraja maharaṇaji śrī arasihaji rī surat ro ghode megapopa? asavar aṅdari khaju rame sura ūpare barachi khavata thaka ītra sardar śrī hajur sathe barachi khavata thaka/ vigat/ baboji sagat sighji/ kura samat sighji/ dhaabhai rupaji/ mia aku? khadu?/ coth ko ghode ca..yo thako/ muli khali sura vatavati thaki/ pano kalami citara jugarasi ro ki do thako vile prohet anop ram re* [in another hand:] *pano ori jama mha sud 10 samat 1818 vars.*

169

Maharana Ari Singh with Sardars
Udaipur, 1765. By Shiva
36.3 x 28 cm

The Maharana, with nimbus, wearing an orange *pagri* and blue-grey *jama* with gold quatrefoil pattern, is seated against a magenta and gold bolster. He receives Raja Raghodev and Rawat Durjan Singh, who fold their hands in respect. On the left are the Maharana's *dhabhai*, Rupji, and Pancholi Gumani Ram holding the *morchal*. Green background with multi-coloured cloud above. Good quality; some flaking. Blue-grey inner and outer margins with gold decoration; salmon-pink border with gold quatrefoil decoration, inscribed in gold: *śrī ekaliṅga sada mahata: maharaji ..? ve raja maharana śrī ari siṅhaji cidaje?*

Inscribed on the back: *śrī ramji. pano 1 śrī maharajadhiraja maharaṇaji śrī arasihaji rī surat ro śriji birajya thaka sama raja ragodeji ravat durjan sighji betho thaka pache dhaabhai rupaji betha thaka pancoli gumani ram morchal rakhto thako śrī pano citare sive śrī hajur nijar ki do* [in another hand:] *samat 1822 ra huti caitra sud 6 mhe ori jma.*

170

Maharana Ari Singh Riding
Udaipur, c. 1765
29.5 x 20.1 cm

The Maharana, bearded and with nimbus, wears a *pagri* with chevron pattern and a deep blue *jama* and rides a pale brown stallion. Yellowish-green background with cloud above. Some discolouration, repairs and repainting. Red border with black and white rules.

Inscribed on the back: *maharaṇaji śrī arsiji.*

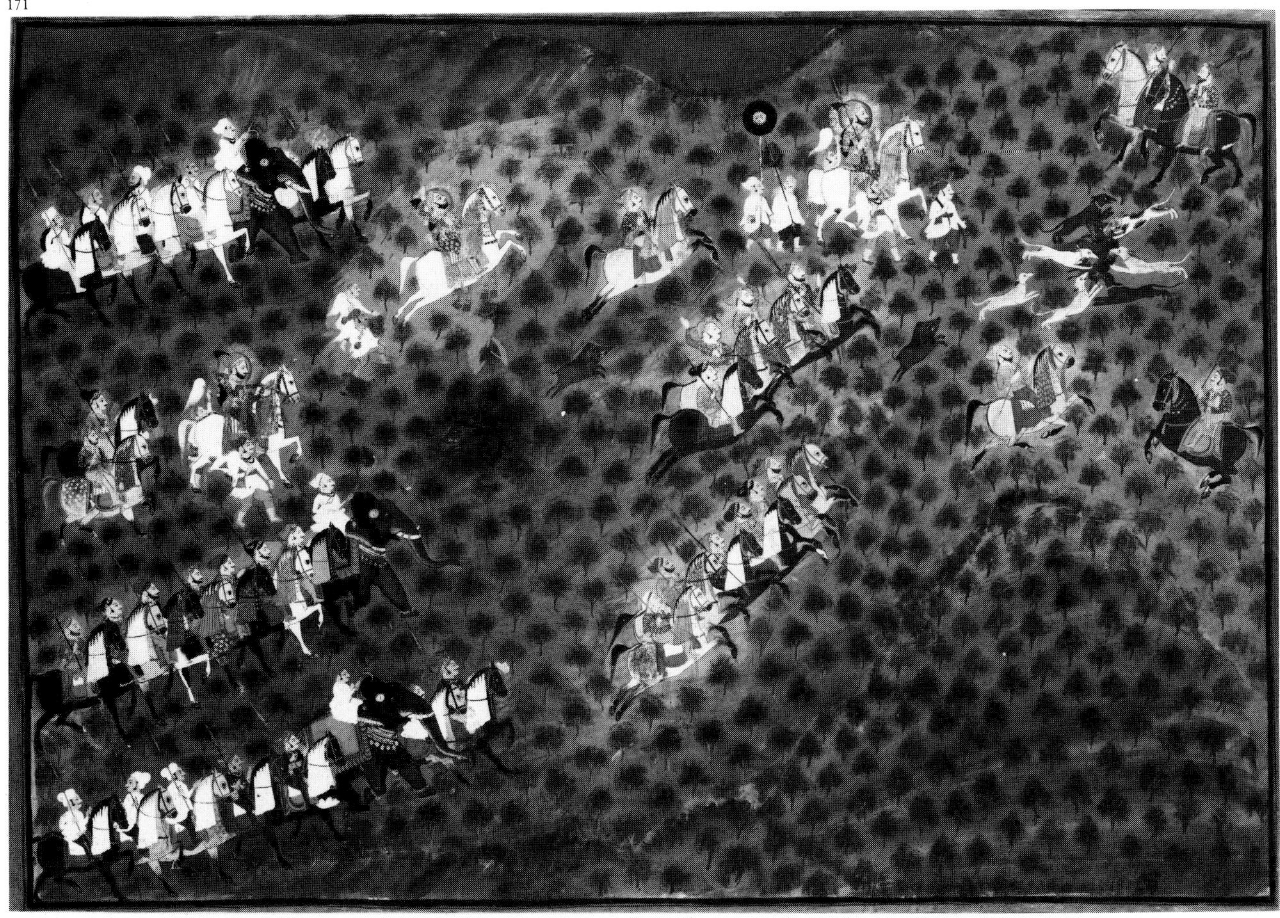

171
Maharana Ari Singh Hunting Boar at Nahar Magra
Udaipur, 1765. By Bhopa
46 x 67.3 cm

The Maharana, with nimbus, riding a white horse, is
seen thrice, shooting at a boar, pursuing it with a spear
and watching as the hounds make a kill at the far right.
Among the sardars accompanying him are his uncles,
Baghji and Durjan Singh, his *dhabhais*, Rupji, Kikaji
and Jodaji, and many others; mounted attendants and
three elephants make up the escort. The hilly landscape
of Nahar Magra is shown covered with dense even rows
of stylized trees dabbed in with a cloth-pad. Red border.

Inscribed on the back: *śri ramji. pano 1 śri
maharajadhiraja maharanaji
śri arasihaji ri surat ro ghore chaba sudar asavar hua
thaka nare magare sura ri sikar khelta thaka itra sirdar
sikar me base ani śri hajur* [del.] *sirdar kako bagji
kako durjan sighji dhaabhai rupaji dhaabhai
kikoji dhaabhai jodoji maraja sagat sighji
jalo samat sighji jalo ude sighji ranavat ?vavasan
sighji cudavat bhim sighji ravat durjan sighji cahuan
nathji babo surat sighji babo sagat sighji ranavat
dhirat sighji pa?. ar amar candji babo sambhuji ani
?duji 2 me ?meto kano ani tiji ume solanki bhavani das
pano citare bhope śri hajur najar ki do* [in another
hand:] *pano ori jma samat 1822 ra asoj vid 13 mhe jma.*

172
Maharana Ari Singh
Udaipur, 1766. By Bhopa (?)
24.1 x 16.5 cm

The Maharana, with nimbus, wearing an orange-red
jama, stands facing right, holding a lotus. Green
background. Some flaking and damage. Black margin
with silver meander; red border.

Inscribed on the back: *śri ramji. pano 1 śri
maharajadhiraja mahaji śri
arasihaji ri surat śriji ubha thaka pano
citare bhope? śri hajur nijar ki do pane ..?ar ro* [in
another hand:] *pano ori jama samat 1823 ra asoj vid 3.*

173
Maharana Ari Singh Hunting Boar
Udaipur, 1766
22.5 x 30.5 cm

The Maharana, with nimbus, riding a grey stallion,
transfixes a boar with a spear, while another boar lies
bleeding on its side. Pale blue-grey background. Red
border; inscribed above: *ghodo helala.*

Inscribed on the back: *maharanaji śri arasihaji. pano 1
śriji ri surat ro ghode helala asavar sura ?upe barachi
vavata thaka ro babat asavari mhe thi avyo so jma samat
1822 ra maha sud 6 mhe jma.*

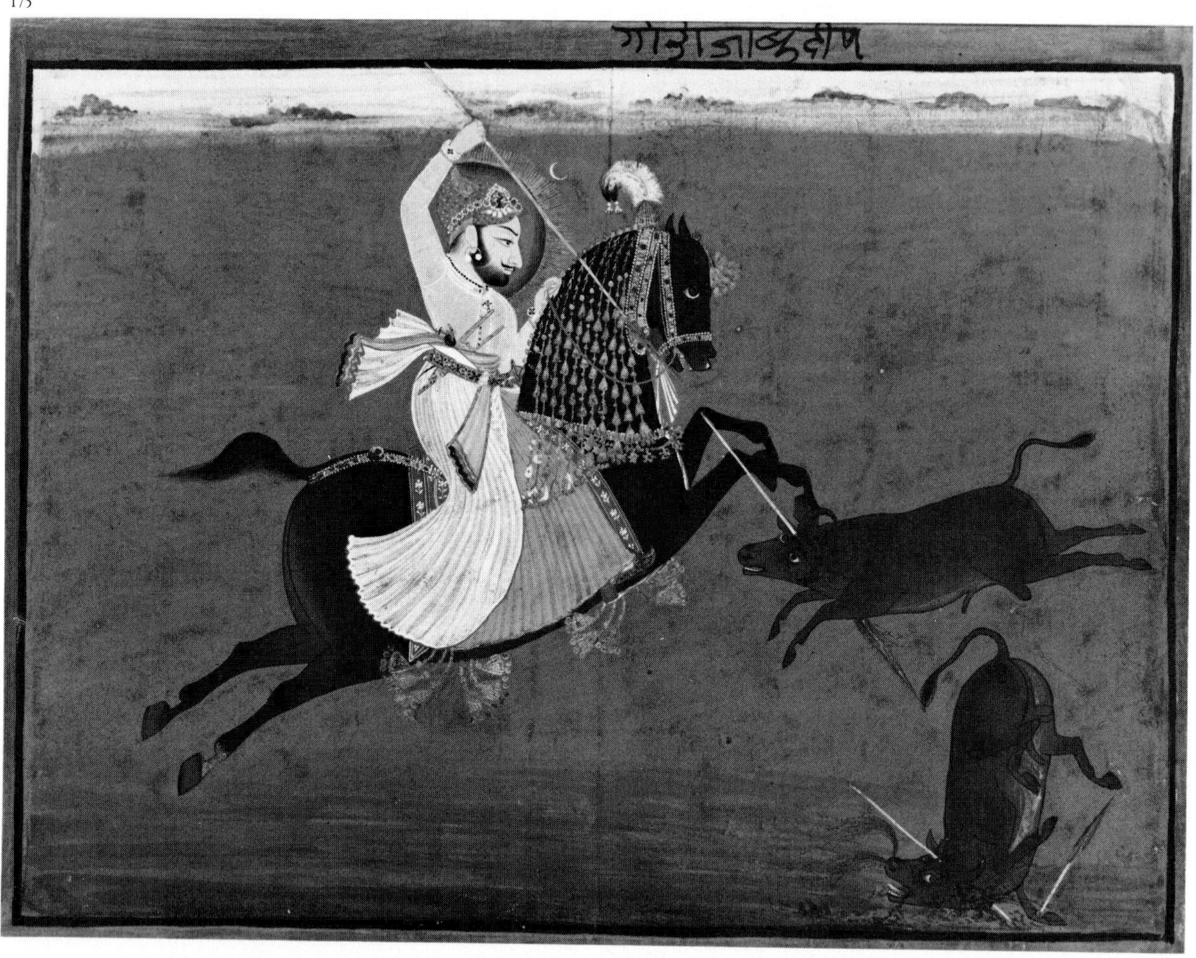

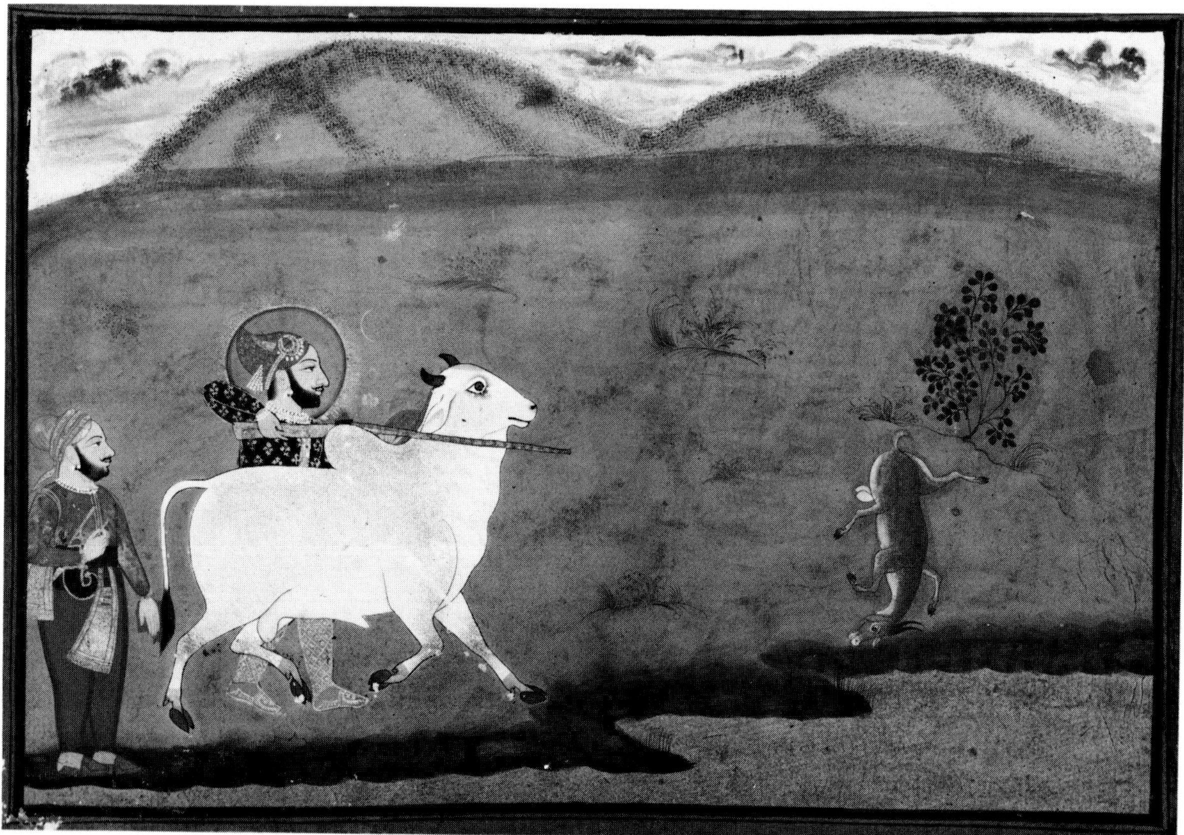

174
Maharana Ari Singh Riding
Udaipur, 1765
21.6 x 29 cm

The Maharana, with nimbus, in red *pagri* and red and
orange *jama*, rides a galloping dark stallion, Tilak
Sundar. Green background. Red border; inscribed
above: *ghodo talank sundar.*

Inscribed on the back: *maharajadhiraja maharanaji
sri arsi sihaji ri surat ro pano ghode tilak sudar asavar
citra* [artist's name omitted] *ro ki do so babat asavari
mhe thi avyo so ori jma samat 1822 ra asoj sud 7 sinau
mhe jma.*

175
Maharana Ari Singh Hunting Buffalo
Udaipur, 1765
22.6 x 30.9 cm

The Maharana, with nimbus, wearing a transparent
white *jama* over an orange skirt, rides a dark stallion,
Jambudvipa, and transfixes two buffaloes with spears.
Green background, with clouds above. Red border,
inscribed: *godo jabudip.*

Inscribed on the back: *maharajadhiraja maharana sri
arasihaji ri surat ro ghode jabudip asavar asavari mhe thi
avyo so ori jama samat 1822 varse asoj sud 5 mhe jma.*

176
Maharana Ari Singh Shooting Deer
Udaipur, 1765. By Naga
22 x 32.8 cm

The Maharana, with nimbus, has stalked and shot a
blackbuck from the cover of a white bull. He is
accompanied by his *dhabhai*, Jodaji. A river in the
foreground; green landscape background with heavily
outlined mauve hills. Red border.

Inscribed on the back: *sri ramji. pano sri
maharajadhiraja maharanaji
sri arasihaji ri surat ro balad re asare haran ri sikar
khelata thaka sriji ne dhabhai jodoji sakar khelata thaka
pano citare nago sri hajur nijar ki do* [in another hand:]
pano ori jma samat 1822 ra bhadava sud 2 mhe jma.
See also cat. no. 111.

177
Maharana Ari Singh
Udaipur, c. 1765
21 x 11.2 cm

The Maharana, with nimbus, in a gold-printed greenish-
yellow *jama*, stands facing right, holding a flower and a
sword. Green foreground with flowering plants; pale
turquoise background with a dark blue band above.
Indifferent quality. Much flaking. Red border.

Inscribed on the back: *liaja jaganath. maharanaji sri
arasihaji.*

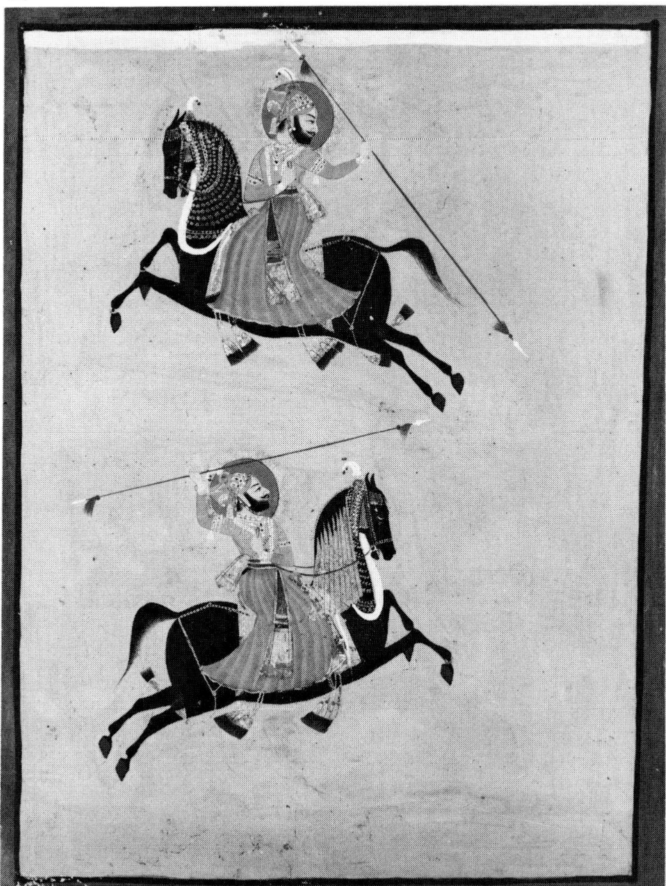

178
Maharana Ari Singh Riding
Udaipur, 1766. By Nathu
23 x 19.8 cm

The Maharana, with nimbus, wearing an orange *jama*
and *pagri*, rides a brown stallion with gold tassels and
trappings. Green background. Some damage and
discolouration. Trimmed red border.

Inscribed on the back: *ghoro tilak sudar citra nathu ro ki
do so ori jma sam 1823 ra asadh vid 5 me karakhana
thi jma* [in another hand:] *maharanaji sri
arasihaji.*

179
Two Views of Maharana Ari Singh Riding
Udaipur, 1767
48 x 36.8 cm

The Maharana is seen twice, in orange *pagri* and *jama*,
riding a black horse with gold harness and tassels,
holding the reins in one hand and wielding a spear in
the other. Plain green background. Red border.

Inscribed above: *maharajadhiraja maharana sri arsiji*
Inscribed on the back: *pano ori jma samat 1824 ra
bhadava sud 2.*

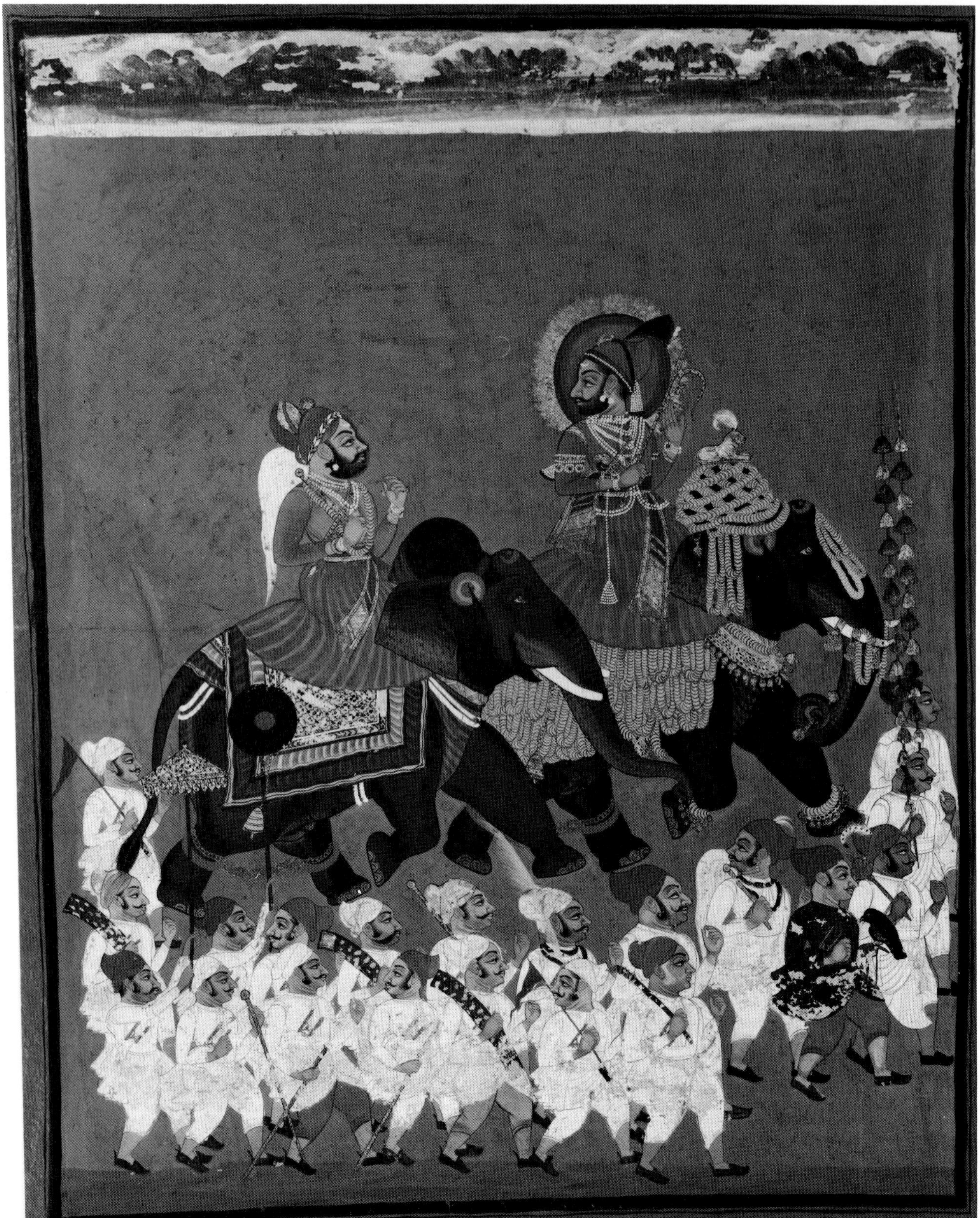

180

Maharana Ari Singh and Rupaji Riding Elephants
Udaipur, 1767. By Jiva
48 x 37.5 cm

The Maharana, with nimbus, in crimson *jama* and *pagri*, holds an ankus as he rides a garlanded elephant. His *dhabhai*, Rupaji, dressed in orange, accompanies him on another elephant, holding a chowry. Numerous attendants on foot. Green background with a band of cloud above. Some flaking. Red border.

Inscribed on the back: *maharanaji śri arasihaji* [in another hand:] *pano 1 śriji ri surat ro hathi pritabar bagas ri asavar gulab ra phulari ?jula tha ?i sudhintha dha: rupaji duje hathi asavar camar rakhta thaka citra jiva ro ki do so ori jama samat 1824 ra vaisak vid 4 mhe jama.*

181

Maharana Jai Singh (1680-98)
Udaipur, 1761. By Sahaji
23.5 x 16.5 cm

The Maharana, with nimbus, in a transparent four-pointed *jama* over striped *paijama*, stands holding his sword-hilt in one hand and a flower in the other. Blue-green background. (Oxidised) silver margin; tan border flecked with grey, numbered 7. Blue text panel with a verse inscribed in gold.

Inscribed on the back: *7 maharajadhiraja maharanaji śri je sighji* [in another hand:] *pano 1 citra sahaji ro ki do so ori jama samat 1818 ra asadh vid 4 me jma.*

This picture and cat. no. 182 belong to a series of portraits of earlier Maharanas which was presented to Maharana Ari Singh shortly after his accession by the painter Sahaji; other examples are in private collections. In the Tod collection of the Royal Asiatic Society there is a later, similar portrait of Rana Kumbha, probably by Ghasi, described by Tod as 'after an original in the Durbar by Sabji [?Sahji]'.

182

Maharana Amar Singh II, (1698-1710)
Udaipur, 1761. By Sahaji
23 x 16.4 cm

The Maharana, with nimbus, in white *pagri* and transparent *jama* over orange and gold, stands with one hand on his sword-hilt and a flower in the other. Dark green background. Silver margin; red border, numbered 8; a blue panel above, inscribed with a eulogistic verse in gold. Inscribed below (incorrectly) in a 19th century English hand: *Muha Rana Umur Singh 1st.*

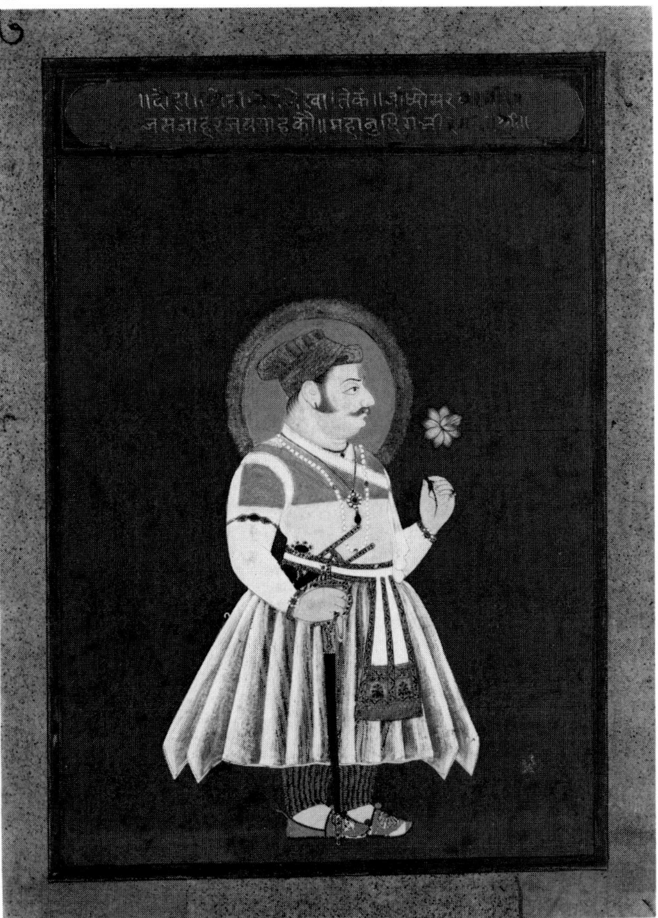

181

Inscribed on the back: *maharajadhiraja maharanaji śri amar sighji raj sighot* [in another hand:] *pano 1 ori jama sam 1818 ra asadh vid 4 mhe citra ?shaji thi.*

The same English hand is found on the border of a portrait of Maharana Jawan Singh (cat. no. 234), and is therefore too late to be that of Tod, who is known to have consulted this series of portraits while at Udaipur (see cat. no. 181).

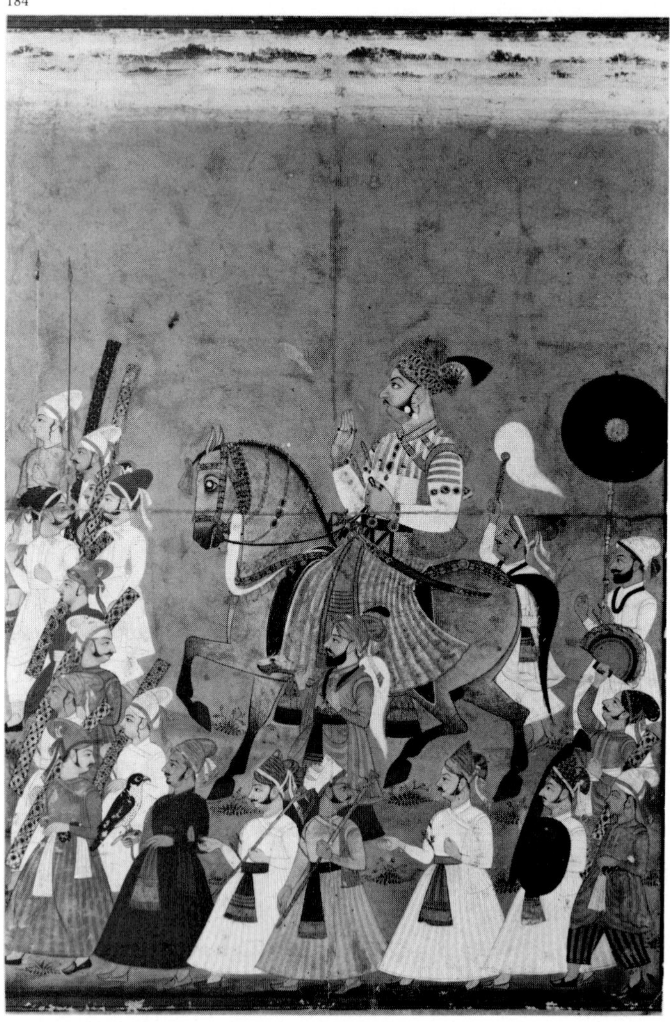

184

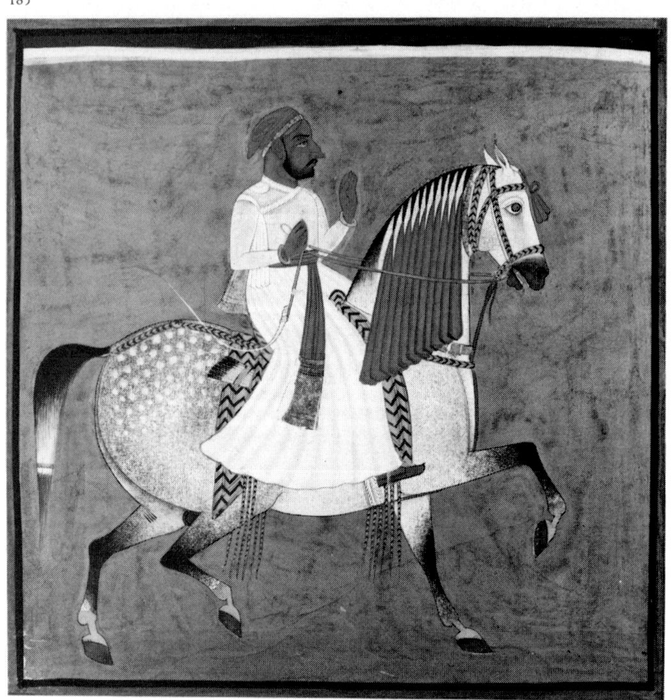

185

183

Maharaja Madho Singh of Jaipur
Udaipur, c. 1760-65. Style of Bakhta
21 x 13 cm

The Maharaja (b. 1727, r. 1751-68), with nimbus, in orange *jama* and magenta and gold *patka,* stands holding a string of pearls and the hilt of his sword. Green background with orange and white bands above. Yellow margin; dark indigo border with a white compartment, inscribed: *mhāraja śrī mādhe syaṅghjī rī;* numbered 55.

An Udaipur version of a Jaipur portrait (cf. cat. nos. 27 and 28); the palette and execution with fine stippling are reminiscent of the work of Bakhta (see cat. nos. 130 and 167). Madho Singh was the son of a Mewar princess, and Maharana Jagat Singh incurred several expensive defeats in support of his claim to the throne of Jaipur after the death of Sawai Jai Singh in 1743. Madho Singh's thanks, when finally helped to power by the Marathas, was to sequestrate Rampura, hitherto part of Mewar, as a gift to them.

184

Maharaja Bijai Singh of Jodhpur Riding
Udaipur, c. 1760-65
50.5 x 36 cm

The Maharaja (b. 1729; r. 1753-93) rides, accompanied by numerous attendants with chowries, regalia etc. Pale green background with cloud above. Silver margin; trimmed buff border.

Inscribed above: *mhārāja vije sīghjī jodpur.*

185

A Horse Portrait
Udaipur, 1762
21.1 x 21.1 cm

A dappled grey stallion with red tassels on his mane and hennaed ankles, ridden by a dark-skinned syce. Green background. Red border, inscribed: *ghoḍo he sanagārasa gokal dās ṭīlī ro najar kī do.*

Inscribed on the back: *orī jamā mhā sud 8 samat 1818 vars.*

Cat. no. 186 appears to be a portrait of the same horse.

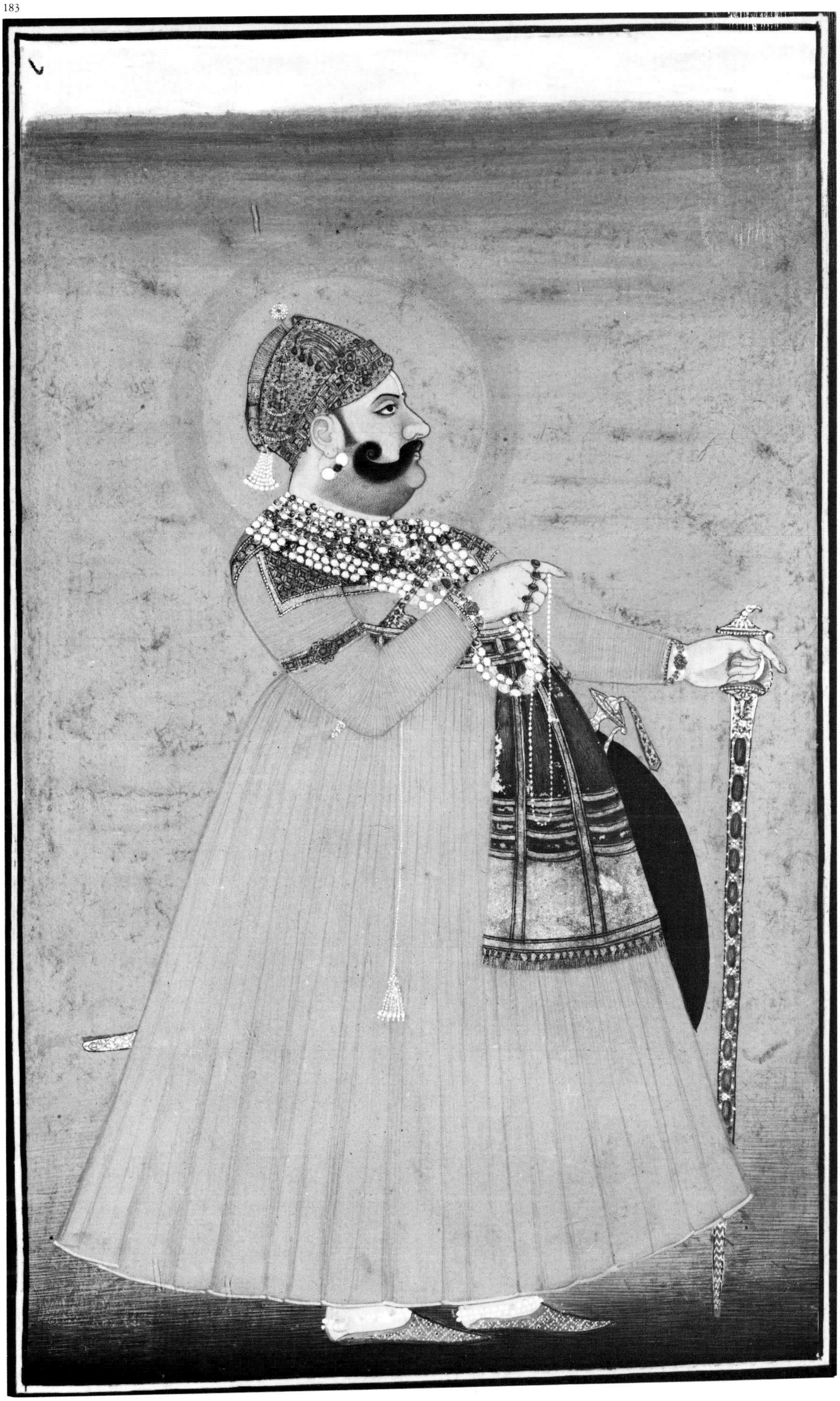

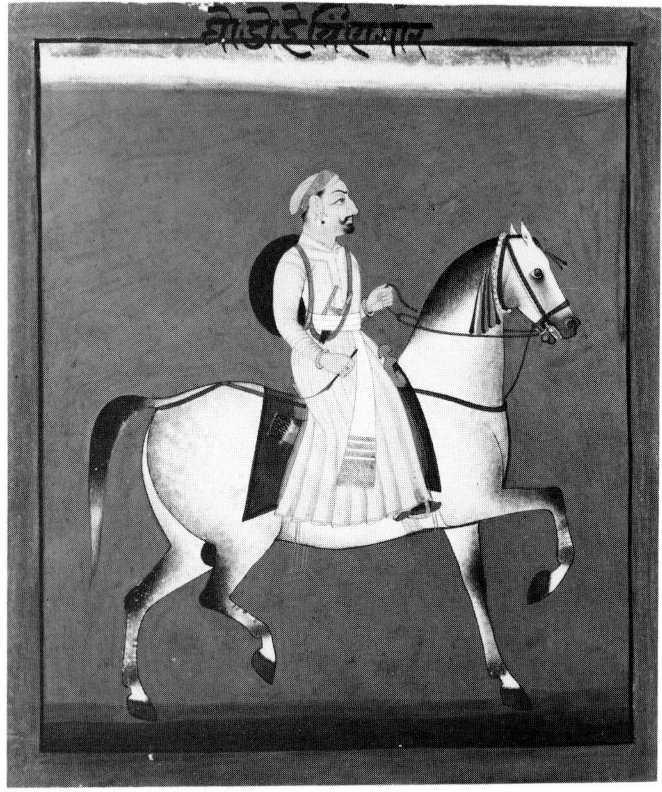

186

A Horse Portrait
Udaipur, c. 1761-65
23.2 x 20.3 cm

The dappled grey horse is ridden by a syce in a pink *jama*. Green background. Trimmed red border, inscribed above: *ghoḍo he siṅgār*.

187

A Horse Portrait
Udaipur, 1762
19.9 x 20.7 cm

An off-white stallion, its lower half stained with henna, with yellow tassels on its mane; its rider wearing a white *jama* and *pagri*. Green background. Red border, inscribed: *ghoḍo hasaraj kharīd ru 1200 rī* (the horse Hasaraj, bought for 1200 rupees).

Inscribed on the back: *orī jamā mhā sud 8 samat 1818 vars.*

188

A Horse Portrait
Udaipur, 1762
20.6 x 20.6 cm

A piebald stallion with gold harness; its rider wears a dark pink *pagri* and a white *jama* striped with lemon-yellow. Green background. Red border, inscribed: *ghoḍo raga jadav raṇāvat sava?ayajī tīla ro najar ki do.*

Inscribed on the back: *pāno orī jamā mhā sud 8 samat 1818 vars.*

189

A Horse Portrait
Udaipur, c. 1762
18.9 x 21.6 cm

A trotting chestnut stallion with white legs and long grey and white mane. The rider wears a transparent white *jama* and yellow *patka*. Blue-green background. Red border.

Inscribed on the back: *aladaraj.*

190

A Horse Portrait
Udaipur, c. 1762
20.1 x 22.3 cm

The orange-brown stallion, with green saddle-cloth is ridden by a syce in white *jama* and *pagri*. Pale turquoise background. Much flaking. Red border, trimmed and inscribed: *ghoḍo yara?dharo.*

191

The Elephant Rinasobha
Udaipur, c. 1730-60
21.5 x 36 cm

The elephant, with a mahout and a keeper on its back, runs forward after breaking its ankle-chain. Three other keepers make way for him. Pale green background. Yellow margin; red border with black ruling, inscribed: *mahārana śrī je sīghjī rī var ro* [in another hand:] *hathī riṇasobha.*

Inscribed on the back: *riṇasobhā.*

The elephant entered the royal stable in the reign of Maharana Jai Singh (1680-98).

192

The Elephant Verisal
Udaipur, c. 1761-65
18.5 x 21.5 cm

The elephant, with a green, orange and red covering, trots towards the right, ridden by a mahout in white holding an ankus in both hands. Green background. Red border.

Inscribed on the back: *hathī verī sāl;* [in another hand:] *mahāraṇajī śrī sagrām sīghjī rī vagat.*
Numbered: 91.

191

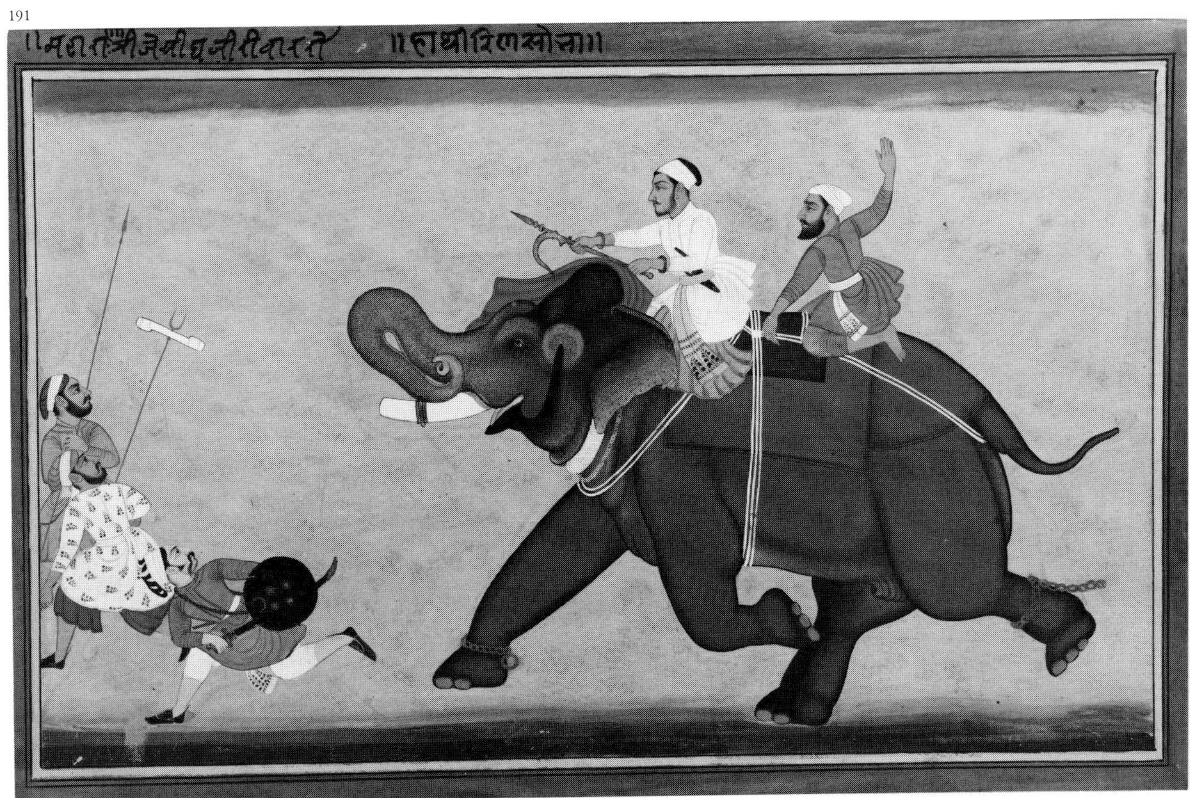

192

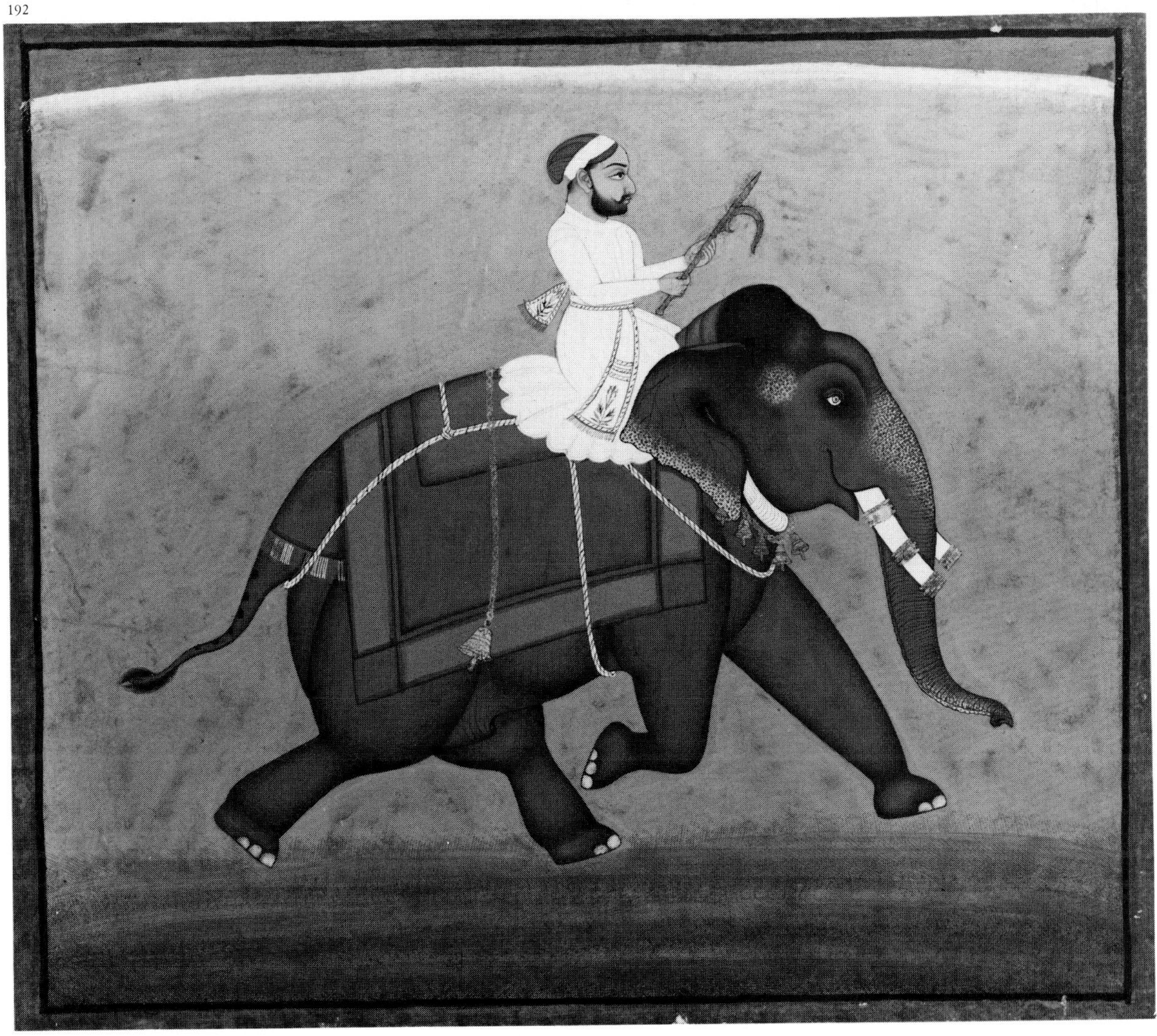

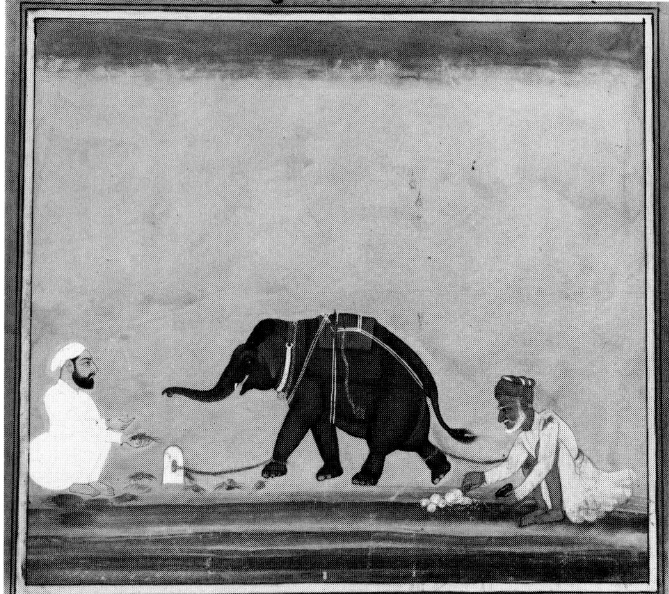

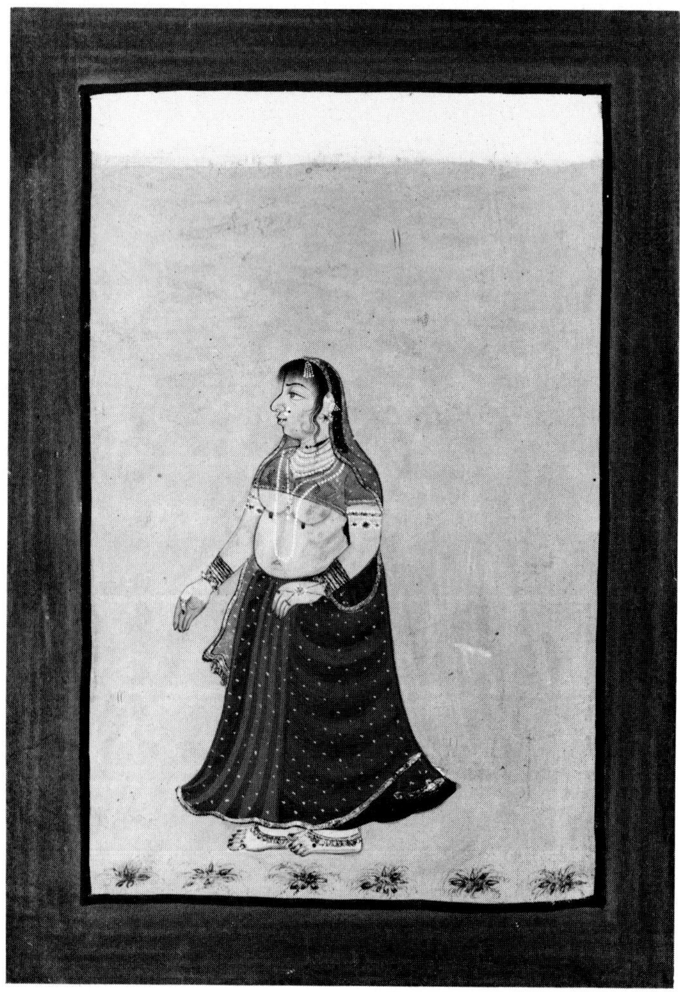

193

The Elephant Phundo
Udaipur, c. 1761-65
19.5 x 22.3 cm

The baby elephant stands tethered while a keeper offers him handfuls of grass and another spreads food(?) for him on the ground. Pale green background. Yellow margin; red border, inscribed above: *hathī phundo* [in another hand:] *mharaṇa śrī raj sighjī rī var ko.*

Inscribed on the back: *phudo.*

194

The Elephant Mrigavati
Udaipur, c. 1761-65
21 x 26 cm

The female elephant, spread with a green cloth, trots to the right, ridden by a mahout in white holding an ankus. Bluish-green background. Yellow margin; red border, inscribed above: *hathanī miragāvatī* [in another hand, partly deleted:] *maharaṇajī śrī raj sighjī rī var rī.*

Inscribed on the back: *mragāvatī.*

195

The Elephant Zulfikar
Udaipur, c. 1762
20.5 x 23.3 cm

The elephant, ridden by his mahout, stands near a tree to which his leg is being chained by a keeper, while two other attendants stand by holding restraining spears with a fire-cracker, and a taper in case of need. Pale green background. Yellow margin; red border, inscribed: *hathī julafikar.*

Inscribed on the back: *maharaṇajī śrī sagrām sighjī rī var ro.*

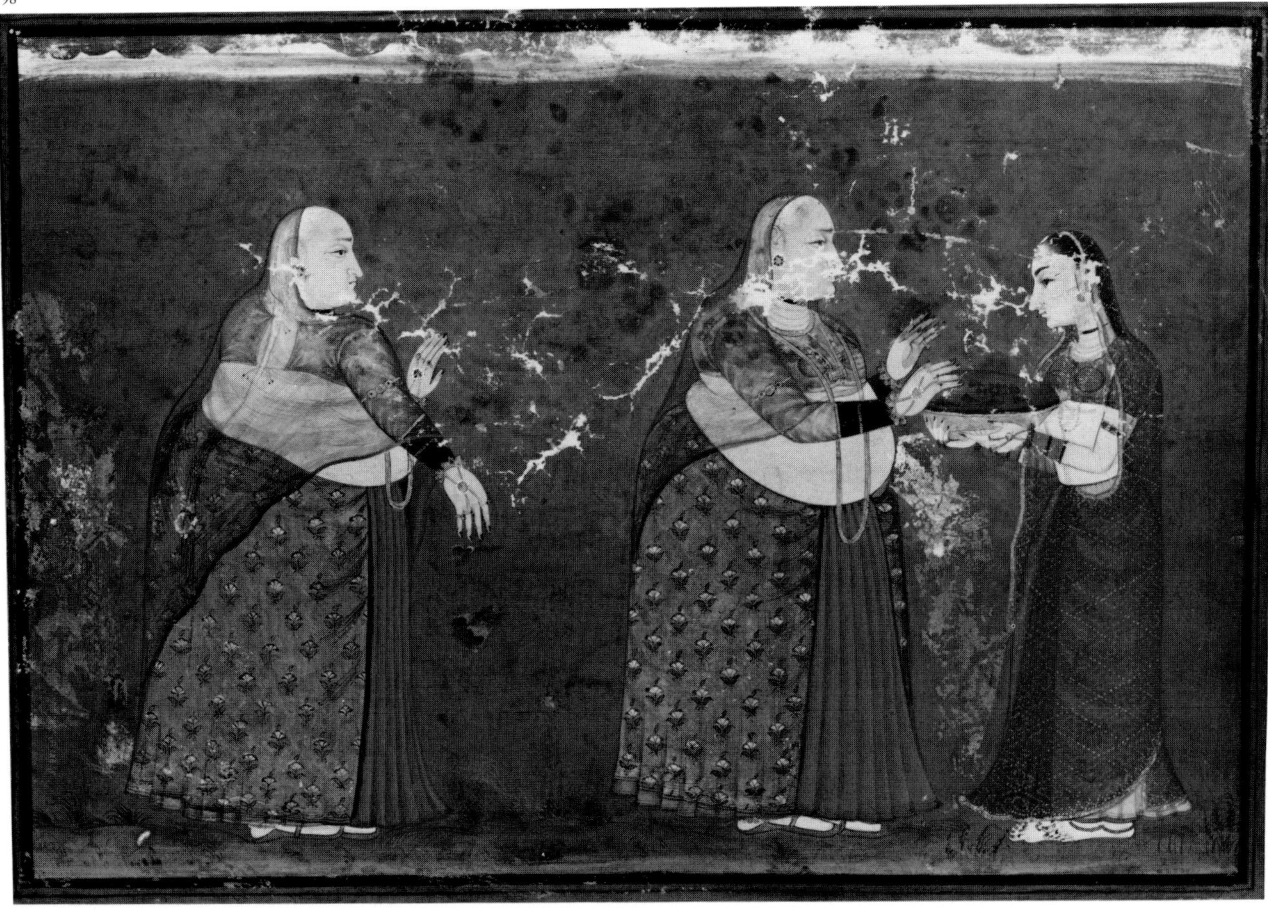

196

Two Ladies on a Terrace

Udaipur, 1761

22 x 10.8 cm

Two ladies stand on a terrace staring into each other's eyes. One holds a wine-flask and cup, the other two garlands. Flower-beds with a pool and water-courses in the foreground; green background with two trees. Coarsely painted. Orange-red border.

Inscribed on the back: *pāno orī jmā bābat jatī jaganath thī jmā samat 1818 rā asādh vid 12 mhe jmā.*

197

A Lady of *Śankhini* Type

Udaipur, 1763. By Bhopa

18.7 x 12.5 cm

The *śankhini* is one of the less pleasing types of women in the Indian classification. Plump and ill-favoured, she stands against a pale green background. Verses on the back describe her as angry and deceitful, and having a sweaty and hairy body. Red border.

Also inscribed on the back: *pāno citrā bhopā ro kī do so orī jamā samat 1820 rā sāvan sud 5 mhe.*

198

A Fat Old Lady

Udaipur, c. 1765

22.1 x 32.5 cm

A very obese old lady in green *choli*, transparent *odhni*, and silver *ghaghra* with floral pattern, is seen twice, standing and on the right taking *pan* from a tray held by a maid. Blue-green background. Damaged. Red border.

Inscribed on the back: *khadārana kujakalī* [in another hand, in red:] *kujakalī v..ṇa.*

Unconventional studies of women were perhaps popular with Maharana Ari Singh. Cf. cat. no. 197. A curious picture of men outside a brothel, dated 1767, was also painted for him (private collection).

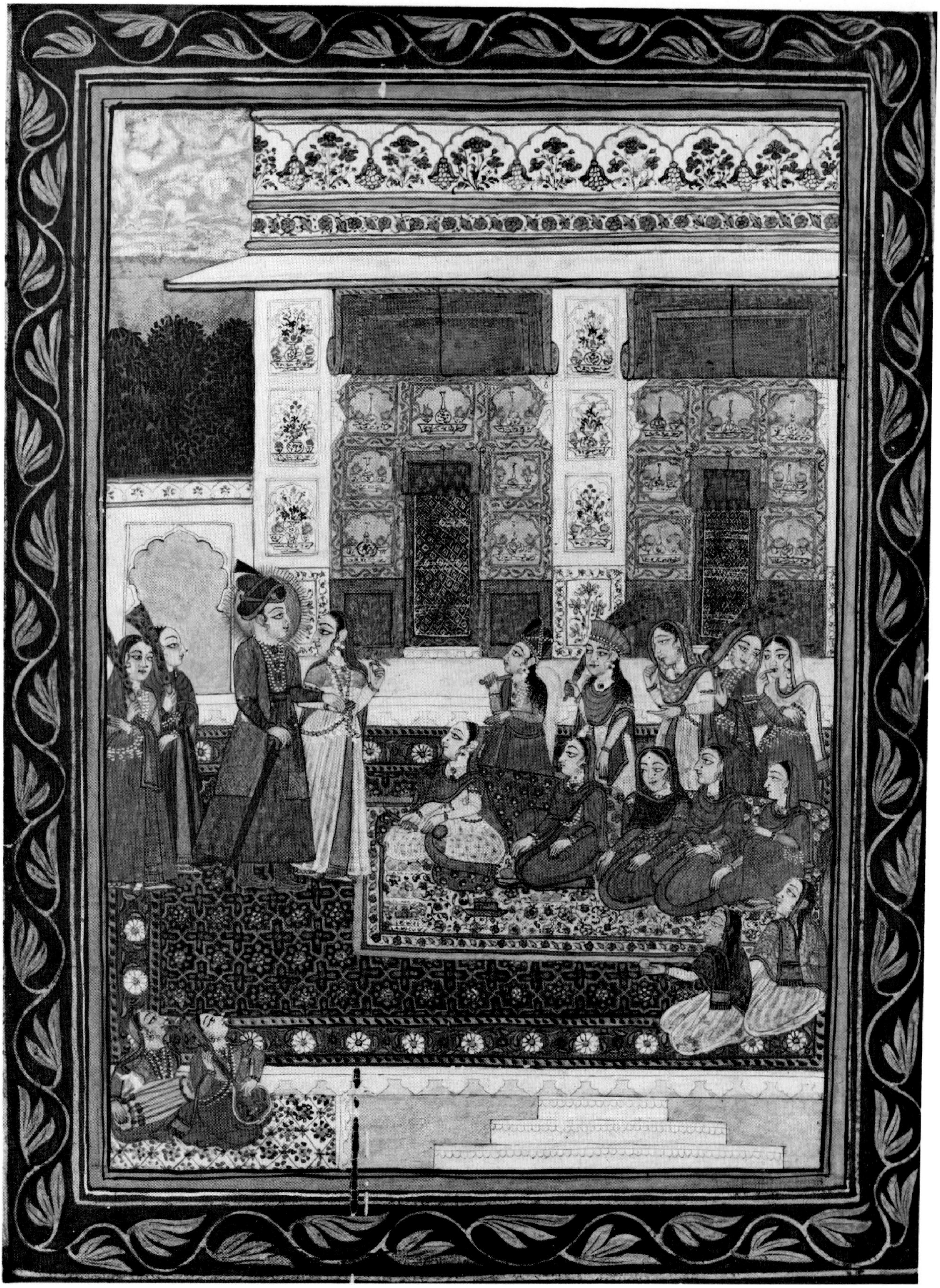

199

A Domestic Mishap
Mewar sub-style, mid-18th century
24.3 x 19.2 cm

An unidentified scene, in which a young male child
walks into the kitchen fire, watched with alarm by his
mother, who is fanning her husband, sleeping after his
meal, and another woman standing in a doorway.
Yellow margin; orange border with white ruling,
numbered 60.
A largely unintelligible two-line inscription on the back
appears to mention the name of (the poet?) Sur Das.

200

Yusuf and Zulaikha
Mewar sub-style, 1761. By Chitar Bagas(?)
27.4 x 19 cm

An illustration, perhaps after a Mughal model, of the
Persian romance of Yusuf (the Biblical Joseph) and
Zulaikha; Yusuf's beauty causes Zulaikha's maids, who
are peeling fruit, to cut their own hands in astonishment
when he is first led before them. The palace terrace is
highly decorated, and the light palette with dominant
yellowish-greens is unusual. Yellow margin; blue border
with yellow meander pattern.

Inscribed on the back: *pano śri hajur nijar ki do kalami
citare chitar ?vagasa ramapure* [in another hand:] *pano
ori jma samat 1818 ra asoj sud 14 sukrai.*

The reading of this otherwise unknown artist's name
(Chitar ??Bagas, of Rampura) is uncertain.

201

The Month of Magha
Mewar sub-style, c. 1770
27 x 19.5 cm

From a *Barahmasa,* or series of the months of the year;
Magha runs from January to February. A ruler and
sardars sit on a terrace watching a nautch girl. They and
the musicians are stained with red powder after playing
Holi. A lady attended by maids watches from a roof.
Flower-beds and water-courses in the foreground. Yellow
margin; red border with blue and white rules and white,
yellow and blue decoration.

Inscribed above: *maha*; numbered 59.
Inscribed on the back: *śri. idar ko raja* [= raja of Idar??]
*rage? bhana masa mha me takhat upare barya ?jye che
patarya? narata ?kararahi che saradar betha che*...etc.
(the meaning is obscure).

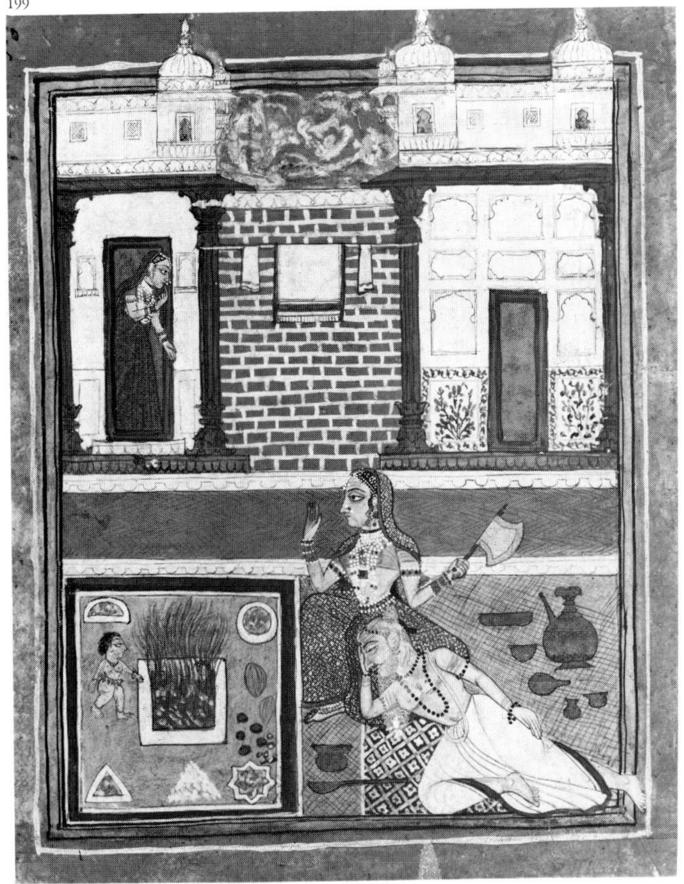

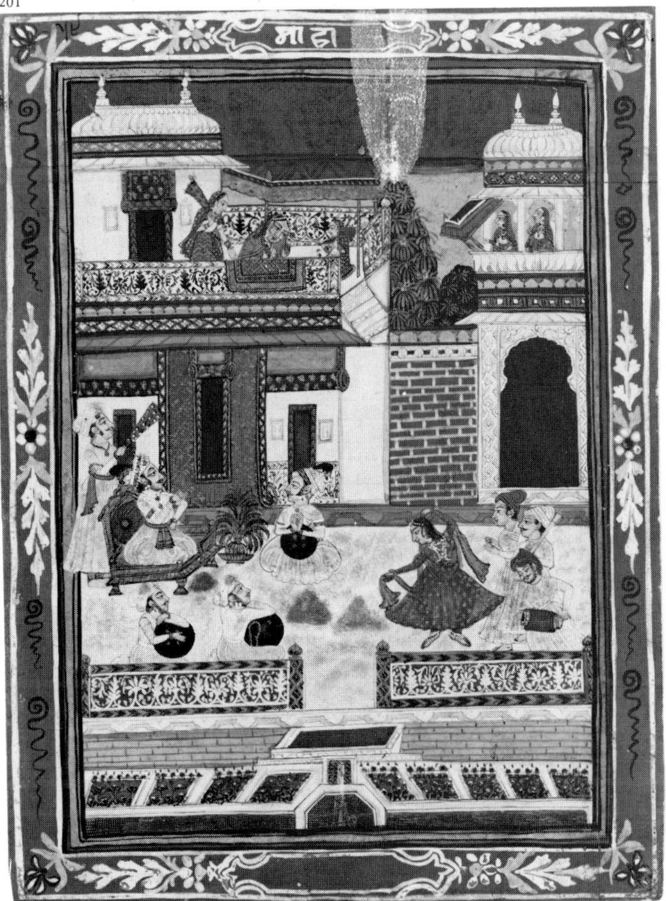

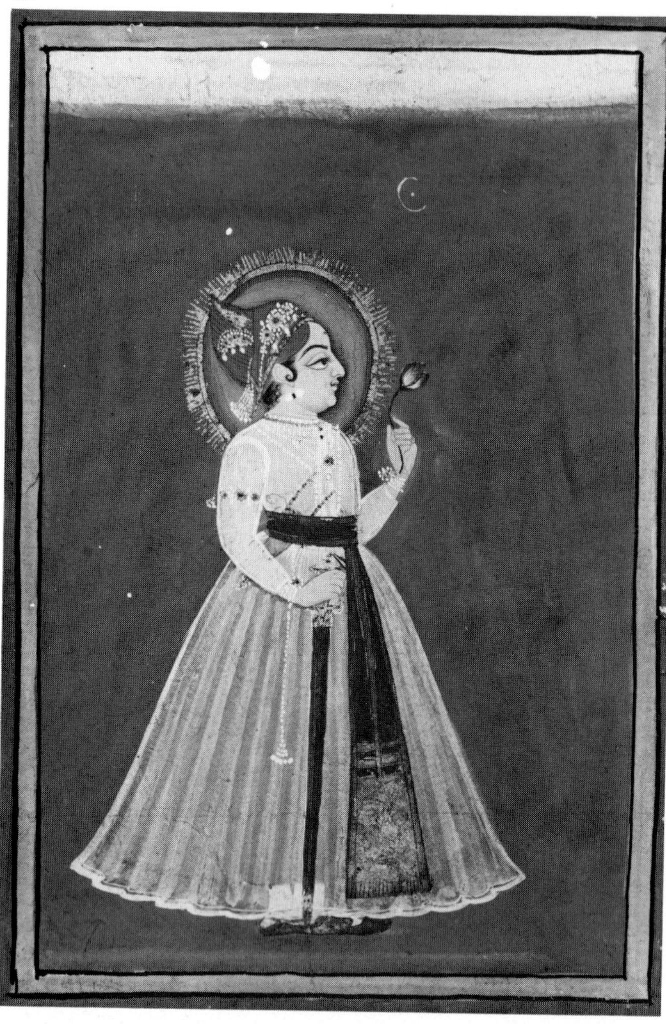

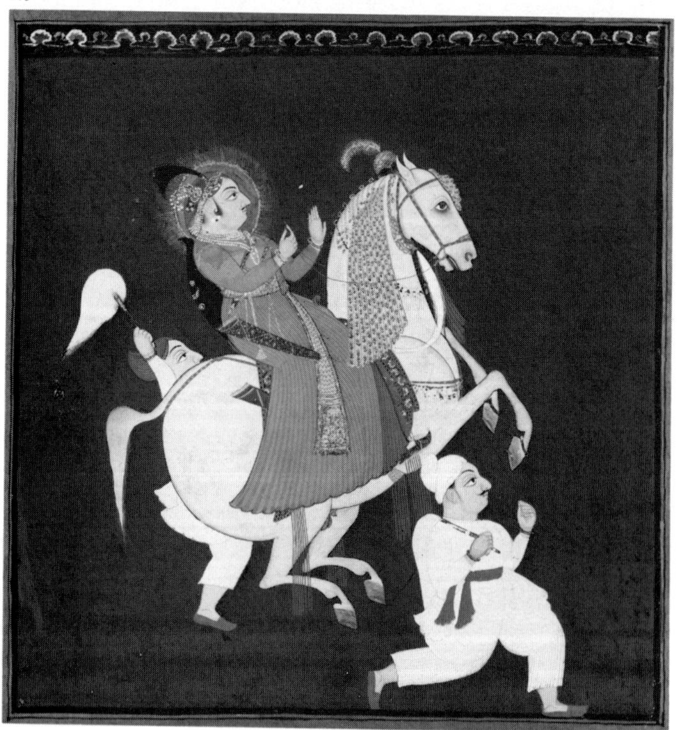

202

Maharana Bhim Singh
Udaipur, 1782
16 x 10.5 cm

The youthful Maharana, with nimbus, in pink *pagri* and transparent white *jama,* stands holding a flower in one hand and a sheathed sword in the other. Pale green background. Yellow margin; red border with some obscured writing, beginning: *74. rana śri...*

Inscribed on the back: *maharanaji śri bhim sighji;* [in another hand:] *pano 1 śriji surat ro babat asavari mhe thi avyo so jma samat 1839 ra bhadava vid 5 bhome.*

203

Maharana Bhim Singh Riding
Udaipur, 1784
23 x 22.2 cm

The Maharana, with nimbus, wearing an orange *jama,* rides a grey stallion, accompanied by two chowry-bearers. Dark green background with a band of stylized cloud above. Red border.

Inscribed on the back: *?pra: cet bid 7 re din śriji tija pohara asavar huva so cogan padharyo so asavari mhe nijar huvo sambat 1841* [in another hand:] *maharanaji śri bhim singhji.*

A similar painting in a private collection is dated 1785.

204

Maharana Bhim Singh and a Lady
Udaipur, 1788. By Mialalotar(?)
24 x 19.1 cm

The Maharana, in orange *pagri* and white *jama,* sits on a swing-bed and offers *pan* to a concubine (*pasavan:* the illegitimate offspring by Rajputs of women attendants in the *zenana;* Tod, *Annals and Antiquities of Rajasthan,* vol. II, p. 1076, fn.). A carpet with yellow ground in the foreground. Blue-grey background enclosed by an engrailed arch. Red border with black ruling.

Inscribed on the back: *śri ramji. maharajadhiraja maharana śri bhim sighji re pasavan ?suaji santidasji kapadadar surat ro pana caro 1 phutali ro siga lata mhe betha thaka citaro mialalotar ki do cham 1845 ra savan sud 3 some re dan ki do nagar.*

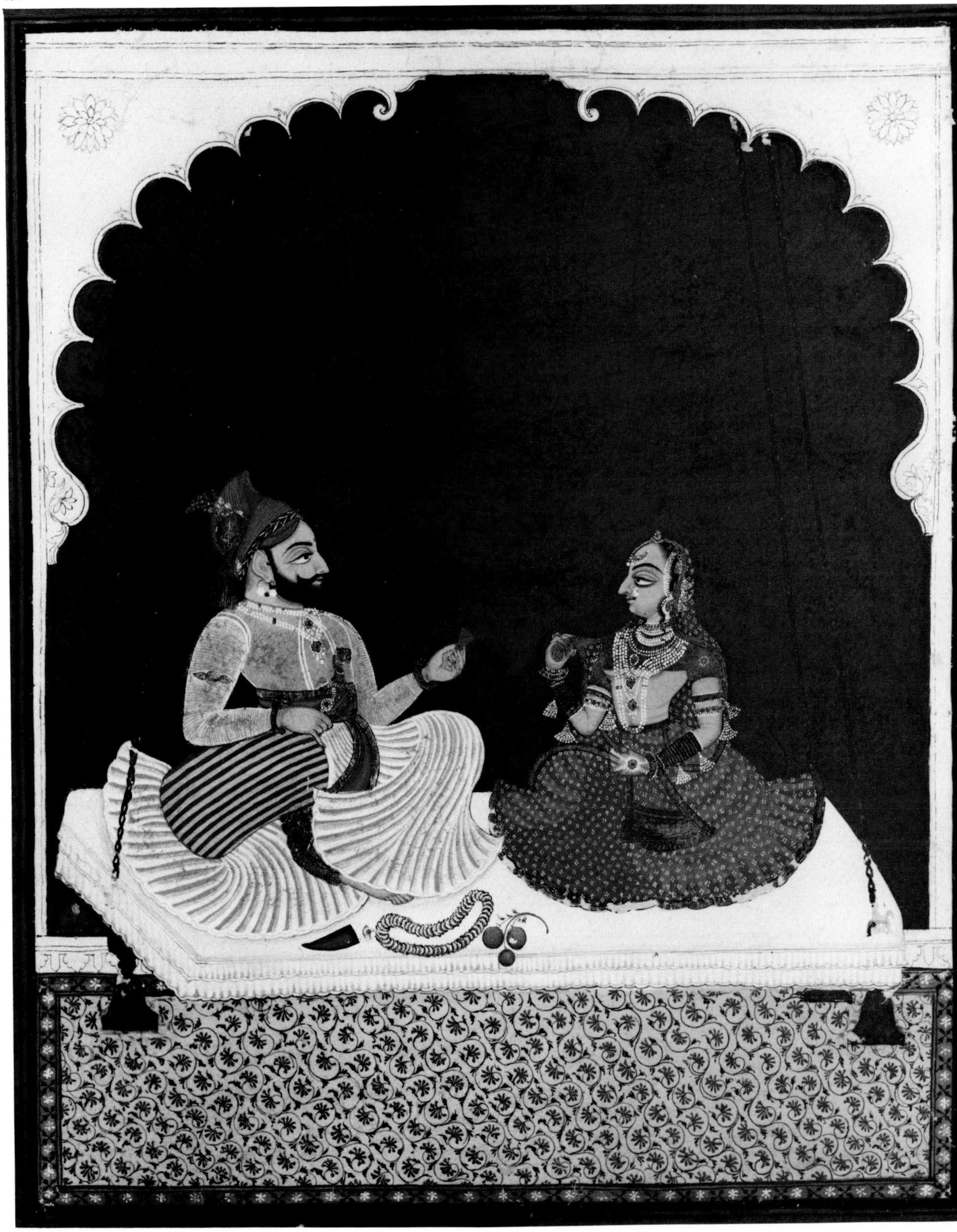

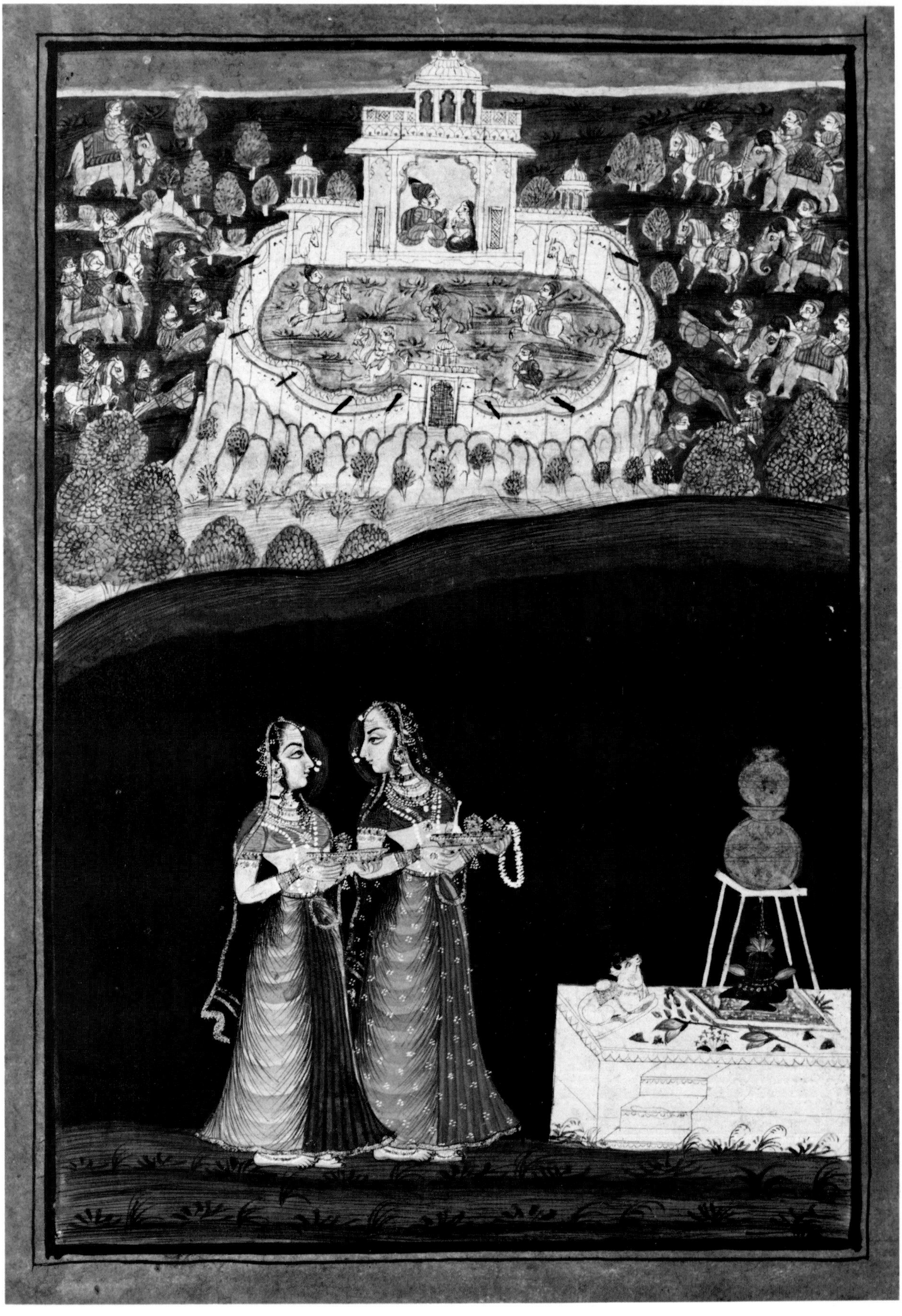

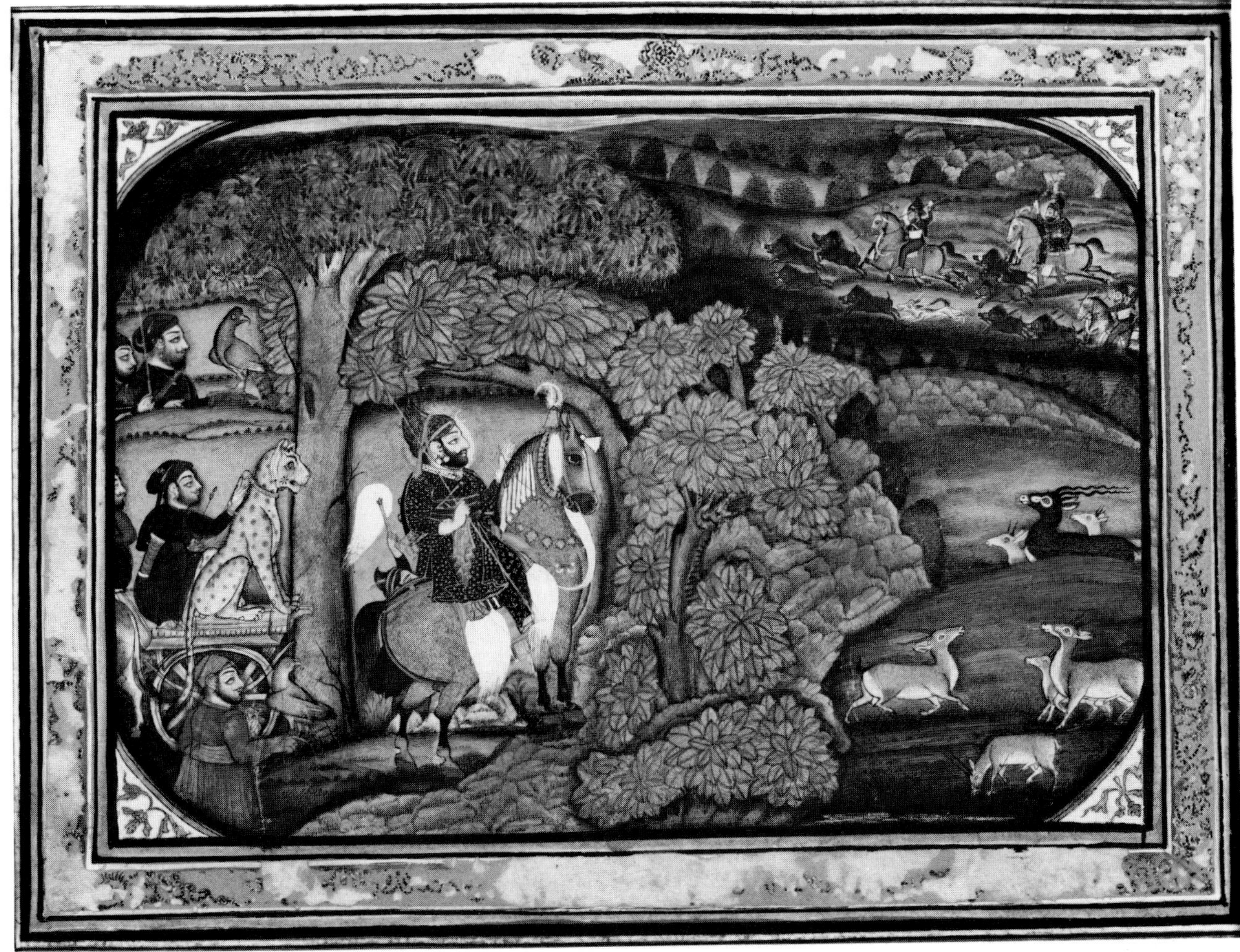

205

Two Ladies at a Shiva Shrine
Udaipur, 1781
17.3 x 12 cm

Two ladies bearing offerings on gold trays stand gazing at one another in front of a *lingam* shrine. Dark green background. Above, painted in a coarser hand, an army besieges a hilltop fort in which a prince and a lady are seated. Red border.

Inscribed on the back: *pāno phutalī ra ro bābat asavarī mhe thī āvyo so orī jmā samat 1838 rā asoj sud 3 mhe jmā.*

206

Maharana Bhim Singh Hunting
Udaipur, c. 1800. Attributed to Chokha
10.9 x 16.2 cm

The Maharana, on horseback, accompanied by attendants and *shikaris* with hawks and a cheetah, surveys a group of grazing deer and blackbuck from the cover of trees. The Maharana is seen again in the background riding with two sardars in hot pursuit of a herd of boar. The picture is rounded off at the corners. Pale blue inner border with gold decoration (damaged) and thick gold, black and white rules; red outer border, much trimmed.

Inscribed on the back: *surat rāṇā bhīm sīgh ri gho: phate turag.*

This painting is effectively a companion picture to cat. no. 207. It is however more highly finished, with the use of heavily stippled modelling typical of Chokha's work. The trees are also delineated in his more detailed manner and finished with gold, whereas in cat. no. 207 they have been rapidly dabbed in with a cloth-pad, an expedient often used by Mewar artists.

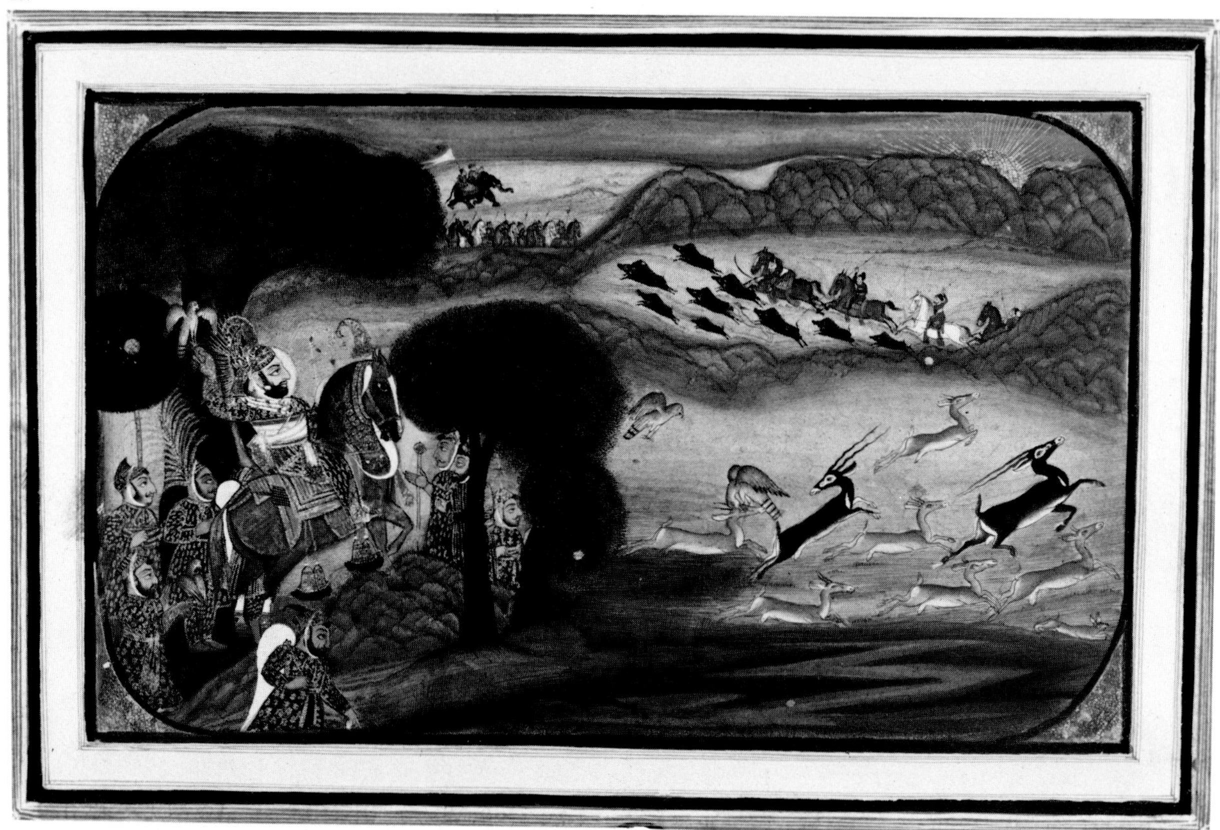

207

208

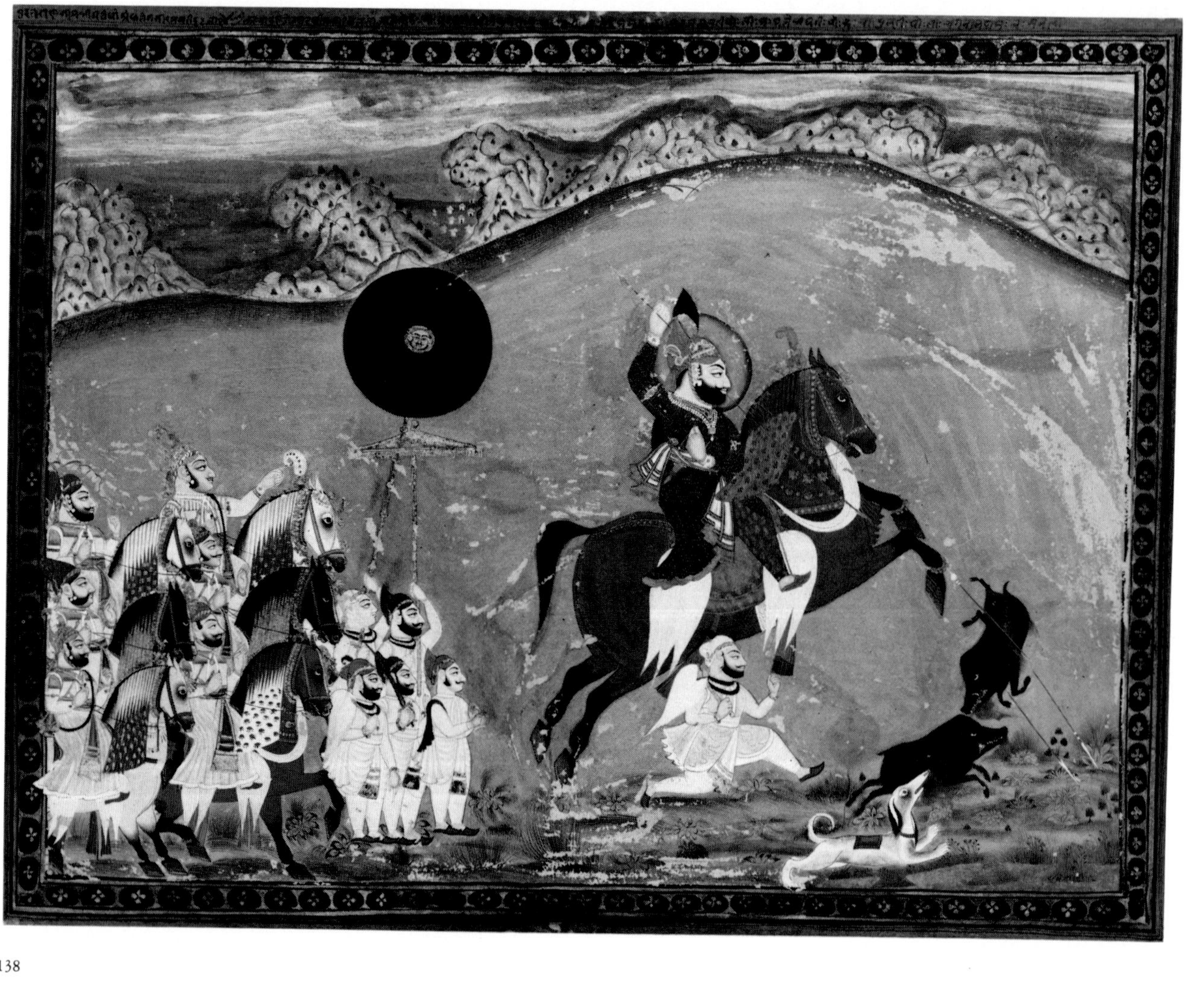

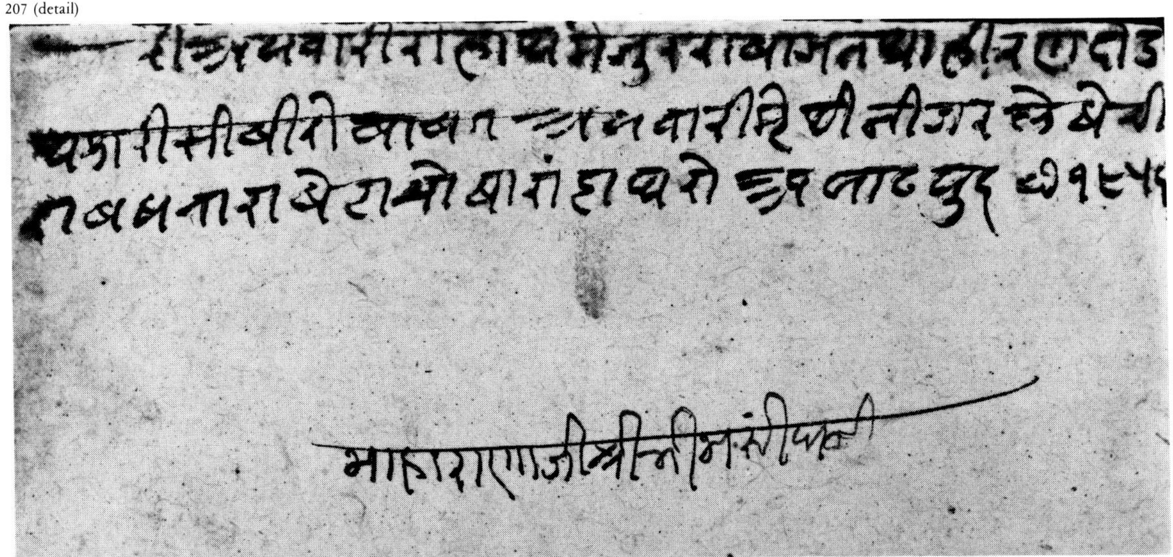

207

Maharana Bhim Singh Hawking
Udaipur, 1799(?). By Chokha
11 x 18.6 cm

The Maharana, on horseback, accompanied by
attendants in green and gold, raises his hawk aloft; it
flies and attacks one of a group of deer and blackbuck.
In the distance a boar hunt is in progress. A gold sun in
a red sky appears behind the hills. The picture is
rounded off at the corners with gold inserts; white inner
border with black, yellow and red rules; trimmed red
outer border with white rules and vacant yellow boxes
for inscriptions.

Inscription on the back has been mutilated by trimming
of the edges: *ri asavari ra hath me jurara bajat tha hiran
dod... ?thaka ri sibi ro babat asavari mhe thi nijar lekhe
ci [ta] ra bakhata ra beta cokha ra hath ro
asadh sud cha? 1856?* (see detail).

This is the earliest dated painting yet known by Chokha,
son of the artist Bakhta who worked for Maharana Ari
Singh at Udaipur in the 1760s (see cat. nos. 130, 167)
and later for the Rawats of Deogarh from c. 1769-1811.
It can be assumed that Chokha served his apprenticeship
with his father at Deogarh, and in his maturity (around
1811 especially) he produced some excellent pictures for
Rawat Gokul Das (e.g. Andhare and Singh, *Deogarh
Painting,* pl. III, and Andhare, ''Painting from the
Thikana of Deogarh'', *Prince of Wales Museum
Bulletin,* 10, 1967, fig. 46, in which he portrays himself
and his father). There is, however, as in the case of
Bakhta, sufficient evidence to render untenable the
hypothesis of earlier writers that Chokha was exclusively
a Deogarh painter. For it seems that he was if anything
more active at Udaipur than Deogarh between c. 1799
(the most likely reading of the date of this picture) and
c. 1824 (the date of a picture of a young European
hunter with a lynx, inscribed as the work of Chokha, son
of Bakhta, and presented as *nazar* at Udaipur: National
Museum, New Delhi, acc. no. 58.45/28). Much of

Chokha's production in the intervening period consists
of portraits of Maharana Bhim Singh: e.g. Beach,
'Painting at Devgarh', *Archives of Asian Art,* XXIV,
1970-71, fig. 14 (dated 1803: wrongly identified by
Beach as Gokul Das — Chokha's renderings of the two
rulers do in fact show a great similarity; Bhim Singh is
chiefly distinguishable by his royal nimbus and by the
shortness of his legs in the saddle) and Pal, *The Classical
Tradition in Rajput Painting,* no. 48 (Pal here follows
the inadequate argument of Andhare and Singh,
Deogarh Painting, pp. 3-4, that such portraits were
made to commemorate a visit by Bhim Singh to
Deogarh). Several other portraits by Chokha of Bhim
Singh and his sons in private collections remain
unpublished; one late example, dated 1823, was sold at
Sotheby's on 24 April 1979, lot 117 (see also cat.
nos. 210-213 etc.). Wall-paintings in Chokha's style also
survive in the palace at Udaipur.

208

Maharana Bhim Singh Hunting Boar
Udaipur, c. 1815
35 x 48.2 cm

The Maharana, with nimbus, wearing an orange *pagri*
and a green coat, rides a brown horse and hurls spears at
two boars. He is followed by attendants on foot with
chowries and regalia and by six mounted sardars,
Savdanji, Ajit Singh, Suraj Mal, Fateh Singh, Pulji and
Bhagvan Das. Pale green background with distant rocky
landscape. Gold and black margin with gold rules and
quatrefoil pattern; red border with gold floral designs.

Inscribed on the border: *surat rana bhim sigh ri ghodo
kalem marakh kharid hajar 4000 ka caran jeth sur thi
sakar khelta lale ghode: bha: savdanji ghode kumet: cu:
ajit sighji ghode samad: bha: suraj malji gho: la: sa: fate
saghji: gho: ku: ca: pulji: gho: la: bhagvan das: ca:
sanalau.*

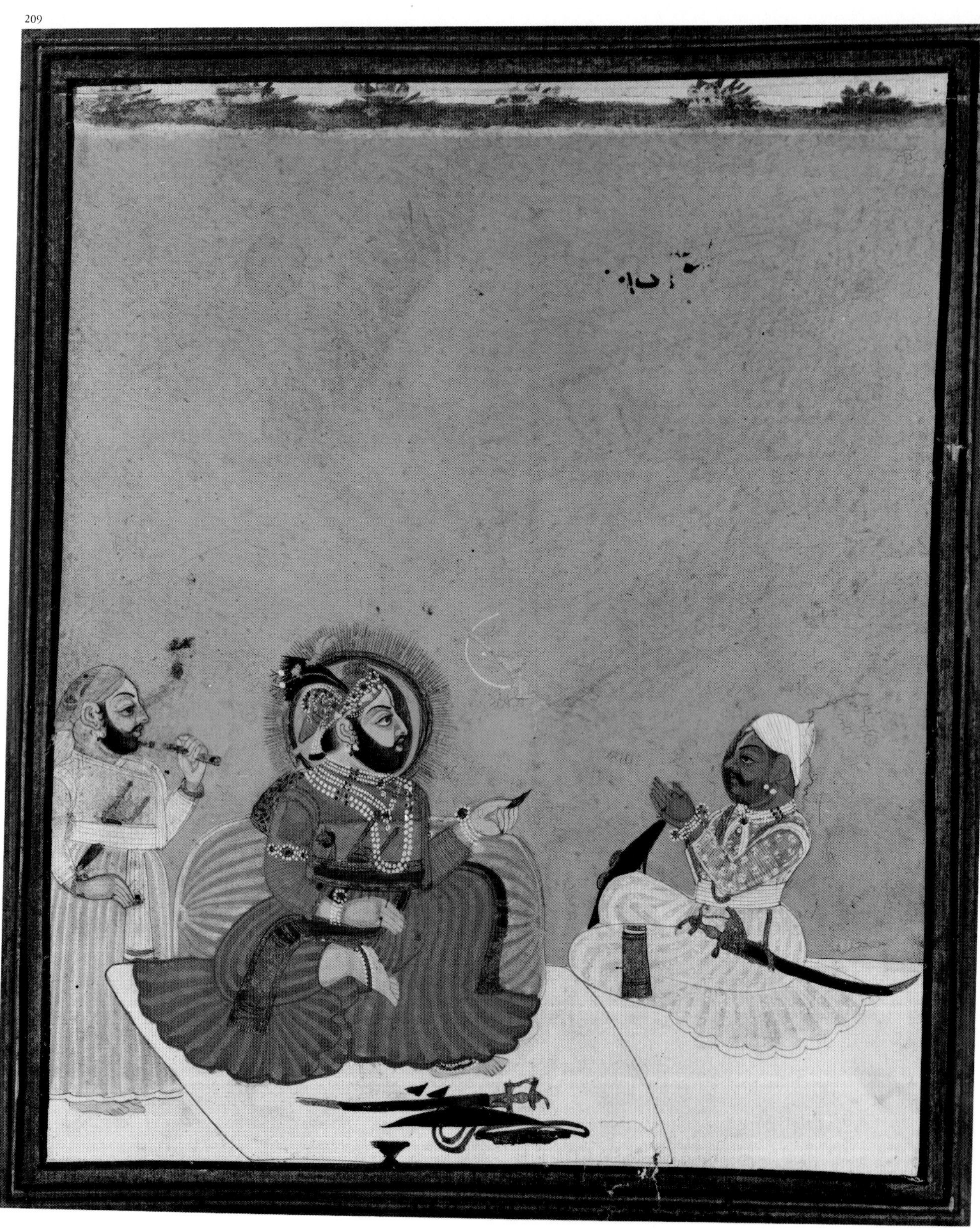

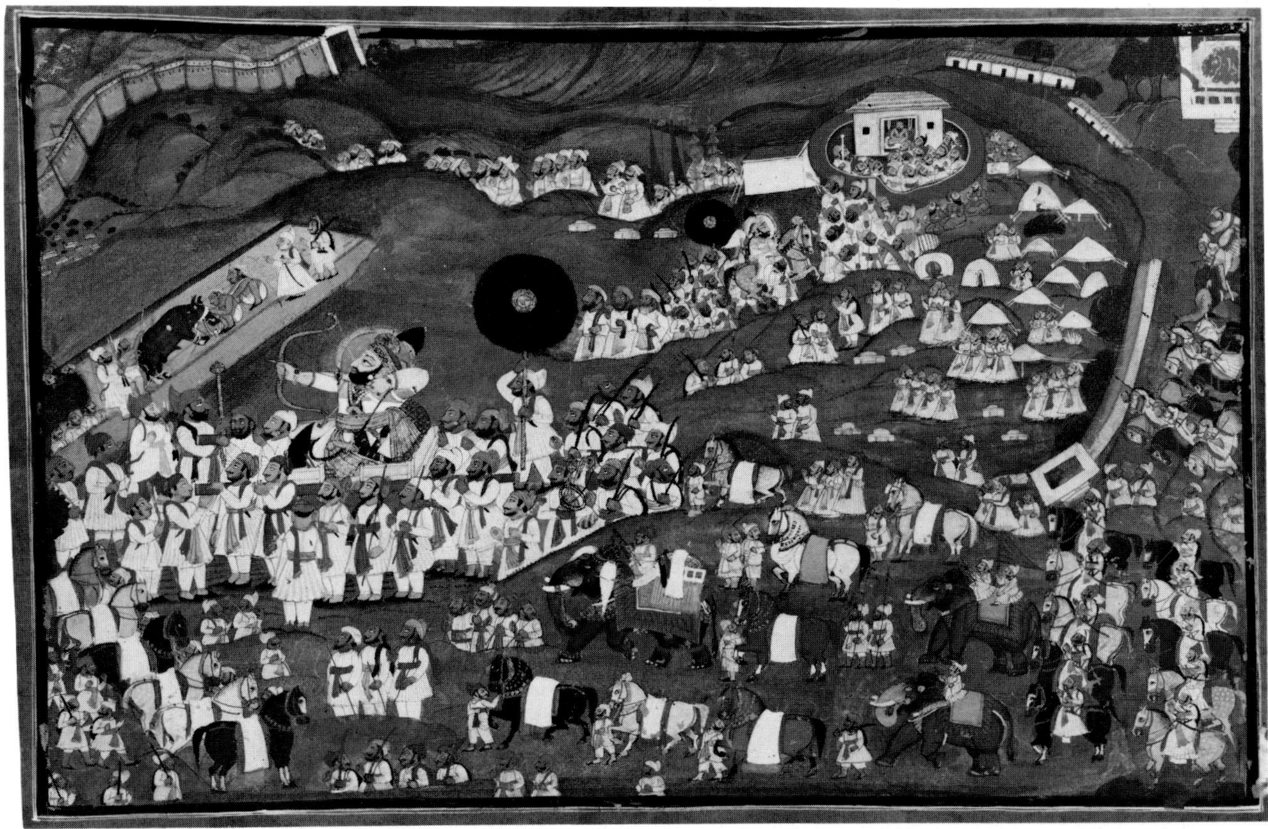

209

Maharana Bhim Singh and a Sardar
Udaipur, early 19th century
21.6 x 17.6 cm

The Maharana, with nimbus, orange *pagri* and *jama,* sits
against a bolster on a white floor-spread, attended by a
chowry-bearer. He offers *pan* as a token of dismissal to a
sardar who folds his hands in respect. Pale green
background. (Oxidised) silver margin; red border with
white and black rules.

Inscribed on the back: *maharajadhiraja
maharanaji śri bhim sighji ri sabi
ro pano sama.*

210

Maharana Bhim Singh Performing a Buffalo Sacrifice
Udaipur, c. 1815-20. Attributed to Chokha
25 x 39.5 cm

The Maharana, with nimbus, wearing a white and yellow
jama, is shown accompanied by mounted sardars and
numerous attendants performing the main observances
prescribed for the fourth day of the bright half of Asvina
during the autumnal martial festival of Navaratri. In the
distance he goes on horseback to visit a *yogi,* while in
the foreground he aims an arrow at a tethered buffalo
from his palanquin. Colonel Tod, who witnessed these
scenes, writes: '...the day opens with the slaughter of a
buffalo. The Rana proceeds to the temple of Devi, when
he worships the sword, and the standard of the Raj Jogi,
to whom, as the high-priest of Siva, the god of war, he
pays homage and makes offerings of sugar, and a
garland of roses. A buffalo having been previously fixed
to a stake near the temple, the Rana sacrifices him with
his own hand, by piercing him from his travelling
throne (raised on men's shoulders and surrounded by his
vassals) with an arrow. In the days of his strength he
seldom failed almost to bury the feather in the flank of
the victim; but on the last occasion his enfeebled arm
made him exclaim with Prithiraj, when, captive and
blind, he was brought forth to amuse the Tartar despot,
''I draw not the bow as in the days of yore'' ' (*Annals
and Antiquities of Rajasthan,* vol II, pp. 681-82).
According to Shyamaldas, whose father had also
witnessed the ceremony (after which the day was called
bhalka cauth), the sacrifice was discontinued after the
reign of Bhim Singh (*Vir Vinod,* vol. I, pp. 128-29).
Brown border with white rules.

Inscribed on the back: *mahajadhiraja mahara śri bhim
sigji ri chabi bhalaka cori pada upare bhalako vata thaka
ri pada ratanalal gajadhar jivan ram tir kubana liya thaka
ora si ri asavari ubi thaki.*

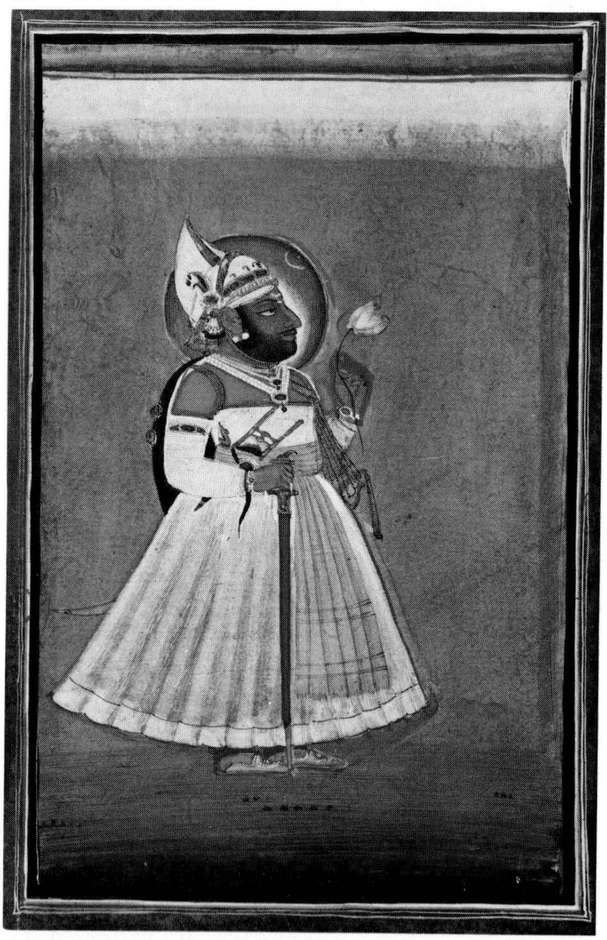

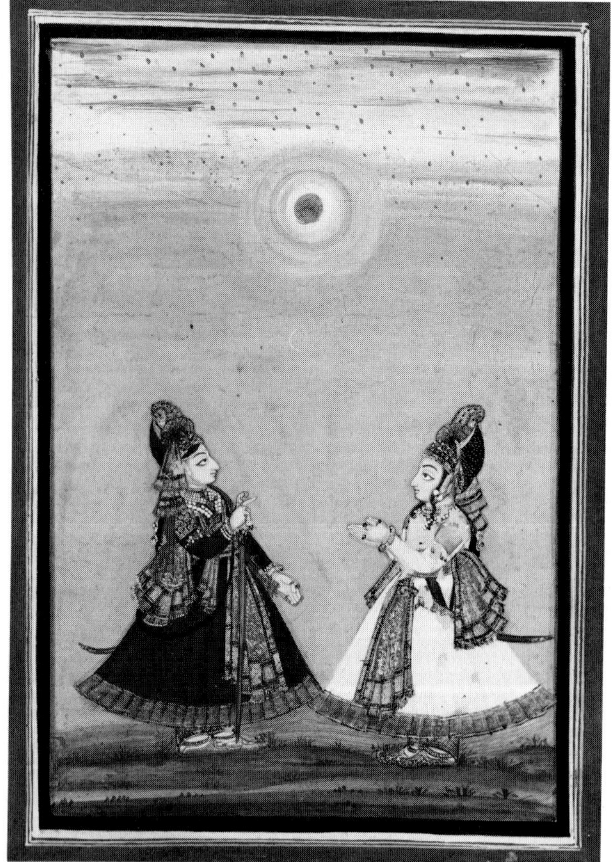

211

Maharana Bhim Singh
Udaipur, c. 1820. Style of Chokha
18.5 x 12 cm

The Maharana, with nimbus, white *pagri*, orange and white *jama* and yellow *patka*, stands facing right, holding a flower in one hand and a sheathed sword in the other. Blue-grey background with white, red and orange bands above. Red border with white ruling.

Inscribed on the back: *mahārāṇaji śrī bhīm sigji.*

212

Prince Amar Singh
Udaipur, c. 1815. Attributed to Chokha
20 x 13.5 cm

The youthful prince, in crimsom *pagri* and *jama* edged with silver, stands holding a long-stemmed flower in one hand and the hilt of a sheathed sword in the other. White background with streaky cloud above. Blue, black and yellow marginal bands. Wide green border with white rules.

Inscribed on the back: *mhārāja kuvar śrī amra sigh bhīm sīghot.*

According to Tod (*Annals and Antiquities of Rajasthan*, vol. I, pp. 542-43) Maharana Bhim Singh had ninety-five children, but only one son (Maharana Jawan Singh) survived him. The elder prince, Amar Singh, died in 1818, after being entertained on his death-bed by Colonel Tod's demonstration of the properties of the camera obscura (Tod, *Travels in Western India*, repr. Delhi, 1971, p. 263). Cf. cat. no. 213.

213

Prince Amar Singh and a Companion
Udaipur, c. 1815. Attributed to Chokha
20 x 13.8 cm

The youthful prince, in deep blue *pagri* and *jama* with silver and gold *patka*, stands holding a sheathed sword with another noble youth (perhaps his brother Jawan Singh), in a white *jama* (somewhat flaked), who performs *namaskar*. Pale verdigris background, with moon and stars shown against streaky cloud. Wide red border with white rules and a vacant blue compartment for an inscription.

Inscribed on the back: *mhārāja kunva śrī amra sīghji bhīm sīghot.*

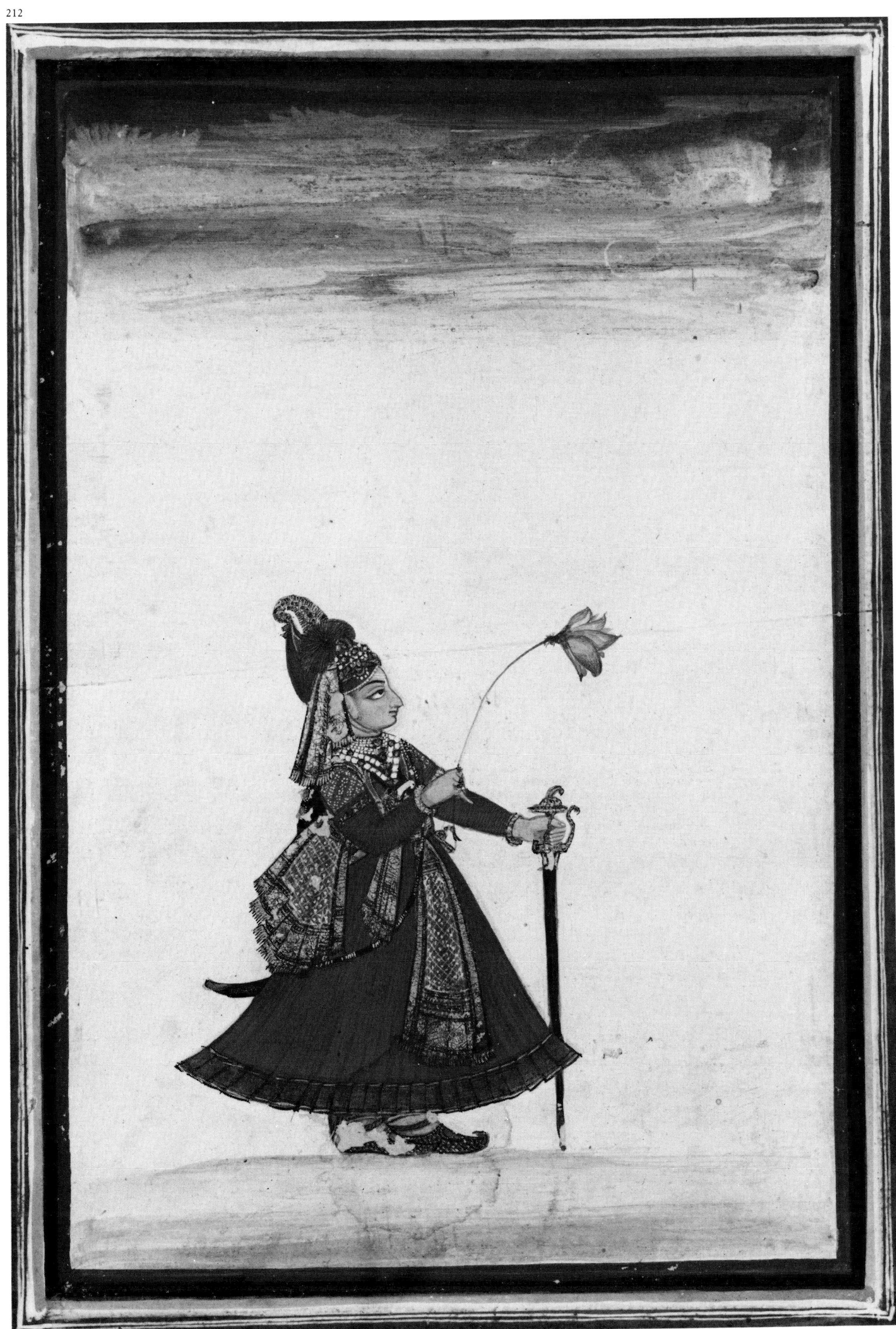

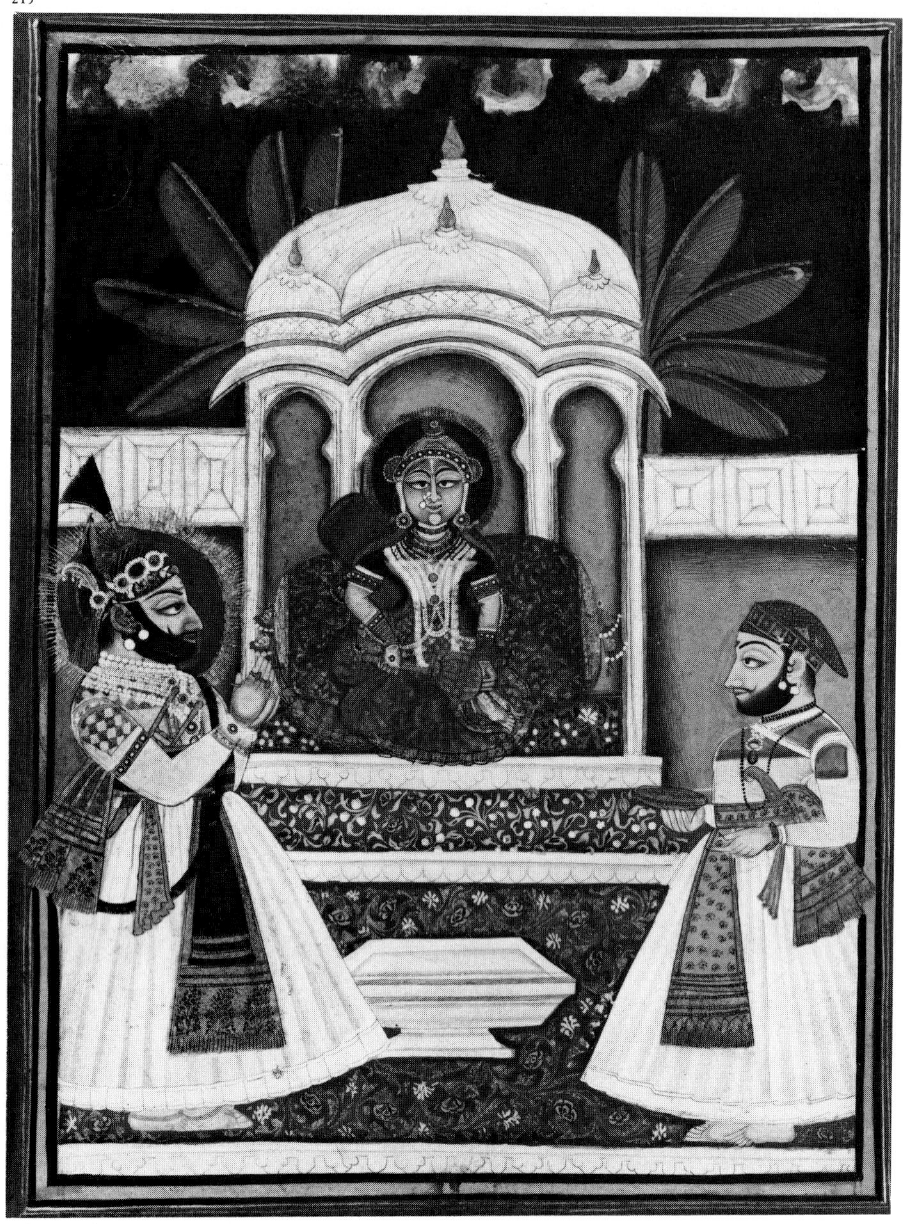

214

Maharana Bhim Singh Seated on a Lion-throne
Udaipur, c. 1820
22.5 x 16.5 cm

The Maharana, with nimbus, wearing a crimson and
gold *jama* and *pagri,* sits on a gold lion-throne on a
terrace, smoking a blue and white ceramic *huqqa.* Two
chowry-bearers stand behind him. Dark green
background. Blue margin with black rules; red border
with white rules.
Inscribed above: *śrī śrī ranāji śrī hajur ri subā rau
pāno sigasana barāja he nara ro.*

Inscribed on the back: *mharanaji śrī bhim syanghji ri
sibī* [in another hand:] *thaka sona rayagaro sigasana.*

215

Maharana Bhim Singh Worshipping Annapurna
Udaipur, c. 1825
24 x 17.7 cm

The Goddess is shown frontally, with a nimbus, seated
against a bolster in a shrine, holding a gold ladle, her
usual attribute. The Maharana, with nimbus, stands on
the left performing *namaskar;* a nobleman with a gold
dish stands on the right. Plantains appear behind a wall
against a deep blue sky with rain-clouds above. Yellow
margin; red border with white rules.

Inscribed on the back: *maharanaji śrī bhīm singhji
mataji śrī anapurnaji darsan karvaya dhasa(?)*

This subject recalls the similar scenes in a bound volume
of paintings of different Maharanas having darshan of
the gods which was prepared for Maharana Bhim Singh,
probably by Chokha among other artists (Government
Museum, Udaipur, no. 1097/25).

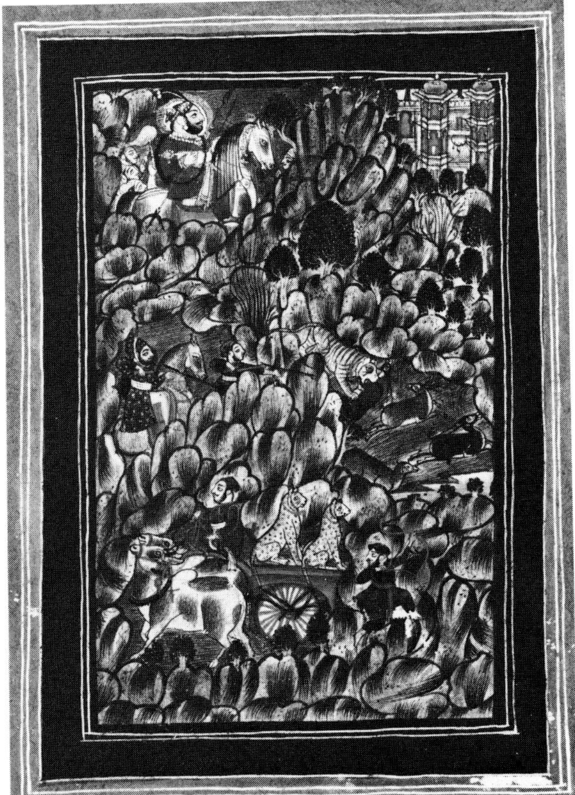

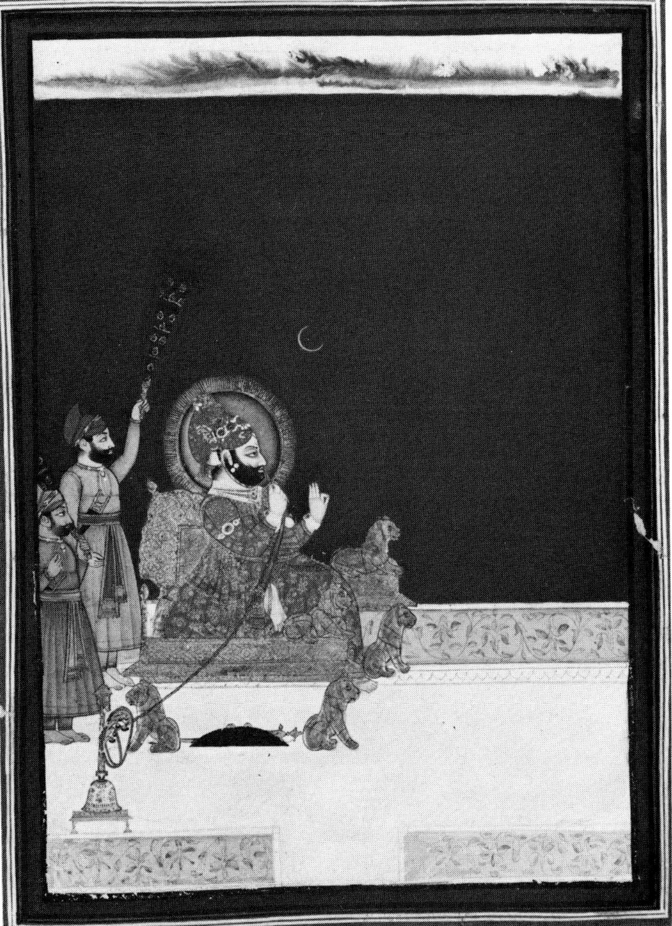

216

Prince Jawan Singh Shooting a Hare
Udaipur c. 1825. Attributed to Chokha
23.3 x 17.6 cm

Prince Jawan Singh, garlanded and wearing a dark blue
bandhana pagri and a gold-edged white *jama,* fires an
arrow from horseback at a fleeing hare. Pale green
background with cloud above. Dark green marginal
band; speckled pink border with white rules, inscribed:
*mahārāja kuvar śrī javan sīghjī goḍo chada galī
asavar.*

217

Maharana Bhim Singh Hunting
Udaipur, c. 1820. By a follower of Chokha
11 x 7 cm

A small scene of the Maharana and companions, dressed
in hunting green, at shikar in a greenish rocky
landscape. The Maharana, with nimbus, rides a piebald
horse. A palace is seen on the right. Hunting cheetahs
sit on a bullock-cart in the foreground. Black margin
with white rules; red border with white rules.

Inscribed on the back: *mahāraṇajī śrī bhīm
sīnghjī.*

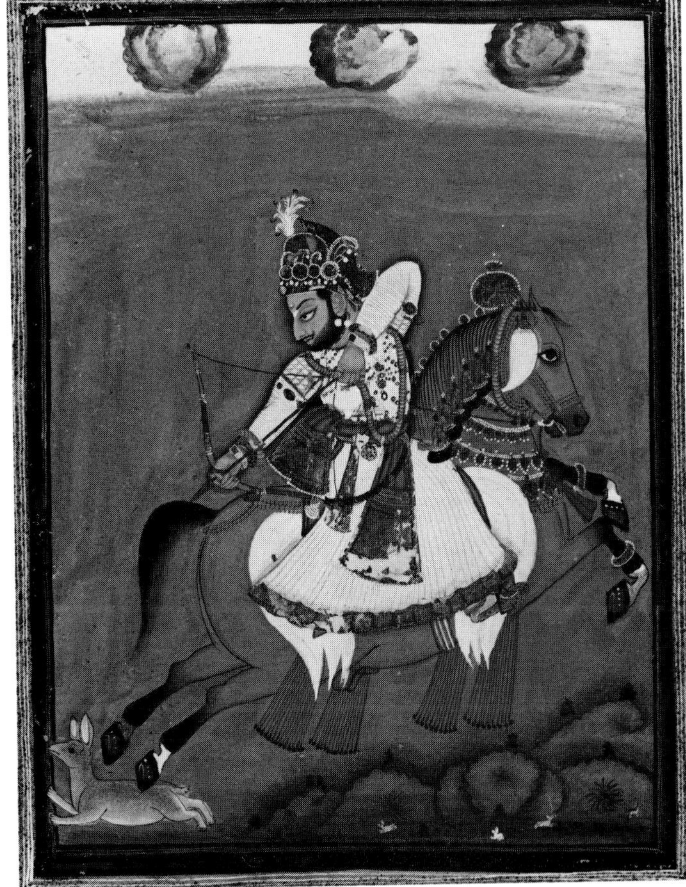

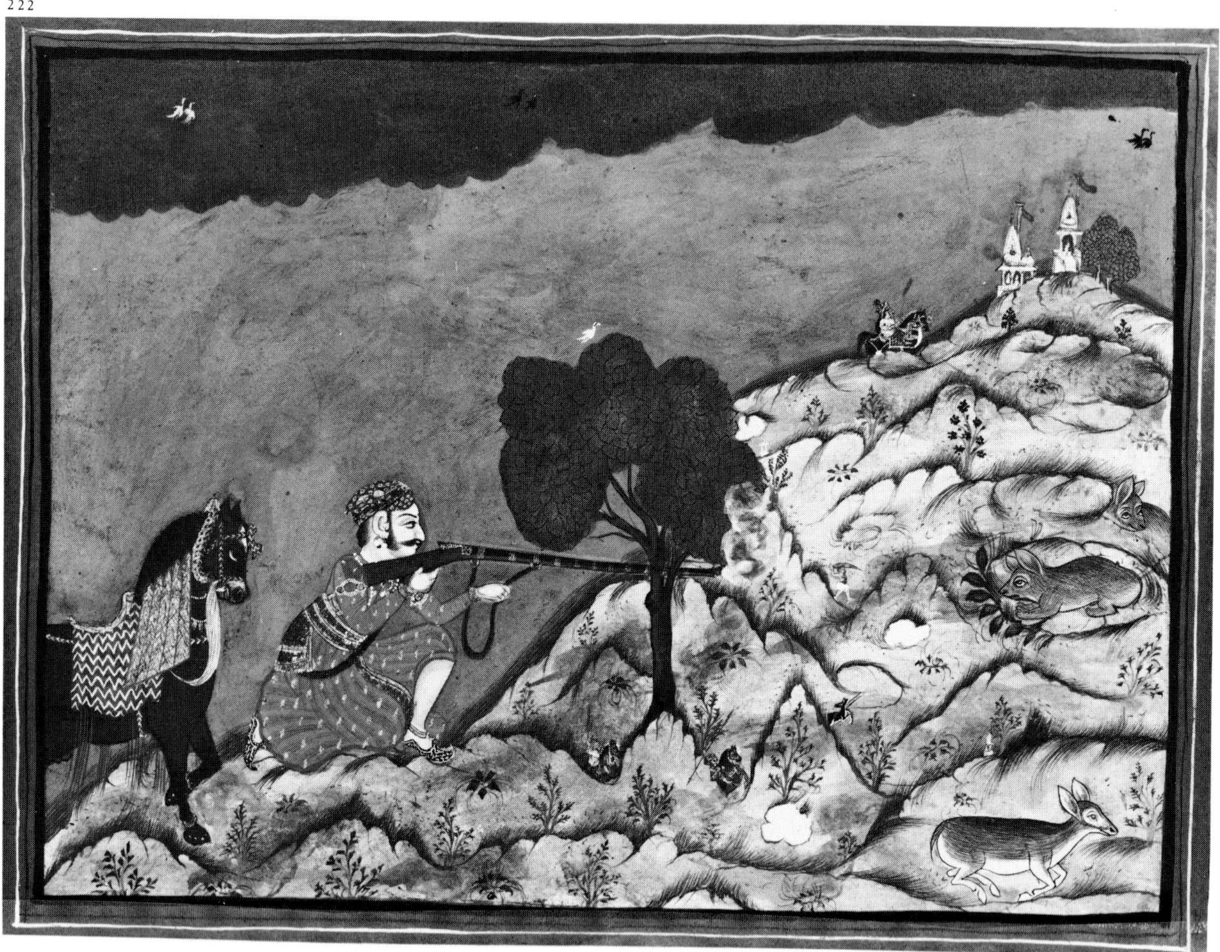

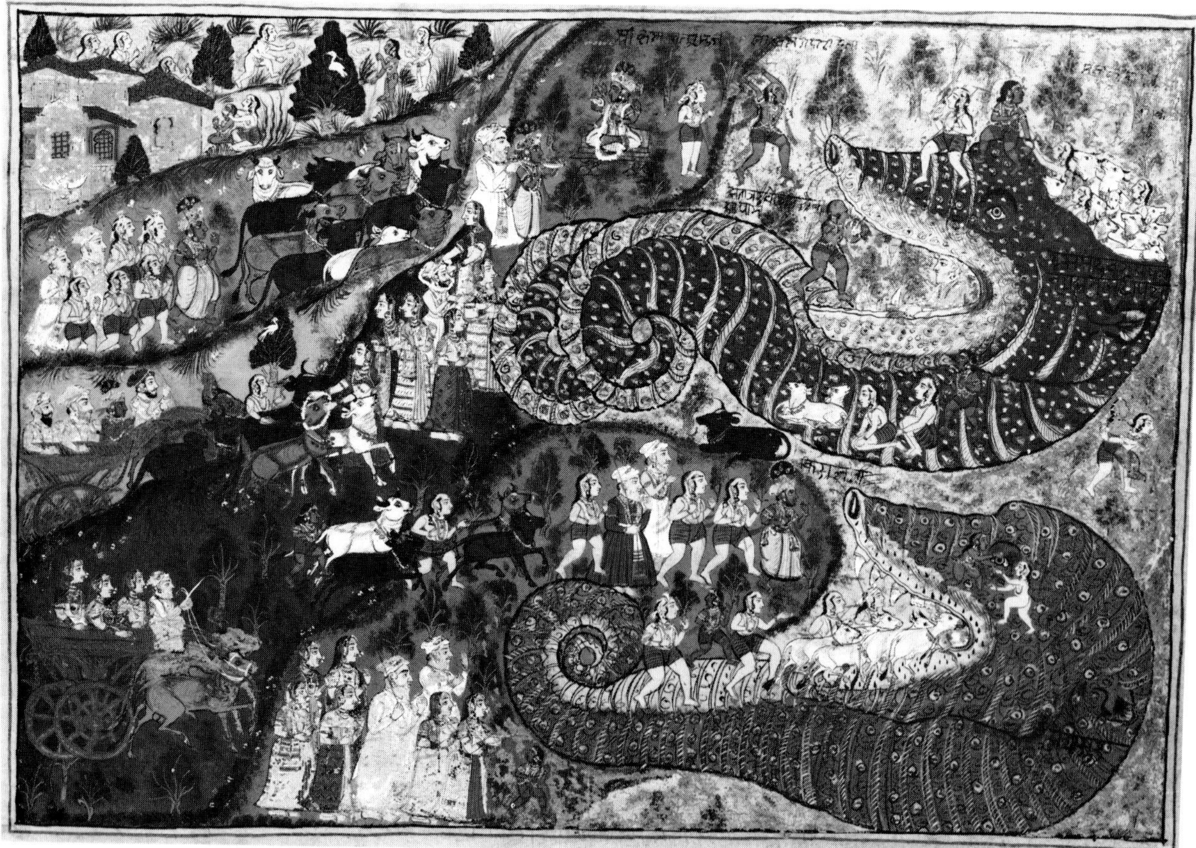

146

218

Maharana Bhim Singh Riding

Udaipur, c. 1820

22.5 x 17.2 cm

The Maharana, with nimbus, in gold-printed green *jama*
and red *pagri,* rides a pale brown stallion and holds a
spear, accompanied by two chowry-bearers on foot. Pale
green background. Red border.

Inscribed on the back: *maharanaji śri bhim
singhji.*

219

Maharana Bhim Singh Riding

Udaipur, c. 1820-25. Style of Chokha

17 x 11.5 cm

The Maharana, with nimbus, dressed in hunting green,
rides a brown stallion and carries a spear, accompanied
by two chowry-bearers in white. Pale green background
with white and blue-grey cloud above. Red border with
white ruling.

Inscribed on the back: *maharanaji śri bhim sighji.*

220

Maharana Bhim Singh Riding an Elephant

Udaipur, c. 1820-25

18.6 x 22.5 cm

The Maharana, with nimbus, orange *pagri* and *jama,*
rides in the howdah of an elephant, with mahout,
chowry-bearers and attendants on foot dressed in white.
Murky green background. Coarsely painted. Red border
with white ruling.

Inscribed on the back: *maharanaji śri bhim
singhji.*

221

Prince Man Singh of Jodhpur (?) Hawking

Udaipur, c. 1800

14.4 x 14.4 cm

A nobleman, identified as Prince Man Singh of Jodhpur
(b. 1783, r. 1803-43) rides a white stallion, holding a
hawk, accompanied by an attendant and a white hound,
in a rocky landscape with a red barge on a lake in the
distance. Indifferent quality. Trimmed at the edges.

Inscribed on the back: *jodapur rajaji ra kuvarji man
singhji ra hā..? upare kulang betho* [in another hand:]
thako ?dili cakari śri patasa?ji hajur jave he.
An indistinct sketch of a nobleman also appears on the
back.

222

A Nobleman Shooting Hares

Mewar, early 19th century

14 x 19.2 cm

A kneeling nobleman in orange *jama* shoots from
behind a tree at hares crouching in a rocky landscape;
his horse stands behind him. Other tiny figures of
huntsmen appear out of proportion in the landscape,
with a temple in the distance. Green background with
blue cloud above. Red border with black and white
rules; yellow outer border.

223

Krishna Slaying Aghasura

Udaipur, late 18th century

34 x 50 cm

Krishna and Balarama are seen several times proceeding
from left to right along with the villagers and cows of
Gokula, who stray into the mouth of the giant serpent
Aghasura, mistaking it for a mountain cave. They are
delivered from this trap by Krishna and Balarama above.
Possibly from a *Bhagavata Purana* series. Buff border
with grey ruling.

Inscribed on the back: *pano dasama ro agasara ro bhava;*
inscriptions on the painting identify the main
protagonists.

This subject was treated quite frequently in Udaipur
illustrations of Vaishnava manuscripts (see Gangoly,
*Critical Catalogue of the Miniature Paintings in the
Baroda Museum,* pl. XXIVa). For one of the earliest
versions of it see R. Parimoo, 'A New Set of Early
Rajasthani Paintings', *Lalit Kala,* 17, fig. 7.

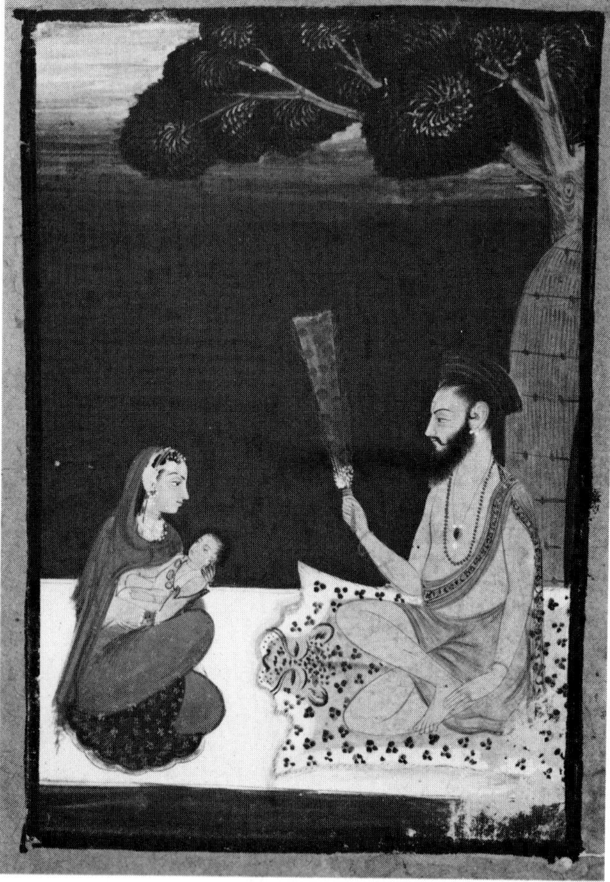

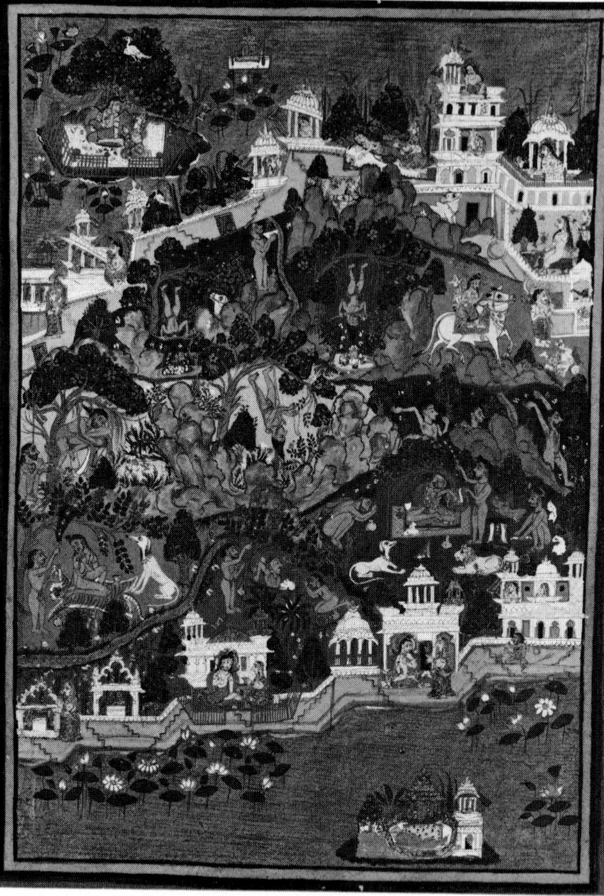

224

A Mother and Child Visiting a *Yogi*
Mewar, c. 1800(?)
16.3 x 11.5 cm

A mother has brought her baby for blessing to a *yogi* who sits holding a *morchal* on a leopard-skin in front of his ashram. Dark grey background with streaky cloud above. Plain buff border.

225

Sadashiva
Udaipur, late 18th century
21.5 x 16.2 cm

Shiva, in his five-faced form, sits holding a trident on a gold throne before Mt Kailasa, sketched in gold. Rajas, deities and demons stand and kneel in attendance in two rows on either side. Shiva also appears airborne in the sky above, seated on a tiger-skin and also in his androgynous form. In the foreground a raja and lady make an offering at a riverside *lingam* shrine, their horse and elephant waiting behind them. Red border. Damaged.

226

Shiva and Parvati on Mt Kailasa
Udaipur, late 18th century
28.7 x 20.5 cm

Shiva and Parvati are seen together in several scenes, dallying in a palace on Mt Kailasa and by a lakeside and riding on the bull Nandi. Ash-smeared *yogis* perform various types of ascetic practices on the hilly slopes. Yellow margin; red border.

227

A Lady Looking in a Mirror
Mewar, late 18th century
21 x 12.2 cm

Partially coloured study of a lady seated against a bolster on a carpeted terrace regarding herself in a mirror; heavy shadow around her facial profile. A slender tree against a plain background with clouds above. Red border.

228

A Yearning Lady
Udaipur, late 18th century
19.8 x 12.2 cm

A lady in green *choli* and orange *ghaghra* stands stretching her arms behind her head in love-longing (in the manner of *Desavarati ragini*), while a maid stands before her playing a *tanpura*. Green foreground; deep blue background. Red border.

229

Rama and Lakshman(?) at a Riverside Ashram
Mewar, late 18th century
24.3 x 17.5 cm

Probably a scene from the *Ramayana,* although
inscriptions on both sides of the picture identify it as a
Krishna story (another shorter, illegible inscription on
the back begins: *śrī ramacandraji...*). Rama, Lakshman
and a rishi stand before a lady (Sita?) who greets them.
In the background a boatman poles a boat across a river
and a rishi sits meditating on a deer-skin near a blazing
fire outside his ashram on the further bank. Yellow
margin; red border.

230

Krishna and Radha Embracing
Mewar, early 19th century
23.6 x 19.3 cm

Krishna and Radha stand embracing in a pale green
field, attended by five maids, four cows and a cowherd.
Red railings in the background, with trees and a red
love-bower beyond. Red border. Crude work.

231

A Lady Performing Surya Puja
Mewar, early 19th century
17.5 x 9.2 cm

A lady stands beside a stretch of water with lotuses,
pouring water from a vessel and contemplating the sun,
shown with a human face amid streaky cloud. Border
with gold stripes and an unrelated verse in Persian
script.

232

Scenes from the Life of Krishna
Udaipur, c. 1820. Attributed to Chokha
45 x 58 cm

The composition is a compressed anthology of incidents
from the early life of Krishna, from his rescue as a baby
by his foster-father Nanda from the persecution of King
Kansa to his childhood among the cowherds of Gokula
and the slaying of the various demons which molested
him, culminating in the eventual overthrow of King
Kansa himself.
In the four compartmented chambers to the left:
Yashoda churns while Krishna milks a cow; Krishna
steals butter from a jar; Nanda presents the infant
Krishna to Yashoda; three seated figures. To the left of
the central river: Krishna slays the ass-demon Dhenuka
and the whirlwind demon Trinavartta; he sports with the
gopas and miraculously drags a heavy mortar; he slays
the demoness Putana by sucking at her breast and the
demon Aghasura. Above the central river: a female deity
clutches severed human arms, while below Krishna
quells the snake-demon Kaliya, whose wives intercede
for him; a rishi sits with attendant ladies; Nanda bears
the infant Krishna safely across the river, protected by a
tiger and the snake Shesha; to the right of the river,

Krishna raises Mt Govardhana, consumes the forest-fire
and slays the horse, bull and crane demons as well as
Kansa's wrestlers and elephant, while his brother
Balarama looks on.
In the four compartmented chambers to the right,
Krishna and Balarama kill Kansa; Krishna's real parents
Vasudeva and Devaki stand before an image of Shri
Nathji; Nanda substitutes his own child for the infant
Krishna, while two demonic guards sleep at the door
below. Yellow margin; narrow red border.
Some of the figures, e.g. Putana and the two demonic
guards, appear to be by Chokha himself, although
others are more weakly painted and may be by a
follower.

233

Shiva and Parvati Embracing
Udaipur, c. 1830-40
19.8 x 11.5 cm

Shiva and his consort Parvati sit embracing in a palace
room with a floral carpet and yellow walls with a red
niche behind; the scene is partly framed by an engrailed
arch with heavy green shadow surround. Lime-green
margin with black rules; red border with white rules.

234

Maharana Jawan Singh Riding
Udaipur, c. 1830-35
49.5 x 36 cm

The Maharana, with nimbus, in gold-edged white *jama,*
rides a dark stallion, Eklinga Baksh , accompanied by
numerous attendants on foot with regalia, *huqqa,*
chowries, etc. Blue-green background, with distant hills
and large indigo, white and grey clouds piled above.
Green margin; red border.
Inscribed above: *maharajadhiraja maharana śrī javan
sīghji ri chabi ro pano ghode ekaliga bagas asavar.*

Inscribed below in a 19th century English hand: *Muha
Rana Juwan Singh* (cf. cat. no. 182).

235

Maharana Jawan Singh Riding
Udaipur, c. 1835. By Khaja (?)
39.2 x 27 cm

The Maharana, with nimbus, in a white *jama* edged
with gold, rides a white stallion accompanied by four
attendants. Green background; indigo clouds in a white
sky. Deep blue margin; dull crimson border with white
rules and sketchy silver floral pattern.

Inscribed on the back: *pano 1 maharana śrī 108 śrī javan
sigji ri chavi ro ghode sabataj asavar catara khajo saradari
puran vasi re ..? jma?*

Similar composition and border to cat. no. 236, dated
1835. The artist Khaja(?), an inhabitant of Sardari
Purna(?), is otherwise unknown.

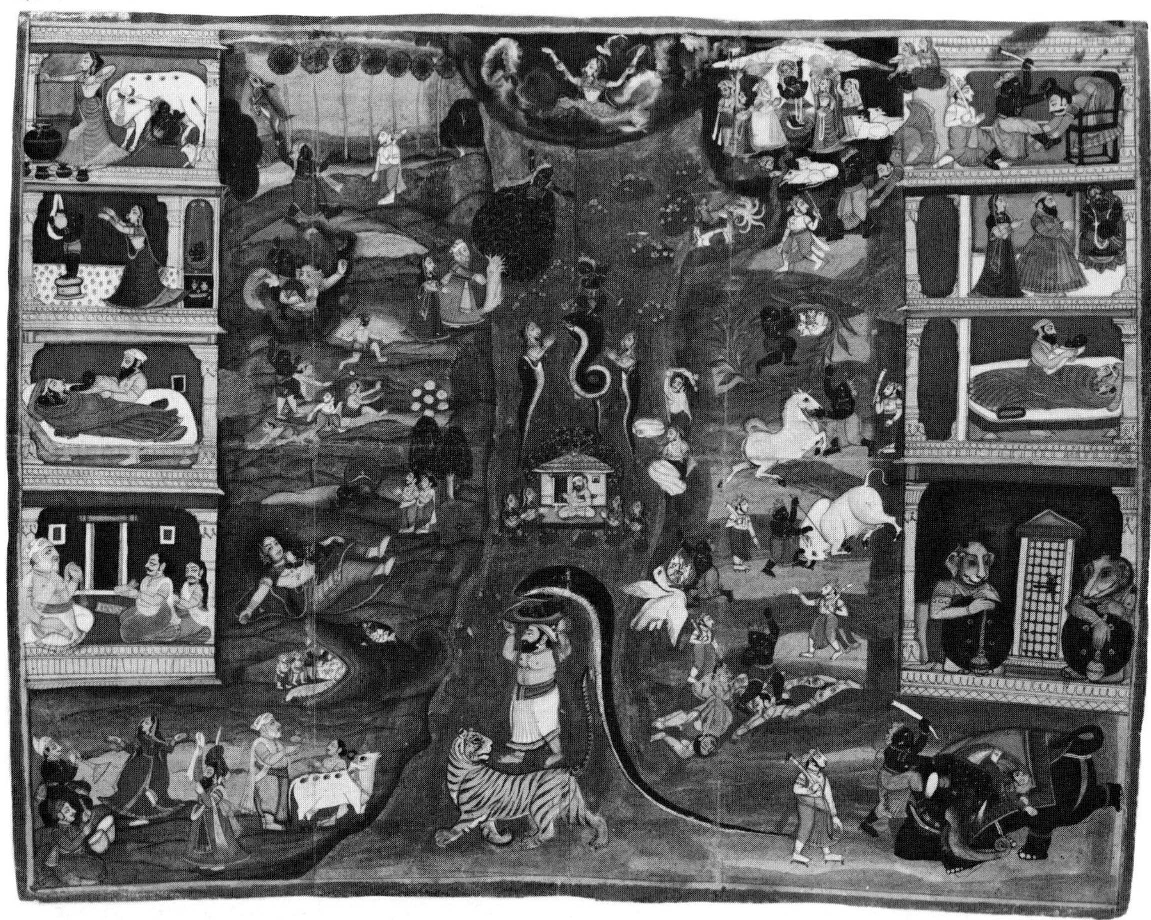

232

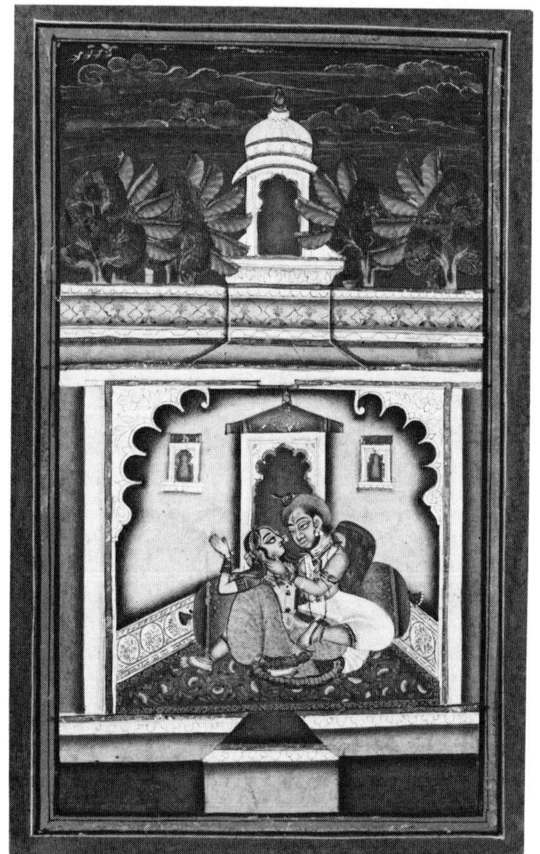

233

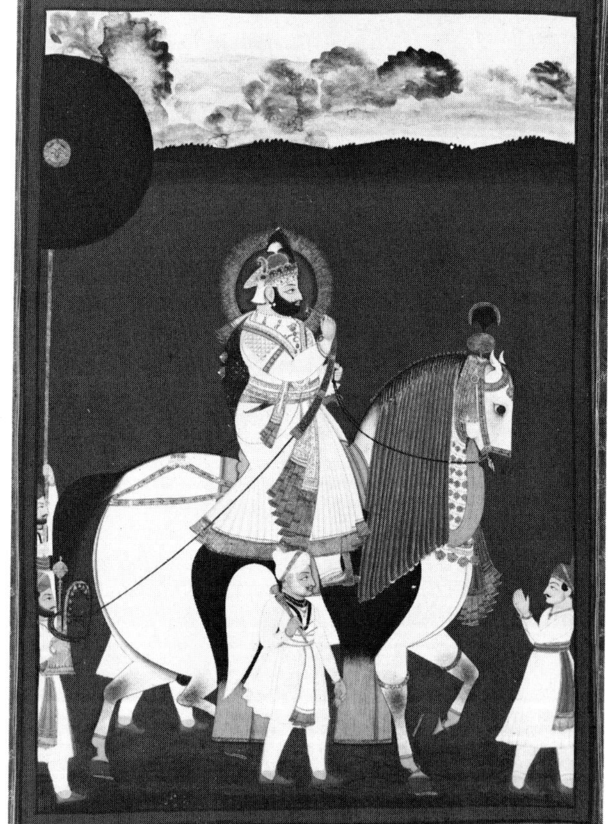

235

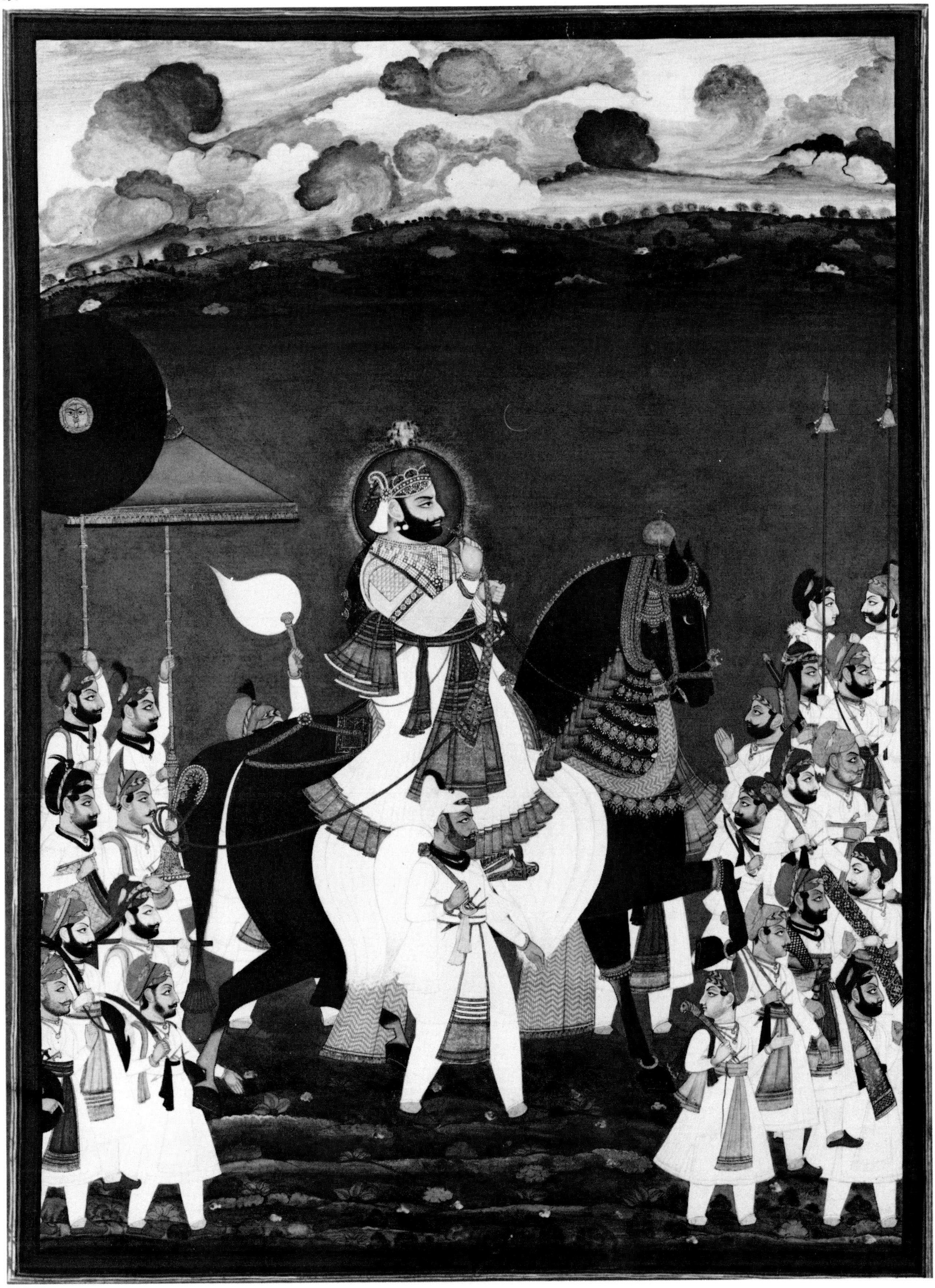

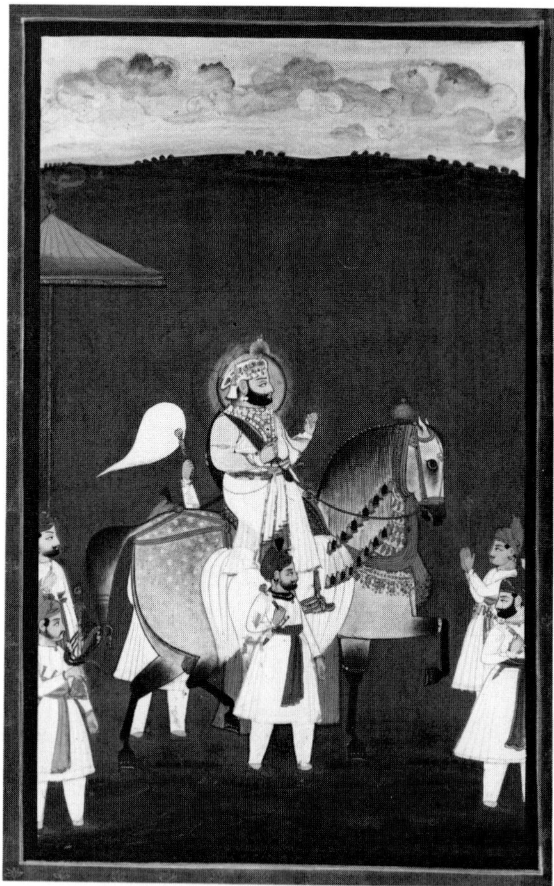

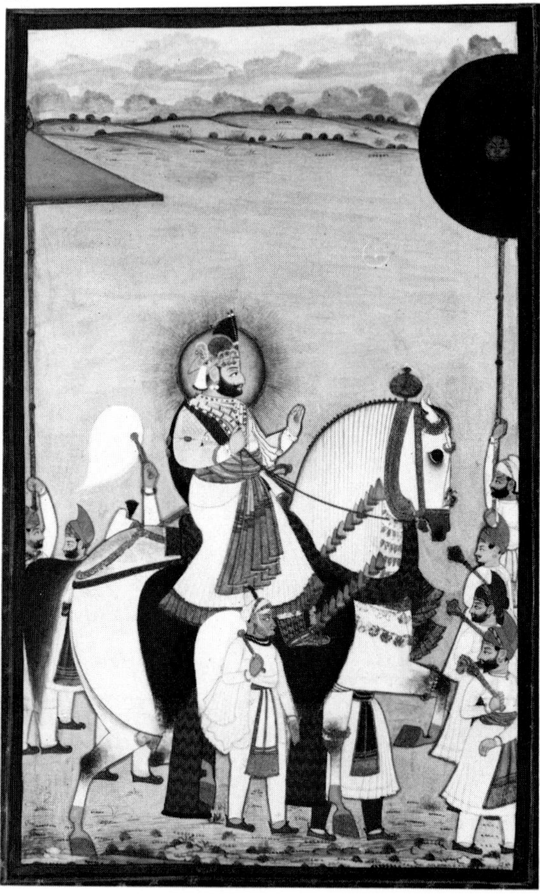

236
Maharana Jawan Singh Riding
Udaipur, 1835. By Rama
38.7 x 23.6 cm

The Maharana, with nimbus, in white *jama* and *pagri*,
rides a grey stallion, Jag Jeth , accompanied by six
attendants on foot with *huqqa,* chowry and regalia.
Olive-green background with cloudy sky. Olive-green
margin; dull crimson border with white rules and
sketchy silver floral pattern.

Inscribed on the back: *pano 1 maharana śrī 108 śrī javan
sigjī rī chabī ro ghode jag jeth asavar cataro rāmo sambat
1892 vrṣe katī sud 5.*

237
Maharana Jawan Singh Riding
Udaipur, c. 1835
31.4 x 19.6 cm

The Maharana, with nimbus, rides a brown stallion,
accompanied by numerous attendants on foot with
huqqa, chowries and regalia. Cream background with
cloudy sky above. Pale turquoise margin, dull crimson
border with silver floral motifs.

Inscribed on the back: *mharaṇajī śrī juvān sīghjī.*

238
Maharana Jawan Singh Riding
Udaipur, 1835. By Nathu
43.5 x 25.5 cm

The Maharana, with nimbus, rides a white stallion,
accompanied by nine attendants on foot with chowries
and regalia. Pale green landscape background with
cloudy sky. Olive-green margin, dark cerise border with
white rules and perfunctory silver floral motifs,
numbered 88.

Inscribed on the back: *pano 1 mharajadhiraja maharana
śrī śrī 108 śrī śrī śrī maharana śrī
javan sigjī rī chabī ra pano ghode asavar ghodo sabataj
kalamī cataro nathu(?) sabat 1892 vrṣe jeth sud 5.*

239
Maharana Jawan Singh Riding
Udaipur, c. 1835
23 x 15 cm

The Maharana, with nimbus, wearing a white *jama* and
a shield on his back, rides a dark brown stallion,
accompanied by four attendants on foot with chowries
and regalia. Green background with distant hills and
white sky suffused with crimson. Grey-blue with silver
decoration and green margins; trimmed dark crimson
border flecked with silver.

Inscribed on the back: *maharaṇajī śrī 108 śrī javān sigjī.*

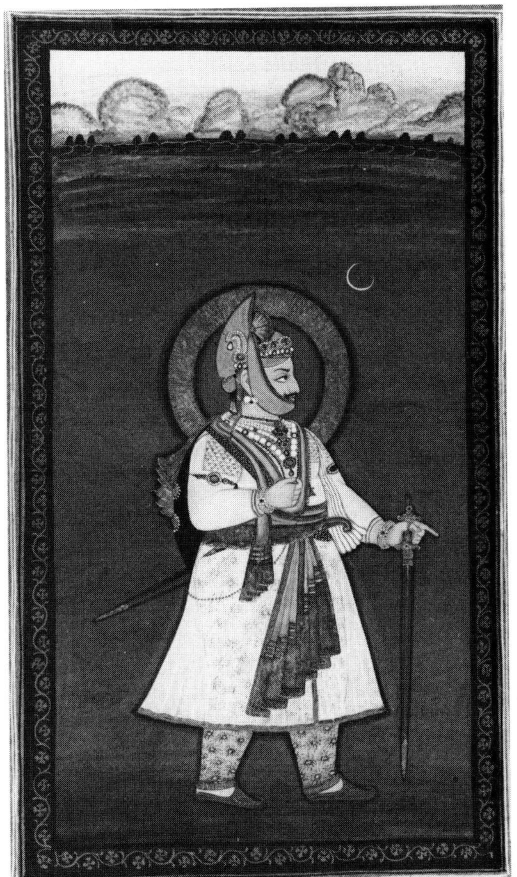

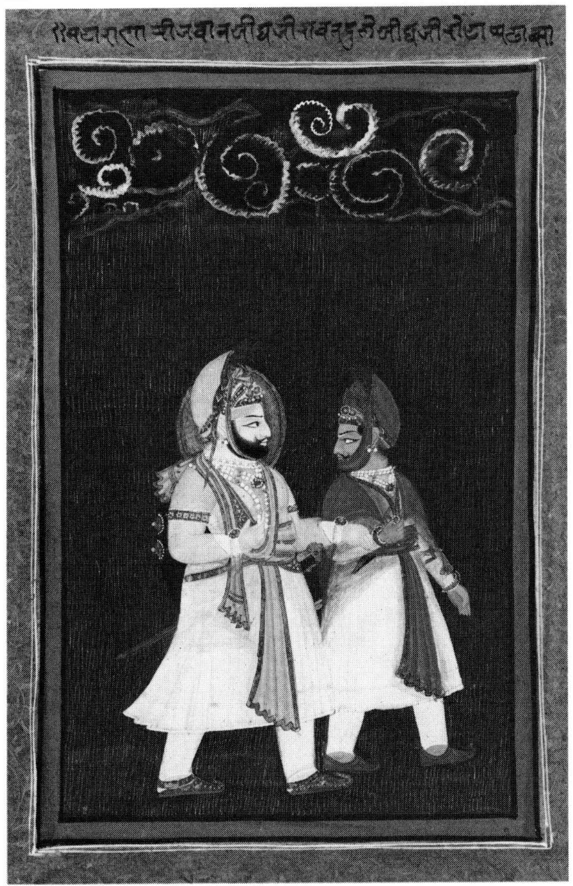

240

Maharana Jawan Singh

Udaipur, c. 1830-35

24.5 x 13.3 cm, 47.6 x 32.9 with border

The Maharana, with nimbus, yellow *pagri* and beard-cover and transparent white *jama*, stands holding a sheathed sword against a green landscape background with cloudy sky above. Olive-green margin with silver meander; dull crimson border with silver diaper pattern enclosing gold circles, with white and silver rules; numbered 20.

Inscribed on the back: *mahāraṇā śrī javan sighji ubha thaka.*

This portrait bears many similarities to those prepared for Colonel Tod by the artist Ghasi, who worked for him at Udaipur (e.g. Victoria and Albert Museum, R.A.S. Loan 16).

241

Maharana Jawan Singh Riding with Rawat Dule Singh

Udaipur, c. 1835

26.3 x 19.2 cm

The Maharana, with nimbus, and Rawat Dule Singh, seen greeting the Maharana respectfully with folded hands, are both mounted. They are accompanied by mace-bearers, chowry-bearers, a *huqqa*-bearer and other attendants. Pale green background with distant hills and cloudy sky above. Green margin with black and white rules; border trimmed.

Inscribed above: *mhāranaji śri javan sighji ghoḍo berojode rāvat dule sighji ghoḍo jobana chaka.*

242

Maharana Jawan Singh with Rawat Dule Singh

Udaipur, c. 1835

21.2 x 14 cm

The Maharana, with nimbus, walks holding the wrist of Rawat Dule Singh, the Thakur of Asind, in a rainstorm at night. Their white *jamas* are stained with dye running from their *pagris* and *patkas*, which are yellow and red respectively. Each wears a green sprig in his *pagri*. Dark grey background with falling rain and convoluted clouds. Blue margin; dull crimson border with silver floral meander pattern.

Inscribed above: *mahāraṇā śri javan sighji rāvat dule sighji ro hath dhabya.*

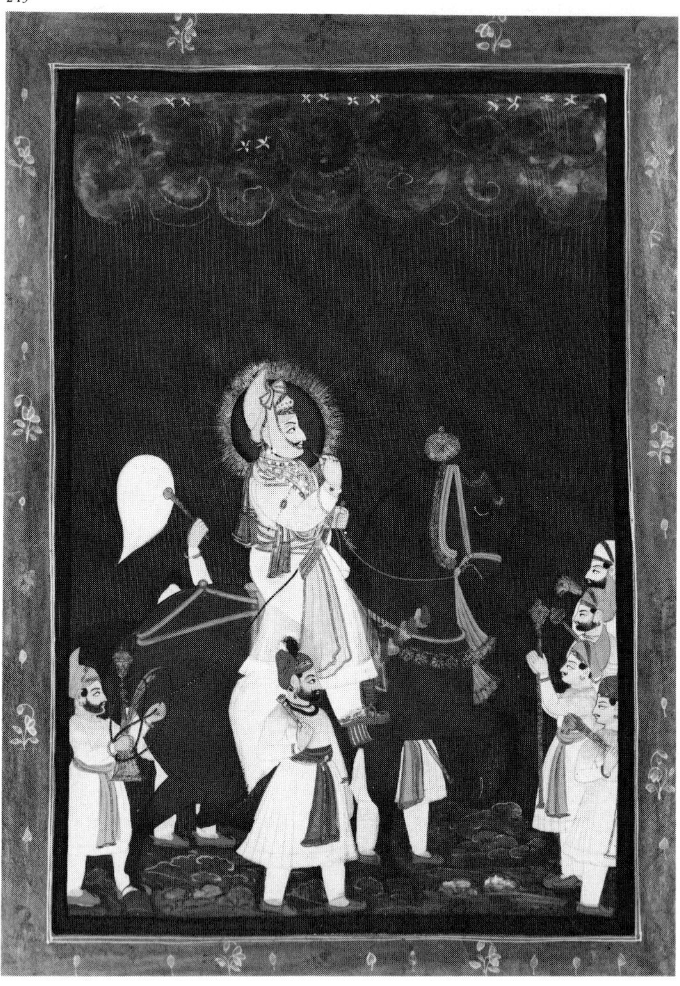

Blue margin with gold quatrefoil pattern; magenta border speckled with gold. A long and poorly written inscription on the back is essentially a list of nearly fifty names of sardars and other figures in the picture; the Maharana's immediate companions are Sirdar Singh, Rawat Dule Singh, Idar Singh, Rawat Isari Singh, Rawat Amar Singh and Raja Sangram Singh. A similar composition with far fewer figures is in a private collection.

245

Maharana Jawan Singh with Two Sardars
Udaipur, c. 1835
24 x 17 cm

The Maharana, with nimbus, white *jama* and yellow *pagri* and *patka,* sits against a bolster on a carpeted terrace under a *shamiana,* while a sardar offers him a drink and another fans him with a *morchal.* Pale green background with clouds above. Red border with white rules.

246

Maharana Jawan Singh
Udaipur, c. 1835
18.3 x 11.6 cm

The Maharana, with nimbus, dressed in hunting green, stands facing right with a gun cradled in his arm. White background with blue cloud. Dull crimson border with white rules and pattern of silver circles.

Inscribed on the back: *mharaṇa śrī javan sīghjī.*

247

Maharana Jawan Singh Riding
Udaipur, c. 1835
26 x 17 cm

The Maharana, with nimbus, gold *pagri* and gold and green overcoat, rides a dark brown stallion, Manak, accompanied by attendants on foot with chowries, *huqqa,* regalia and a hound in a red jacket. Cream background, with distant hills streaked with gold. Blue margin with black and white rules and gold meander pattern; pale brown border with gold, black and white rules, much trimmed.
Inscribed above: *mharaṇajī śrī javan sīghjī ghoḍo mānak.*

248

Maharana Jawan Singh Riding
Udaipur, c. 1835
22.3 x 15.1 cm

The Maharana, with nimbus, rides a galloping dark chestnut stallion and looks backwards over his shoulder as he wields a spear in his right hand. Pale green background. Gold inner and outer margins; buff inner border with gold quatrefoil pattern, outer border trimmed.
Inscribed above: *maharaṇojī śrī javan sīghjī goḍo mānak.*

243

Maharana Jawan Singh Riding in the Rain
Udaipur, c. 1835
40 x 26.5 cm

The Maharana, with nimbus, in a transparent white *jama,* rides a dark brown stallion accompanied by attendants on foot with a *huqqa,* chowry and regalia. Storm clouds above with flying cranes, and rain falling against a black background. Olive-green margin, red border with white rules and white and gold floral motifs.

Inscribed on the back: *pāno 1 maharaṇa śrī 108 śrī javan sīgjī ghoḍe asavar.*

244

Maharana Jawan Singh Bathing with his Sardars
Udaipur, c. 1835
42.6 x 28.8 cm

The Maharana, with nimbus, stands chest-deep in a palace pool, accompanied by numerous sardars, some of whom hold vessels or boards to aid their buoyancy; one of them holds the Maharana's *huqqa* above water. Attendants, ladies and musicians watch from the sides.

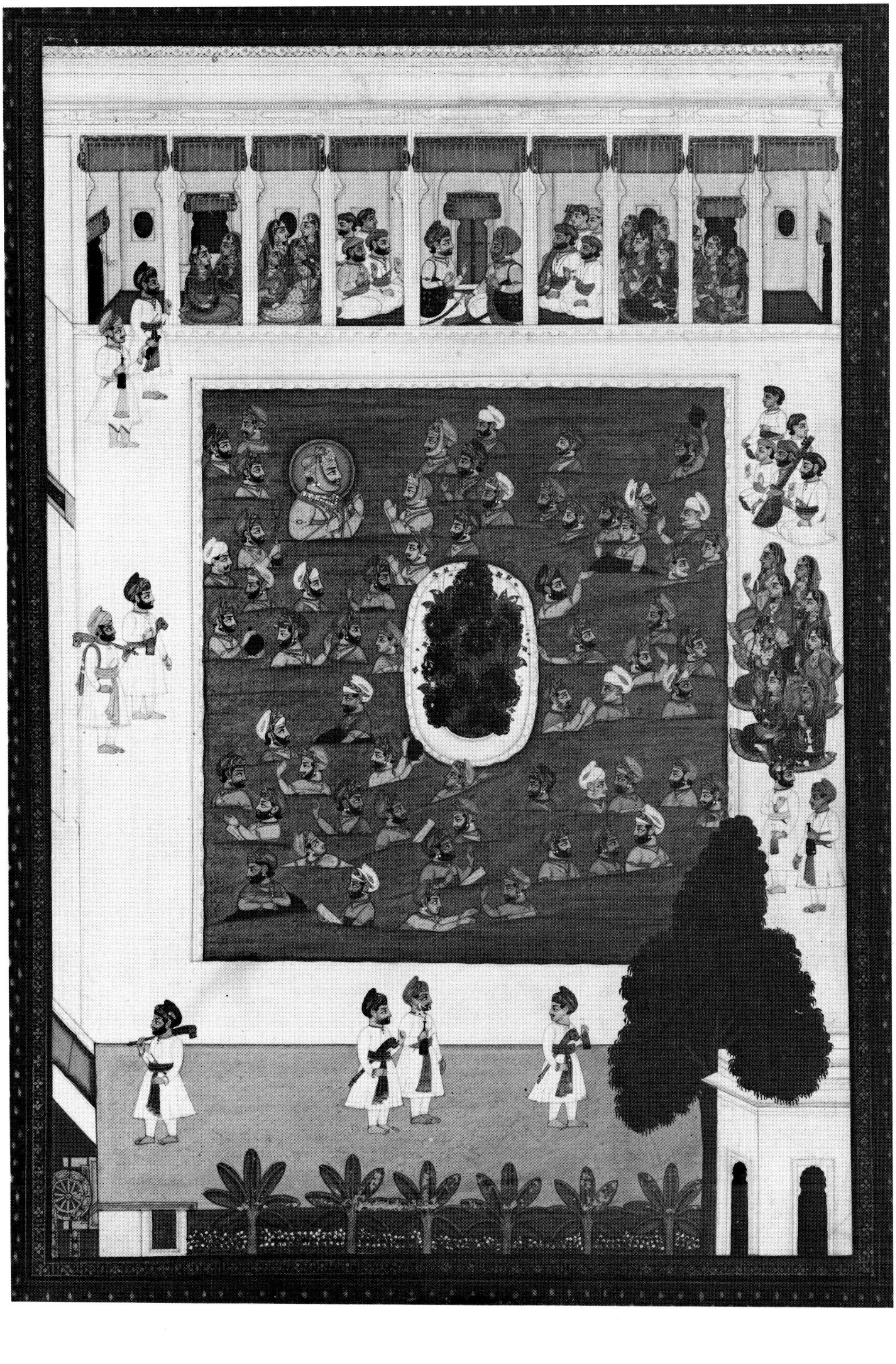

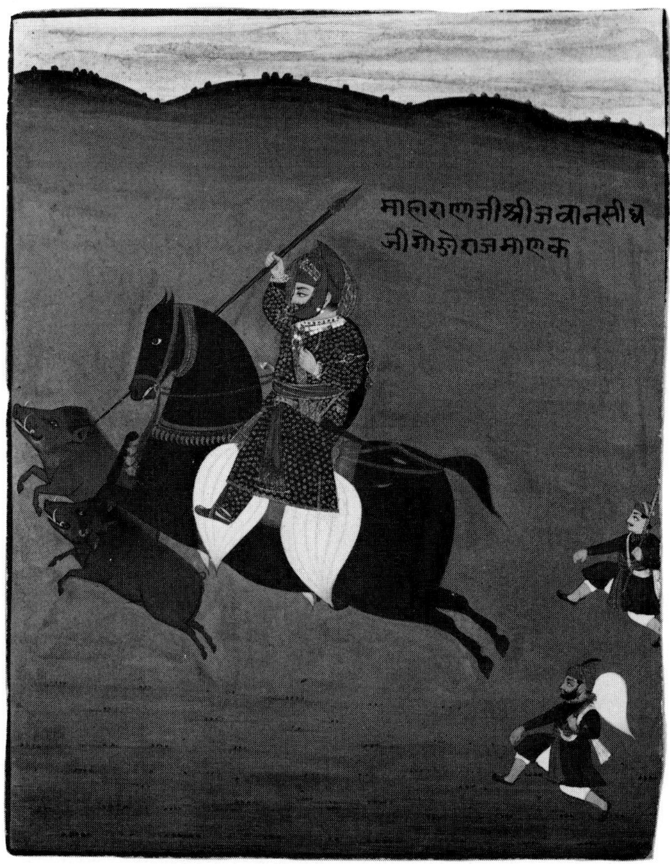

249

Maharana Jawan Singh Hunting Boar
Udaipur, c. 1835
26.5 x 21.1 cm

The Maharana, with nimbus, rides a brown stallion and strikes at two fleeing boars with a spear. Two attendants run behind; all are dressed in hunting green. Bluish-green landscape. Black margin; edges severely trimmed.
Inscribed: *maharanaji sri javan sighji godo raj manak.*

250

Maharana Jawan Singh Killing a Boar
Udaipur, c. 1835
18.6 x 15.2 cm

The Maharana, with nimbus and dressed in hunting green, rides a chestnut stallion and strikes at a boar with a sword. Blue margin; buff border, much trimmed at top and bottom.
Inscribed above: *mharanaji sri javan sighji ghodo gopal bagas.*

251

Maharana Sardar Singh Killing a Boar
Udaipur, c. 1840
17.3 x 15.7 cm

The Maharana, with nimbus and dressed in hunting green, rides a grey horse and strikes at a fleeing boar with a sword. White background. Green margin; trimmed buff border with black ruling.
Inscribed above: *maharajadhiraja maharana sri saradar sighji ghodo ravat pasav.*

252

Krishna Taking Toll *(Danalila)*
Udaipur, 1836. By Rama
22.9 x 15.6 cm

One of the youthful sports of Krishna was to waylay the milkmaids and demand a toll before letting them pass. Here Krishna and Balarama stand on the further bank of the Jumna with a townscape to the left. The milkmaids with their cows and empty pitchers are in the foreground. Two of them are about to cross the river, when they will be waylaid by Krishna. Olive-green, buff and olive-green margins; ultramarine border with white and black rules, flecked with silver.

Inscribed on the back: *sri krasna(?) ri sabi ro pano bansi bajavata thaka citare rame pane najar ki do karapo(?)he samat 1893 ka asoj sud 2 najar huvo.*
Numbered: 116.

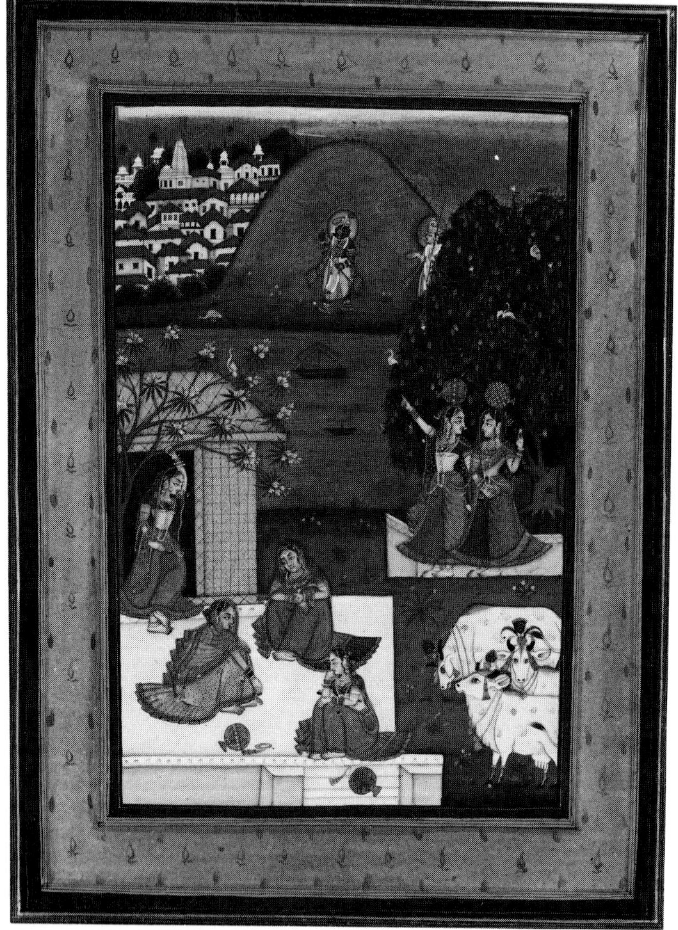

253

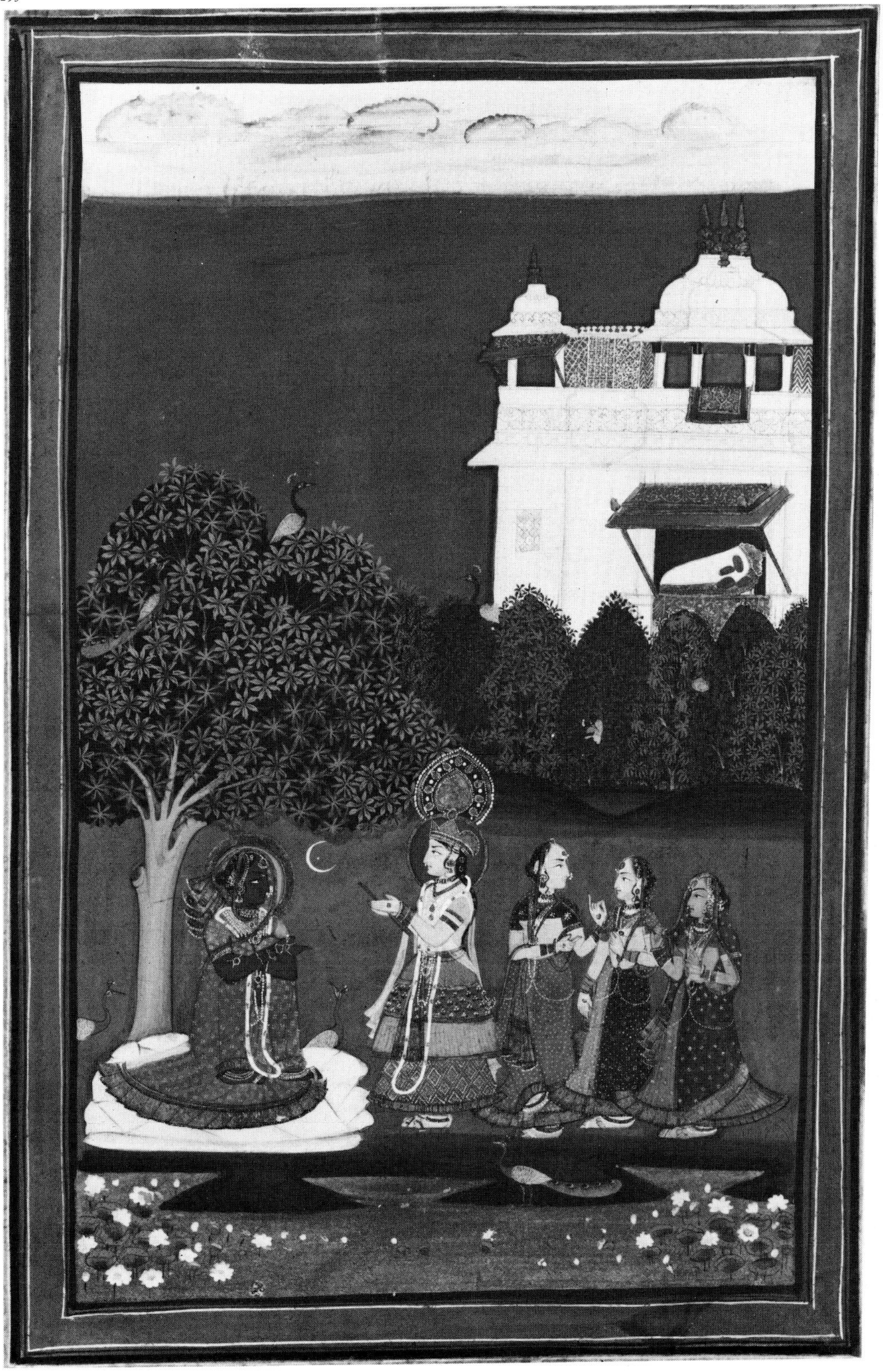

253
Radha and Krishna Exchange Clothes
Udaipur, c. 1835
24.1 x 15.1 cm

As part of their love-play Radha and Krishna have exchanged their clothing. Radha stands before Krishna, seated under a tree. Three maids stand in attendance, and peacocks perch in the trees; in the distance a palace with an empty bed-chamber. Grey-blue margin; trimmed pale cerise border with ruling and silver meander pattern.

Cf. cat. nos. 254 and 255; a picture of Rama and Sita enthroned, dated 1840 and by Baijnath, son of Chokha, in the National Museum, New Delhi, is related in style but of somewhat better quality.

254
Krishna Waking Radha
Udaipur, c. 1835-40
20.7 x 13.1 cm

Krishna awakens Radha, who is sleeping on a terrace
attended by two dozing maids with fans, by touching
her belly with his flute. Pale blue sky with crescent
moon and streaky cloud. Trimmed pale orange border.
By the same clumsy follower of Chokha as cat. no. 255.

255
Krishna and Radha Looking in a Mirror
Udaipur, c. 1835-40
29.8 x 17.8 cm

Krishna and Radha sit together on a lion-throne
(through which their legs seem to protrude) on a terrace;
they gaze at their reflection in a mirror held by a maid.
Three other maids attend them with chowries and *pan*.
Two silver candle-holders in the form of women stand in
the foreground. Pale blue sky with silver moon and
stars. Dark viridian margin; sepia border with black and
white rules and vacant cartouche for an inscription.
Cf. cat. no. 254.

256
Krishna and Radha on the Riverbank
Udaipur, c. 1830-40
16 x 14.2 cm

Krishna, with nimbus and wearing a layered dancing-
skirt, stands on a lotus to the left of a creeper-entwined
tree, while Radha performs *namaskar* to him on the
right. Flowering plantains are on either side, and the
river Jumna in the foreground with ducks and lotuses.
Yellow margin; red border with black and white ruling.
The lush treatment of this subject, with the curving,
elongated eyes of the figures, is related to the style of
picchavai or temple-hanging paintings of Krishna as Shri
Nathji which is still practised at Nathdwara, an
important pilgrimage centre to the north of Udaipur (see
R. Skelton, *Rajasthani Temple-Hangings of the Krishna
Cult,* New York, 1973).

257
Laila Visiting Majnun
Udaipur, c. 1835-40
24.2 x 17.2 cm

An episode from the well-known Islamic love story of
Laila and Majnun; a reinterpretation of a common
Mughal theme, in the bluish-green palette typical of
Jawan Singh's reign. Laila, visiting Majnun in the
wilderness, is accompanied by five maids, and he by a
blue dog, a lion and a nilgai. Cloudy sky, streaked with
gold. Blue inner border with gold quatrefoils; trimmed
reddish-brown outer border with black and white rules.

258
A Lady Performing Surya Puja
Udaipur, c. 1835
17.5 x 11.8 cm

A lady, nude except for a transparent waist-cloth, stands
on a silver stool in a landscape pouring water from a
gold vessel as the sun rises from behind a hill. Her
clothes are hung on a tree and other vessels stand
nearby. Green, pale blue and reddish-brown borders.
This subject was popular at Udaipur in the early 19th
century, combining as it does the theme of worship of
the sun, of whom the Maharanas were considered to be
descendants, and erotic elements deriving from Mughal
paintings of women at their toilet. Cf. cat. no. 231; also
Bulletin, Baroda Museum and Picture Gallery, XII,
pl. XV; J. L. Davidson, *Art of the Indian Subcontinent
from Los Angeles Collections,* Los Angeles, 1968,
no. 133; Andhare and Singh, *Deogarh Painting,* fig. 2.

259
A Lady
Udaipur, c. 1830-40
14.1 x 9.1 cm

Drawing, with some colouring, of a lady in a printed
dress holding a flask and cup and standing beside an
attenuated drooping tree. Plain background; green band
in foreground; dark blue band above. Indifferent
quality. Yellow margin; red border; yellow outer
margin.

260
A Lady Playing a *Vina*
Udaipur, c. 1830-40
21.7 x 14.7 cm

A lady sits on a chair on a terrace playing the *vina* while
a young boy in a yellow *jama* approaches her. Treetops
appear behind a wall with blue sky and white cloud
above. Black margin; red border. Crudely painted.

261
A Lady at her Toilet
Udaipur, c. 1835-40
24.5 x 15.7 cm

A bare-breasted lady stands combing her hair on a gold
stool under a flowering tree on a terrace beside a
pavilion. Pale green background with white and blue
cloud-band. Deep blue margin; trimmed buff border
with gold and black rules.

262
Two Ladies Embracing
Udaipur, c. 1840
20.3 x 12.4 cm

One lady offers a drink to the other as they stand
embracing on a carpeted terrace near a pavilion, a
nimbus encircling both their heads. Blue-green
background with distant hills. White, blue and green
margins; tan border with ruling and gold flecks.
Indifferent quality.

263
A Lady on a Terrace
Udaipur, c. 1835-40
14.5 x 9.8 cm

A lady sits against a bolster on a carpeted terrace
holding a *tanpura*. Trees in the background with gold-
streaked cloudy white and blue-grey sky above.
Indifferent quality. Dark umber margin and dirty pale
brown border.

264
A Lady Listening to Music on a Terrace
Udaipur, c. 1840-50
22.9 x 15.5 cm

A lady sits on a terrace under a canopy drinking and
listening to female musicians; maids stand in
attendance. Buff inner border with vine scroll pattern;
gold and green margins; outer border trimmed.
Painted in the dull palette of some mid-19th century
Udaipur work, this composition is probably based on a
Mughal composition of c. 1700 or a later Deccani
composition.

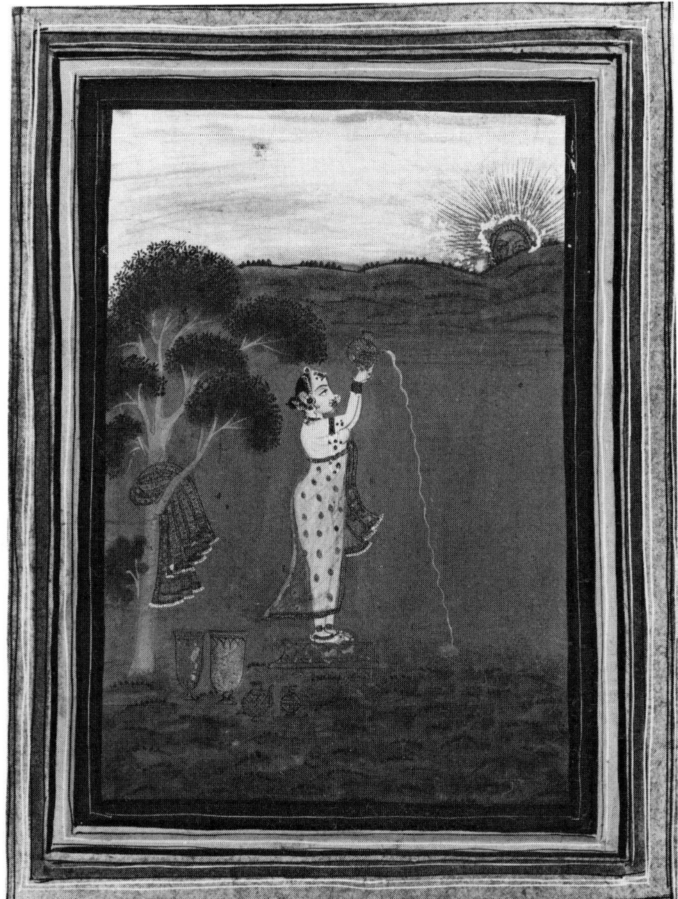

258

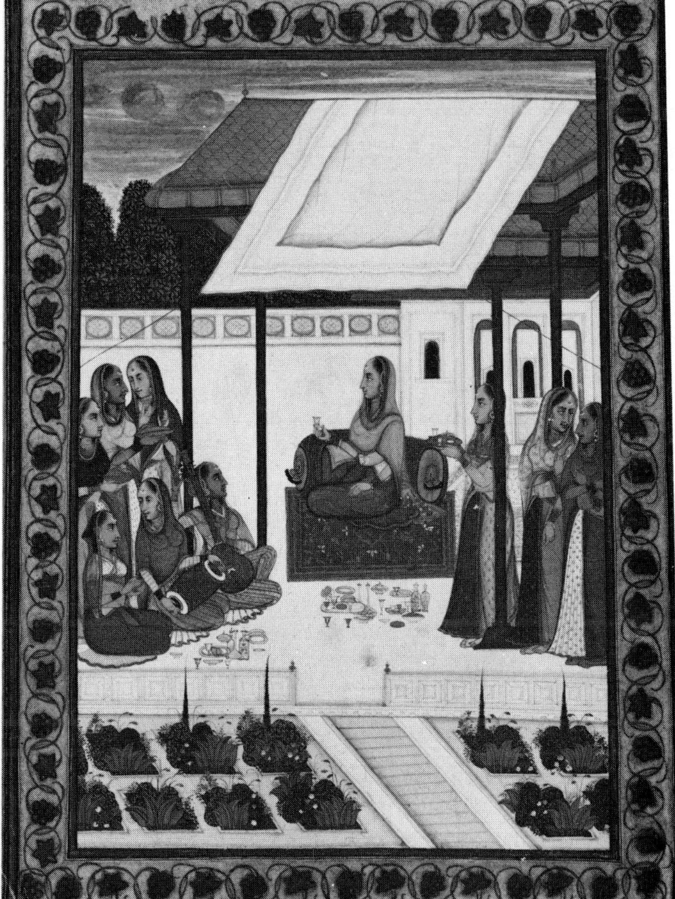

264

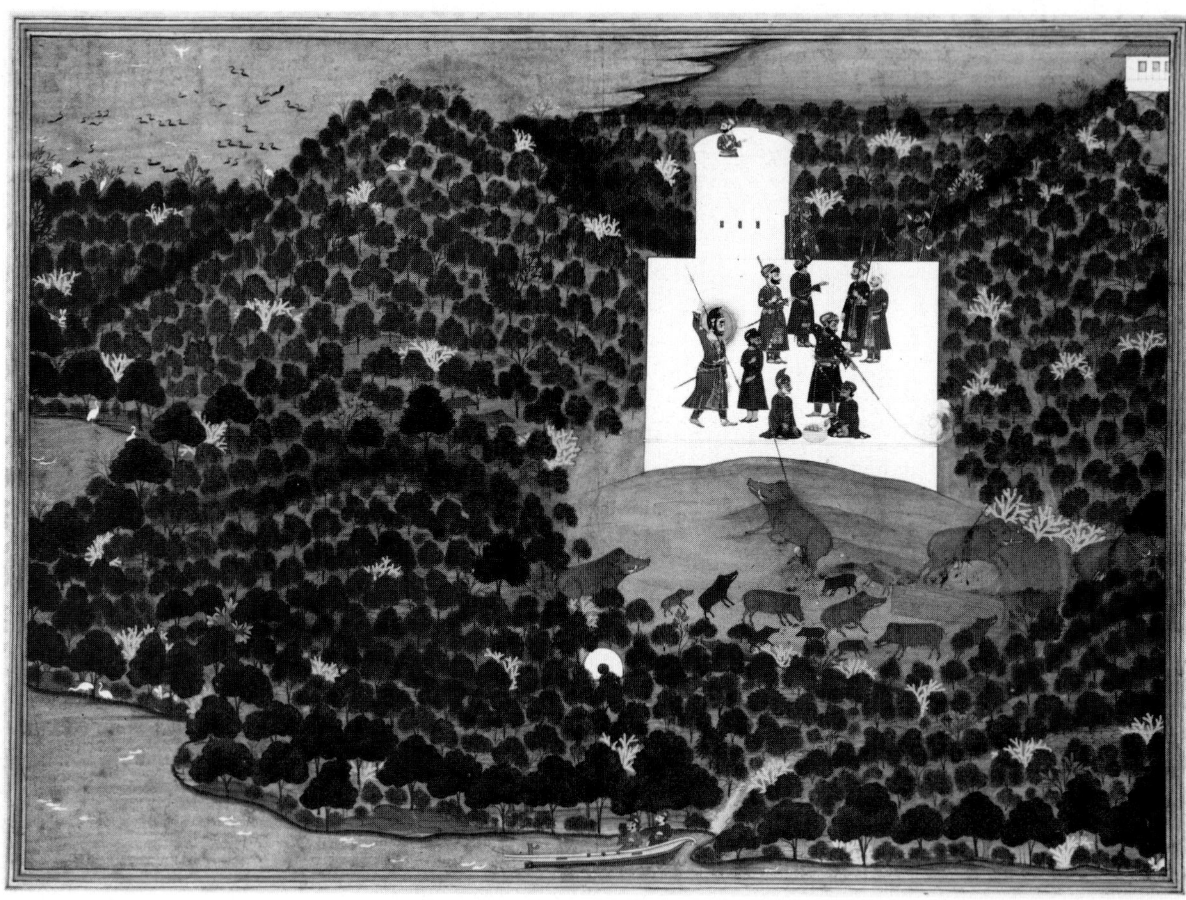

265

Maharana Sarup Singh at a Hunting-Lodge
Udaipur, 1845. By Tara
43.5 x 61.5 cm

The Maharana and several sardars, wearing hunting
green and khaki, are killing boar which have been lured
with food to a hunting-lodge on a wooded hillock on
the northern shore of the Pichola lake. The Maharana,
with nimbus, has transfixed the largest boar with a spear
and it flees bleeding into the undergrowth while a sardar
with a gun fires after it. Two boatman await the party in
the foreground. Gold and pink margins; buff border
with gold floral pattern.

Inscribed on the back: *mharajadhiraja mharanaji śrī
sarup sīghjī rī sabī ro panau barachī su sura maryau
mangari me jathe atra sardar pasavan hajar baba
candjī golī khavata thaka meta bagatavar sīgh nakhe
banduk solakhī mokhau coi? ?syau savalal a..? ?dova
nakhe barachya buraj parapane rī ganga ram chaidīdar
harīdas bethau thakau aur dujau sakar kau laug hajar
sambat 1901 rā paus bīd 14 kau kalamī cataro taryau
panau pāde kī orī jama sambat 1901 rā cet sud pacam
jma hasate pāde santok das kī orī jama.*

A hunting-lodge standing on this spot is nowadays
known as Haridas ki Magari, after the *shikari* Haridas
who appears here as one of the two seated figures. The
few remaining boar, protected in the Maharana's
preserve, are still summoned to be fed each evening by
the ululating cry of a palace servant.

266

Maharana Sarup Singh Riding
Udaipur, 1847. By Tara
28.2 x 19.3 cm

The Maharana, with nimbus, wearing a white *jama* and
gold-bordered *patka*, rides a dark brown stallion and
holds a jewelled wand. Pale green background with
cloud above. Gold and red margins; buff border with
cerise floral meander.

Inscribed on the back: *maharajadhiraja maharanaji śrī
sarup sighjī rī chabī ro pano ghodo alijo sambat 1904 rā
katī vid 7 sinu najar kī do cataro taro hasate ?pāde
santok das.*

267

Maharana Sarup Singh Riding
Udaipur, c. 1845-50. Attributed to Tara
39 x 26.5 cm

The Maharana, with nimbus, in green *pagri* and maroon
jama, is mounted on a pale brown stallion with black
yak-tails under the saddle, and accompanied by
numerous attendants with maces, a *huqqa,* regalia and a
hound in a red and gold jacket. Green landscape
background with distant gold hills and cloudy sky. Dark
umber margin, pink border with black rules, inscribed:
*maharajadhiraja maharanaji śrī sarup sighjī
rī tasbir ro pano ghod* [del.] *banamasant.*

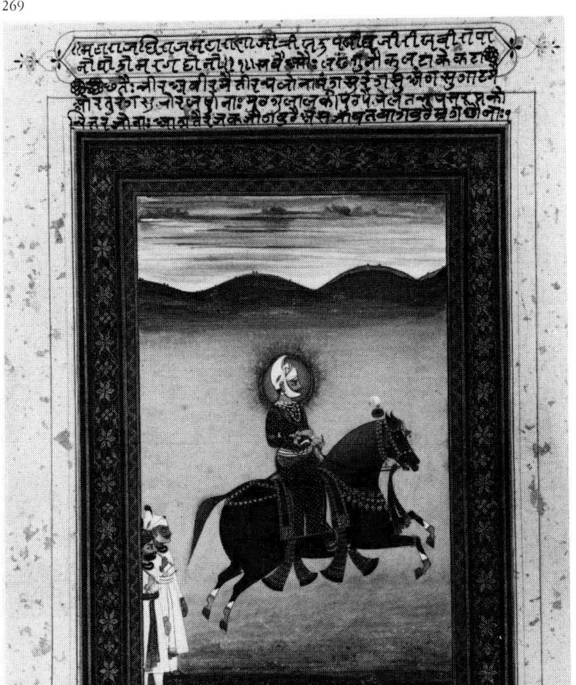

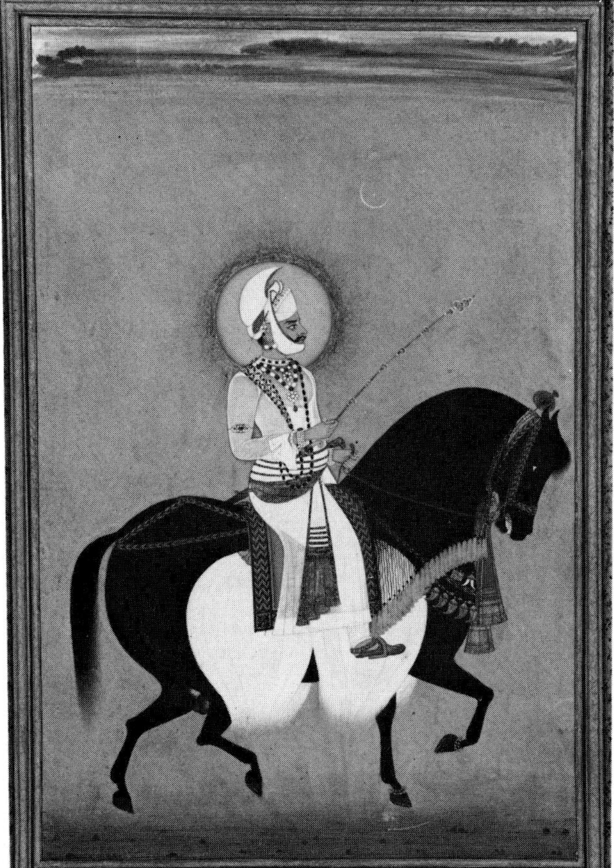

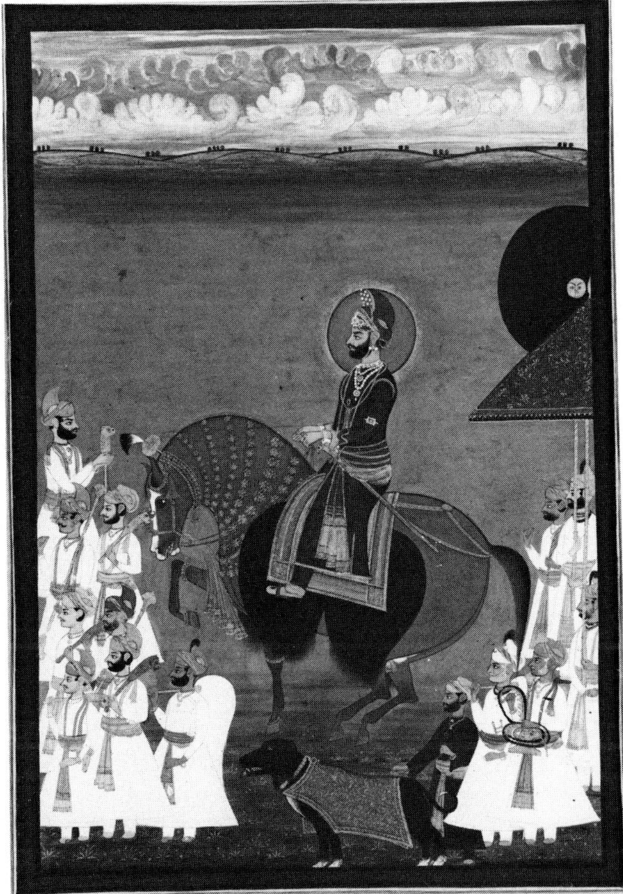

268

Maharana Sarup Singh Playing Holi on Horseback
Udaipur, 1850. By Tara
23.4 x 37.3 cm

The Maharana, with nimbus, is seen twice, riding
forward and flinging a trail of red powder into the air
from a bag tied to his wrist. Pale green background.
Blue-green and brown margins with gold meander
pattern and black, white and gold rules; pale brown
border with gold decoration.

Inscribed on the back: *maharajadhiraja maharanaji śrī
śrī 108 śrī sarup sighji rī tasbīr ro pano ghodo
mragachono. savaiyo...* [verses follow, identical to those
on no. 269] *kalamī cataro taro samat 1906 ra phagan vid
2 najar kī do haste pande ekaligadas.*

269

Maharana Sarup Singh Riding
Udaipur, c. 1850. Attributed to Tara
26 x 16.6 cm

The Maharana, with nimbus, wearing a white *pagri* and
magenta and gold *jama,* rides a brown stallion,
accompanied by two chowry-bearers, partially hidden by
the margin. Pale green background with distant hills
and cloud-streaked sky. Blue inner margin with gold and
black rules and gold meander pattern; brown outer
margin with gold floral pattern; buff border with black
rules and gold flecks.

Inscribed above: *maharajadhiraja maharanaji śrī sarup
sighji rī sabi ro pano ghodo maragachono...* (verses
follow, identical to those which appear, in a better
hand, on cat. no. 268, dated 1850. The Maharana
appears on the same horse, Maragachono , and in
similar postures, in both pictures).

270

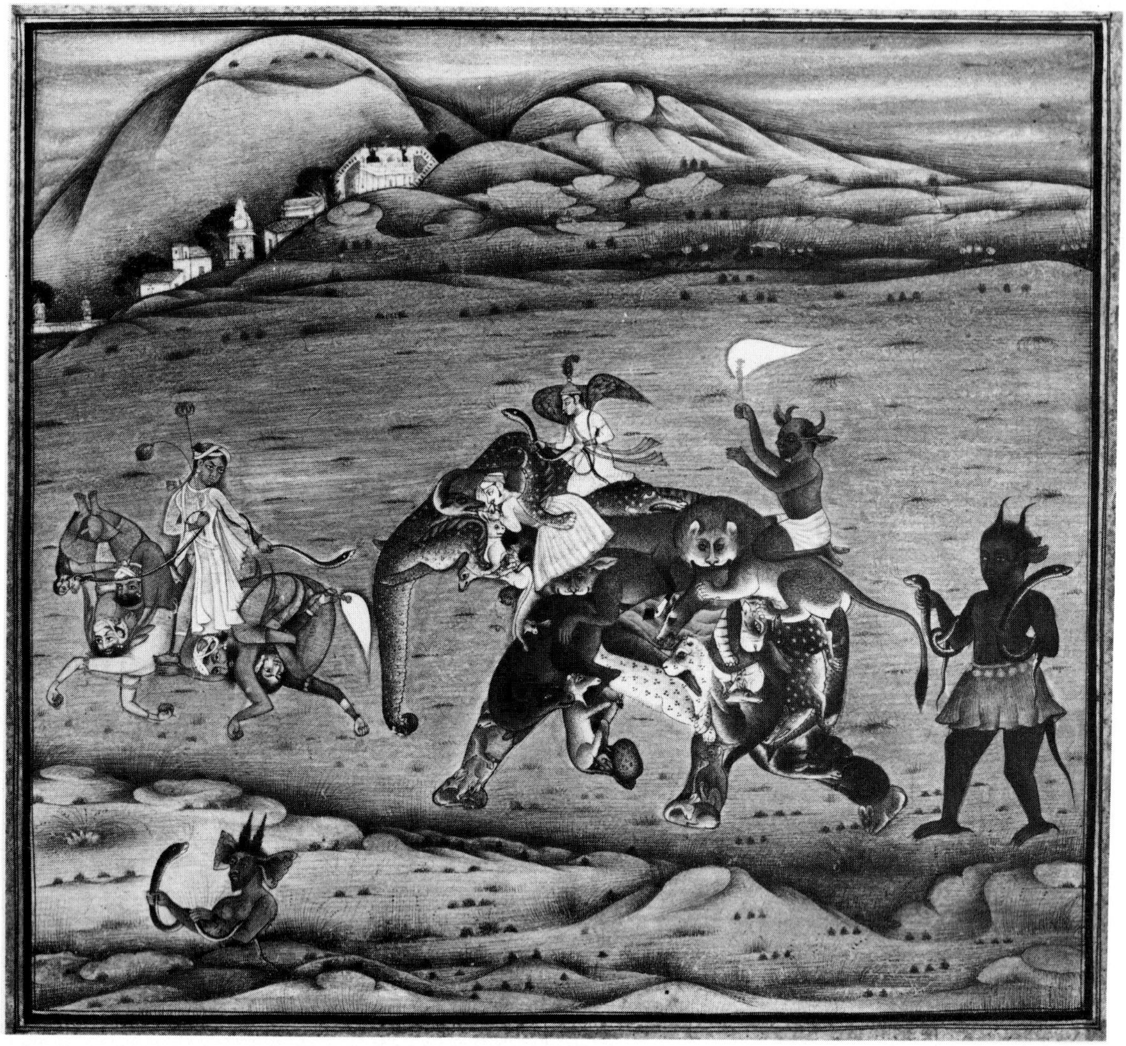

272

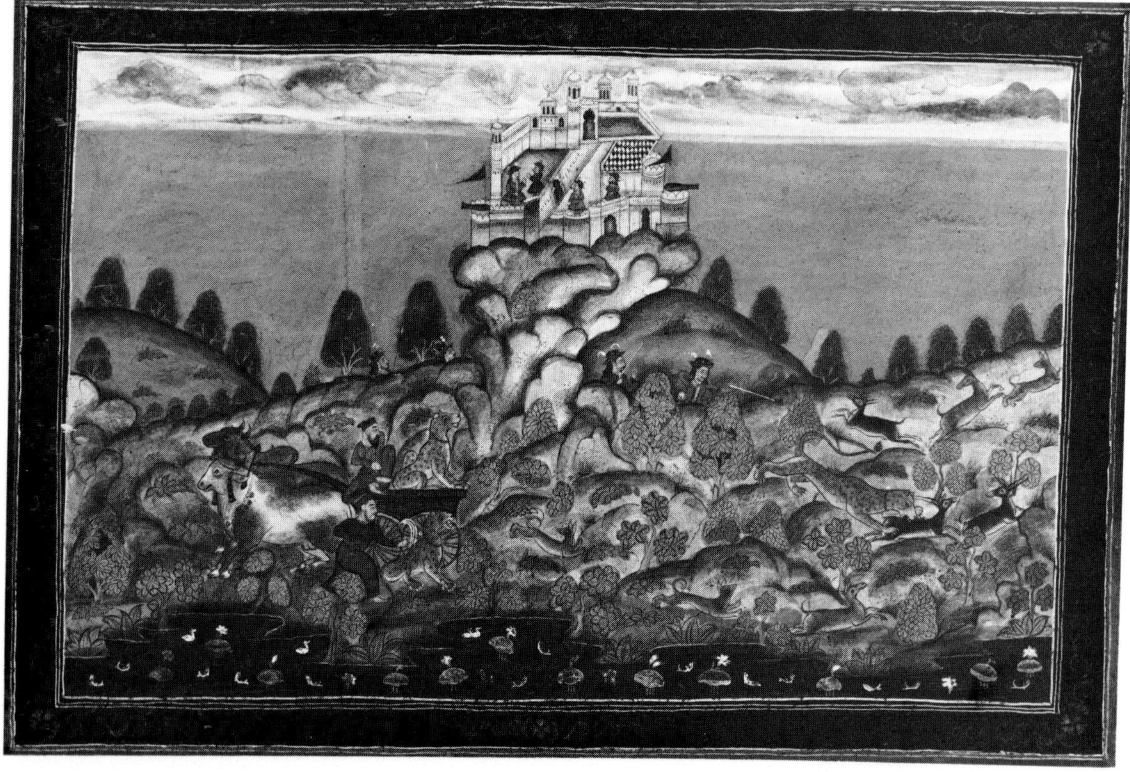

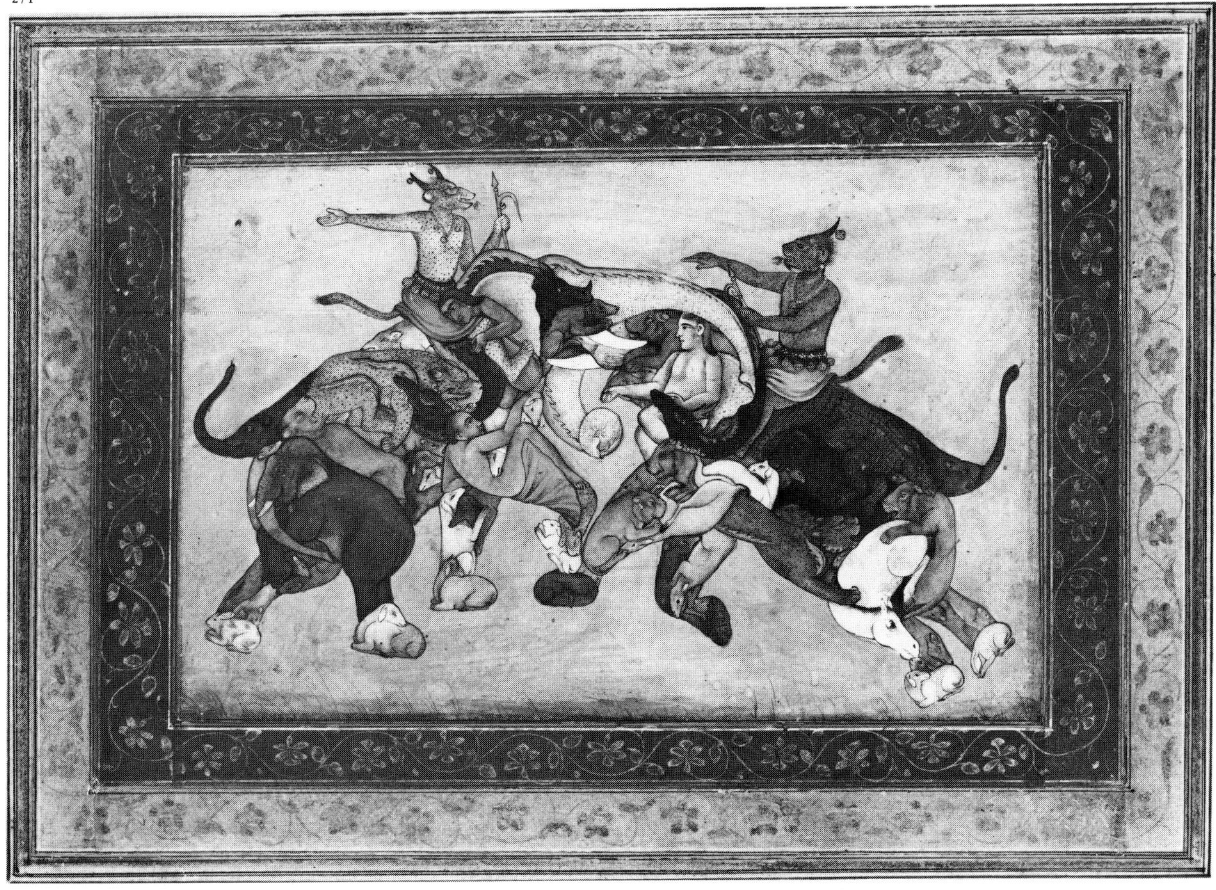

270

Composite Animals in a Landscape
Udaipur, 1851. By Deva
20.6 x 23 cm

A lady holding a snake and flowers rides a horse
composed of male and female figures, in front of an
elephant composed of animal and human figures, ridden
by a peri with a snake and a demon with a chowry. Two
other demons holding snakes are on foot. Hilly
landscape in the background with a palace, temple and
houses.

Inscribed on the back: *pano 1 hatī dantu lagajaro o
pano citāre deve nazar kī do smat 1908 āsoj bīd
1…janāvarā kiar ādamrā (?) ki nārīkujar.*
Inscribed on an attached leaf: *pāno 1 hatī datulajar ro o
pana citāre deve nijar kī do bars 1908 āsaj vīd 1.*

Composite animals *(narikunjara)* were a popular subject
in many schools of Indian painting, often being copied
from *charbas* or pounces. They were depicted at Udaipur
at least from the early 18th century, when a picture of a
Dutchman riding a composite camel was painted
(Victoria and Albert Museum; see J. Auboyer, 'Un
maître hollandais s'inspirant des miniatures mogholes',
Arts Asiatiques, II, 1955, fig. 10). See also cat. no. 271.

271

Composite Elephants Fighting
Udaipur, c. 1850
12.8 x 19.9 cm

Each of the two elephants, composed of animal and
human figures, is ridden by a demon holding an ankus.
Dull yellow background. Pale blue and salmon-pink
margins with gold floral meander pattern and gold,
orange and black rules. Buff border with blue, black and
gold rules, inscribed above: *jatugaj* (magic elephant).

Inscribed on the back: *nārikunjra ko ādmi janavarā ko.*
See cat. no. 270.

272

Europeans Hunting Deer
Udaipur, c. 1850
15.2 x 24.5 cm

Four Europeans, modelled on early 18th century
Dutchmen, shoot deer and blackbuck in a rocky
landscape. Four other Europeans appear in a hilltop fort.
Two *shikaris* with a bullock-cart hold hunting cheetahs.
Pale green background. Dark mauve margin with white
rules and gold decoration. Rust-coloured border.
The Europeans in this picture are distant descendants of
the periwigged Dutch East India Company officers who
visited Udaipur in the early 18th century and lived on
subsequently in the native artistic imagination (cf. cat.
no. 70).

273
Maharana Sarup Singh Receiving Sir Henry Lawrence in Durbar

Udaipur, 1855. By Tara
43 x 59.2 cm

The Maharana, with nimbus, sits against deep red
cushions in an arcade of the lower *Chitrashala* in the
palace, holding a shield to his knee and attended by
servants with *morchals*. In the courtyard the Governor-
General's Agent for Rajputana, Sir Henry Lawrence,
kneels before him, accompanied by his brother, Colonel
George St. Patrick Lawrence, the Political Agent for
Jaipur(?) and Captain J. C. Brooke. Seated facing them
on the right are Rao Bakhat Singh of Bedla, Rao
Lakshman Singh of Parsoli, Ravat Khuman Singh of
Asind, Sare Singh of Bagor, Dal Singh of Sivarati, Ravat
Bakhtavar Singh of Banera, Mehta Sher Singh and
Purohit Samanath. Narrow blue margin with black,
gold, green, red and white rules; bright green border.

Inscribed on the back: *mharajadhiraja mharanaji śri 108
śri sarup sighji ri sabi ro panau hetali catrasali
suraj copad ri taka me virajya saaib a..? so darikhana me
atari sirdar pasavan saaib betha thaka sama
jimani baju rajidand karanel sir hinari larans
saaib jyahate ajat mevad ra karanel jaraj satapatrak larans
saaib jyahete jepur ka ajant jyahete kapatan burak saaib
davi baju sadi ola sare rao bagat sighji bedale rao
lachman sighji pirasoli ravat khuman sighji asid
kaka sare sighji bagor kaka dal sighji sivarati
ravat bagatavar sighji baneda sama meta ser
sighji prota samanath moda pache kaka cadji samo
morachal liyyo? ....? ude ram dujo morachal ...? tej ram
saaib log pachadi uba thaka shivalo acaldas surano nath
mal shivalo durjan sigh ukilat karata kalami cataro
tarau 1911 ra śri ri jma pada kasare raai.*

The occasion for Sir Henry Lawrence's visit to Udaipur
during the second fortnight in February 1855 was the
signing of a treaty *(kaulnama)* to settle the long-standing
disputes between the Maharana and his sardars (see J. C.
Brooke, *History of Meywar,* pp. 68-71; Shyamaldas, *Vir
Vinod,* vol. II, p. 1955; C. U. Aitchison, *A Collection of
Treaties, Engagements and Sunnuds Relating to India
and Neighbouring Countries,* vol. IV, Calcutta, 1864,
pp. 21-28). Lawrence had recently written in a private
letter: 'I am sorry to say that time has not improved my
opinion of the Rajputs...The kings are tyrants, the
thakurs are rebels, and at the same time hardly less
tyrannical than their sovereigns...For years past Mewar
has been in tacit rebellion. Four-fifths of the thakurs
have cut the Rana, and now that all parties have begged
our interference, the thakur gentlemen tell my brother,
and indeed me, that they will abide by no decision that
does not give them all their own rights, meaning
thereby all they want and have been contending for the
last 50 years... I have pitched into the Mewar thakurs
frightfully as also into the Alwar raja...' (quoted in
M. Edwardes, *The Necessary Hell,* London, 1958,

p. 129). After several years' service in the Punjab (where
he was also portrayed by native artists; see F. S.
Aijazuddin, *Pahari Paintings and Sikh Portraits in the
Lahore Museum,* London, 1977, p. 90 and refs.)
Lawrence had been transferred to Rajputana against his
will in 1853. In 1857 he was moved to Oudh, where he
died in the siege of Lucknow.

It is interesting to compare Tara's version of the Udaipur
durbar with an oil-painting of the same event by
Frederick Christian Lewis in the India Office Library (see
William Foster, *A Descriptive Catalogue of the
Paintings, Statues, etc. in the India Office,* 5th ed.,
London, 1924, no. 213). Lewis (1813-75), a pupil of (the
artist) Lawrence, made four visits to India, where he
specialized in princely durbar scenes. His work on the
Udaipur durbar scene is referred to in a letter dictated
by Lawrence's little daughter Honoria which begins,
'18 Feb. 1855. Camp. Oodypore, Meywar. My dear
brothers, Papa sits for his picture and I sit with him. He
looks very nice, and say he puts his star on; and Dr
Ebden our doctor — and Capt. Brooke and Uncle he
sits...' (I.O.L. MSS. Eur. F.85.112, notebook no. 18). It
can be inferred that the third European figure in Tara's
picture may also be the Residency surgeon, Dr Ebden,
rather than the Agent for Jaipur, as the inscription
states; there is however a certain sameness about Tara's
Europeans — all four have blue eyes for example. They
are shown holding handkerchiefs (because of the heat?)
and kneeling in a markedly humbler attitude than in
Lewis' probably more faithful version. Tara's grouping
of the figures in the durbar is altogether more strictly
formal. He has also avoided showing the Mewar sardars'
voluminous whiskers, or else Lewis has exaggerated
them. On the other hand Tara's palace setting is
scrupulously observed (with attention to both perspective
and modelling), whereas Lewis has brought in an
imaginary lake scene as a backdrop.

Fig. 2.
Maharana Sarup Singh Receiving Sir Henry Lawrence in Durbar
by F. C. Lewis, 1855
India Office Library, London

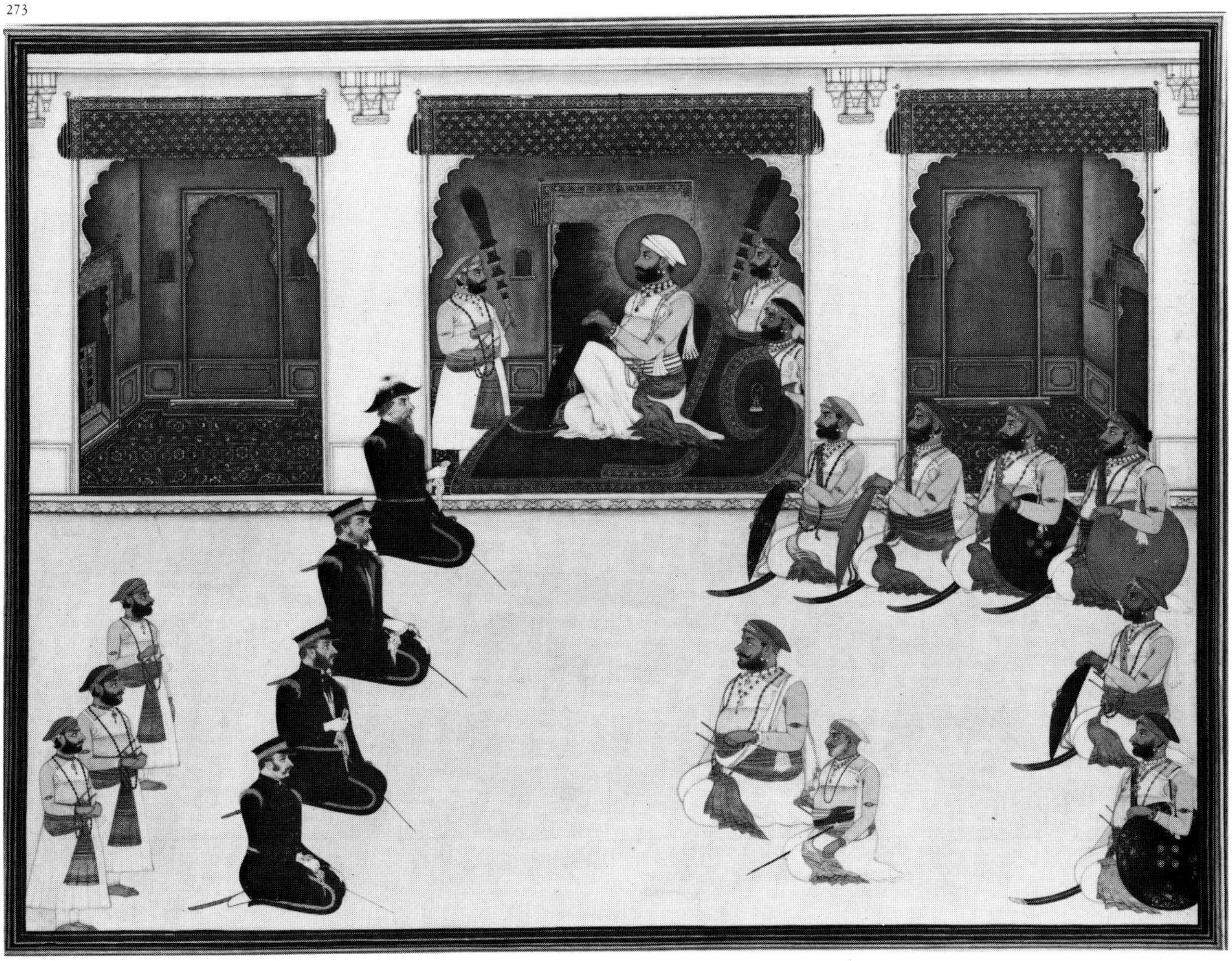

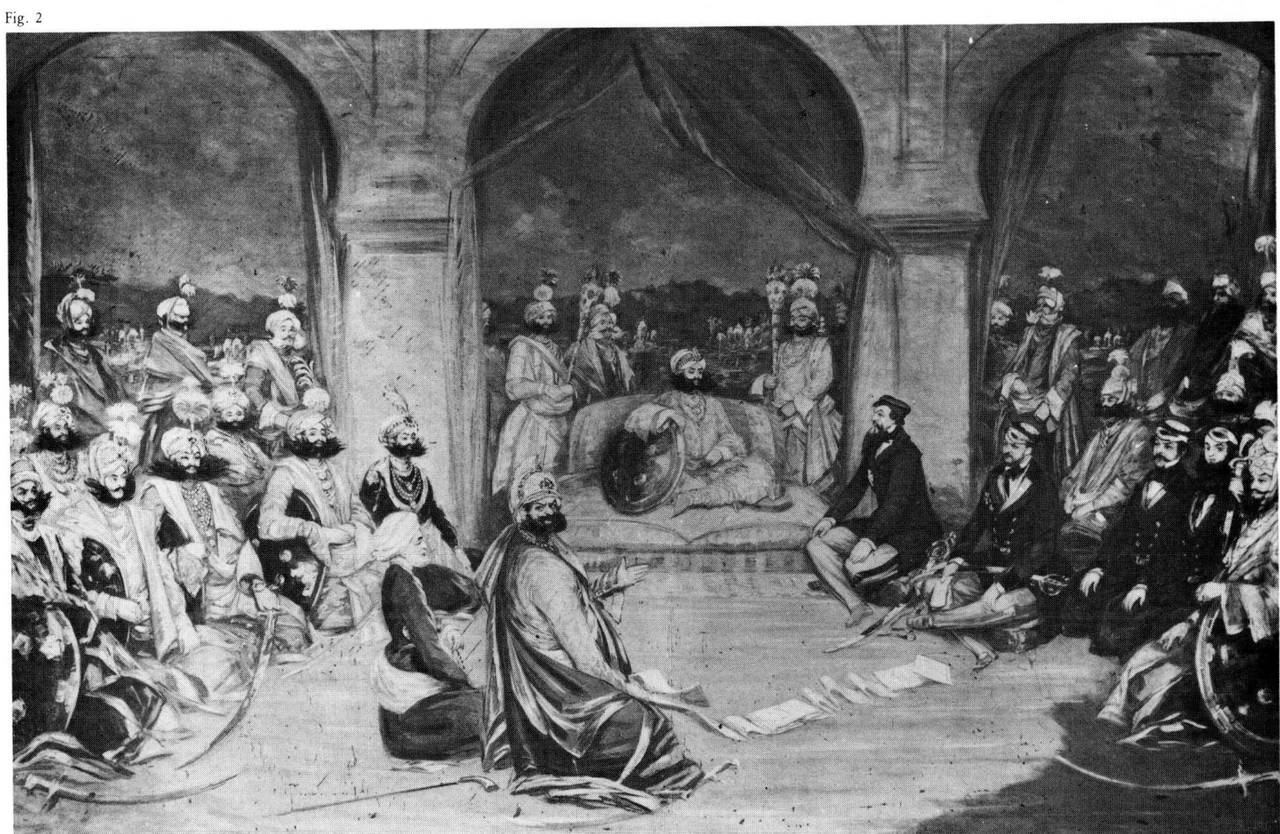

Fig. 2

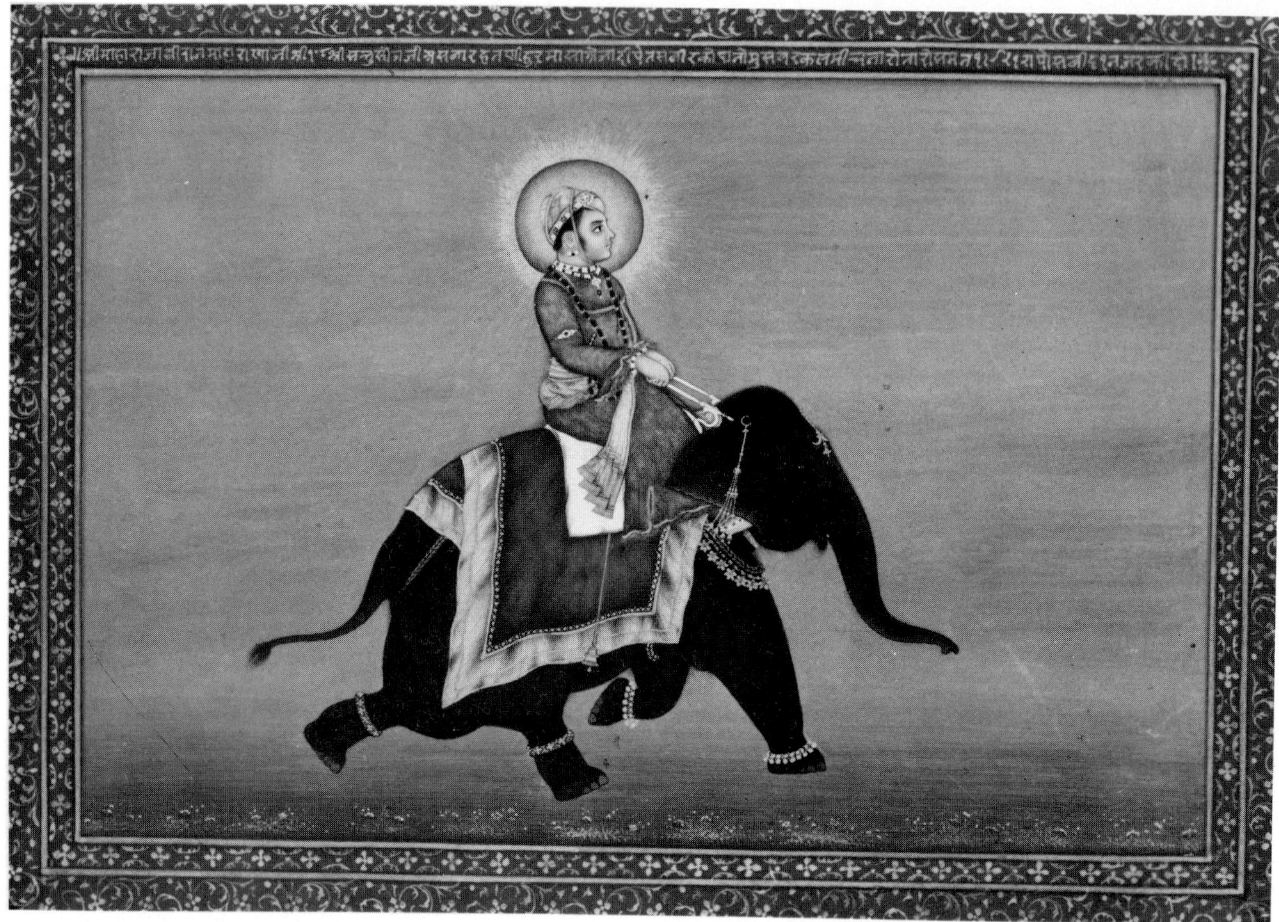

274

Maharana Shambhu Singh Riding a Young Elephant
Udaipur, 1864. By Tara
13.8 x 21.1 cm

The Maharana, with nimbus, wears a cerise *jama* and rides a young female elephant with a red and yellow saddle-cloth. Vivid green background. Pale blue margin with gold ruling and quatrefoil pattern; chocolate border with gold scrollwork.
Inscribed above: *śrī mahārājādhirāja maharānāji śrī 108 śrī sabhu siṅgji asavar hatani huramāsā ?ojadi pe tasabir ko pāno musavar kalami cataro taro samat 1921 rā pos bid 1 najar kī do.*

A very similar inscription appears on the back.

This painting was evidently presented on the seventeenth birthday of the Maharana, who was born on the first of the dark half of Pausa, V.S. 1904 (1847 A.D.). it is one of Tara's latest paintings; a procession scene of Shambhu Singh (r. 1861-74), in an American collection (see P. Chandra, *Indian Miniature Painting*, no. 106), is most likely a slightly earlier work by him. The frontispiece of a manuscript of the *Rasikapriya* of Keshav Das dated 1866 in the Rajasthan Oriental Research Institute, Udaipur, showing Shambhu Singh on a lion-throne, attended by sardars in the palace, may also be attributed to Tara.

Index of Artists

Bibliography

Historical and General Works

Bhatnagar, V. S., *Life and Times of Sawai Jai Singh*, Delhi, 1974.
Brooke(s), J. C., *History of Meywar*, Calcutta, 1859.
Erskine, K. D., *Rajputana Gazetteers: the Mewar Residency*, Ajmer, 1908.
Gahlot, J. S., *Rajputane ka Itihas*, vol. 1, Jodhpur, 1937.
Gupta, K. S., *Mewar and the Maratha Relations*, New Delhi, 1971.
Hendley, T. H., *The Rulers of India and the Chiefs of Rajputana*, London, 1897.
Mehta, F. L., *Handbook of Mewar*, Bombay, 1888.
Ojha, G. H., *Rajputane ka Itihas*, Ajmer, 1927.
Paliwal, D. L., *Mewar and the British, 1857-1921*, Jaipur, 1971.
Reuther, O., *Indische Paläste und Wohnhäuser*, Berlin, 1925.
Rousselet, L., *India and its Native Princes*, rev. ed., London, 1878.
Sarkar, Sir Jadunath, *Fall of the Mughal Empire*, 3rd ed., 4 vols., Calcutta, 1964.
Sharma, G. N., *Social Life in Medieval Rajasthan*, Agra, 1968.
Shyamaldas, Kaviraj, *Vir Vinod*, 2 vols., Udaipur, 1886.
Singh, K., *The Relations of the House of Bikaner with the Central Powers*, New Delhi, 1974.
Somani, R. V., *History of Mewar*, vol. 1, Jaipur, 1976.
Tod, J., *Annals and Antiquities of Rajasthan*, ed. W. Crooke, 3 vols., London, 1920; repr. Delhi, 1971.

Works Relating to Painting

Andhare, S., 'Painting from the Thikana of Deogarh', *Prince of Wales Museum Bulletin*, 10, 1967, pp. 43-53.
Andhare, S. and Singh, N., *Deogarh Painting*, Lalit Kala Akademi portfolio, New Delhi, 1977.
Archer, W. G., *Indian Paintings from Rajasthan*, London, 1957.
Archer, W. G., *Indian Painting in Bundi and Kotah*, London, 1959.
Archer, W. G., *Indian Miniatures*, London, 1960.
Archer, W. G. and E. Binney 3rd, *Rajput Miniatures from the Collection of Edwin Binney 3rd*, Portland, 1968.
Barrett, D. and Gray, B., *Painting of India*, Geneva, 1963.
Beach, M. C., 'Painting and the Minor Arts', in *Arts of India and Nepal: the Nasli and Alice Heeramaneck Collection*, Boston, 1966.
Beach, M. C., 'Painting at Devgarh', *Archives of Asian Art*, XXIV, 1970-71, pp. 23-35.
Beach, M. C., *Rajput Painting at Bundi and Kota*, Ascona, 1974.
Beach, M. C., 'The Context of Rajput Painting', *Ars Orientalis*, 10, 1975, pp. 11-17.
Beach, M. C., *The Grand Mogul*, Williamstown, 1978.
Chandra, M., *Mewar Painting*, New Delhi, 1957.
Chandra, P., *Bundi Painting*, New Delhi, 1959.
Chandra, P., *Indian Miniature Painting*, Madison, 1971.
Coomaraswamy, A. K., *Rajput Painting*, 2 vols., London, 1916.
Coomaraswamy, A. K., *Catalogue of the Indian Collections in the Museum of Fine Arts, Boston*, vol. 5, Cambridge, Mass., 1926.
Czuma, S., *Indian Art from the George P. Bickford Collection*, Cleveland, 1975.
Dahmen-Dallapiccola, A. L., *Indische Miniaturen*, Baden-Baden, 1976.
Das, A. K., 'Miniatures' in "Homage to Jaipur", *Marg*, XXX, 4, 1977, pp. 77-94.
Devkar, V. L., 'Some Recently Acquired Miniatures in the Baroda Museum', *Bulletin, Museum and Picture Gallery, Baroda*, XII, 1955-56, pp. 19-24.
Dickinson, E. and Khandalavala, K., *Kishangar Painting*, New Delhi, 1959.
Dwivedi, V. P., 'Some Inscribed and Dated Rajasthani Miniatures in the Collection of State Museum, Lucknow', *Journal of the Indian Society of Oriental Art*, n.s., VIII, 1976-77, pp. 48-56.

Ebeling, K., *Ragamala Painting*, Basle, 1973.

Formijne, P., *Minaturen uit India: de verzameling van dr. P. Formijne*, Amsterdam, 1978.

Gangoly, O. C., *Critical Catalogue of the Miniature Paintings in the Baroda Museum*, Baroda, 1961.

Gangoly, O. C., 'Some New Acquisitions of Rajput Miniatures', *Bulletin, Museum and Picture Gallery, Baroda*, XIV, 1962, pp. 9-18.

Goetz, H., *The Art and Architecture of Bikaner State*, Oxford, 1950.

Goetz, H., 'The First Golden Age of Udaipur', *Ars Orientalis*, II, 1957, pp. 427-37.

Gray, B., 'Painting', in *The Art of India and Pakistan*, ed. L. Ashton, London, 1950.

Khandalavala, K. and Chandra, M., *Miniatures and Sculptures from the Collection of the Late Sir Cowasji Jehangir, Bart.*, Bombay, 1965.

Khandalavala, K. and Chandra, M. and Chandra, P., *Miniature Paintings from the Sri Motichand Khajanchi Collection*, New Delhi, 1960.

Lee, S. E., *Rajput Painting*, New York, 1960.

McNear, E. and A., *Persian and Indian Miniatures*, Chicago, 1974.

Pal, P., *The Classical Tradition in Rajput Painting*, New York, 1978.

Sharma, O. P., *Indian Miniature Painting*, Brussels, 1974.

Skelton, R., 'The Tod Collection of Rajasthani Paintings', *Roopa Lekha*, XXX, 1959, pp. 5-11.

Skelton, R., *Indian Miniatures*, Venice, 1961.

Skelton, R., *Rajasthani Temple-hangings of the Krishna Cult*, New York, 1973

Skelton, R., 'Shaykh Phul and the Origins of Bundi Painting', in *Chhavi 2*, ed. A. Krishna, Banaras (forthcoming).

Topsfield, A., 'Sahibdin's *Gita Govinda* Illustrations', in *Chhavi 2*, ed. A Krishna, Banaras (forthcoming).

Waldschmidt, E. and R. L., *Miniatures of Musical Inspiration*, vol. 2, Berlin, 1975.

Welch, S. C., *The Art of Mughal India*, New York, 1963.

Welch, S. C., *A Flower from Every Meadow*, New York 1973.

Welch, S. C., *Indian Drawings and Painted Sketches*, New York, 1976.

Welch, S. C. and Beach, M. C., *Gods, Thrones and Peacocks*, New York, 1965.

Glossary

ashram	A secluded abode of *yogis* or ascetics.
bait	A couplet of Persian verse.
bandhana	Tie-dyed cloth (hence English 'bandana').
bhat	A bard, performing the function of genealogist.
charba	A pounce, used for tracing the outlines of paintings.
chattri	A small kiosk or pavilion with umbrella-like dome.
choli	A short bodice worn by women.
chowry *(chauri)*	A fly-whisk, consisting of the tail of a yak set in a handle.
dhabhai	A foster-brother of a Rajput ruler.
dhoti	A waist-cloth, passed between the legs and tucked; the most common male dress in northern India.
durree *(dari)*	A thick cotton floor covering.
ghaghra	An ankle-length gathered skirt worn by Rajasthani women.
gopa (f. *gopi*)	Cowherd/milkmaid; companions of Krishna in his youth spent at the village of Gokula.
gosain	'Master of the senses' or 'master of cows'; a member of one of the ten orders of Shaivite ascetics; or, a Vaishnavite priest.
haveli	A town house or mansion.
Holi	The spring festival, celebrated with the throwing of coloured powder and water.
huqqa (hookah)	A water-pipe.
jama	A coat or over-garment worn by noblemen.
katar	A type of dagger.
lingam	Sacred phallic emblem of the god Shiva, usually standing in the *yoni,* or female organ.
makara	A mythical aquatic beast resembling a crocodile.
morchal	A ceremonial fan made of peacock feathers.
nasta'liq	A cursive variety of the Arabic script developed in Persia.
nautch	A dance performance.
nayaka (f. *nayika*)	A type of ideal lover, as classified in Indian poetry and rhetoric.
pagri	A turban.
paijama (pyjama)	Loose trousers, tied at the waist.
pan	Betel leaf, which together with areca nut and lime is formed into a quid and chewed; often stored in a *pandan* or special box.
pargana	A district.
patka	A waist-sash worn by the nobility.
qanat	A canvas tent wall round an encampment.
ragamala	A 'garland of *ragas*' or musical modes (f. *ragini*), whose supposed essential characteristics are personified, both in verse and in visual images, in series of thirty-six or more illustrations.
sadhu	A wandering ascetic.
sakhi	A lady's confidante, acting as a go-between for separated lovers.
sardar	A Rajput chieftain.
shikari	A huntsman.
syce *(sais)*	A groom.
talwar	A sword with long curved blade.
tanpura	A stringed instrument, used to provide a drone accompaniment for a singer or instrumentalist.
thikana	A Rajput fief or barony.
vahana	A 'vehicle': a particular animal or bird with which the major Hindu deities are associated.
vina	A stringed instrument.
yogi (f. *yogini*)	An ascetic, or practitioner of yoga.
yoni	See *lingam.*
zenana	The women's quarters of a palace.